SIXTH EDITION

GRAMMAR 2
IN CONTEXT

SANDRA N. ELBAUM

NATIONAL GEOGRAPHIC LEARNING | CENGAGE Learning

Australia • Brazil • Mexico • Singapore • United Kingdom • United States

Grammar in Context 2, Sixth Edition
Student Book
Sandra N. Elbaum

Publisher: Sherrise Roehr

Executive Editor: Laura Le Dréan

Managing Editor: Jennifer Monaghan

Development Editor: Claudi Mimó

Executive Marketing Manager: Ben Rivera

Product Marketing Manager: Dalia Bravo

Senior Director, Production: Michael Burggren

Content Project Manager: Mark Rzeszutek

Manufacturing Planner: Mary Beth Hennebury

Interior Design: Brenda Carmichael

Compositor: SPi Global

Cover Design: Brenda Carmichael

Cover Photo: Arches National Park, Utah.
   Photo by Chad Liddell.

For permission to use material from this text or product, submit all requests online at **www.cengage.com/permissions**

Further permissions questions can be emailed to **permissionrequest@cengage.com**

ISBN 13: 978-1-305-07538-2

National Geographic Learning
20 Channel Center Street
Boston, Massachusetts 02210
USA

Cengage Learning is a leading provider of customized learning solutions with office locations around the globe, including Singapore, the United Kingdom, Australia, Mexico, Brazil, and Japan. Locate our local office at international.cengage.com/region

Cengage Learning products are represented in Canada by Nelson Education, Ltd.

Visit National Geographic Learning online at **ngl.cengage.com**
Visit our corporate website at **www.cengage.com**

Printed in the United States of America
Print Number: 02   Print Year: 2016

CONTENTS

GRAMMAR   **The Simple Past**
            The Habitual Past with *Used To*
CONTEXT   **What is Success?**

GRAMMAR   **Possessive Forms**
            Object Pronouns
            Reflexive Pronouns
            Questions
CONTEXT   **Weddings**

5

GRAMMAR   **Nouns**
There + Be
Quantity Words
CONTEXT   **Thanksgiving, Pilgrims, and Native Americans**

GRAMMAR   **Gerunds**
             Infinitives
CONTEXT   **Jobs**

APPENDICES

GLOSSARY OF GRAMMATICAL TERMS

INDEX

ACKNOWLEDGMENTS

I am grateful to the team at National Geographic Learning/Cengage Learning for showing their faith in the *Grammar in Context* series by putting their best resources and talent into it. I would especially like to thank Laura Le Dréan for driving this series into an exciting, new direction. Her overall vision of this new edition has been a guiding light. I would also like to thank my development editor, Claudi Mimó, for managing the difficult day-to-day task of polishing and refining the manuscript toward its finished product. I would like to thank Dennis Hogan, Sherrise Roehr, and John McHugh for their ongoing support of *Grammar in Context* through its many editions.

I wish to acknowledge the immigrants, refugees, and international students I have known, both as a teacher and as a volunteer with refugee agencies. These people have increased my understanding of my own language and taught me to see life from another point of view. By sharing their observations, questions, and life stories, they have enriched my life enormously.

This new edition is dedicated to the millions of displaced people in the world. The United States is the new home of many refugees, who survived unspeakable hardships in Burundi, Rwanda, Iraq, Sudan, Burma, Bhutan, and other countries. Their resiliency in starting a new life and learning a new language is a tribute to the human spirit.
—*Sandra N. Elbaum*

The author and publisher would like to thank the following people for their contributions:

Pamela Ardizzone, Rhode Island College;

Dorothy S. Avondstondt, Miami Dade College—Wolfson Campus;

Patricia Bennett, Grossmont College;

Mariusz Bojarczuk, Bunker Hill Community College;

Rodney Borr, Glendale Community College;

Nancy Boyer, Golden West College;

Charles Brooks, Norwalk Community College;

Gabriela Cambiasso, Harold Washington College;

Julie Condon, St. Cloud State University;

Anne Damiecka, Lone Star College — CyFair;

Mohammed Debbagh, Virginia Commonwealth University;

Frank DeLeo, Broward College;

Jeffrey DiIuglio, Boston University Center for English Language and Orientation Programs;

Monique Dobbertin Cleveland, Los Angeles Pierce College;

Lindsey Donigan, Fullerton College;

Jennifer J. Evans, University of Washington;

Norm Evans, Brigham Young University—Hawaii;

David Gillham, Moraine Valley Community College;

Martin Guerra, Mountain View College;

Eric Herrera, Universidad Técnica Nacional;

Cora Higgins, Bunker Hill Community College;

Barbara Inerfeld, Rutgers University;

Barbara Jonckheere, California State University, Long Beach;

Gursharan Kandola, University of Houston;

Roni Lebrauer, Saddleback College;

Dr. Miriam Moore, Lord Fairfax Community College;

Karen Newbrun Einstein, Santa Rosa Junior College;

Stephanie Ngom, Boston University Center for English Language and Orientation Programs;

Charl Norloff, International English Center, University of Colorado Boulder;

Gabriella Nuttall, Sacramento City College;

Fernanda Ortiz, University of Arizona;

Dilcia Perez, Los Angeles City College;

Stephen Peridore, College of Southern Nevada;

Tiffany Probasco, Bunker Hill Community College;

Natalia Schroeder, Long Beach City College;

Elizabeth Seabury, Bunker Hill Community College;

Maria Spelleri, State College of Florida, Manatee-Sarasota;

Susan Stern, Irvine Valley College;

Vincent Tran, University of Houston;

Karen Vlaskamp, Northern Virginia Community College—Annandale;

Christie Ward, Intensive English Language Program, Central Connecticut State University;

Colin Ward, Lone Star College—North Harris;

Laurie A. Weinberg, J. Sargeant Reynolds Community College

My parents immigrated to the United States from Poland and learned English as a second language as adults. My sisters and I were born in the United States. My parents spoke Yiddish to us; we answered in English. In that process, my parents' English improved immeasurably. Such is the case with many immigrant parents whose children are fluent in English. They usually learn English much faster than others; they hear the language in natural ways, in the context of daily life.

Learning a language in context, whether it be from the home, from work, or from a textbook, cannot be overestimated. The challenge for me has been to find a variety of high-interest topics to engage the adult language learner. I was thrilled to work on this new edition of *Grammar in Context* for National Geographic Learning. In so doing, I have been able to combine exciting new readings with captivating photos to exemplify the grammar.

I have given more than 100 workshops at ESL programs and professional conferences around the United States, where I have gotten feedback from users of previous editions of *Grammar in Context*. Some teachers have expressed concern about trying to cover long grammar lessons within a limited time. While ESL is not taught in a uniform number of hours per week, I have heeded my audiences and streamlined the series so that the grammar and practice covered is more manageable. And in response to the needs of most ESL programs, I have expanded and enriched the writing component.

Whether you are a new user of *Grammar in Context* or have used this series before, I welcome you to this new edition.

Sandra N. Elbaum

For my loves
Gentille, Chimene, Joseph, and Joy

Grammar in Context presents grammar in interesting contexts that are relevant to students' lives and then recycles the language and context throughout every activity. Learners gain knowledge and skills in both grammar structures and topic areas.

New To This Edition

NATIONAL GEOGRAPHIC PHOTOGRAPHS
introduce unit themes and draw learners into the context.

LESSON

7

Time Words
The Past Continuous

IMMIGRANTS AND REFUGEES

Celebrity Cesar Millan (center) during his citizenship ceremony

America was born as a nation of immigrants who have always contributed to its greatness.
—Charles B. Rangel

New To This Edition

EVERY LESSON OPENER
includes a quote from an artist, scientist, author, or thinker that helps students connect to the theme.

NEW AND UPDATED READINGS
many with National Geographic content, introduce the target grammar in context and provide the springboard for practice.

Second Careers

Read the following article. Pay special attention to the words in bold.

Judy Perlman, of Chicago, **is starting** a new career—making dolls. She sells most of them before Christmas, at holiday fairs all over Illinois. "I**'m having** more fun than ever before. I**'m traveling** in my new job and **meeting** new people. Right now I**'m preparing** for my next show. I**'m not earning** a lot of money, but I don't care." Why isn't she worried about making money? Perlman is a retired teacher, and she**'s getting** a pension.[1]

Many older people **are starting** new careers in their retirement. Americans **are living** longer than ever before. The average life expectancy in the United States is seventy-six years for men and eighty-one years for women. Most people retire in their midsixties. That means that retired people can have many years ahead of them. Some people are content just relaxing. But many seniors[2] **are getting** involved in interesting hobbies or second careers. If they **are getting** a pension or **living** off savings from their work years, many can afford to find rewarding work without worrying about money. "I**'m enjoying** every minute of my new career. I think this is the best time of my life," says Perlman.

Some senior citizens decide not to retire at all. Frank Babbit of Newark is a carpenter, and he**'s still working**. He has his own business and works fifty hours a week. And he's almost eighty-eight years old.

Today healthy retirees **are exploring** many options, from relaxing to starting a new business or making a hobby into a new career. How do you see yourself as a retiree?

[1] *pension:* a regular payment made by a business or government to a retired employee
[2] *senior:* an older person; this usually refers to people over 65.

42   Lesson 2

NEW LISTENING EXERCISES
reinforce the grammar through natural spoken English.

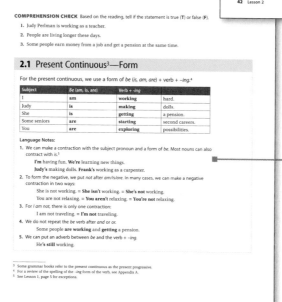

COMPREHENSION CHECK Based on the reading, tell if the statement is true (**T**) or false (**F**).

1. Judy Perlman is working as a teacher.
2. People are living longer these days.
3. Some people earn money from a job and get a pension at the same time.

2.1 Present Continuous[3]—Form

For the present continuous, we use a form of *be* (*is, am, are*) + verb + *-ing*.[4]

Subject	Be (am, is, are)	Verb + -ing	
I	**am**	**working**	hard.
Judy	**is**	**making**	dolls.
She	**is**	**getting**	a pension.
Some seniors	**are**	**starting**	second careers.
You	**are**	**exploring**	possibilities.

Language Notes:

1. We can make a contraction with the subject pronoun and a form of *be*. Most nouns can also contract with *is*.[5]
   I**'m** having fun. We**'re** learning new things.
   Judy**'s** making dolls. Frank**'s** working as a carpenter.
2. To form the negative, we put *not* after *am/is/are*. In many cases, we can make a negative contraction in two ways:
   She is not working. = **She isn't** working. = **She's not** working.
   You are not relaxing. = **You aren't** relaxing. = **You're not** relaxing.
3. For *I am not*, there is only one contraction:
   I am not traveling. = **I'm not** traveling.
4. We do not repeat the *be* verb after *and* or *or*.
   Some people **are working** and **getting** a pension.
5. We can put an adverb between *be* and the verb + *-ing*.
   He**'s still** working.

[3] Some grammar books refer to the present continuous as the present progressive.
[4] For a review of the spelling of the *-ing* form of the verb, see Appendix A.
[5] See Lesson 1, page 5 for exceptions.

The Present Continuous, The Future   43

NEW REDESIGNED GRAMMAR CHARTS offer straightforward explanations and provide contextualized clear examples of the structure.

TEST/REVIEW

Fill in the blanks to complete the conversation. Use the words given and context clues to help you. Use contractions wherever possible.

A: There _____ was _____ a good program on TV last night. _Did you see_ it?
  1. be   2. you/see

B: No, I _____. What _____ about?
  3.   4. be

A: It was about successful people who _____ at first.
  5. fail

B: Who _____ about?
  6. they/talk

A: One success was Bill Gates. Gates _____ a company with a friend when he

_____ 17 years old.
  8. be

B: What kind of company _____?
  9. they/start

A: They _____ software to help regulate traffic. They _____ to sell it
  10. build   11. try

to the city, but they _____ successful.
  12. not/be

B: Why _____ successful?
  13. they/not/be

END-OF-LESSON ACTIVITIES

help learners review and apply the target grammar to writing.

SUMMARY OF LESSON 3

The Simple Past of *Be*

AFFIRMATIVE STATEMENT:	Dawson **was** happy
NEGATIVE STATEMENT:	He **wasn't** rich.
Yes/No QUESTION:	**Was** he from a large family?
SHORT ANSWER:	Yes, he **was**.
Wh- QUESTION:	Where **was** he born?
NEGATIVE *Wh-* QUESTION:	Why **wasn't** he in school?

The Simple Past of Regular Verbs

AFFIRMATIVE STATEMENT:	Andrée **wanted** to go to the North Pole.
NEGATIVE STATEMENT:	He **didn't want** to go over land.
Yes/No QUESTION:	**Did** he **want** to go by balloon?
SHORT ANSWER:	Yes, he **did**.
Wh- QUESTION:	Why **did** he **want** to go to the North
NEGATIVE *Wh-* QUESTION:	Why **didn't** he **want** to go over land?

The Simple Past of Irregular Verbs

AFFIRMATIVE STATEMENT:	Dawson **felt** happy.
NEGATIVE STATEMENT:	He **didn't feel** lonely.
Yes/No QUESTION:	**Did** he **feel** good when he learned to
SHORT ANSWER:	Yes, he **did**.
Wh- QUESTION:	How **did** he **feel** about his life?
NEGATIVE *Wh-* QUESTION:	Why **didn't** he **feel** lonely?

The Habitual Past with *Used To*

AFFIRMATIVE STATEMENT:	Black children **used to attend** separa
NEGATIVE STATEMENT:	They **didn't use to attend** schools wi
Yes/No QUESTION:	**Did** baseball teams **use to have** blac
SHORT ANSWER:	No, they **didn't**.
Wh- QUESTION:	Why **did** schools **use to segregate** st

Robinson born in 1919 in the South. His family was very poor. When he was just a baby,
                                5.   6.

his father leaved the family and his mother decided to moved the family to California. When he
              7.   8.   9.

were in high school and college, he interested in several different sports. After junior college, he
  10.   11.

went to the University of California, where he was won awards in baseball, basketball, football,
  12.   13.

and track. He didn't finished college. He taked a job as athletic director of a youth organization.
              14.   15.

Then he enter the army in 1942. After he left the army in 1944, he accepted an offer to be the
         16.   17.

athletic director at a college in Texas. In 1945, the Kansas City Monarchs, an African American

baseball team, sended him an offer to play professional baseball. In 1947, the Brooklyn Dodgers
               18.

offered him a contract. The manager of the team knowed that Robinson would face racial
  19.   20.

discrimination. He didn't wanted Robinson to fight back. Some people in the crowds yelled
                 21.   22.

racial insults to him. Even some of his teammates objected to having an African American
                                                23.

on their team. Robinson didn't surprised. He knew this would happen. Some other teams
                      24.   25.

threatened not to play against the Dodgers. How the manager of the team reacted?
  26.   27.

The manager, Leo Durocher, supported Robinson. He sayed that he would rather keep Robinson
                          28.   29.

than some of them. In one game, when people yelled racial insults at Robinson, the team

captain come over and putted his arm around Robinson to show his support.
        30.   31.

Robinson succeeded in breaking the racial barrier. He become the highest paid player in
            32.   33.

_____ e door for other African American athletes

_____ 7. He was died in 1972.
                       36.

_____ xtraordinary (like George Dawson). It can be

_____ at did you learn from your failure?

_____ Edit your writing from Part 3.

The Simple Past, The Habitual Past with *Used To* **91**

WRITING

PART 1 Editing Advice

1. Use *was/were* with *born*.
                    was
   Dawson ̄born in the South.
          ^

2. Don't use *was* or *were* with *die*.

   He ~~was~~ died in 2001.

3. Don't use a past form after *to*.
                    swim
   Nyad decided to ~~swam~~ from Cuba to Florida.

4. Don't use *was* or *were* to form the simple past.
      accomplished
   She ~~was accomplish~~ her goal.

5. Use a form of *be* before an adjective. Remember, some *-ed* words are adjectives.
          was
   Dawson ̄excited about going to school.
          ^

6. Don't use *did* with an adjective. Use *was* or *were*.
                          weren't
   Andrée and his men ~~didn't~~ successful.

7. Form the past question correctly.
           didn't you
   Why ~~you didn't~~ read the article?
        did   write
   Why Dawson ~~wrote~~ a book?

8. Use the base form after *didn't*.

   He didn't learn~~ed~~ to read when he was a child.

9. Don't forget the *d* in *used to* in affirmative statements.
         d
   He use ̄to live in the South.
         ^

10. Don't add the verb *be* before *used to* for habitual past.

   Nyad ~~is~~ used to be a sportscaster.

11. Use the correct past form.
         swam
   Nyad ~~swimmed~~ from Cuba to Florida.

PART 2 Editing Practice

Some of the shaded words and phrases have mistakes. Find the mistakes and correct them. If the shaded words are correct, write C.

      C   was
   I recently read an article about Jackie Robinson. He were the first African American to play
                                 1.

on a major league baseball team, the Brooklyn Dodgers. Major league baseball teams use to
                                                                                        3.

have only white players. Blacks were used to have their own teams.
                                 4.

90 Lesson 3

Updated For This Edition!

ENHANCED WRITING SECTION

is divided into two sections which provide students with editing and writing activities to consolidate the grammar structures learned in each lesson.

Updated For This Edition!

ONLINE WORKBOOK

powered by MyELT provides students with additional practice of the target grammar and greater flexibility for independent study.

- Engages students and supports classroom materials by providing a variety of interactive grammar activities.

- Tracks course completion through student progress bars, giving learners a sense of personal achievement.

- Supports instructors by maximizing valuable learning time through course management resources, including scheduling and grade reporting tools.

Go to NGL.Cengage.com/MyELT

Lesson 7 Practice 4

INSTRUCTIONS ▲
Rewrite the sentences to make them more formal. Click the PDF icon to see the chart for this exercise.

1. The teacher I spoke to is here. _____
2. The website that I got the information from was a news organization. _____
3. The store that we bought the computer from closed. _____
4. The house they're interested in has a swimming pool. _____
5. There's a piece of property we want to invest in. _____
6. I'd like you to meet someone I work with. _____
7. That's the professor that I grade papers for. _____
8. She's the friend I talk to about my problems. _____

Lesson 3 Pre-Test

INSTRUCTIONS ▲
Choose the best answer to complete the sentences.

1. ___ *Avatar* directed by James Cameron?
   - ○ Did
   - ○ Was
   - ○ Have

2. It ___ by millions of people since its release in 2009.
   - ○ saw
   - ○ has been seen
   - ○ was seen

3. The film ___ billions of dollars.
   - ○ was brought in
   - ○ is brought by
   - ○ has brought in

4. *Avatar* ___ for nine Oscars and ___ three.

Show Answers   Submit

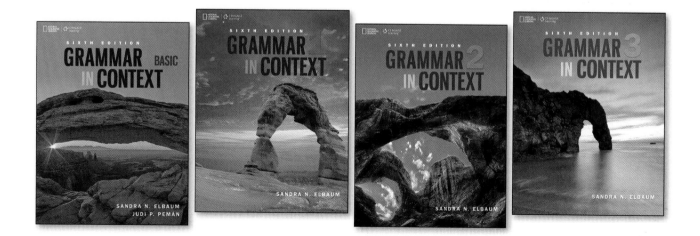

LESSON

1

The Simple Present
Frequency Words

ANIMALS

A black rhino and two zebras roam
a savanna under cloudy skies.

Some people talk to animals. Not many listen though. That's the problem.

—A.A. Milne

Special Friends

Read the following article. Pay special attention to the words in bold.

They **are** our friends. We play with them. We talk to them. We spend a lot of money on them. We love them. Who **are** they? Our pets, of course. About 56 percent of Americans **live** with one or more animals. There **are** about 74 million pet cats and 70 million pet dogs in the United States. There **are** more pets than children in the United States! The most popular pets **are** dogs and cats. Other popular pets **are** fish, birds, and rabbits.

Pet ownership **isn't** cheap. Americans spend more than $55 billion a year on their pets. There **are** schools, toys, hotels, clothes, and cemeteries for pets. The average dog owner spends over $200 a year on vet[1] bills.

For many Americans, pets **are** part of the family. Many owners sleep with their dogs or cats. Some people travel with their pets. (The average cost to fly with a pet is $125 each way.) Some hotels allow guests to bring their pets.

Pets are great for your health. Contact with an affectionate[2] dog or cat can lower a person's blood pressure. Also, pets **are** a comfort to lonely people.

Animals need a lot of attention. Before you buy a pet, it **is** important to answer these questions:
- **Are** you patient?
- **Are** you home a lot?
- If you have children, **are** they responsible?
- **Is** this a good animal for children?
- **Are** pets allowed where you live?
- **Are** you or your family members allergic[3] to pets?

It **is** important to understand that a pet **is** a long-term responsibility—and a long-term friend.

---

1 *vet*: short for veterinarian; an animal doctor
2 *affectionate*: loving
3 *allergic*: very sensitive to a particular animal or plant

A man plays with his affectionate dog.

COMPREHENSION CHECK Based on the reading, tell if the statement is true (**T**) or false (**F**).

1. The most popular pets in the U.S. are dogs and cats.

2. About 74 percent of Americans have a pet.

3. Pets are not allowed on an airplane.

1.1 *Be* Simple Present—Form

Examples			Explanation
Subject	**Form of *Be***		**Forms of *be*: *am*, *is*, *are***
I	**am**	happy with my dog.	We use *am* with *I*.
The child He She The cat It That There	**is**	responsible. intelligent. lonely. happy. cute. a friendly cat. a dog in the yard.	We use *is* with *he, she, it, this, that*, and singular subjects (*the child, the cat, this, that*, etc). We use *there is* with a singular noun.
We You Pets They Those There	**are**	responsible. home a lot. fun. good friends. cute kittens. schools for dogs.	We use *are* with *we, you, they, these, those*, and plural subjects (*pets, cats*, etc.). We use *there are* with a plural noun.

1.2 Contractions with *Be*

Examples		Explanation
I am You are She is He is It is We are They are	**I'm** responsible. **You're** patient. **She's** happy. **He's** kind. **It's** necessary. **We're** busy. **They're** cute.	A contraction combines two words. We can make a contraction with the subject pronoun and *am, is,* or *are*. We put an apostrophe (') in place of the missing letter.
There is Here is That is	**There's** a pet store near my house. **Here's** an idea. Let's get a dog. **That's** a friendly cat.	We can make a contraction with *there is, here is,* and *that is*.
cat is dog is	The **cat's** hungry. Your **dog's** cute.	We can make a contraction with most singular nouns and *is*.
A fo**x** **is** a relative of a dog. A mou**se** **is** a small animal. Thi**s** **is** a cute cat.		We don't make a contraction with *is* if the preceding word ends in *s, se, ce, ge, ze, sh, ch,* or *x*.

♀ ♀ EXERCISE 1 Listen to the conversation. Fill in the blanks with the words you hear.

A: I want a dog. My friend has a dog with new puppies. There _____are_____ nine puppies,

1.

and they need a home. The puppies _____are_____ two months old. They _____are_____

2. 3.

so cute. I want one. Look—this _____is_____ a picture of my favorite puppy.

4.

B: Dogs _____are_____ a big responsibility.

5.

A: Mom, I _____am_____ nine years old now, and I _____am_____ responsible. I love

6. 7.

dogs. They _____are_____ so affectionate. They _____are_____ great friends. And

8. 9.

dogs _____are_____ fun.

10.

B: They _____are_____ expensive too. For example, there _____is_____ the cost of

11. 12.

food.

EXERCISE 2 Fill in the blanks with the correct form of *be* to finish the conversation from Exercise 1.
Use contractions wherever possible.

B: There _____ vet bills.

1.

A: Vet bills?

B: Yes. A vet _____ an animal doctor. Dogs need doctors just like we do. It _____

2. 3.

important to think about that too.

A: But the puppies _____ healthy.

4.

B: You _____ healthy too. But sometimes you _____ sick and

5. 6.

you need a doctor. Also, your little brother _____ only three years old.

7.

He _____ afraid of dogs. Here _____ another problem:

8. 9.

It _____ summer now, so it _____ easy to take the dog out.

10. 11.

But in winter, it _____ so cold.

12.

A: Please, Mom.

B: Let me think about it. I have to talk to Dad. We _____ your parents, and we want

13.

to make the right decision.

A: Thanks, Mom.

1.3 Be—Use

Examples	Uses
I **am** patient.	With a description (an adjective)
A vet **is** an animal doctor.	With a classification or definition of the subject
My dog **is** in the yard.	With a location
This dog **is** from Alaska.	With a place of origin
The dog **is** cold. It **is** cold outside.	With a physical reaction to the temperature (*hot, cold, warm*) and with weather. The subject for sentences about weather is *it*.
My dog **is** three (years old).	With age
The cat **is** hungry. I **am** afraid of dogs.	With a physical or emotional state: *hungry, thirsty, afraid*
There **are** toys for dogs. There **is** an animal hospital near my house.	With *there*, to show that something exists
It **is** ten o'clock now.	The subject for time is *it*.
It **is** important to be responsible with a pet.	With certain expressions beginning with *it*

Language Note:

Some words that end in *-ed* are adjectives: *tired, married, worried, interested, bored, excited, crowded, located.*

> The pet shop is **located** on the corner.
> The children are **excited** about the new puppy.

EXERCISE 3 Fill in the blanks with the correct form of *be*. Then write **D** for description, **C** for classification, **L** for location, **O** for origin, **W** for weather, **A** for age, **P** for a physical or emotional state, **TH** for *there*, **T** for time, **I** for expressions beginning with *it*. Use contractions wherever possible.

1. My dog <u>'s</u> small. <u>D</u>

2. You _____ home a lot. _____

3. This dog _____ friendly. _____

4. There _____ a lot of pets in the U.S. _____

5. It _____ fun to own a pet. _____

6. It _____ hot today. _____

7. The dog _____ thirsty. _____

8. The puppies _____ three months old. _____

9. It _____ 7 a.m. _____

10. I _____ from Vietnam. _____

11. Vietnam _____ a country in Asia. _____

1.4 Negative Statements with *Be*

Examples	Explanation
The dog owner **is not** home now. She **isn't** home during the day. You **are not** ready for a pet. You **aren't** patient.	To make a negative statement with *be*, we put *not* after a form of *be*. The negative contractions are *isn't* and *aren't*.

We can make contractions in negative statements with most subject pronouns + a form of *be* or with a form of *be* + *not*. (Exception: *I am not*)

I am not	I'm not		—
you are not	you're not	OR	you aren't
he is not	he's not	OR	he isn't
she is not	she's not	OR	she isn't
it is not	it's not	OR	it isn't
we are not	we're not	OR	we aren't
they are not	they're not	OR	they aren't

Language Notes:

1. We can make contractions with most nouns:

   The dog is not friendly. = The **dog's not** friendly. = The **dog isn't** friendly.

2. Remember: We cannot make a contraction with certain words + *is*. (See 1.2)

   This is not a good pet. = This isn't a good pet. (NOT *This's not*)

EXERCISE 4 Fill in the first blank with the correct form of *be*. Then fill in the second blank with a negative form. Use contractions wherever possible. In some cases, more than one answer is possible.

1. Today <u>'s</u> my daughter's birthday. It <u>isn't</u> a holiday.
     a.   b.

2. My daughter and I _____ at the pet shop. We _____ at home.
                           a.   b.

3. My husband _____ at work now. He _____ with me.
                     a.   b.

4. I _____ patient with dogs. I _____ patient with cats.
        a.   b.

5. This puppy _____ for my daughter. It _____ for my son.
                    a.   b.

6. My daughter _____ responsible. My son _____ responsible.
                      a.   b.

7. Dogs _____ good for protection. Cats _____ good for protection.
            a.   b.

8. This _____ a small dog. It _____ a big dog.
           a.   b.

9. There _____ a lot of puppies here. There _____ a lot of kittens here.
              a.   b.

EXERCISE 5 Circle the correct words to complete the sentences. In some cases, both answers are possible, so circle both options.

1. My dog (*is* / *are*) sick.

2. (*She's not* / *She isn't*) young.

3. She (*is* / *'s*) 15 years old.

4. She (*isn't* / *not*) hungry.

5. This (*is* / *'s*) a serious problem.

6. My dog and I (*am* / *are*) at the vet.

7. (*I'm not* / *I amn't*) happy.

8. We (*is* / *are*) worried about the dog.

9. (*The vet's* / *The vet*) a good doctor.

10. There (*'s* / *are*) many dogs in the waiting room.

11. (*They aren't* / *They're not*) all sick.

12. There (*are* / *is*) one cat in the waiting room.

13. (*It's* / *It*) in a box.

14. The box (*is* / *'s*) small.

15. There (*are* / *'re*) pet magazines in the waiting room.

16. (*Is* / *It's*) important to have a healthy pet.

17. (*It's* / *It*) my turn with the vet now.

18. (*I'm* / *I*) next.

1.5 Yes/No Questions and Short Answers with *Be*

Compare statement word order with yes/no question word order.

Statement Word Order	Yes/No Question	Short Answer
I am patient.	**Am I** patient with pets?	Yes, you are.
You are happy.	**Are you** happy with the new dog?	Yes, I am.
The vet is kind.	**Is the vet** patient?	Yes, she is.
It is important to take the dog to the vet.	**Is it** important to give the dog exercise?	Yes, it is.
We are at the vet.	**Are we** in her office?	No, we're not.
Pets are fun.	**Are pets** interesting?	Yes, they are.
They are interested in a pet.	**Are they** interested in a bird?	No, they aren't.
Those are cute puppies.	**Are those** your puppies?	Yes, they are.
That is a friendly dog.	**Is that** your dog?	No, it's not.
There are dogs at the vet.	**Are there** birds at the vet?	No, there aren't.

Language Notes:

1. In a question, we put *am, is,* or *are* before the subject.
2. We use a contraction for a short *no* answer. We don't use a contraction for a short *yes* answer.

   Is your son responsible? No, he isn't. **OR** No, he's not.

   Is your daughter responsible? Yes, she is. (NOT Yes, she's.)
3. We use a pronoun (*he, we, you,* etc.) in a short answer.
4. When the question contains *this* or *that*, the answer uses *it*, even for people.

   Is that the vet? Yes, **it** is.

Pronunciation Note: We usually end a *yes/no* question with rising intonation.

EXERCISE 6 Fill in the blanks to complete each item. Use contractions wherever possible.

1. **A:** _____Is a bird_____ a good pet?

   B: Yes, it is. A bird is a very good pet.

2. **A:** _____Are you_____ happy with your new kitten?

   B: Yes, I am. My new kitten is fun.

3. **A:** _Is your son_____ interested in birds?

   B: No, he _____isn't_____. My son's interested in fish.

4. **A:** _Is there_____ a vet near here?

   B: Yes, _there is_____. There's a vet on the next block.

5. **A:** _Is your dog____ in the yard?

   B: No, she _____isn't_____. The dog is in the house.

6. **A:** _Are you_ ready for a dog?

   B: No, I'm not. _I'm_ not home enough.

7. **A:** _~~Are yo~~ Am I_ good with pets?

   B: No, you _aren't_. You're not patient enough.

EXERCISE 7 Fill in the blanks to complete this conversation. Use contractions wherever possible. In some cases, more than one answer is possible.

A: _Is_ this your dog?
   1.

B: Yes, it _is_.
   2.

A: He _He's_ beautiful.
   3.

B: Thanks. But it's a "she."

A: _Is she_ friendly?
   4.

B: Yes, she _is_.
   5.

A: She's so small. _Is she_ a puppy?
   6.

B: No, she _isn't_. _She's_ four years old.
   7.   8.

A: _Is it_ hard to take care of a dog?
   9.

B: No, it _isn't_.
   10.

A: _Are you_ home a lot?
   11.

B: No, _I'm not_. _I'm_ a student. But my parents _are_
   12.   13.   14.

home a lot.

A: I love dogs, but I _~~am not~~ I'm not_ home very much, and I live alone. So that _is_
   15.   16.

a problem.

B: Cats _are_ good pets too. With a cat, it _isn't_ necessary to be
   17.   18.

home a lot. I think a cat _is_ the perfect pet for you. _~~Is that~~ Am I_
   19.   20.

right?

A: No, you _aren't_. I'm allergic to cats.
   21.

1.6 Wh- Questions with Be

Compare statement word order with wh- question word order.

Affirmative Statements	Affirmative Wh- Questions
I am lost.	Where **am I**?
You are lonely.	Why **are you** lonely?
That is a nice dog.	What kind of dog **is that**?
The cat is old.	How old **is the cat**?
It is important to choose the right pet.	Why **is it** important to choose the right pet?
She is at work.	When **is she** at home?
There are a lot of dogs in my neighborhood.	How many dogs **are there** in your neighborhood?
Negative Statements	**Negative Wh- Questions**
The dogs aren't friendly.	Why **aren't the dogs** friendly?
You aren't happy with the dog.	Why **aren't you** happy with the dog?

Language Notes:

1. Most question words can contract with *is*. (Exceptions: *which is; how much is*)

> What's a vet?

> Where's your cat?

> Which is bigger, my dog or your dog?

3. After *what*, we can use a noun:

> what kind, what color, what country, what time

4. After *how*, we can use an adjective or adverb:

> how long, how hard, how old, how big, how much, how many

5. After *which*, we can use a noun:

> which dog, which vet, which animal

🎧 CD 1 TR 4 **EXERCISE 8** Fill in the blanks with the words you hear.

A: _____Is that_____ your dog?

 1.

B: No. It's my neighbor's dog.

A: _What kind of dog is it_____? It's so cute.

 2.

B: I think it's a mutt.

A: _What's_____ a mutt?

 3.

B: It's a mixed breed dog.

A: My daughter wants a dog. But dogs are so expensive.

B: A mutt isn't so expensive.

A: _why isn't it_____ expensive?

 4.

B: Because a mutt isn't so popular. You can get a mutt at an animal shelter. Dogs aren't expensive there.

A: _What's_ an animal shelter?
5.

B: It's a place for unwanted pets. Those animals need a loving family.

A: _are they_ healthy?
6.

B: Yes, they _are_ . The vets check the animals' health.
7.

A: Why _are there_ so many unwanted pets?
8.

B: There are a lot of unwanted pets because some people aren't responsible. They get a pet and then realize it's too much trouble to take care of it. What about your daughter?

Is she responsible?
9.

A: Yes, _she is_ .
10.

B: _How old is she_ ?
11.

A: She's almost ten years old.

B: I love dogs, but it's not a good idea for our family.

A: _why isn't it_ a good idea?
12.

B: We're all too busy.

EXERCISE 9 Fill in the blanks to complete the phone conversation.

A: Hello?

B: Hi, Betty. This is Lara. How _are you_ ?
1.

A: I'm fine. I'm not home now.

B: Where _are you_ ?
2.

A: I'm at the animal hospital with the cat.

B: You have two cats. Which cat _is_ sick?
3.

A: Fluffy.

B: _What's_ wrong with Fluffy?
4.

A: He isn't hungry or thirsty.

continued

B: _How old is he_ ?
     5.

A: He's only four years old.

B: _Are you_ alone?
     6.

A: No, I'm not.

B: _Who is_ with you?
     7.

A: My daughter's with me.

B: Why _isn't she_ at school?
              8.

A: She's on spring break now. She's very worried.

B: Why _is she_ worried?
              9.

A: Fluffy is tired all the time. Oh, I have to go. The vet is ready to see us now.

B: OK. Call me later.

EXERCISE 10 About You Find a partner. Ask each other these questions and share your answers.

1. Are pets popular in your native country? What kind?

2. What's a popular name for dogs in your native culture?

3. What's a better pet—a dog or a cat?

GUIDE DOGS

CD 1
TR 5

Read the following article. Pay special attention to the words in bold.

Most pet dogs have an easy life. They **eat, play,** and **sleep.** But guide dogs **work** hard. They **go** to school for training. They **learn** to help blind people move from place to place safely.

Guide dog training **lasts** five months. The dogs **take** difficult tests to graduate. If they **graduate,** they **get** a job. Only about 72 percent of dogs in the training program **graduate.** In pet dog training, trainers **use** food as a reward. In guide dog training, the trainers **don't use** food. They **use** physical and verbal affection.

Guide dogs **don't** completely **lead** their owners, and their owners **don't** completely **control** the guide dogs. They **work** together as a team. A guide dog **doesn't know** where its owner wants to go, so it **follows** the owner's instructions. Dogs **don't see** color, so they **don't know** if a traffic light is red or green. A guide dog **stops** at all curbs[4] and intersections and **waits** for the owner's command. The owner **decides** if it **is** time to cross the street by listening to the sound of traffic. The dog **doesn't decide.**

A guide dog **works** in all kinds of situations: noisy places, bad weather, crowds of people, and other difficult situations. Guiding **is** very complicated, and it **requires** a dog's full attention. When you **see** a guide dog, don't pet it or talk to it. The dog **needs** to concentrate on its job.

Most guide dogs **are** golden retrievers, Labrador retrievers, or German shepherds. These three breeds are very intelligent, obedient,[5] and friendly.

Like other dogs, guide dogs **like** to play too, but only after the work is finished. How **do** dogs **know** when their work is finished? When the harness[6] is on, they **know** there is work to do. When it is off, they can play.

---

[4] *curb*: the edge between the sidewalk and the street
[5] *obedient*: willing to follow rules
[6] *harness*: a strap and collar that some dogs wear

A woman walks with her guide dog.

COMPREHENSION CHECK Based on the reading, tell if the statement is true (**T**) or false (**F**).

1. A guide dog decides when it is time to cross the street.

2. Trainers use food to train a guide dog.

3. It takes five months to train a guide dog.

1.7 The Simple Present Affirmative Statements—Form

A simple present tense verb has two forms: the base form and the -s form.

Examples			Explanation
Subject	**Base Form**	**Complement**	We use the base form of the verb when the subject is *I, you, we, they,* or a plural noun. **NOTE:** *People* is a plural noun.
I You We They Some people	**work**	hard.	
Subject	**-s Form**	**Complement**	We use the -s form of the verb when the subject is *he, she, it,* or a singular noun. **NOTE:** *Everyone* and *family* are singular words.
He She It The dog Everyone My family	**works**	hard.	

Language Notes:

1. *Have* is an irregular verb. The -s form is *has.*

   I **have** a pet dog. My friend **has** a guide dog.

2. We use the -s form in the following expression: It **takes** (time) to do something.

   It **takes** time to train a guide dog.

3. We use the -s form after an *-ing* subject (gerund).

   Training a dog **starts** early.

4. For the spelling of the -s form, see Appendix A.

EXERCISE 11 Fill in the blanks with the words you hear.

Most people _____think_____ of a dog as a pet. But people _____use_____ dogs
1.   2.

for all kinds of reasons. Guide dogs _____help_____ people with disabilities. Another
3.

kind of helpful dog is a search and rescue dog. *Search* _____means_____ "look for." *Rescue*
4.

_____means_____ "to help someone in a dangerous situation." In a disaster, such as an
5.

earthquake or a flood, it is important to find missing people quickly. You probably

_____Know_____ that dogs _____have_____ an excellent sense of smell. Their sense of
6.   7.

smell _____makes_____ them great in search situations. They _____work_____ with
8.   9.

humans to try to find missing people. They _____save_____ many lives. They
10.

_____find_____ people that humans can't find. I _____love_____ dogs. And I
11.   12.

_____love_____ to help other people.
13.

I _____plan_____ to enter a training program for search and rescue dogs. The
14.

training program for people _____lasts_____ twelve weeks. The training program for dogs
15.

usually _____begins_____ when the dog is twelve weeks old.
16.

The trainer and the dogs _____work_____ together to save lives.
17.

1.8 The Simple Present—Use

Examples	Uses of the Simple Present
A dog **has** a good sense of smell. Guide dogs **help** people. Americans **love** pets. Some people **sleep** with their pets.	To talk about general truths, habits, or customs
I **walk** my dog three times a day. He **feeds** his cat every morning and every night.	To show regular activity or repeated action

EXERCISE 12 Fill in the blanks with the base form or the *-s* form of the verb given.

1. A guide dog _____needs_____ to take a test to graduate.
need

2. Training a guide dog _____ time and patience.
take

3. Trainers _____ affection to teach the dogs.
use

4. A guide dog _____ at all curbs.
stop

5. It _____ to wait for the owner's instructions.
need

6. When you _____ a guide dog, don't play with it.
see

7. Everyone _____ to understand this.
need

8. My neighbor _____ a guide dog.
have

1.9 The Simple Present—Negative Statements

Examples	Explanation
The owner **decides** when to cross the street. The dog **doesn't decide** when to cross the street. The dog **stops** at a curb. It **doesn't stop** because of a red light.	We use *doesn't* + the base form with *he, she, it,* or a singular subject. **Compare:** decides doesn't **decide** stops doesn't **stop** *Doesn't* is the contraction for *does not*.
Some trainers **use** food to reward a dog. Guide dog trainers **don't use** food. We **have** a cat. We **don't have** a dog.	We use *don't* + the base form with *I, you, we, they,* or a plural subject. **Compare:** use don't **use** have don't **have** *Don't* is the contraction for *do not*.

EXERCISE 13 Fill in the blanks with the negative form of the underlined verb.

1. A guide dog <u>needs</u> a lot of training. A pet dog ___*doesn't need*___ a lot of training.

2. Most dogs <u>play</u> a lot. Guide dogs _____ during their work time.

3. A guide dog <u>works</u> hard. A pet dog _____ hard.

4. People <u>see</u> colors. Dogs _____ colors.

5. A guide dog <u>goes</u> on public transportation. A pet dog _____ on

    public transportation.

6. *Search* <u>means</u> "look for." *Rescue* _____ "look for."

7. A dog <u>has</u> a good sense of smell. A person _____ a good sense of

    smell (compared to a dog).

8. Training <u>begins</u> with young dogs. Training _____ when a dog

    is an adult.

9. I <u>want</u> to train rescue dogs. I _____ to train family dogs.

10. You <u>work</u> with guide dogs. You _____ with search and rescue dogs.

EXERCISE 14 Fill in the blanks with the correct negative form of one of the verbs from the box.

make	allow	help✓	know	work	graduate
like	want	leave	use		

1. Rescue dogs ___*don't help*___ people with disabilities. They try to find people in danger.

2. Most restaurants _____ pets, but they permit guide dogs.

3. A dog _____ if a traffic light is green or red.

4. About 28 percent of dogs _____ from a guide dog training program.

5. Guide dogs _____ when the harness is off.

6. The dog _____ the decision to cross the street.

7. Guide dog trainers _____ food as a reward. They use affection.

8. Don't pet or play with a guide dog. The owner _____ the dog to

   lose concentration on the job.

9. Dogs _____ to be alone. They enjoy people.

10. Some people _____ their pets when they go on vacation.

    They travel with their pets.

A rescue dog prepares for a training exercise.

LUCY COOKE, ZOOLOGIST

Read the following article. Pay special attention to the words in bold.

CD 1
TR 7

Which animal **do** you **prefer** to see? A baby panda, a toad, or a snake? Most people choose the baby panda. Why **do** people **choose** this animal? Most people like cute, furry animals with big eyes, like the panda. These animals get a lot of attention. Why **don't** people **like** snakes and toads? They're just not cute like pandas.

Lucy Cooke wants people to respect all animals. Who is Lucy Cooke? Why **does** she **want** to show people the importance of other animals? Cooke is a zoologist, a scientist who studies animals. She worries about the future of all animals. Scientists need money to study and protect these animals, but they get less money for toads and snakes than for pandas.

"There are so many television shows about koala bears and kittens," Cooke says. To get people interested in less popular animals, Cooke writes stories about them in a blog. She also makes videos about them and puts them online. People love her videos. Many of them are fun to watch.

Cooke is especially interested in frogs and other amphibians.[7] Some of these are in danger of disappearing. She wants to save these animals. Why **does** she **want** to save these animals? Other animals depend on them for food. If we save frogs, we save other animals too.

Do you **know** about the flying frog in Borneo? It has wings. It lives in the treetops and goes from tree to tree without going down to the ground. **Do** you **know** about the poison[8] dart frog? It is only one centimeter long. But it has enough poison to kill ten people.

Scientists need research money to protect all animals. Cooke's videos and blog make people aware of all kinds of animals.

---

[7] *amphibian*: an animal that can live on the land or in the water
[8] *poison*: a substance that harms or kills people or animals

COMPREHENSION CHECK Based on the reading, tell if the statement is true (**T**) or false (**F**).

1. Cooke makes videos about animals.

2. The Borneo frog needs to go to the ground to get food.

3. Cooke writes a blog about animals.

1.10 The Simple Present—Questions

Compare statements, *yes/no* questions, and short answers.

Statement	Yes/No Question & Short Answer	Explanation
Cooke **studies** animals. She **writes** a blog.	**Does** she **study** frogs? Yes, she **does**. **Does** she **write** about pets? No, she **doesn't**.	For *yes/no* questions with *he, she, it,* or a singular subject, we use *Does* + subject + base form.
People **like** cute animals. Koala bears **get** attention.	**Do** people **like** insects? No, they **don't**. **Do** pandas **get** attention? Yes, they **do**.	For *yes/no* questions with *I, we, you, they,* or a plural subject, we use *Do* + subject + base form.

Language Note:

Compare *yes/no* questions and short answers with *be* and other simple present verbs:

> **Is** Cooke a zoologist? Yes, she **is**.
> **Does** Cooke do research? Yes, she **does**.

Compare statements and *Wh-* questions.

Statement	Wh- Question	Explanation
Cooke **studies** frogs. She **makes** videos.	How **does** Cooke **study** frogs? Why **does** she **make** videos?	For *wh-* questions with *he, she, it,* or a singular subject, we use *Wh-* word + *does* + subject + base form.
Some frogs **live** in trees. Some frogs **have** wings.	Where **do** other frogs **live**? Why **do** these frogs **have** wings?	For *wh-* questions with *I, we, you, they,* or a plural subject, we use *Wh-* word + *do* + subject + base form.
Cooke **doesn't study** plants. Borneo frogs **don't live** on the ground.	Why **doesn't** Cooke **study** plants? Why **don't** Borneo frogs **live** on the ground?	For negative *wh-* questions, we use *Wh-* word + *don't* or *doesn't* + subject + base form.

Language Note:

Compare *wh-* questions with *be* and other simple present tense verbs:

> What kind of animals **are** you interested in?
> What kind of animals **do** you **like**?
> Why **aren't** people interested in some animals?
> Why **don't** people **like** some animals?

EXERCISE 15 Listen to the conversation. Fill in the blanks with the words you hear.

A: There's a program on TV tonight about search and rescue dogs. _Do you want_ (1.) to watch it with me?

B: I _know_ (2.) about guide dogs. But I _don't know_ (3.) anything about search and rescue dogs. What _does_ (4.) search _mean_ (5.)?

A: Search _means_ (6.) "look for."

B: _How do you spell_ (7.) search?

A: S-E-A-R-C-H.

B: What _do_ (8.) these dogs _do_ (9.)?

A: When there is a disaster, like an earthquake, they _help_ (10.) the workers find missing people. They _save_ (11.) people's lives.

B: How _do_ (12.) they _do_ (13.) that?

A: They _have_ (14.) a great sense of smell. They can find things that people can't.

B: _Do they need_ (15.) a lot of training?

A: Yes, they _do_ (16.).

B: What kind of dogs _do they use_ (17.)?

A: They usually _are_ (18.) large, strong dogs. Labrador retrievers or golden retrievers are often search and rescue dogs. Let's watch the program together tonight.

B: What time _does it begin_ (19.)?

A: At 9 p.m.

B: _Does_ (20.) your dog _want_ (21.) to watch the program with us?

A: Ha! I _don't_ (22.) think so. My dog is lazy. She just _likes_ (23.) to eat, play, and sleep.

EXERCISE 16 Fill in the blanks to complete the conversation. Use context clues to help you.

A: Do you _like_ (1.) animals?

B: Yes, I _____ (2.). In fact, I like animals very much, especially dogs.

A: _____ (3.) a dog?

B: No, I don't have a dog, but my sister has two Labradors. I love to play with them when I visit her.

A: If you love dogs, why _____ a dog?
4.

B: Because my landlord _____ dogs.
5.

A: That's too bad. _____ he permit cats?
6.

B: Yes, he _____.
7.

A: Why _____ cats but not dogs?
8.

B: He says dogs make a lot of noise. I have a cat, but I have to find a new home for her.

_____ you know anyone who wants a cat?
9.

A: No, I _____. Sorry. Why _____ your cat?
10.   11.

B: I want my cat, but my girlfriend doesn't.

A: Why _____ your cat?
12.

B: She's allergic to cats.

A: That's a problem.

EXERCISE 17 About You Choose Part 1 to interview a student who has a dog, or Part 2 to interview a student who has a cat.

PART 1: Use the words below to interview a student with a dog.

1. your dog / big
   A: Is your dog big?
   B: Yes, she is.

2. your dog / sleep a lot (how many hours)
   A: Does your dog sleep a lot?
   B: Yes, she does.
   A: How many hours does she sleep?
   B: She sleeps about fifteen hours a day.

3. how old / your dog

4. it / a male or a female

5. what / your dog's name

6. what / your dog / eat

7. how often / you / take your dog out

8. your dog / do tricks (what kind)

9. your dog / have toys (what kind)

continued

10. your dog / friendly

11. your dog / bark a lot (when)

12. why / you / like dogs

PART 2: Use the words below to interview a student with a cat.

1. how old / your cat

2. it / a male or a female

3. what / your cat's name

4. your cat / eat special food (what kind)

5. your cat / friendly

6. your cat / sit on your lap a lot

7. your cat / have toys (what kind)

8. your cat / sleep with you (where)

9. why / you / like cats

EXERCISE 18 Circle the correct words to complete the conversation.

A: We're late. Hurry. The train is ready to leave.

B: Let's go . . . (on the train) . . . Why (*that dog is*/*is that dog*) on the train? (*Are/Do*) they allow
1.   2.

dogs on trains?

A: Not usually. But that's not an ordinary dog. That's a guide dog. It's a dog that helps people

with disabilities.

B: How (*do they help*/*they help*) people?
3.

A: They (*help*/*helps*) blind people move from place to place, on foot and by public transportation.
4.

B: (*Are/Do*) they need a lot of training?
5.

A: Yes, they (*are/do*).
6.

B: Where (*do/are*) they get their training?
7.

A: They get their training at special schools. There are guide dogs for the blind, the deaf,[9] and

people in wheelchairs.

B: Why (*are you*/*you are*) such an expert on guide dogs?
8.

A: My cousin is blind. He has a guide dog.

B: Then you know a lot about guide dogs.

---

9 *deaf:* not able to hear

A: Yes, I (*am/do*). A guide dog (*need/needs*) to concentrate.
  9.   10.

B: When (*are/do*) they play?
  11.

A: They (*play/plays*) when the owner (*take/takes*) off the dog's harness. Then the dog
  12.   13.

(*know/knows*) its work is finished.
  14.

B: It's amazing what a dog can do.

1.11 *Wh-* Questions with a Preposition

Examples	Explanation
A: What does Lucy Cooke write **about**? **B:** She writes about animals in danger. **A:** What are these animals in danger **of**? **B:** They're in danger of disappearing.	In conversation, most people put the preposition at the end of the *wh-* question.
A: Where does Lucy Cooke **come from**? **B:** She comes from England. **A:** Where **is** she **from**? **B:** She's from England.	For place of origin, we use *be from* or *come from*.
A: What time does the program begin? **B:** It begins **at** 9 p.m.	We omit *at* in a question about time.

Language Note:

Putting the preposition before a question word is very formal. When the preposition comes at the beginning, we use *whom*, not *who*.

FORMAL: **With whom** does the dog sleep?

INFORMAL: **Who** does the dog sleep **with**?

EXERCISE 19 Complete each question using the underlined words as clues.

1. Lucy Cooke <u>comes from</u> England. What city _____*does*_____ she ___*come from*___ ?

2. <u>I'm interested in</u> pandas. What animals _____ you _____ ?

3. What _____ Lucy Cooke _____ ? She <u>writes</u> a blog <u>about</u>

   animals in danger.

4. Who _____ ? She <u>studies</u> animals <u>with</u> other zoologists.

5. She <u>travels to</u> other countries. Which countries _____ ?

6. Cooke <u>worries about</u> certain animals. Which animals _____ ?

7. I <u>want to learn</u> more <u>about</u> tree frogs. What animals _____ you _____

   _____ ?

1.12 Questions About Meaning, Spelling, Cost, and Time

Wh- Word	Do/Does	Subject	Verb (Base Form)	Complement
What	does	"puppy"	mean?	
How	do	you	spell	"puppy"?
How	do	you	say	"puppy" in Spanish?
How much	does	a puppy	cost?	
How long	does	it	take	to train a puppy?

Language Note:

Questions about meaning, spelling, cost, and *take* + time follow usual question word order.

EXERCISE 20 Fill in the blanks to complete the conversation.

A: <u>Do you have</u> a pet?
1.

B: Yes. I have a new kitten.

A: I don't know the word "kitten." What _____?
2.

B: Kitten means "baby cat."

A: Oh. What's his name?

B: Romeo.

A: How _____?
3.

B: R-O-M-E-O. _____ any pets?
4.

A: Yes, I do. I have a bird.

B: What kind of bird _____?
5.

A: I have a bird that talks. I don't know the name in English.

How _____ "loro" in English?
6.

B: Parrot. So you have a parrot.

A: Yes. His name is Chico.

B: How old _____?
7.

A: He's almost twenty years old.

B: How long _____?

8.

A: They live a long time. Some live up to eighty years.

B: How much _____?

9.

A: It depends on what kind you get. But they usually cost between $175 and $1,000.

B: Wow! _____ parrots affectionate?

10.

A: Oh, yes. They're very affectionate. Chico sits on my shoulder all the time.

B: What _____?

11.

A: He eats fruit, vegetables, rice, nuts, and seeds.

B: _____ a lot?

12.

A: Yes. He talks a lot.

B: What _____?

13.

A: He says, "Good-bye," "Hello," "I love you," and many more things. He speaks Spanish and

English.

B: How long _____ to teach the parrot a word?

14.

A: My parrot is very smart. It takes a few weeks to teach him one word.

A woman goes grocery shopping with her pet parrot.

Bottlenose Dolphins

CD 1
TR 9

Read the following article. Pay special attention to the words in bold.

Bottlenose dolphins are very popular animals. We **often** see them in aquariums, sea parks, TV shows, and movies. Because of the shape of their nose, they look like they **always** have a smile on their faces.

Bottlenose dolphins live in warm climates. They live underwater, but they **rarely** stay there for more than seven minutes. Humans are involuntary[10] breathers. We don't **usually** think about breathing. But dolphins have to remember to breathe. One side of their brain is **always** active. This means they **never** fully sleep.

Dolphins have an excellent sense of hearing. They use clicking sounds to find food. The sound echoes[11] back and tells them where the food is.

Bottlenose dolphins are social animals. They **usually** swim in groups of ten to fifteen. Together they hunt[12] for food. They **sometimes** hunt with fishermen near their fishing boats. **Once in a while** a dolphin hunts alone. **Sometimes** a dolphin gets lost. Each dolphin has a unique[13] whistle, so it uses its whistle to call out to the group.

Bottlenose dolphins **usually** live about forty to fifty years.

---

[10] *involuntary*: done without thinking
[11] *to echo*: to be repeated by bouncing off a surface
[12] *to hunt*: to search for
[13] *unique*: one of a kind; not like anything else

COMPREHENSION CHECK Based on the reading, tell if the statement is true (**T**) or false (**F**).

1. Bottlenose dolphins are involuntary breathers.

2. Bottlenose dolphins usually hunt alone.

3. The whistle of the bottlenose dolphin helps it find other dolphins.

1.13 Frequency Words with the Simple Present

Examples	Explanation
Dolphins **never** fully sleep. They **always** come up for air. They **sometimes** hunt with fishermen.	We use the simple present with frequency words to show a regular activity.
Whenever a dolphin gets lost, it uses sound to find its group.	*Whenever* shows a regular activity. It means "any time."

Frequency Words	Frequency	
always	100%	
usually/generally	↑	
often/frequently		
sometimes/occasionally		
rarely/seldom/hardly ever	↓	
never/not ever	0%	

Language Note:

Hardly ever is more informal than *rarely* or *seldom*.

FORMAL: Dolphins **rarely** hunt alone.

INFORMAL: Dolphins **hardly ever** hunt alone.

EXERCISE 21 Fill in the blanks with a phrase from the box.

always come	is always	are never✓	usually live	sometimes get	usually think

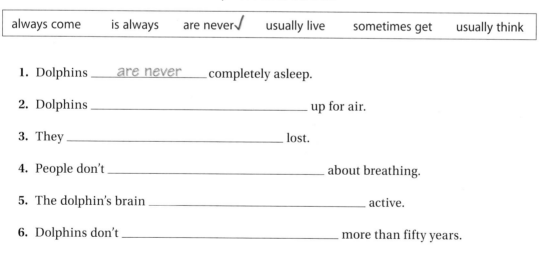

1. Dolphins _____*are never*_____ completely asleep.

2. Dolphins _____ up for air.

3. They _____ lost.

4. People don't _____ about breathing.

5. The dolphin's brain _____ active.

6. Dolphins don't _____ more than fifty years.

EXERCISE 22 About You Fill in the blanks with an appropriate frequency word to talk about your native country or culture. Find a partner and compare your answers.

1. People in my native culture _____*rarely*_____ have cats in the house.

2. Dogs in my native culture _____ sleep with their owners.

3. Dogs are _____ part of the family.

4. Cats are _____ part of the family.

5 People _____ feed pet food to cats and dogs.

6. People _____ travel with their pets.

7. People _____ take dogs into restaurants.

8. Blind people _____ use dogs to help them.

9. People are _____ kind to animals.

EXERCISE 23 Look again at the sentences in Exercise 22. Does the frequency word come before or after the verb? Write *B* for *before* or *A* for *after*.

1. ____B____   4. _____   7. _____

2. _____   5. _____   8. _____

3. _____   6. _____   9. _____

1.14 Position of Frequency Words

Examples	Explanation
A dolphin's brain **is always** active.	A frequency word can come after the verb *be*.
A dolphin **rarely stays** under water for more than 7 minutes.	A frequency word can come before other verbs.
Sometimes a dolphin gets lost. A dolphin **sometimes** gets lost. Dolphins **usually** swim in groups. **Usually** dolphins swim in groups.	*Sometimes* and *usually* can come close to the verb or at the beginning of the sentence.

Language Note

Always and *never* are rarely at the beginning of the sentence.

      I'm **always** interested in animal TV programs. (NOT: *Always* I'm interested....)

      Fish **never** live on land. (NOT: *Never* fish live...)

EXERCISE 24 Rewrite the sentence, adding the word given.

1. A guide dog stops at an intersection. (*always*)

   A guide dog always stops at an intersection.

2. Dogs like to play. (*often*)

   _____

3. Lucy Cooke is excited about animals. (*always*)

   _____

4. Dolphins hunt with fishermen. (*sometimes*)

   _____

5. Dolphins come up for air. (*always*)

   _____

6. People go to sea parks to see dolphins (*sometimes*)

   _____

7. Sea parks are crowded in the summer. (*always*)

   _____

8. A dolphin hunts alone. (*rarely*)

   _____

9. A dolphin is awake. (*always*)

   _____

10. A dolphin leaves its group. (*hardly ever*)

    _____

1.15 Questions about Frequency

Yes/No Questions with *Ever*

Do/Does	Subject	*Ever*	Verb		Short Answer
Do	you	**ever**	sleep	with your cat?	No, I **never** do.
Does	the teacher		talk	about her dog?	Yes, she **often** does.

Be	Subject	*Ever*		Short Answer
Are	dogs	**ever**	lonely?	Yes, they **sometimes** are.
Is	your cat		home alone?	Yes, she **often** is.

Language Notes:

1. In a short answer, the frequency word comes between the subject and the verb.

2. The verb after *never* is affirmative.

> Does your cat ever drink milk?
>
> No, she never **does**.

EXERCISE 25 Answer the questions with a short answer and the frequency word given.

1. Do dogs ever bark? (*sometimes*)

   <u>Yes, they sometimes do.</u>

2. Do people ever travel with their dogs? (*sometimes*)

   _____

3. Do fish ever make noise? (*never*)

   _____

4. Do birds ever make noise? (*always*)

   _____

5. Do parrots ever live for more than twenty years? (*usually*)

   _____

6. Do dogs ever live for more than twenty years? (*hardly ever*)

   _____

7. Does a dolphin ever swim alone? (*sometimes*)

   _____

8. Are parrots ever affectionate? (*sometimes*)

   _____

9. Do dolphins ever hunt in groups? (*usually*)

_____

10. Are pets ever lonely? (*sometimes*)

_____

1.16 Questions with How Often

Examples	Explanation
How often do you take your dog out? I take her out **three times a day**. **How often** do you take your cat to the vet? I take my cat to the vet **twice a year**.	We use *how often* when we want to know about the frequency of an activity. We answer with a frequency expression.
Once in a while, a dolphin gets lost. A dolphin gets lost **once in a while**. **Every seven minutes**, a dolphin needs air. A dolphin needs air **every seven minutes**.	A frequency expression can come at the beginning or at the end of a sentence. When it comes at the beginning of the sentence, we sometimes separate it from the rest of the sentence with a comma.

Language Note:

Some frequency expressions are:
- every (other) day/week/month/year
- several/many/a few/five times—a day/week/month/year
- once/twice—a day/week/month/year
- from time to time
- once in a while

EXERCISE 26 Fill in the blanks to complete each item.

1. **A:** How _____*often*_____ do you take your dog to the vet?

        a.

   B: I take her to the vet _____ a year, in April.

              b.

2. **A:** Do guide dogs _____ play?

         a.

   B: Yes. They usually play when they finish their work.

3. **A:** Do dolphins _____ swim in groups?

         a.

   B: Yes. They usually swim in groups.

4. **A:** _____ often do dolphins come up for air?

      a.

   B: They come up for air _____ seven minutes.

            b.

5. **A:** _____ do you put your dog in a pet hotel?

      a.

   B: I never _____.

        b.

continued

6. **A:** _____ does your dog want to go out?

            a.

   B: She wants to go out three times _____ .

                                     b.

7. **A:** Does your dog _____ sleep with you?

                        a.

   B: Yes. My dog sleeps with me _____ night.

                             b.

8. **A:** _____ in a while, I take my dog to a dog park. What about you?

            a.

   B: I hardly _____ go there. It's too crowded.

                b.

EXERCISE 27 Fill in the blanks to complete the conversation.

A: I know you love dogs. ___*Do you have*___ a dog now?

                                       1.

B: No, I _____ . But I have two cats. I don't have time for a dog.

                      2.

A: Why _____ time for a dog?

                          3.

B: Because I'm not at home very much. I work in the day and go to school in the evening.

A: How _____ ?

                          4.

B: I have class three nights a week. I love dogs, but dogs need a lot of attention.

A: Cats need attention too.

B: When I'm not home, sometimes my sister comes to play with them.

A: _____ often does she come?

               5.

B: Two or three times _____ week. What about you? _____

                                 6.   7.

any pets?

A: I have several tropical fish.[12]

B: How _____ ?
8.

A: Some tropical fish cost more than $100.

B: Wow! How many fish _____ ?
9.

A: I have about fourteen or fifteen. My favorite is my Oranda.

B: How _____ "Oranda"?
10.

A: O-R-A-N-D-A. It's a kind of a goldfish.

B: You spend a lot of money for a boring pet.

A: Fish _____ boring. It _____ interesting to look at them. And
11. 12.

they _____ easy to take care of. When I go to work, they _____
13. 14.

get lonely, like dogs and cats.

B: Yes, but they _____ affectionate like dogs and cats.
15.

A: They _____ make noise like dogs do, so neighbors never complain about fish.
16.

One thing isn't easy: cleaning the fish tank.

B: _____ clean the tank?
17.

A: About once _____. I usually clean the tank every Saturday.
18.

---

[12] *Fish* can be singular or plural. In this case it is plural.

SUMMARY OF LESSON 1

The Simple Present with *Be*

	With *Is*	With *Are*
Affirmative Statement	Your dog **is** beautiful.	Dolphins **are** smart animals.
Negative Statement	It **isn't** big.	They **aren't** afraid of fishermen.
Yes/No Question	**Is** it friendly?	**Are** dolphins fish?
Short Answer	No, it **isn't**.	No, they **aren't**.
Wh- Question	What kind of dog **is** it?	How smart **are** they?
Negative *Wh-* Question	Why **isn't** it friendly?	Why **aren't** they afraid of fishermen?

The Simple Present with Other Verbs

	Base Form	-s Form
Affirmative Statement	My friends **have** a dog.	She **likes** birds.
Negative Statement	They **don't have** a cat.	She **doesn't like** cats.
Yes/No Question	**Do** they **have** a bird?	**Does** she **like** small birds?
Short Answer	No, they **don't**.	Yes, she **does**.
Wh- Question	What kind of dog **do** they **have**?	Why **does** she **like** birds?
Negative *Wh-* Question	Why **don't** they **have** a cat?	Why **doesn't** she **like** cats?

Frequency Words and Expressions

Frequency Words	Frequency	Frequency Expressions
always	100%	once in a while
usually/generally		from time to time
often/frequently		every day
sometimes/occasionally		once a year
rarely/seldom/hardly ever		several times a day
never/not ever	0%	every other month

Questions and answers with frequency words

Question	Answer
Does he **ever** take his dog to the park?	Yes, he often does.
How often does he feed his dog?	Twice a day.

A: Your dog (*is/are*) very friendly.
1.

B: Yes, he (*love/loves*) people. His name is Buddy.
2.

A: How (*do you spell/you spell*) "Buddy"?
3.

B: B-U-D-D-Y. He's a therapy dog.

A: What (*a therapy dog does/does a therapy dog do*)?
4.

B: He (*make/makes*) sick people feel better.
5.

A: How (*does a therapy dog make/is a therapy dog make*) sick people feel better?
6.

B: People (*feel/feels*) happy when they're with a nice dog. Buddy and I (*often visit/visit often*)
7.   8.

patients in the hospital. Everyone at the hospital (*love/loves*) him.
9.

A: How (*does a dog become/a dog becomes*) a therapy dog?
10.

B: First, the owner (*need/needs*) to answer a few questions such as these:
11.

"(*Is your dog likes/Does your dog like*) people?" or "Does he (*have/has*) a calm personality?"
12.   13.

But that's not enough. (*Always the dog/The dog always*) needs training.
14.

A: How much (*costs the training/does the training cost*)?
15.

B: (*It's cost/It costs*) $150.
16.

A: (*How long it takes/How long does it take*) to train the dog?
17.

B: That (*depend/depends*) on the dog.
18.

A: (*Are/Do*) the dog owners make money?
19.

B: No. We (*work/are work*) as volunteers.
20.

A: How (*often/ever*) (*do you visit/you visit*) the hospital with Buddy?
21.   22.

B: (*We once a week go/Once a week we go*) to the hospital. For more information, check the
23.

TDI website.

A: What (*means TDI/does TDI mean*)?
24.

B: (*It's mean/It means*) "Therapy Dogs International."
25.

A: (*Do you ever/Do ever you*) get tired of working with sick people?
26.

B: No, I (*don't never/never do*). I have to go now. Buddy (*needs/is needs*) water.
27.   28.

A: How (*does you know/do you know*) that?
29.

B: His tongue is out. That's dog talk for "(*I/I'm*) thirsty."
30.

WRITING

PART 1 Editing Advice

1. Don't use *have* with age. Don't use *years* without *old*.

   The dog ~~has~~ is ten years. old

2. Don't use *have* with *hungry, thirsty, hot, cold,* or *afraid*.

   The dog ~~has~~ is thirsty. She wants water.

3. Don't forget the verb *be*. Remember that some words that end in *-ed* are adjectives, not verbs.

   We are excited about our new puppy.

4. Use the correct question formation.

   Why ~~your sister doesn't~~ doesn't your sister like dogs?

   Why ~~Lucy Cooke studies~~ does Lucy Cooke study animals?

5. Don't use *be* with another present verb.

   ~~We're~~ have a new cat.

6. Use the *-s* form when the subject is *he, she, it,* a singular noun, *everyone,* or *family*.

   The cat sleep**s** all day.

   Everyone love**s** the new puppy.

   My family want**s** a cat.

7. Use *doesn't* when the subject is *he, she, it,* a singular noun, or *family*.

   He ~~don't~~ doesn't have a pet.

   My family ~~don't~~ doesn't like cats.

8. Use the base form after *does*.

   My brother doesn't ~~has~~ have a pet.

   How does a dolphin gets~~~~ air?

9. Use normal question formation for *spell, mean, cost,* and *take*.

   What ~~means "obey"~~ does "obey" mean?

   How do you spell "dolphin"?

   How much ~~costs~~ does a parrot cost?

   How long ~~it takes~~ does it take to train a guide dog?

11. Use the correct word order with frequency words.

    ~~Never my dog~~ My dog never sleeps with me.

12. Don't put longer frequency expressions between the subject and the verb.

    She ~~all the time~~ plays with her cat. all the time

PART 2 Editing Practice

Some of the shaded words and phrases have mistakes. Find the mistakes and correct them. If the shaded words are correct, write C.

The relationship between people and pets in the U.S. is sometimes strange to me.
1.

I surprised that Americans thinks of their pets as part of the family. I'm have a new American
2.   3.   4.

friend, Marianne. She live alone, but she's has a dog, Sparky. Marianne treats him like a child.
5.   6.   7.

I not very interested in him, but always she wants to show me pictures of him on her phone.
8.   9.

She thinks everyone want to see them, but I think she wrong. She often buy toys for him,
10.   11.   12.

especially on his birthday. He has twelve years old, so she spends a lot of money on vet bills
13.   14.

too. How much cost a visit to the vet? At least $100!
15.

She have several coats for him for the winter weather, but he don't like to wear them. So
16.   17.

when they go outside in winter, he has cold. She buys sometimes expensive food for him. (He
18.   19.   20.

likes steak.) She sometimes calls him on the telephone when she not home and talks into the
21.   22.   23.   24.

answering machine. Sparky always sleeps in bed with her.
25.

When she goes to work, she uses a dog-walking service. Someone twice a day comes to
26.   27.   28.

her house to play with Sparky and take him for a walk. She says that he gets lonely if he's
29.

home alone all day.

Once a month, she takes him to a dog groomer. What means "dog groomer"? This is a
30.   31.

professional that gives Sparky a bath and cuts and paints his nails. Nothing cost too much
32.

money when it comes to Sparky.

Sometimes I'm think American dogs live better than most people in the world.
33.

PART 3 Write About It

1. Look for a Lucy Cooke video online. Watch the video and describe the behavior of the animal. What does this video teach you about the animal? (Provide the teacher with a link to the video.)

2. Describe the behavior of an animal you know about. This can be a pet or a wild animal.

PART 4 Edit Your Writing

Reread the Summary of Lesson 1 and the editing advice. Edit your writing from Part 3.

2

The Present Continuous
The Future

Frank Shearer, 99, waterskis. He was a championship polo player until he was 70.

GENERATIONS

Youth is wasted on the young.

—Oscar Wilde

Second Careers

Read the following article. Pay special attention to the words in bold.

Judy Perlman, of Chicago, **is starting** a new career—making dolls. She sells most of them before Christmas, at holiday fairs all over Illinois. "I**'m having** more fun than ever before. I**'m traveling** in my new job and **meeting** new people. Right now I**'m preparing** for my next show. I**'m not earning** a lot of money, but I don't care." Why isn't she worried about making money? Perlman is a retired teacher, and she**'s getting** a pension.[1]

Many older people **are starting** new careers in their retirement. Americans **are living** longer than ever before. The average life expectancy in the United States is seventy-six years for men and eighty-one years for women. Most people retire in their midsixties. That means that retired people can have many years ahead of them. Some people are content just relaxing. But many seniors[2] **are getting** involved in interesting hobbies or second careers. If they **are getting** a pension or **living** off savings from their work years, many can afford to find rewarding work without worrying about money. "I**'m enjoying** every minute of my new career. I think this is the best time of my life," says Perlman.

Some senior citizens decide not to retire at all. Frank Babbit of Newark is a carpenter, and he**'s** still **working**. He has his own business and works fifty hours a week. And he's almost eighty-eight years old.

Today healthy retirees **are exploring** many options, from relaxing to starting a new business or making a hobby into a new career. How do you see yourself as a retiree?

---

1 *pension*: a regular payment made by a business or government to a retired employee
2 *senior*: an older person; this usually refers to people over 65.

COMPREHENSION CHECK Based on the reading, tell if the statement is true (**T**) or false (**F**).

1. Judy Perlman is working as a teacher.

2. People are living longer these days.

3. Some people earn money from a job and get a pension at the same time.

2.1 Present Continuous[3]—Form

For the present continuous, we use a form of *be* (*is, am, are*) + verb + *–ing*.[4]

Subject	*Be* (am, is, are)	Verb + *-ing*	
I	**am**	**working**	hard.
Judy	**is**	**making**	dolls.
She	**is**	**getting**	a pension.
Some seniors	**are**	**starting**	second careers.
You	**are**	**exploring**	possibilities.

Language Notes:

1. We can make a contraction with the subject pronoun and a form of *be*. Most nouns can also contract with *is*.[5]

   I'm having fun. **We're** learning new things.

   Judy's making dolls. **Frank's** working as a carpenter.

2. To form the negative, we put *not* after *am/is/are*. In many cases, we can make a negative contraction in two ways:

   She is not working. = **She isn't** working. = **She's not** working.

   You are not relaxing. = **You aren't** relaxing. = **You're not** relaxing.

3. For *I am not,* there is only one contraction:

   I am not traveling. = **I'm not** traveling.

4. We do not repeat the *be* verb after *and* or *or*.

   Some people **are working** and **getting** a pension.

5. We can put an adverb between *be* and the verb + *–ing*.

   He**'s still** working.

---

[3] Some grammar books refer to the present continuous as the present progressive.
[4] For a review of the spelling of the *–ing* form of the verb, see Appendix A.
[5] See Lesson 1, page 5 for exceptions.

EXERCISE 1 Fill in the blanks with the words you hear to complete the conversation between a 59-year-old man (A) and the manager of a retirement home (B).

A: I _'m thinking_____ about moving into this retirement village. Can you give me some information?

_____1.

B: Sure. This is a village for people over 55 years old.

A: _____ now. I'm retired. _____ for activities to keep me busy.

_____2. _____3.

B: Most of the people here are very active. Let me give you a tour. This is our fitness center.

A: What _____ those people _____?

_____4. _____5.

B: _____ yoga. It's very popular here. And here's our pool. As you can see,

_____6.

some people _____ .

_____7.

A: What about those people in the pool? _____ .

_____8.

B: _____ a water aerobics class. Now let's go to the computer center.

_____9.

That's Nicole. She's the teacher. _____ a photo-editing course.

_____10.

_____ Marge make a photo album for her grandchildren. And Bob and

_____11.

Cindy over there travel all over the world. _____ together a Web page

_____12.

with their vacation pictures. Let me show you our game room. As you can see, some people

_____ chess.

_____13.

A: What about those women? What game _____?

_____14.

B: That's called MahJongg. It's especially popular among the women.

A: I'm a widower. Maybe I can meet a woman here.

B: That's possible. We have a singles group that meets once a week. In fact,

_____ right now. I can introduce you to Mary Dodge.

_____15.

_____ over there. _____ a red T-shirt. She can

_____16. _____17.

give you more information.

EXERCISE 2 Fill in the blanks with the present continuous form of the verb given. Use the correct spelling. Make contractions wherever possible.

1. Jack _'s visiting_____ a retirement village.
   visit

2. He _____ a tour.
   take

3. He _____ at the different activities.
   look

4. The manager of the village _____ him information.

give

5. Some people _____ .

relax

6. Some people _____ the exercise equipment.

use

7. One man _____ weights.

lift

8. Some people in the pool _____ .

not/swim

9. Nicole _____ a class. She _____ a class.

not/take   teach

10. Some people _____ anything.

not/do

2.2 The Present Continuous—Use

Examples	Explanation
Some people **are doing** yoga over there. Those women **are playing** a game.	We use the present continuous to describe an action in progress at this moment.
Mary **is standing** over there. She**'s wearing** a red T-shirt.	We use the present continuous to describe a state or condition that we can observe now, using the following verbs: *sit, stand, wear,* and *sleep.*
Judy **is meeting** new people. She **is getting** her pension and **earning** money from her new job.	We use the present continuous to show a long-term action that is in progress. It may not be happening at this exact moment.
More and more retired Americans **are starting** a second career. People **are living** longer.	We use the present continuous to describe a trend. A trend is a behavior that many people in society are doing at this time. It describes a change in behavior from an earlier time.

EXERCISE 3 Fill in the blanks with the present continuous form of one of the verbs from the box.

retire	return	work✓	discover	start	volunteer	live	spend

1. More and more older people ___are working___ at second careers these days.

2. Many people _____ at a younger age.

3. They _____ time doing interesting things.

4. Some people _____ new careers.

5. Other people _____ . They are helping others without pay.

6. People _Are living_ longer and healthier lives.

7. Some people _____ new talents and abilities.

8. Some older women _are ~~volunteering~~ returning_ to work after raising a family.

EXERCISE 4 Are these things happening at this point in time in the United States, in the world, or in another country you know about? Discuss your ideas with a partner.

1. People are living healthier lives.

2. People are living longer.

3. The world is becoming a safer place.

4. Medical science is advancing quickly.

5. A lot of people are losing their jobs.

6. People are working harder than before.

7. People are doing more and enjoying less.

8. Kids are growing up faster than before.

2.3 Questions with the Present Continuous

Compare statements, *yes/no* questions, short answers, and *wh-* questions.

Statement	Yes/No Question and Short Answer	Wh- Question
You **are working** as a carpenter.	**Are** you **working** full time? Yes, I **am**.	How many hours **are** you **working**?
They **are doing** an exercise.	**Are** they **doing** yoga? No, they**'re** not.	What kind of exercise **are** they **doing**?
Judy **isn't earning** a lot of money.	**Is** she **earning** enough money? Yes, she is.	Why **isn't** Judy **earning** a lot of money?

Language Notes:

1. We sometimes leave a preposition at the end of a question.

   What kind of career is he thinking **about**?

2. When the question is "What . . . doing?" we usually answer with a different verb.

   What are they **doing**? They're **taking** an aerobics class.

EXERCISE 5 Use the words given to make a *yes/no* question. Fill in the second blank to complete the short answer.

1. those/men play

   A: ___Are those men playing___ checkers?

   B: No, they _____aren't_____. They're playing chess.

2. you/consider

   A: _____ this retirement home?

   B: Yes, I _____. I'm considering it now that my wife is gone.

3. Marge/design

   A: _____ a website?

   B: Yes, she _____. She's designing a website with pictures of her

   vacations.

4. Marge/take

   A: _____ pictures now?

   B: No, she _____. She's putting her pictures on her website.

5. your wife/do

   A: _____ something now?

   B: No, _____. She's just relaxing.

6. Betty and Charles/take

   A: _____ art classes?

   B: Yes, they _____. They love art.

7. I/ask

   A: _____ too many questions?

   B: No, _____. You can ask as many questions as you want.

8. you/write

   A: _____ down this information?

   B: No, _____. I can check your website later.

EXERCISE 6 Read each statement. Then write a question using the word(s) given.

1. Some retirees are discovering new interests. (*how*)

   How are they discovering new interests?

2. Judy is having more fun. (*why*)

   _____

3. Jack is taking piano lessons. (*where*)

   _____

4. I'm starting a new career. (*what kind of career*)

   _____

5. Some seniors are studying new things. (*what*)

   _____

6. My father is thinking about retirement. (*why*)

   _____

7. Those women are playing a game. (*what game*)

   _____

8. We're not planning to retire. (*why*)

   _____

9. People are living longer nowadays. (*why*)

   _____

10. I'm doing interesting things. (*what kinds of things*)

    _____

11. My father isn't working now. (*why*)

    _____

EXERCISE 7 Fill in the blanks with the present continuous to complete the conversation between two neighbors. Use contractions wherever possible.

A: What ___are you doing___ , Jack?
                    1. you/do

B: I _____ at some brochures.
           2. look

A: What kind of brochures _____ ?
                           3. you/look at

B: They're from a retirement village.

A: _____ about moving?
          4. you/think

B: Yes, I am.

A: Why?

B: Now that Rose is gone, I feel lonely.

A: But you have a lot of good neighbors here. And your daughter lives with you.

B: Most of the neighbors are young. My next-door neighbors are always busy. Right now

they _____ . And the neighbors across the street are never home.
         5. work

A: They're older people. _____ too?
                       6. work

B: No. They _____ now.
              7. travel

A: But I'm here. I _____ my lawn, as usual. And my wife is inside.
                   8. water

She _____ on the phone, as usual.
          9. talk

B: I'm sorry I'm complaining so much.

A: You _____ . You _____ for
            10. not/complain   **11.** just/look

something to do.

B: There's a lot to do. I just don't want to do things alone.

A: What retirement village _____ to go to?
                        12. you/plan

B: Sun Valley Senior Village seems nice.

A: What about your daughter?

B: She _____ to move in with a friend of hers.
          13. plan

Digital Natives and Digital Immigrants

Read the following article. Pay special attention to the words in bold.

They're everywhere: in coffee shops, on the train, in restaurants, at work. They**'re texting**; they**'re tweeting**; they**'re googling**; they**'re checking** social media; they**'re taking** selfies; they**'re listening** to music. And yes, **they're** even **working**. They're always connected. These are the "digital natives."

Born at the end of the twentieth century and the beginning of the twenty-first century, digital natives **don't know** life without technology. The first generation of digital natives **is** now **entering** the workforce and **changing** the way we work. More and more younger people **are working** from home, in coffee shops, or anyplace. They**'re bringing** their personal equipment into the workplace too. They **switch** back and forth between their social and professional lives. They **don't see** the need to separate the two.

Some older people **are adapting** well to technology. Some people call them "digital immigrants." Others **are having** trouble. Some **are refusing** to use any new technology. Older people often **think** that technology **is** growing too fast. Look at the older people around you. **Do** they **have** smartphones? **Do** they **have** earbuds in their ears? **Are** they **texting**? Many older people **prefer** to share information with a small group of friends. Digital natives **share** information globally.[6]

The younger generations **want** high-tech devices that do everything: take pictures, send texts and photos, provide music and videos, and connect them with friends around the world. What **does** the older generation **want** from technology? In many cases, Grandma and Grandpa **want** a device that **connects** them to family and friends. They **like** to see pictures of grandchildren. Some even **love** to have a video chat with family.

As more and more technology **is entering** every aspect of our lives, the digital divide between generations **is widening**.

---

6 *globally*: throughout the world

COMPREHENSION CHECK Based on the reading, tell if the statement is true (**T**) or false (**F**).

1. Many digital natives are always connected.

2. Seventy-five percent of older people use smartphones.

3. Digital immigrants usually want a device that does many things.

2.4 Contrasting the Simple Present and the Present Continuous

Form

The Simple Present	The Present Continuous
Grandma **uses** e-mail.	Marc **is receiving** a message.
She **doesn't use** a smart phone.	He **isn't getting** a phone call.
Does she **use** the Internet? Yes, she **does**.	**Is** he **receiving** a message from his friend? Yes, he **is**.
When **does** she **use** the Internet?	How **is** he **receiving** a message?
Why **doesn't** she **use** a smart phone?	Why **isn't** he **receiving** a message from his friend?

Use

Examples	Explanation
People **use** their phones to text. I sometimes **send** photos to my grandmother. Older people **prefer** to talk on the phone.	We use the **simple present** for: • a general truth. • a habitual activity. • a custom.
I'm getting a text message right now. My grandfather **is learning** about technology. Technology **is growing** quickly.	We use the **present continuous** for: • an action that is in progress now. • a longer action in progress at this general time. • a recent trend.
My grandparents **live** in a retirement home. My sister **is living** in a dorm this semester.	We use *live* in the simple present to indicate a person's home. We use *live* in the present continuous to indicate a temporary, short-term residence.
A: What does she do (for a living)? **B:** She's an English teacher. **A:** What is she doing now? **B:** She's texting her grandson.	"What does she do?" asks about a job or profession. "What is she doing?" asks about an activity now.

EXERCISE 8 Fill in the blanks with the simple present or the present continuous form of the verb given.

1. Conversation between a grandmother and grandson:

   A: You <u>'re eating and working</u> on your essay at the same time.
            a. eat and work

   B: That's not a problem, Grandma.

   A: What _____? Is that a hamburger?
            b. you/eat

   B: No, it isn't. It's a veggie burger. I never _____ meat.
            c. eat

continued

A: You don't eat enough. Look at you. You're so thin.

B: I _____ to lose weight.
    d. try

A: You always _____ in front of your computer. Take a break.
    e. eat

I _____ soup now. When it's ready, please come to the table.
    f. make

B: But I _____ on something important now.
    g. work

A: How is that possible? You _____ to music too.
    h. eat and listen

B: I always _____ to music when I _____.
    i. listen   j. work or study

A: Whenever I _____, I _____ on my work.
    k. work   l. concentrate

I _____ other things at the same time.
    m. not/do

B: You _____ the world of young people. We often multitask.
    n. not/understand

A: You're right. I don't.

2. Conversation between two brothers:

A: _____? Wake up. It's almost time for class.
    a. you/sleep

B: I'm so tired. I never _____ enough sleep.
    b. get

A: That's because you're always on your computer or phone. How many hours

_____ a night?
    c. you/sleep

B: About four or five.

A: That's not enough. You _____ more sleep. Turn off your computer
    d. need

and phone at night, and get some sleep.

B: I never _____ my devices. I always _____
    e. turn off   f. want

to know when I get a message.

A: That's ridiculous! Let's go get breakfast. Mom _____ pancakes.
    g. make

B: I _____ breakfast. I just _____ coffee.
    h. not/want   i. drink

A: That's not good. You _____ to live a healthier life.
    j. need

3. Conversation between two friends:

A: What _____ for a living?
    a. your mother/do

B: She's retired now.

A: _____ old?
    b. she/be

B: No. She's only fifty-eight.

A: What _____ with her free time?
         c. she/do

B: A lot of things. In fact, she _____ any free time at all.
                          d. not/have

She _____ a course at the art center this semester. Right now
       e. take

she _____ a picture of me.
     f. paint

2.5 Action and Nonaction Verbs

Examples	Explanation
He **is texting** his friend. I **am listening** to music.	Some verbs are action verbs. These verbs express physical or mental activity (*text, call, work, share,* etc.).
Young people **know** a lot about technology. Many people **have** a smart phone now. **Do** you **remember** a time without cell phones?	Some verbs are nonaction verbs. These verbs express a state, condition, perception, or feeling, not an action. We do not usually use the present continuous with nonaction verbs. We use the simple present even if we are talking about now.
She**'s looking** at the text message. I want to learn about technology, but it **looks** hard. Your photo **looks like** a selfie.	Some verbs can express an action or a perception. When they express an action (for example, *look at*), they are action verbs. When they express a perception (for example, *look* + adjective or *look like*), they are nonaction verbs.
I'm looking at my cell phone. I **see** a text from my father. She **is listening** to music. She **hears** her favorite song.	*Look* and *listen* are action verbs. *See* and *hear* are nonaction verbs.
Grandma **is thinking** *about* getting an e-reader. She **thinks** *that* technology is a good thing.	When we think *about* or *of* something, *think* is an action verb. *Think that* shows an opinion about something. It is a nonaction verb.
My grandfather **is having** a hard time with technology. He**'s having** lunch with his friends now. Grandma **has** free time now. She **has** five grandchildren. I can't visit her now. I **have** a cold.	When *have* means to experience something or to eat or drink something, it is an action verb. When *have* shows possession, relationship, or illness, it is a nonaction verb.

Some common nonaction verbs are:

- Perception verbs: *smell, taste, look, sound,* followed by an adjective or *like*
- Feelings and desires: *like, dislike, love, hate, hope, want, need, prefer, agree, disagree, care about, expect, matter*
- Mental states: *believe, know, hear, see, notice, understand, remember, think that, suppose, recognize*
- Other nonaction verbs: *mean, cost, spell, weigh*

EXERCISE 9 Circle the correct words to complete the conversation between a grandmother and her grandson.

A: Listen, Marco, (*I'm thinking*/ *I think*) about getting a new computer. Can you help me pick one
1.

out?

B: Sure, Grandma. How about on Saturday?

A: Saturday's good. What's that noise? It (*sounds* / *is sounding*) like rock music (*comes* / *is coming*)
2.   3.

from your pocket.

B: It's my cell phone. It's my new ringtone. (*I receive* / *I'm receiving*) a text message now.
4.

It's a message from Dad. See?

A: It (*looks* / *is looking*) like Greek to me. What does it say?
5.

B: (*He tells* / *He's telling*) me to come home early. (*He wants* / *He's wanting*) to give me another
6.   7.

driving lesson. (*I learn* / *I'm learning*) to drive, you know.
8.

A: When (*I have* / *I'm having*) something to say, (*I use* / *I'm using*) the phone.
9.   10.

B: (*I prefer* / *I'm preferring*) to text. (*It saves* / *It's saving*) time. You can text me too, Grandma.
11.   12.

A: OK. (*It looks* / *It's looking*) hard. Teach me. Let me send a note to Grandpa. "Jim. Where are you?
13.

See you later."

B: Grandma, (*you're writing* / *you write*) so slowly. And (*you use* / *you're using*) whole words. Use
14.   15.

abbreviations, like this: "where r u c u later." Don't use punctuation. (*You need* / *You're needing*)
16.

to write fast.

A: You know I'm an English teacher, and (*I don't like* / *I'm not liking*) to write without punctuation.
17.

B: Text messages don't need punctuation.

A: (*I don't think* / *I'm not thinking*) I can do it.
18.

B: But (*you send* / *you're sending*) e-mail every day.
19.

A: That's different. (*I write* / *I'm writing*) slowly, and (*I check* / *I'm checking*) my spelling.
20.   21.

B: You're so old-fashioned!

A: No, I'm not. This month (*I study* / *I'm studying*) photo editing at the senior center.
22.

(*I make* / *I'm making*) a digital family album.
23.

B: That's great, Grandma! I'm proud of you.

EXERCISE 10 Fill in the blanks with the simple present or the present continuous form of the verb given.

1. **A:** My grandfather is a volunteer. Twice a week he _____*reads*_____ for blind people.
                                                  a. read

   B: That's great! My grandmother _____ part-time in a bookstore. She _____
                                       b. work   **c.** love

   books. She usually _____ her bike to work. She _____ the exercise.
                                 d. ride   **e.** like

   A: Where is she now? _____?
                                           f. she/work

   B: Right now she's on vacation. She _____ her sister in Florida.
                                                        g. visit

2. **A:** Can I borrow your dictionary?

   B: I'm sorry. I _____ it now. Where's your dictionary?
                                     a. use

   A: I never _____ it to class. It's too heavy.
                                 b. bring

   B: _____ to use my dictionary all the time? You _____
                                  c. you/expect   **d.** need

   a dictionary app for your phone.

   A: I _____ a smart phone.
                                     e. not/have

3. **A:** What _____? She _____ too fast, so
                                   a. the teacher/say   **b.** talk

   I _____ her.
                               c. not/understand

   B: I don't know. I _____. I _____ a friend.
                                       d. not/listen   **e.** text

   A: I _____ you should pay attention in class.
                             f. think

4. **A:** What _____?
                                   a. you/write

   B: I _____ an essay about my grandparents. I _____
                                     b. write   **c.** love

   them very much.

   A: _____ with you?
                             d. they/live

   B: No, they don't. They live in Pakistan. They _____ us once a year.
                                                      e. visit

   A: How _____? By e-mail?
                                   f. you/communicate

   B: We usually _____ a video chat once a week. But right now their computer
                                    g. do

   _____, so we _____ the phone.
                                 h. not/work   **i.** use

continued

5. A: _____ that guy over there? Who is he?
       a. you/see

B: That's my technology teacher.

A: He _____ jeans and running shoes. And he _____ an
          b. wear   c. have

earring in his ear. He _____ like a student.
                          d. look

B: I _____ . Everyone _____ he's a student. But he's a very
         e. know   f. think

professional teacher.

6. A: My parents _____ to put Grandma in a nursing home. Mom _____
                        a. plan   b. think

she'll receive better care there.

B: It _____ like a difficult decision.
          c. sound

A: It is. Mom _____ what else to do. Grandma _____ .
                    d. not/know   e. sometimes/fall

B: Maybe she _____ a cane or a walker.
                    f. need

A: Her memory is bad too. She _____ where she puts things.
                                    g. never/remember

B: Can I call you back later? I _____ my other phone. My son
                                      h. hear

_____ me.
      i. call

THE FUTURE
UNITED STATES POPULATION

CD 1
TR 13

Read the following article. Pay special attention to the words in bold.

The population of the United States is growing slowly. Today it's about 320 million. By 2050, it**'s going to be** about 440 million. This is not a big growth, but one group is growing very fast— the elderly. The sixty-five and over population **will** more than **double** by 2050. The eighty-five and over population **will** more than **triple**.

There are two reasons for this increase of older Americans. First, the "baby boomers" are getting old. Baby boomers are people born between 1946 and 1964. During that time, a very large number of babies were born. The oldest are now entering their senior years. Many more **will** soon **be** elderly. As these people retire, young people **are going to have** many more job opportunities. In fact, there**'s going to be** a shortage[7] of workers to take their place. The number of jobs in health care **will increase**. There **will be** many jobs for pharmacists, physical therapists, and home health aides.

There is another reason for the increase in older Americans: life expectancy is increasing. Some scientists predict that half the babies born in 2007 **will live** to be 104 years old. But according to Dr. Harrison Bloom of the Longevity Center of New York, many young people **won't reach** this age because they don't have a healthy lifestyle. Or, if they do live a long time, they**'re going to need** a lot of medical help.

When today's young people retire at age sixty-five or seventy, they**'ll have** a lot of years ahead of them. They need to think about how they**'ll spend** their later years. If they expect to have good health, they need to think about it now.

---

[7] *shortage*: a state of not having enough

COMPREHENSION CHECK Based on the reading, tell if the statement is true (**T**) or false (**F**).

1. There will be a shortage of jobs in health care.

2. The biggest growth in population will be in people over eighty-five.

3. The baby boomers will live longer than younger generations.

2.6 The Future with *Will*

Examples	Explanation
The number of older people **will increase**. My grandfather **will be** 85 next week.	We use *will* + the base form for the future.
I'll be 72 years old in 2050. **We'll** retire at age 65.	We can contract *will* with the subject pronouns. The contractions are *I'll, you'll, he'll, she'll, it'll, we'll,* and *they'll*.
The population **will not decrease**. I **won't retire** soon.	To form the negative, we put *not* after *will*. The contraction for *will not* is *won't*.
You'll **probably** have a long retirement.	We can put an adverb between *will* and the main verb.

Compare statements, *yes/no* questions, short answers, and *wh-* questions.

Statement	Yes/No Question and Short Answer	Wh- Question
She **will help** her parents.	**Will** she **help** her grandparents? Yes, she **will**.	How **will** she **help** her parents?
You **will retire** soon.	**Will** you **retire** next year? No, I **won't**.	When **will** you **retire**?
There **won't be** enough health workers.	**Will** there **be** a lot of jobs? Yes, there **will**.	Why **won't** there **be** enough health workers?

🎧 CD 1 TR 14 **EXERCISE 11** Listen to the conversation between a 60-year-old mother and her 29-year-old daughter. Fill in the blanks with the words you hear.

A: Tomorrow _____ will be _____ my last day of work.
1.

B: What _____ with all your free time?
2.

A: Our retired friends all say I _____ any free time. They say

_____ plenty of things to do.
4.

B: So _____ first?
5.

A: Dad and I are planning to travel.

B: _____ first?
6.

A: To the Grand Canyon.

B: That's great! How long _____ 7. _____ there?

A: For about two weeks. Then _____ 8. _____ Grandpa in Nevada.

B: I'm sure _____ 9. _____ happy to see you.

A: _____ 10. _____ eighty-five at the end of August. _____ 11. _____ there for his birthday.

B: What _____ 12. _____ with the dog?

A: Can you take care of her for us while we're gone?

B: Sorry. I _____ 13. _____ here the first week in August.

A: Why _____ 14. _____ here?

B: I'm going to New York. _____ 15. _____ to find someone else to take care of the dog.

A: _____ 16. _____ my neighbor. Maybe _____ 17. _____ it. Don't forget to send Grandpa a birthday card.

B: _____ 18. _____ him an e-mail on his birthday.

A: You know Grandpa. He doesn't use his computer much.

B: All right. _____ 19. _____ him a card then.

A: I'm sure _____ 20. _____ it.

EXERCISE 12 Fill in the blanks with *will* and one of the verbs from the box. You may use the same verb more than once.

spend	have	increase	triple	live✓	need	move	find	be

1. Today's generation _____ will live _____ longer.

2. The population of old people _____ .

3. The over-85 population _____ by 2050.

4. _____ young people _____ more job opportunities?

5. Many young people _____ jobs in health care.

6. Some older people _____ into retirement housing.

continued

7. How _____ you _____ your retirement years?

8. Why _____ we _____ more health care workers?

9. How old _____ you _____ in the year 2050?

2.7 The Future with *Be Going To*

Examples	Explanation
People **are going to live** longer. We **are going to need** more pharmacists in the future.	We can use a form of *be* + *going to* + the base form to express future time.
I'm not going to work after retirement. He **isn't going to retire** soon.	To form the negative, we put *not* after *am, is,* or *are.*
We're **going to go** to the Grand Canyon. We're **going** to the Grand Canyon.	We often shorten *going to go* to *going.*

Compare statements, *yes/no* questions, short answers, and *wh-* questions.

Statement	*Yes/No* Question and Short Answer	*Wh-* Question
We **are going to travel**.	**Are** we **going to travel** by car? Yes, we **are**.	When **are** we **going to travel**?
She **is going to work** as a nurse.	**Is** she **going to work** at a hospital? No, she **isn't**.	Where **is** she **going to work**?
You **aren't going to send** Grandpa a present.	**Are** you **going to send** an e-card? Yes, I **am**.	Why **aren't** you **going to send** Grandpa a present?

Pronunciation Notes:

1. In informal speech, *going to* before another verb often sounds like "gonna." In formal English, we don't write "gonna."

    I'm not "gonna" work after retirement.

2. Only *going to* before another verb sounds like "gonna." We don't pronounce "gonna" before a noun or a noun phrase.

    He's **going to** the store.

EXERCISE 13 Fill in the blanks with *be going to* and one of the verbs from the box. You may use the same verb more than once.

need	spend	study	be	live	find	become	double	have

1. Many people _are going to live_ to the age of 100.

2. Young people _____ a lot of job possibilities.

3. I _____ a nurse because it _____

   easy to find a job.

4. Some people _____ a long retirement.

5. Some old people _____ a lot of medical help.

6. _____ you _____ to be a physician's assistant?

7. Younger people _____ jobs in health care.

8. By 2050, the population of people over sixty-five _____ .

9. _____ your grandparents _____ with your family?

10. You need to think about how you _____ your retirement years.

11. In the future, there _____ a shortage of workers.

12. _____ I _____ to be 100?

EXERCISE 14 Fill in the blanks with *be going to* and the words given to complete the conversation between two co-workers.

A: I'm so excited. I _'m going to retire_ at the end of this year!
        1. retire

B: That's wonderful news. What _____ next?
                                    2. you/do

A: I don't really know yet. I _____ new things.
                                  3. explore

B: What _____ ?
            4. you/explore

A: I think I have a talent for art. I _____ art classes.
                                          5. take

B: _____ part-time?
        6. you/work

A: No way! I want to have fun.

B: Is your husband happy about your retirement?

A: Yes. He _____ too.
                7. retire

B: But you're not that old.

continued

A: I'm 58 and he's 56. Our children _____ us much anymore.
8. not/need

B: Why _____ you?
9. not/need

A: Our youngest son _____ from college in June. And the other
10. graduate

two are already on their own. The oldest _____ married next
11. get

year, and the middle one has her own apartment and a job.

B: I _____ you at work. It _____
12. miss   13. not/be

the same without you.

A: I _____ the boss and the long hours.
14. not/miss

2.8 Choosing *Will* or *Be Going To* or Present Continuous for Future

Examples	Explanation
The U.S. population **will be** 440 million by 2050. The U.S. population **is going to be** 440 million by 2050.	For a prediction about the future, we use either *will* or *be going to*. *Will* is more formal than *be going to*.
Grandpa **will be** 85 years old in August. Grandpa **is going to be** 85 in August.	For a fact about the future, we use either *will* or *be going to*.
A: I'm interested in health care. I **am going to become** a nurse. **B:** My sister's a nurse. I**'ll tell** her about your plan. Maybe she can give you some advice.	When we have a definite plan for the future, we use *be going to*. When we are thinking about the future at the moment of speaking, we use *will*.
Grandma: I want to buy a cell phone. What kind should I buy? Grandson: I**'ll help** you. I**'ll take** you shopping. Grandma: You always say that. But you never have time. Grandson: I**'ll make** time. I promise.	To make a promise or offer to help with no previous plan, we use *will*. The decision comes at the moment of speaking.
My grandmother **is moving** into a retirement home on Friday. I**'m helping** her move. The weather report says it's **going to rain** on Friday, so the move won't be easy.	We can use the present continuous with definite plans for the near future. We don't use the present continuous if there is no plan. (Not: It is raining on Friday.)

Language Note:

For a scheduled event, such as a flight, movie, or class, we often use the simple present.

The semester **begins** in August.

My nursing course **ends** next month.

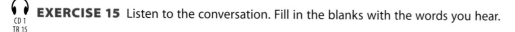

EXERCISE 15 Listen to the conversation. Fill in the blanks with the words you hear.

A: I hear ___you're retiring___ next month.
_{1.}

B: Yes. Isn't it wonderful? _____ sixty-five in September.
_{2.}

A: What _____ after you retire?
_{3.}

B: _____ to Florida.
_{4.}

A: What _____ in Florida?
_{5.}

B: _____ a sailboat. Maybe _____
_{6.}   _{7.}

to play golf. What about you?

A: I don't know. _____ any time soon. I'm only forty-five.
_{8.}

B: I hope _____ me in Florida.
_{9.}

A: Of course _____! Do you need help packing?
_{10.}

B: Yes. _____ to pack this weekend.
_{11.}

A: _____ you.
_{12.}

B: Thanks. _____ my life a lot easier!
_{13.}

EXERCISE 16 Circle the correct words to complete the conversation. In some cases, both choices are possible. If so, circle both.

1. **A:** Do you want to go for a cup of coffee?

   B: Sorry. I don't have time. *(I'm going to visit/I'll visit)* my grandfather this afternoon.
   _{a.}

   (I'm going to help/I'll help) him with his computer. And I need to return some books to the library.
   _{b.}

   A: Give them to me. I'm going that way on my way home. *(I'll return/I'm going to return)* them for you.
   _{c.}

   Do you want to get together for coffee tomorrow?

   B: I'm not sure. *(I'll text/I'm going to text)* you tomorrow to let you know.
   _{d.}

2. **A:** I have to go to the airport. My grandparents' plane *(is arriving/is going to arrive)* at four o'clock this
   _{a.}

   afternoon.

   B: *(I'll go/I'm going)* with you. *(I'll/I'm going to)* stay in the car while you go into the airport.
   _{b.}   _{c.}

   A: Thanks.

   B: How long *(are they going to stay/are they staying)*?
   _{d.}

continued

A: *(They'll come/They're coming)* because *(my sister's graduating/will graduate)* on Sunday. After the
          e.   **f.**

graduation, *(they'll/they're going to)* visit my cousins in Denver.
            g.

3. A: My mother's so happy. *(She's going to retire/She'll)* retire next month.
                                          a.

B: Are you *(going to have/having)* a party for her?
                    b.

A: Yes. Do you want to come to the party?

B: What's the date?

A: June 16.

B: I have to check my calendar. *(I'm going to/I'll)* let you know later.
                                    c.

2.9 Future + Time or *If* Clause

Time or *If* Clause (Simple Present)	Main Clause (Future)	Explanation
When I **retire**,	**I'm going to start** a new hobby.	Some sentences have a time or *if* clause and a main clause. We use the future in the main clause; we use the simple present in the time or *if* clause.
If I **am** healthy,	**I'll continue** to work.	
Main Clause (Future)	**Time or *If* Clause (Simple Present)**	
He**'ll move** to a warm climate	as soon as he **retires**.	
My parents **are going to travel**	if they **have** enough money.	

Punctuation Note:

If the time or *if* clause comes before the main clause, we use a comma to separate the two
parts of the sentence. If the main clause comes first, we don't use a comma.

EXERCISE 17 Choose the correct words to complete the conversation. In some cases, both choices are
possible. If so, circle both choices.

A: What *(are you doing/will you do)* later today?
                     1.

B: After class *(will be/is)* over, I'm going to drive my grandfather to the airport.
                   2.

A: Where *(is he going/will he go)*?
                  3.

B: To Hawaii to play golf.

A: That's great! How old is he?

B: *(He's going to/He'll)* be seventy-eight next month.
            4.

A: He's pretty old.

B: He's in perfect health. *(He's getting/he'll get)* married in two months.
                   5.

A: That's great! What are you and your family *(doing / going to do)* when *(he's / he'll be)* no longer
                                                                    6.   7.

able to take care of himself?

B: We never think about it. He's in great health. I think he's *(outliving / going to outlive)* us all.
                                                                                    8.

A: But *(he's probably going to need / he'll probably need)* help when *(he'll get / he gets)* older.
                                        9.   10.

B: If *(he'll need / he needs)* help, *(he has / he'll have)* his wife to take care of him.
              11.   12.

A: My grandparents are in their sixties now. But when *(they're / they'll be)* older, they're going to
                                                                          13.

live with my parents. In our country, it's an honor to take care of our parents and grandparents.

B: That sounds like a great custom. But I think older people should be independent. I'm glad that

Grandpa doesn't depend on us. And when *(I'm / I'll be)* old, *(I'm going to take / I'm taking)* care
                                                      14.   15.

of myself. I don't want to depend on anyone.

A: *(You'll change / You're changing)* your mind when *(you're / you'll be)* old.
          16.   17.

EXERCISE 18 About You Think about a specific time in your future (when you graduate, when you
get married, when you have children, when you find a job, when you return to your native country,
when you retire, etc.). Write three sentences to tell what will happen at that time. Find a partner who is
close to your age. Compare your answers to your partner's answers.

1. When I have children, I won't have as much free time as I do now.

2. When I retire, I'm going to start a new hobby.

3. _____

4. _____

5. _____

SUMMARY OF LESSON 2

Simple Present	
For general truths	Many people **retire** in their sixties. Some retirees **get** a pension.
For regular activities, habits, customs	Jack **plays** golf twice a week. I **always** visit my grandparents on the weekend.
With a place of origin	My grandfather **comes** from Mexico. My grandmother **comes** from Peru.
In a time clause or in an *if* clause of a future statement	When she **retires**, she'll start a new hobby. If Grandma **needs** help, she'll live with us.
With nonaction verbs	I **care** about my grandparents. Your grandfather **needs** help now. My grandfather **prefers** to live alone now.
For scheduled events	The plane **leaves** at 8 p.m. tonight.

Present Continuous (with action verbs only)	
For an action happening now, at this moment	My friend **is texting** me now. She**'s sending** me her photo.
For a long-term action in progress at this general time	Judy **is earning** money by making dolls. Jack is retired now. He **is starting** a new career.
For a trend in society	The population of the U.S. **is getting** older. Americans **are living** longer.
For a definite plan in the near future	She **is retiring** next month. She **is going** on a long trip soon.
With a descriptive state	Mary **is standing** over there. She **is wearing** jeans and a T-shirt.

Future		
	Will	*Be Going To*
For a plan		He **is going to retire** in two years.
For a fact	The number of old people **will increase**.	The number of old people **is going to increase**.
For a prediction	There **will be** more jobs in health care.	There **are going to be** more jobs in health care.
For a decision made at the time of speaking, usually with a promise or an offer	I**'ll** take care of you when you're old. Grandma, I**'ll carry** your grocery bags for you.	

TEST / REVIEW

Circle the correct words to complete the conversation. If both answers are correct, circle both choices.

A: Hi, Maya.

B: Hi, Liz. How are you?

A: Fine. What *(are you doing/you are doing)*? *(Do/Are)* you want to go out for a cup of coffee?

1.   2.

B: *(I'm not having/I don't have)* time now. *(I pack/I'm packing)*.

3.   4.

(We're moving/We're going to move) next Saturday.

5.

A: Oh, really? Why *(are you/you are)* moving? You *(have/are having)* such a lovely apartment now.

6.   7.

B: Yes, I know we do. But my father *(comes/is coming)* soon, so we're *(going to need/needing)* a

8.   9.

bigger apartment.

A: When *(is he/he is)* going to come?

10.

B: He *(leaves/'ll leave)* as soon as he *(gets/'ll get)* his visa. That *(is probably/will probably be)* in

11.   12.   13.

about four months.

A: But your present apartment *(has/have)* an extra bedroom.

14.

B: Yes. But my husband *(likes/is liking)* to have an extra room for an office.

15.

He usually *(brings/is bringing)* a lot of work home. He doesn't *(likes/like)* noise when he works.

16.   17.

A: *(Is your father/Your father is)* going to get his own apartment after he *(will find/finds)* a job?

18.   19.

B: He's retired now. He's going to *(live/living)* with us. He *(isn't liking/doesn't like)* to live alone.

20.   21.

A: *(Do you need/Are you needing)* help with your packing?

22.

B: No, thanks. Bill and I are *(stay/staying)* home this week to finish the packing. And my sister

23.

(is helping/helps) me now too.

24.

A: I'd like to help. *(I come/I'll come)* over next Saturday to help you move.

25.

B: *(We're going to use/We use)* professional movers on Saturday. We *(aren't/don't)* want to bother

26.   27.

our friends.

A: It's no bother. I *(want/'m wanting)* to help.

28.

B: Thanks. I have to go now. *(I hear/I'm hearing)* Bill now. *(He calls/He's calling)* me.

29.   30.

He *(need/needs)* help in the basement. *(I call/I'll call)* you back later.

31.   32.

A: That's not necessary. *(I see/I'll see)* you on Saturday. Bye.

33.

WRITING

PART 1 Editing Advice

1. Always include a form of *be* in a present continuous verb.

   is
   She ∧ working now.

2. Don't use the present continuous with a nonaction verb.

   like
   I ~~am liking~~ my new hobby.

3. Include *be* in a future sentence that has no other verb.

   be
   You will ∧ busy when you retire.

4. Don't combine *will* and *be going to*.

   He will ~~going to~~ leave. *OR* He's going to leave.

5. Don't use the future after a time word or *if*.

   When I ~~will~~ retire, I'll have more free time.

   If I ~~will~~ have enough money, I'll travel.

6. Use a form of *be* with *going to*.

   is
   He ∧ going to help his grandfather.

7. Use the correct word order in questions.

   will you
   When ~~you will~~ retire?

   isn't she
   Why ~~she isn't~~ going to work part-time?

PART 2 Editing Practice

Some of the shaded words and phrases have mistakes. Find the mistakes and correct them. If the shaded words are correct, write C.

My grandfather is retired now, and he's not happy. He wakes up every day and says,

will I
"What ~~I will~~ do today?" On the other hand, my grandmother is very busy. My grandparents
1.

C
live in a retirement village, and Grandma is learning how to draw. She's also take singing
2. **3.** **4.**

lessons, and she studying photography. Next month, she going to take a trip to India with a
5. **6.**

group of older people. When Grandma will get back from India, she's going to make a photo
7. **8.**

slideshow of her trip.

Grandpa doesn't want to travel. He says, "What I'm going to do in India?" I'm thinking
                                                    9.   10.

that Grandpa is needing to find a hobby. Grandma always tells him, "You will happy if you
                11.   12.

find something to do." Will I going to have a hard time like Grandpa when I will retire?
                            13.   14.

I'll think about it when the time comes.
    15.   16.

PART 3 Write About It

1. Write about the differences in generations and their use of technology. Use examples from your own life or the lives of people you know.
2. Interview a retired person. What is this person doing with his or her life now? What are this person's plans for the future?

PART 4 Edit Your Writing

Reread the Summary of Lesson 2 and the editing advice. Edit your writing from Part 3.

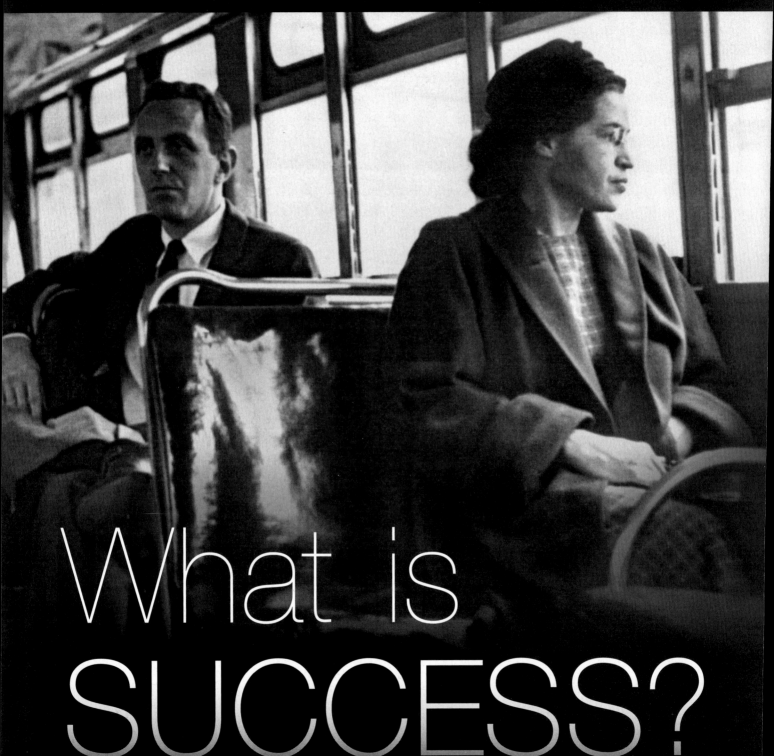

What is SUCCESS?

Rosa Parks sitting on a front seat in a bus (left),
and being processed when she was arrested (right).

Success consists of going from failure to
failure without loss of enthusiasm.

—Winston Churchill

Failure and Success

Two members of the Salomon Andrée expedition look at the remains of their balloon after it crashed in the Arctic.

CD 1
TR 16

Read the following article. Pay special attention to the words in bold.

What is success? What do we learn from failure?[1] When we try something new, failure is always a possibility. In the nineteenth century, many explorers **attempted** to reach the North Pole by land, but they **died** trying. Salomon Andrée **was** a Swedish engineer. He **wanted** to be the first person to arrive at the North Pole. He **knew** that travel over land **was** very dangerous. He **had** an idea. He **thought** he **had** the perfect way to reach the North Pole: by balloon. On a windy day in July 1897, Andrée and two other men **climbed** into the basket of a balloon. They **took** with them enough food for several months. When they **left**, people **cheered** and **waved**.

As soon as they **lifted** off, strong winds **hit** the balloon. Fog[2] **froze** on it, making it too heavy. The men **traveled** by balloon for sixty-five hours. **Were** they successful? **Did** they **arrive** safely? Unfortunately, no. They **landed** almost three hundred miles from the North Pole. No one **heard** from them again. Thirty-three years later, hunters **found** their frozen bodies, their cameras, and their diaries.

Failure is part of all exploration. Robert Ballard, a famous ocean explorer, says that success and failure go together. Failure helps us do things differently the next time. Mountain climber Peter Athans said, "I **learned** how *not* to climb the first four times I **tried** to summit[3] Everest."

In 1914, a polar explorer, Ernest Shackleton, **led** an expedition across Antarctica. His ship became trapped in the ice. However, he **brought** the twenty-seven men on his team home safely. The expedition **was** a failure but the rescue of his men **was** a success.

Failure helps us on our next try. Failure is a good teacher. Without failure, success would be impossible.

---

1 *failure*: an activity or project that does not succeed
2 *fog*: a heavy gray vapor near the ground that makes it difficult to see
3 *to summit*: to reach the top of a mountain

COMPREHENSION CHECK Based on the reading, tell if the statement is true (**T**) or false (**F**).

1. Salomon Andrée was the first person to reach the North Pole.

2. The weather caused problems with the balloon.

3. Robert Ballard successfully climbed Mt. Everest.

3.1 The Simple Past—Form

Examples	Explanation
Andrée's balloon **landed** far from the North Pole. Peter Athans **learned** from his mistakes.	Some simple past verbs are regular. Regular verbs end in –*ed*. **Base Form** **Past Form** land landed learn learned
They **had** bad weather. Hunters **found** the bodies.	Some simple past verbs are irregular. Irregular verbs do not end in –*ed*. **Base Form** **Past Form** have had find found
Shackleton's expedition **was** a failure. The men **were** safe.	The verb *be* is irregular. It has two forms in the past: *was* and *were*.

Language Notes:

1. Except for *be*, the simple past form is the same for all subjects.

> **I had** an idea. **He had** an idea.

2. The verb after *to* does not use the past form.

> He wanted to **reach** the North Pole.

🎧 **EXERCISE 1** Fill in the blanks with the words you hear.

CD 1
TR 17

The famous ship *Titanic* _____sank_____ in 1912. It _____ on the ocean
                                                 1.   **2.**

floor for over seventy years. There _____ many attempts to find it—all of them
                                                 3.

unsuccessful. Oceanographer Robert Ballard _____ to look for it.
                                                             4.

Ballard _____ up in California near the ocean. When he _____
                         5.   **6.**

young, he _____ interested in ocean exploration. He _____ to
                     7.   **8.**

find the *Titanic*. He _____ money for his exploration. He _____
                               9.   **10.**

the U.S. Navy for money, and they _____ it to him. Ballard _____
                                               11.   **12.**

a submersible called the *Argo*. He _____ a French research team to join his
                                             13.

continued

exploration. His team _____ on a ship called the *Knorr* while the *Argo*

14.

_____ underwater for many weeks. The *Argo* _____ pictures to

15.   16.

Ballard and his team. On September 1, 1985, the *Argo* _____ the *Titanic*.

17.

It _____ the first view of the *Titanic* in seventy-three years.

18.

3.2 The Simple Past—Use

Examples	Explanation
In 1897, Andrée **left** for the North Pole in a balloon.	We use the simple past with a single, short past action.
The balloon **traveled** for 65 hours.	We use the simple past with a longer past action.
Peter Athans **climbed** Mt. Everest 7 times.	We use the simple past with a repeated past action.

EXERCISE 2 In Exercise 1, underline the regular verbs once and the irregular verbs twice. Circle the forms of the verb *be*.

EXERCISE 3 Write the base form of the verbs. Write *R* for a regular verb. Write *I* for an irregular verb. Write *B* for the verb *be*.

1. ___cheer___ cheered ___R___
2. ___be___ were ___B___
3. _____ attempted _____
4. _____ thought _____
5. _____ died _____
6. _____ waved _____
7. _____ froze _____
8. _____ lifted _____

9. _____ heard _____
10. _____ learned _____
11. _____ took _____
12. _____ left _____
13. _____ climbed _____
14. _____ brought _____
15. _____ traveled _____
16. _____ was _____

George Dawson holds a copy of his book.

Never TOO LATE TO LEARN

Read the following article. Pay special attention to the words in bold.

George Dawson **was** a successful man. **Was** he famous? No, he **wasn't**. He **was** just an ordinary man who **did** something extraordinary.

George Dawson **lived** in three centuries—from 1898 to 2001. He **was** born in 1898 in Texas, the grandson of slaves. At that time, there **were** fewer opportunities for African Americans.[4] Dawson **was** the oldest of five children. His family **was** very poor, so George **had** to work to help his family. He **started** working for his father when he **was** only four years old. As a result, he **didn't have** a chance to get an education. He **didn't learn** to read and write. He **signed** his name with an X.

When Dawson **was** ninety-eight years old, he **decided** to go to school. He **wanted** to learn to read and write. He **went** to adult literacy[5] classes. The teacher **asked** him, "Do you know the alphabet?" When he **answered** "no," his teacher **was** surprised. Over the next few years, his teacher **taught** Dawson to read and write. Dawson **said**, "Every morning I get up and I wonder what I might learn that day."

In 1998, Richard Glaubman, **read** an article about Dawson in the newspaper and **wanted** to meet him. Glaubman helped Dawson write a book about Dawson's life, called *Life is So Good*. Dawson wrote about what makes a person happy. He **learned** from his father to see the good things in life. They **had** a close family, and George never **felt** lonely. Dawson says in the book, "People worry too much. Life is good, just the way it is."

Was George Dawson a success? He definitely **was**. He **enjoyed** life and **accomplished** his goal: learning to read and write.

---

4 *African American*: an American whose ancestors came from Africa as slaves
5 *literacy*: the ability to read and write

COMPREHENSION CHECK Based on the reading, tell if the statement is true (**T**) or false (**F**).

1. George Dawson was born a slave.

2. Richard Glaubman wrote a book about Dawson.

3. Dawson learned to enjoy life from his father.

3.3 The Past of *Be*

Examples	Explanation
Dawson **was** from a poor family. His grandparents **were** slaves.	The past of the verb *be* has two forms: *was* and *were*. I, he, she, it → **was** we, you, they → **were**
There **was** an article about Dawson in the newspaper. There **were** many changes in his lifetime.	After *there*, we use *was* or *were* depending on the noun that follows. We use *was* with a singular noun. We use *were* with a plural noun.
Dawson's life **wasn't** easy. Education and books **weren't** available to him as a child.	To make a negative statement, we put *not* after *was* or *were*. The contraction for *was not* is *wasn't*. The contraction for *were not* is *weren't*.
Dawson **was born** in 1898.	We use a form of *be* with *born*.
Dawson **was able** to live a happy life.	We use a form of *be* with *able to*.

Compare statements, *yes/no* questions, short answers, and *wh-* questions.

Statement	Yes/No Question and Short Answer	Wh- Question
Dawson **was** poor.	**Was** he successful? Yes, he **was**.	How **was** he successful?
His grandparents **were** slaves.	**Were** they from the North? No, they **weren't**.	Where **were** they from?
Dawson **wasn't** unhappy.	**Was** he in school as a child? No, he **wasn't**.	Why **wasn't** he in school?

EXERCISE 4 Fill in the blanks to complete these affirmative and negative statements and questions.

1. George Dawson _____*was*_____ poor.

2. Dawson _____ born in 1898.

3. At that time, there _____ many opportunities for him.

4. His parents _____ poor.

5. Dawson's father used to tell him, "We _____ born to die."

6. He _____ unhappy.

7. George Dawson wasn't able to write his name. Why _____ able to write his name?

8. George Dawson _____ lonely.

9. _____ happy to go to school? Yes, he _____ .

10. How old _____ when he learned to read? He _____ ninety-eight years old.

11. _____ slavery in the U.S. when Dawson was born? No, there wasn't.

12. _____ a lot of opportunities for African Americans at that time? No, there weren't.

13. Dawson's teacher was surprised. Why _____ surprised?

EXERCISE 5 About You Find a partner and discuss your answers to these questions.

1. Were you interested in the story about George Dawson? Why or why not?

2. Were you surprised that he learned to read when he was 98 years old?

3. In your opinion, was George Dawson a success? Why or why not?

3.4 The Simple Past of Regular Verbs

Examples	Explanation	
Dawson **signed** his name with an X. He **learned** a lot from his father. Dawson **accomplished** his goal.	**Base Form** sign learn accomplish	**Past Form** sign**ed** learn**ed** accomplish**ed**

Language Notes:

1. If the verb ends in an *e*, we add only –*d*.

   Dawson decide**d** to get an education. He die**d** in 2001.

2. For a review of the spelling and pronunciation of the –*ed* past form, see Appendix A.

EXERCISE 6 Fill in the blanks with the simple past form of one of the verbs from the box. In some cases, more than one answer is possible.

fail	ask	live	decide	discover	try
land	attend	want	attempt	learn	
die	occur	rescue	help	start	

1. Dawson _____*lived*_____ from 1898 to 2001.

2. He _____ to work when he was four years old.

3. Many changes _____ during his long life.

4. His teacher _____ him, "Do you know the alphabet?"

5. He _____ school when he was ninety-eight.

6. Richard Glaubman _____ Dawson write a book.

7. Salomon Andrée _____ to explore the North Pole.

8. Many people _____ to reach the North Pole by land, but they weren't successful.

9. Andrée _____ to use a balloon.

10. The balloon _____ far from the North Pole.

11. Andrée and his men _____ .

12. In 1914, Ernest Shackleton _____ when he tried to cross Antarctica.

13. He _____ from his failure.

14. He _____ his men.

15. Robert Ballard _____ the *Titanic* on the ocean floor.

3.5 The Simple Past of Irregular Verbs[6]

Many verbs are irregular in the past. An irregular verb does not use the –*ed* ending.

Examples	Explanation	
A teacher **taught** Dawson to read. Dawson **had** a close family. Andrée and his men **went** up in a balloon.	**Base Form** teach have go	**Past Form** taught had went

---

[6] For an alphabetical list of irregular past verbs, see Appendix K.

Notice the different kinds of changes to form the simple past of irregular verbs.

Verbs With No Change				Final *d* Changes to *t*	
beat	fit	put	spit	bend—bent	send—sent
bet	hit	quit	split	build—built	spend—spent
cost	hurt	set	spread	lend—lent	
cut	let	shut			

Verbs with Vowel Changes			
feel—felt	mean—meant[7]	dig—dug	sting—stung
keep—kept	sleep—slept	hang—hung	strike—struck
leave—left	sweep—swept	spin—spun	swing—swung
lose—lost	weep—wept	stick—stuck	win—won

Verbs with Vowel Changes			
awake—awoke	speak—spoke	begin—began	sing—sang
break—broke	steal—stole	drink—drank	sink—sank
choose—chose	wake—woke	ring—rang	spring—sprang
freeze—froze		shrink—shrank	swim—swam
bring—brought	fight—fought	blow—blew	grow—grew
buy—bought	teach—taught	draw—drew	know—knew
catch—caught	think—thought	fly—flew	throw—threw
arise—arose	rise—rose	bleed—bled	meet—met
drive—drove	shine—shone	feed—fed	read—read[8]
ride—rode	write—wrote	flee—fled	speed—sped
		lead—led	
sell—sold	tell—told	find—found	wind—wound
mistake—mistook	take—took	lay—laid	say—said[9]
shake—shook		pay—paid	
swear—swore	wear—wore	bite—bit	light—lit
tear—tore		hide—hid	slide—slid
become—became	forgive—forgave	fall—fell	run—ran
come—came	give—gave	hold—held	sit—sat
eat—ate	lie—lay	see—saw	
forget—forgot	shoot—shot	stand—stood	
get—got		understand—understood	

Miscellaneous Changes			
be—was/were	go—went	hear—heard	
do—did	have—had	make—made	

---

[7] There is a change in the vowel sound. *Meant* rhymes with *sent*.
[8] The past form of *read* is pronounced like the color red.
[9] *Said* rhymes with *bed*.

EXERCISE 7 Fill in the blank with the simple past form of the verb given.

1. Andrée _____flew_____ to the Arctic in a balloon.
   <u>fly</u>

2. Andrée _____ he could reach the North Pole in a balloon.
   <u>think</u>

3. He and his men _____ in July 1897.
   <u>leave</u>

4. Fog _____ the balloon heavy.
   <u>make</u>

5. Strong winds _____ Andrée's balloon.
   <u>hit</u>

6. They _____ problems with the weather.
   <u>have</u>

7. No one _____ what happened to the men.
   <u>know</u>

8. The *Titanic* _____ in 1912.
   <u>sink</u>

9. Robert Ballard _____ up near the ocean.
   <u>grow</u>

10. He _____ an oceanographer.
    <u>become</u>

11. He _____ the *Titanic* on the ocean floor.
    <u>find</u>

12. Earnest Shackleton _____ an expedition to Antarctica.
    <u>lead</u>

13. He _____ all of his men home safely.
    <u>bring</u>

EXERCISE 8 Fill in the blanks with the simple past form of one of the verbs from the box. You may use the same verb more than once.

teach	write	begin	see
say	have	go	become

1. Dawson _____had_____ a hard life.

2. He _____began_____ to work for his father when he was four years old.

3. He _____saw_____ many changes in his lifetime.

4. He _____became_____ interested in reading when he was 98.

5. He _____went_____ to school when he was 98.

6. His teacher _____taught_____ him the alphabet.

7. Dawson _____, "I wonder what I might learn today."

8. Dawson _____ a book about his life.

If at First You Don't Succeed

Read the following article. Pay special attention to the words in bold.

Diana Nyad was a professional swimmer. She was in her twenties when she decided to swim around Manhattan. The first time she tried, she **didn't succeed**. But she **didn't give** up. She tried again and swam the twenty-eight miles in less than eight hours. Then she had another goal: to swim from Cuba to Florida, a distance of 110 miles. She swam seventy-nine miles in forty-two hours. She **didn't stop** to sleep. But she **didn't finish**. Jellyfish attacked her, and the weather threw her off course.[10] **Did** she **try** again? Yes, but not until thirty-three years later.

Nyad retired from competitive swimming in her twenties. For the next thirty years, she **didn't swim** at all. She became a sportscaster[11] and a journalist. But she **didn't stop** all physical activity. She always kept in shape. Every Friday she took a one-hundred-mile bike ride.

In 2007, when Nyad was sixty years old, her mother died. She started to think about her own life. In the thirty years that she **didn't swim**, she always thought about the possibility of trying again. She **didn't want** to die without achieving her goal. She started to train again. By the summer of 2011, she tried again—and failed again—after twenty-nine hours in the water. She tried two more times—and failed to reach Florida each time. What kinds of problems **did** she **face**? There were attacks by jellyfish, bad weather, and breathing problems from asthma.[12] How **did** she **solve** the problem of jellyfish? For her fifth attempt, she wore a bodysuit and mask to protect against jellyfish stings. On August 31, 2013, after fifty-three hours of swimming, she reached the Florida shore, thirty-five years after her first attempt. Nyad achieved[13] what younger and stronger swimmers could not.

Nyad always tells people, "Never give up."

---

[10] *to throw off course*: to send in an unintended direction
[11] *sportscaster*: someone who gives news about sports on the TV or radio
[12] *asthma*: a serious medical condition that causes difficulty in breathing
[13] *to achieve*: to succeed in doing something

Jellyfish

Diana Nyad waves as she starts her fifth attempt to swim from Cuba to Florida.

COMPREHENSION CHECK Based on the reading, tell if the statement is true (**T**) or false (**F**).

1. Nyad made four attempts to swim from Cuba to Florida before she was finally successful.

2. She didn't do any hard physical activity for thirty years.

3. The death of her mother made her think about her own life.

3.6 Negatives and Questions with the Simple Past

Examples	Explanation
Diana **succeeded** on her fifth attempt. She **didn't succeed** on her first attempt.	For the negative of the simple past, we use *didn't* (*did not*) + base form for regular and irregular verbs (except *be*).
She **swam** around Manhattan in her twenties. She **didn't swim** from Cuba to Florida in her twenties.	**Affirmative** **Negative** succeeded didn't succeed swam didn't swim
Did Nyad **face** difficulties? Yes, she **did**. **Did** she **succeed** the first time? No, she **didn't**.	For *yes/no* questions about the past, we use *did* + base form for regular and irregular verbs (except *be*). For a short answer we use *Yes*, + subject pronoun + *did*. *No*, + subject pronoun + *didn't*.
What kind of difficulties **did** Nyad **face**? When **did** she **succeed**?	For *wh-* questions about the past, we use *Wh-* word + *did* + base form.

Compare statements, *yes/no* questions, short answers, and *wh-* questions.

Statement	*Yes/No* Question and Short Answer	*Wh-* Question
Diana **swam** to Florida.	**Did** she **swim** around Manhattan? Yes, she **did**.	When **did** she **swim** around Manhattan?
She **didn't succeed** the first time.	**Did** she **succeed** the second time? No, she **didn't**.	When **did** she **succeed**? Why **didn't** she **succeed** the first time?

Language Note:

We don't use *did* with the verb *be*.

Compare: Nyad **wasn't** successful her first time.   What **was** her goal?

          She **didn't reach** Florida on her first try.   What **did** she **want** to accomplish?

EXERCISE 9 Fill in the blanks with the negative form of the underlined verbs.

1. Andrée and his men <u>landed</u> on ice. They <u> didn't land </u> on the North Pole.

2. George Dawson <u>knew</u> how to do many things. He _____ how to read and write.

3. His father <u>taught</u> him many things. His father _____ him to read or write.

4. He <u>had</u> the chance for an education when he was old. He _____ the chance

   when he was young.

5. He <u>wrote</u> a book about his life. He _____ it alone.

6. Diana Nyad <u>wanted</u> to swim from Cuba to Florida. She _____ to die without

   achieving her goal.

7. She <u>swam</u> a lot when she was young. She _____ for many years.

8. Nyad <u>went</u> to Cuba. She _____ alone.

EXERCISE 10 Fill in the blanks to complete the conversation. Use context clues to help you.

A: <u> Did you read </u> the Harry Potter books?
   _{1.}

B: Yes, I _____. I read all of them. I recently wrote a paper about the author,
   _{2.}

   J.K. Rowling. She's the first author to become a billionaire from her writing. When she first

   started writing, she considered herself a failure. _____ that?
   _{3.}

A: No, I _____. But I'd like to know more. When _____ the first Harry
   _{4.}   _{5.}

   Potter book?

B: She wrote the first one in 1995. She always wanted to be a writer. But her parents

   _____ the idea. They thought she needed a "real" job.
   _{6.}

A: Why _____ that writing novels was a real job?
   _{7.}

B: They were worried that it wouldn't pay the rent for her. She was very poor. She went on welfare.

   At that time in her life, she was very depressed.

A: Why _____ on welfare?
   _{8.}

B: She was divorced and a single parent. She _____ enough money to support her
   _{9.}

   daughter. She was also very depressed because her mother died. She sent her Harry Potter novel

   to twelve publishers, but they all rejected her novel.

continued

The Simple Past, The Habitual Past with *Used To*   83

A: Why _____ her novel?
                    10.

B: They didn't think it would be successful. Finally a publisher agreed to publish it.

A: _____ her a lot of money?
              11.

B: No, they _____. They only offered her about $2,000. They printed only one
                    12.

thousand copies.

A: That's not very many books. _____ their offer?
                                          13.

B: Yes, she _____. She was happy to accept it.
                14.

A: _____ more copies?
              15.

B: Yes, they _____. They had to print more copies because so many people wanted
                  16.

to read about Harry Potter. By 1999, her book went to the top of best-seller lists. When she wrote

the fourth book, the publisher printed lots of copies.

A: How many copies _____?
                          17.

B: They printed over five million copies.

A: Wow! She wasn't a failure. She was a real success.

B: Besides writing, Rowling does other things. For example, she spoke to the graduating class of

Harvard in 2008.

A: _____ about her novels?
              18.

A: No, _____. She spoke about the benefits of failure. She said, "It is impossible to
            19.

live without failing at something." I recently read that she's not a billionaire anymore. She's just

a millionaire.

A: How _____ her money?
              20.

B: She didn't lose her money. She started to give away money to charity.

A: Cool! She sounds like a very interesting person.

Success in CHANGING LAWS

Martin Luther King Jr. waves to supporters from the Lincoln Memorial in Washington, DC, on August 28, 1963.

Read the following article. Pay special attention to the words in bold.

CD 1
TR 20

Today all people in the United States have equal rights under the law. But this was not always the case, especially for African Americans. Even though slavery in the United States ended in 1865, blacks continued to suffer discrimination[14] and segregation,[15] especially in the South. Many hotels and restaurants **used to serve** white customers only. Many businesses **used to have** signs in their windows that said "Blacks Not Allowed." Black children **used to go** to separate, and often inferior, schools. Many professions were for whites only. Even in sports, blacks could not join the major baseball leagues;[16] there **used to be** separate leagues for them. In many places in the South, buses **used to reserve** the front seats for white people. But that all changed.

One evening in December of 1955, Rosa Parks, a forty-two-year-old woman, got on a bus in Montgomery, Alabama, to go home from work. She was tired and sat down. When some white people got on the crowded bus, the bus driver ordered Ms. Parks to stand up. Ms. Parks refused. The bus driver called the police, and they arrested Ms. Parks.

Martin Luther King Jr., a black minister living in Montgomery, Alabama, wanted to put an end to discrimination. When King heard about Ms. Parks's arrest, he told African Americans in Montgomery to boycott[17] the bus company. People who **used to ride** the bus to work decided to walk instead. As a result of the boycott, the Supreme Court outlawed[18] discrimination on public transportation.

In 1964, about 100 years after the end of slavery, Congress passed a new law that officially gave equality to all Americans. This law made discrimination in employment and education illegal. King won the Nobel Peace Prize[19] for his work in creating a better world.

Martin Luther King, Rosa Parks, and other brave people succeeded in changing unfair laws.

---

[14] *discrimination*: unfair treatment, especially because of race, age, religion, etc.

[15] *segregation*: separation of the races

[16] *league*: a group of sports teams that compete against each other

[17] *to boycott*: to refuse to do business with a company

[18] *to outlaw*: to make an action illegal or against the law

[19] *The Nobel Peace Prize*: a prize given once a year for great work in promoting world peace

COMPREHENSION CHECK Based on the reading, tell if the statement is true (**T**) or false (**F**).

1. When slavery ended, blacks gained equality.

2. Rosa Parks refused to obey the law on the bus.

3. The bus boycott in Montgomery was successful in helping change the law.

3.7 The Habitual Past with *Used To*

Examples	Explanation
Black children **used to attend** separate schools. Many professions **used to be** for white people only. There **used to be** separate baseball leagues for black people.	We use *used to* + a base form to show a habit or custom over a past period of time. It refers to custom that no longer exists.

Language Notes:

1. *Used to* is not for an action that happened once or a few times.

   Many restaurants **used to serve** white people only. (This happened over a period of time.)

   In 1955, Rosa Parks **refused** to stand up. (This happened one time.)

2. For negatives and questions, we omit the *d* in *used to*.

   Some restaurants **didn't use** to serve African Americans.

   Where **did** they **use** to eat?

EXERCISE 11 Fill in the blanks with *use(d) to* + one of the verbs from the box.

make	be✓	suffer	give up	ride	travel
consider	have	dream	wonder	support	

1. J.K. Rowling ___used to be___ poor. Now she's rich.

2. Rowling ___used to have___ billions of dollars. But now she gives away a lot of her money.

3. She didn't ___use to consider___ herself a success. She thought she was a failure.

4. How did she ___use to support___ herself and her daughter when she was poor?

5. Peter Athans, who climbed Mt. Everest several times, ___used to make___ a lot of mistakes. Now he's much more experienced and careful.

6. People ___used to wonder___ where the *Titanic* was. Thanks to Robert Ballard, now we know where it is.

7. Diana Nyad ___used to dream___ of swimming from Cuba to Florida. She finally accomplished it.

8. Nyad ___used to ride___ her bike one hundred miles every Friday.

9. It ___used to be___ difficult to arrive at the North Pole. Now it's easy.

10. People ___used to travel___ from Europe to the U.S. by ship. Now people fly across the ocean.

11. Black people in the South ___used to suffer___ discrimination in hotels and restaurants.

12. Black people in the South ___used to give up___ their seats on a bus to white people.

13. Baseball teams didn't ___use to have___ black players. But that changed in 1947.

EXERCISE 12 About You Compare the situation in your country in the past with the situation in your country today. Discuss your answers with a partner.

1. People used to have large families. Now most people have one or two children.

2. _____

3. _____

4. _____

EXERCISE 13 About You Write sentences comparing the way you used to live with the way you live now. Discuss your answers with a partner. Use the ideas from the box for your sentences:

| school | job | hobbies | apartment/house | family | friends |

1. I used to live with my whole family. Now I live alone.

2. I didn't use to speak English at all. Now I speak English pretty well.

3. _____

4. _____

5. _____

6. _____

7. _____

SUMMARY OF LESSON 3

The Simple Past of *Be*

AFFIRMATIVE STATEMENT:	Dawson **was** happy
NEGATIVE STATEMENT:	He **wasn't** rich.
Yes/No QUESTION:	**Was** he from a large family?
SHORT ANSWER:	Yes, he **was**.
Wh- QUESTION:	Where **was** he born?
NEGATIVE *Wh-* QUESTION:	Why **wasn't** he in school?

The Simple Past of Regular Verbs

AFFIRMATIVE STATEMENT:	Andrée **wanted** to go to the North Pole.
NEGATIVE STATEMENT:	He **didn't want** to go over land.
Yes/No QUESTION:	**Did** he **want** to go by balloon?
SHORT ANSWER:	Yes, he **did**.
Wh- QUESTION:	Why **did** he **want** to go to the North Pole?
NEGATIVE *Wh-* QUESTION:	Why **didn't** he **want** to go over land?

The Simple Past of Irregular Verbs

AFFIRMATIVE STATEMENT:	Dawson **felt** happy.
NEGATIVE STATEMENT:	He **didn't feel** lonely.
Yes/No QUESTION:	**Did** he **feel** good when he learned to read?
SHORT ANSWER:	Yes, he **did**.
Wh- QUESTION:	How **did** he **feel** about his life?
NEGATIVE *Wh-* QUESTION:	Why **didn't** he **feel** lonely?

The Habitual Past with *Used To*

AFFIRMATIVE STATEMENT:	Black children **used to attend** separate schools in some places.
NEGATIVE STATEMENT:	They **didn't use to attend** schools with white children.
Yes/No QUESTION:	**Did** baseball teams **use to have** black players?
SHORT ANSWER:	No, they **didn't**.
Wh- QUESTION:	Why **did** schools **use to segregate** students?

TEST/REVIEW

Fill in the blanks to complete the conversation. Use the words given and context clues to help you. Use contractions wherever possible.

A: There _____was_____ a good program on TV last night. _____Did you see_____ it?
1. be   2. you/see

B: No, I _____didn't_____. What _____was it_____ about?
3.   4. be

A: It was about successful people who _____failed_____ at first.
5. fail

B: Who _____did they talk_____ about?
6. they/talk

A: One success was Bill Gates. Gates _____started_____ a company with a friend when he
7. start

_____was_____ 17 years old.
8. be

B: What kind of company _____did they start_____?
9. they/start

A: They _____built_____ software to help regulate traffic. They _____tried_____ to sell it
10. build   11. try

to the city, but they _____were not_____ successful.
weren't
12. not/be

B: Why _____were they not_____ successful?
weren't they
13. they/not/be

A: The software _____did_____ well in the lab, but it _____didn't do_____ well when they
14. do   15. not/do

showed it to the city. Then Gates _____went_____ to college but he _____didn't finish_____.
16. go   17. not/finish

He _____left_____ before graduation.
18. leave

B: I _____didn't know_____ that. Why _____did he leave_____ college?
19. not/know   20. he/leave

A: He _____was_____ very interested in computers, and he _____started_____ Microsoft
21. be   22. start

with his friend. They _____became_____ successful. The program also talked about Thomas
23. become

Edison. He _____invented_____ many things. He _____made_____ 1,000 attempts
24. invent   25. make

before he _____succeeded_____ with the light bulb. A reporter _____asked_____ him
26. succeed   27. ask

how it _____felt_____ to fail so many times. Edison _____replied_____,
28. feel   29. reply

"I _____did not fail_____ 1,000 times. The light bulb was an invention with 1,000 steps."
30. not/fail

B: I _____used to think_____ that successful people succeeded right away.
31. use to/think

I _____didn't use to think_____ of failure as a part of success.
32. not/use to/think

WRITING

PART 1 Editing Advice

1. Use *was/were* with *born*.

　　　　　was
　　　　Dawson ⌃ born in the South.

2. Don't use *was* or *were* with *die*.

　　　　He ~~was~~ died in 2001.

3. Don't use a past form after *to*.

　　　　　　　　swim
　　　　Nyad decided to ~~swam~~ from Cuba to Florida.

4. Don't use *was* or *were* to form the simple past.

　　accomplished
　　　　She ~~was accomplish~~ her goal.

5. Use a form of *be* before an adjective. Remember, some *–ed* words are adjectives.

　　　　　was
　　　　Dawson ⌃ excited about going to school.

6. Don't use *did* with an adjective. Use *was* or *were*.

　　　　　　　　weren't
　　　　Andrée and his men ~~didn't~~ successful.

7. Form the past question correctly.

　　　　didn't you
　　　　Why ~~you didn't~~ read the article?

　　　did　　　*write*
　　　　Why ⌃ Dawson ~~wrote~~ a book?

8. Use the base form after *didn't*.

　　　　He didn't ~~learned~~ to read when he was a child.

9. Don't forget the *d* in *used to* in affirmative statements.

　　　　d
　　　　He use ⌃ to live in the South.

10. Don't add the verb *be* before *used to* for habitual past.

　　　　Nyad ~~is~~ used to be a sportscaster.

11. Use the correct past form.

　　　　swam
　　　　Nyad ~~swimmed~~ from Cuba to Florida.

PART 2 Editing Practice

Some of the shaded words and phrases have mistakes. Find the mistakes and correct them. If the shaded words are correct, write C.

　　　　　　C　　　　　　　　　　　　　　　　*was*
　　　I recently read an article about Jackie Robinson. He were the first African American to play
　　　　　1.　　　　　　　　　　　　　　　　**2.**

　　　　　　　　　　　　　　　　　　　　　　　　　　　　　　used to
on a major league baseball team, the Brooklyn Dodgers. Major league baseball teams use to
　　　　　　　　　　　　　　　　　　　　　　　　　　　　　　3.

have only white players. Blacks ~~were~~ used to have their own teams.
　　　　　　　　　　　　　4.

was
Robinson born in 1919 in the South. His family was very poor. When he was just a baby,
5.   6.
left
his father leaved the family and his mother decided to moved the family to California. When he
7.   8.   9.
was   _was_
were in high school and college, he interested in several different sports. After junior college, he
10.   11.

went to the University of California, where he was won awards in baseball, basketball, football,
12.   13.

took
and track. He didn't finished college. He taked a job as athletic director of a youth organization.
14.   15.

entered
Then he enter the army in 1942. After he left the army in 1944, he accepted an offer to be the
16.   17.

athletic director at a college in Texas. In 1945, the Kansas City Monarchs, an African American

sent
baseball team, sended him an offer to play professional baseball. In 1947, the Brooklyn Dodgers
18.   _knew_

offered him a contract. The manager of the team knowed that Robinson would face racial
19.   20.

discrimination. He didn't wanted Robinson to fight back. Some people in the crowds yelled
21.   22.

racial insults to him. Even some of his teammates objected to having an African American
23.
wasn't
on their team. Robinson didn't surprised. He knew this would happen. Some other teams
24.   25.
did
threatened not to play against the Dodgers. How the manager of the team reacted?
26.   27.
said
The manager, Leo Durocher, supported Robinson. He sayed that he would rather keep Robinson
28.   29.

than some of them. In one game, when people yelled racial insults at Robinson, the team
came   _put_
captain come over and putted his arm around Robinson to show his support.
30.   31.
became
Robinson succeeded in breaking the racial barrier. He become the highest paid player in
32.   33.

Dodgers history. But more importantly, he opened the door for other African American athletes
34.

in professional sports. He retired from baseball in 1957. He was died in 1972.
35.   36.

PART 3 Write About It

1. Write about an ordinary person who did something extraordinary (like George Dawson). It can be someone you read about or someone you know.

2. Write about a time when you failed at something. What did you learn from your failure?

PART 4 Edit Your Writing

Reread the Summary of Lesson 3 and the editing advice. Edit your writing from Part 3.

Possessive Forms
Object Pronouns
Reflexive Pronouns
Questions

Guests cheer for the newlyweds after the wedding ceremony.

WEDDINGS

A successful marriage requires falling in love
many times, always with the same person.

—Mignon McLaughlin

A Traditional American WEDDING

CD 1
TR 21

Read the following article. Pay special attention to the words in bold.

Many young couples consider **their** wedding to be one of the most important days of **their** lives. They often spend a year planning for **it**: finding a place, selecting a menu, buying a wedding dress, ordering invitations and sending **them** to friends and relatives, selecting musicians, and more.

The bride chooses **her** bridesmaids[1] and maid of honor[2], and the groom chooses **his** groomsmen and best man. The bride and groom want to make this day special for **themselves** and for **their** guests. Sometimes the bride and groom use a professional wedding planner so they don't have to do everything by **themselves**.

When the day arrives, the groom doesn't usually see the bride before the wedding. It is considered bad luck for **him** to see **her** ahead of time. When the wedding begins, the groom and groomsmen enter first. Next, the maid of honor and bridesmaids enter. When the bride finally enters in **her** white dress, everyone turns around to look at **her**. Often the **bride's** father or both of **her** parents walk **her** down the aisle to the groom.

During the ceremony, the bride and groom take vows.[3] They promise to love and respect each other for the rest of their lives. The groom's best man holds the rings for **them** until they are ready to place **them** on each **other's** fingers. At the end of the ceremony, the groom lifts the **bride's** veil and kisses **her**.

There is a dinner and dance after the ceremony. The bride and groom usually dance the first dance alone. Then guests join **them**.

Before the bride and groom leave the party, the bride throws **her** bouquet over **her** head, and the single women try to catch **it**. It is believed that the woman who catches **it** will be the next one to get married.

The newlyweds[4] usually take a trip, called a honeymoon, immediately after the wedding.

---

[1] *bridesmaid*: one of a group of women (a good friend or close relative of the bride) who is part of the wedding ceremony
[2] *maid of honor*: one special woman (a good friend or close relative of the bride) who helps the bride during the wedding ceremony
[3] *vow*: a promise
[4] *newlywed*: a recently married person

COMPREHENSION CHECK Based on the reading, tell if the statement is true (**T**) or false (**F**).

1. Some people use a wedding planner to help plan for the wedding.

2. The bride usually enters with the groom.

3. All the women try to catch the bouquet.

4.1 Overview of Possessive Forms and Pronouns

Examples	Explanation
Your wedding was beautiful. **Her** mother looks happy.	A possessive adjective shows ownership or relationship.
You attended my wedding, and I attended **yours**.	A possessive pronoun also shows ownership or relationship.
The **bride's** dress is white.	A noun has a possessive form.
They sent **me** an invitation.	An object pronoun follows the verb.
They want to make the wedding special for **themselves** and their guests.	Some pronouns are reflexive.

EXERCISE 1 This is a conversation between a bride-to-be and a professional wedding planner. Fill in the blanks with the words you hear.

CD 1
TR 22

A: My friend gave _____me your_____ contact information. She said she used _____your_____
 1. 2.

services when she got married last year. My fiancé and _____I_____ are planning
 3.

_____Our_____ wedding now, and we want to know how _____you_____ can help
 4. 5.

_____us_____ .
 6.

B: Some people try to plan _____their_____ wedding _____themselves_____ , but the results are
 7. 8.

often not so good. So I'm glad you contacted _____me_____ . I can help _____you_____
 9. 10.

plan the perfect wedding. Planning a wedding by _____yourselves_____ is stressful. It's
 11.

_____your_____ special day, and I want _____you_____ to enjoy _____it_____ .
 12. 13. 14.

There are a lot of little details in planning a wedding, and it's my job to take care of

_____them_____ for _____you_____ .
 15. 16.

continued

A: My ___Cousins'___ mother helped ___her___ plan ___her___
17.   18.   19.

wedding, but she was so busy that she didn't enjoy ___it___ very much. My cousin
                                                      20.

told ___me___ that ___her___ wedding day was stressful for ___her___
     21.   22.   23.

and ___her___ fiancé. I need help, but ___our___ budget is limited. How
    24.   25.

much is this going to cost ___us___?
                           26.

B: That depends. If you want ___my___ services for every step, it will be about $3,500.
                              27.

If you make ___your___ own arrangements and want ___my___ services for
            28.   29.

the two weeks before the wedding and on the wedding day, ___my___ fee is about
                                                          30.

$1,000. I made a list of all the things I do for a wedding. Please look at ___it___ and
                                                                            31.

give ___me___ a call if ___you___ have any questions.
     32.   33.

4.2 Possessive Forms of Nouns

Noun	Rule	Examples
Singular nouns: bride groom	Add apostrophe + *s*.	The **bride's** dress is white. The **groom's** tuxedo is black.
Plural nouns ending in –*s*: parents guests	Add apostrophe only.	She got married in her **parents'** house. The **guests'** coats are in the coat room.
Irregular plural nouns: men women	Add apostrophe + *s*.	The **men's** suits are black. The **women's** dresses are beautiful.
Names that end in –*s*: Charles	Add apostrophe + *s*.	Do you know **Charles's** wife?
Inanimate objects: the church the dress	Use "*the _____ of the _____.*"	New Hope is **the name of the church.** **The front of the dress** has pearls.
Time words: today this month	Add apostrophe + *s*	**Today's** weddings are very expensive.

Language Note:

Sometimes you will see only an apostrophe when a name ends in –*s*.

Do you know **Charles'** wife?

EXERCISE 2 Fill in the blanks to make the possessive form of the noun given.

1. The ___bride's___ grandfather looks very handsome.
   _{bride}

2. The ___bridesmaids'___ dresses are blue.
   _{bridesmaids}

3. They invited many guests to the wedding. Did they invite the ___guests'___ children?
   _{guests}

4. The ___women's___ dresses are very elegant.
   _{women}

5. ___Ross's___ sister is a bridesmaid.
   _{Ross}

6. ___Today's___ newspaper has the ___newlyweds'___ photo.
   _{Today}   _{newlyweds}

7. Do you know the ___children's___ names?
   _{children}

EXERCISE 3 Fill in the blanks with the two nouns given. Put them in the correct order. Use the possessive form of one of the nouns, except with inanimate objects.

1. ___The bride's name___ is Lisa.
   _{name/the bride}

2. _____ is open.
   _{the door/the church}

3. _____ came to the wedding from London.
   _{the bride/grandmother}

4. _____ is June 1.
   _{the wedding/the date}

5. _____ is crying.
   _{the bride/mother}

6. _____ are black.
   _{the men/tuxedos}

7. _____ is white.
   _{the limousine/color}

8. _____ are pretty.
   _{dresses/girls}

9. Some people get married in their _____ .
   _{house/parents}

10. What is _____ ?
    _{wedding/the cost}

4.3 Possessive Adjectives

Examples	Explanation
I love **my** wife. Where did you buy **your** gift? He chose **his** brother to be **his** best man. She's wearing **her** sister's dress. It's a big restaurant with **its** own reception hall. We planned **our** wedding for over a year. They bought **their** rings at a jewelry store.	Compare subject pronouns and possessive adjectives. **Subject Pronouns**　**Possessive Adjectives** 　　I　　　　　　　　my 　　you　　　　　　　your 　　he　　　　　　　　his 　　she　　　　　　　her 　　it　　　　　　　　its 　　we　　　　　　　our 　　they　　　　　　　their
My sister loves **her** husband. **My brother** loves **his** wife.	A possessive adjective refers to the noun before it. Be careful not to confuse *his* and *her*. 　NOT: My sister loves *his* husband. 　NOT: My uncle loves *her* wife.
The **bride's mother's** dress is blue.	We can use two possessive nouns together.
My brother's wife didn't attend the wedding.	We can use a possessive adjective (*my*) before a possessive noun (*brother's*).

Language Notes:

1. Don't confuse *your* and *you're*. *You're* = *you are*.

2. Don't confuse *their* and *they're*. *They're* = *they are*.

3. Don't confuse *its* and *it's*. *It's* = *it is*.

EXERCISE 4 Fill in the blanks with a possessive adjective.

1. I love _____my_____ parents.

2. I have one sister. _____ sister got married five years ago.

3. She loves _____ husband very much.

4. He's an accountant. He has _____ own business.

5. They have one child. _____ son's name is Jason.

6. My sister and I visit _____ parents once a month. They live two hours away from us.

7. My sister said, "My car isn't working this week. Let's visit them in _____ car."

EXERCISE 5 Fill in the blanks with a possessive adjective.

A: My sister, Nicole, is getting married next month.

B: Will your parents have the wedding at _____*their*_____ home?
1.

A: Oh, no. They live in an apartment. _____ apartment is too small. My sister
2.

invited more than 200 guests. The wedding is going to be at a church. Afterwards, there's going

to be a reception nearby. The church has _____ own reception hall.
3.

B: Did she already buy _____ dress?
4.

A: Dresses are so expensive. We wear the same size, so my sister's going to wear _____
5.

dress. Nicole and _____ fiancé, Kevin, want to save money for _____
6.   7.

honeymoon. They're going to Paris.

B: Wow! Paris is beautiful—and expensive.

A: Yes, it is. But Kevin's aunt lives there. They're going to stay at _____ apartment.
8.

B: Isn't she going to be at her apartment?

A: No. _____ aunt is coming here for _____ wedding. She's going to
9.   10.

stay here an extra week to give Kevin and Nicole _____ apartment.
11.

4.4 Possessive Pronouns

We use a possessive pronoun to avoid repetition of a noun. Compare possessive
adjectives and possessive pronouns.

Example	Explanation		
We had our wedding in a church. They had **theirs** in a garden. (*theirs* = their wedding) Her dress is white. **Mine** is blue. (*mine* = my dress) Their wedding was big. **Ours** was small. (*ours* = our wedding)	**Possessive Adjectives**		**Possessive Pronouns**
	my		mine
	your		yours
	his		his
	her		hers
	its		—
	our		ours
	their		theirs
The groom's parents look happy. The **bride's** do too. (*bride's* = bride's parents)	After a possessive noun, we can omit the noun to avoid repetition.		

EXERCISE 6 Circle the correct words to complete the conversation.

A: I heard your brother got married last month. How was the wedding? Was it anything like your

wedding? I remember (*your/*(*yours*)) very well.
    1.

B: (*My/Mine*) wedding was very different from my (*brother/brother's*). (*His/Hers*) was a very
    2.   **3.**   **4.**

formal wedding in a church. (*My/Mine*) was very informal, in a garden.
                        5.

A: I enjoyed (*your/yours*) wedding. I prefer informal weddings. At most weddings, I have to get
            6.

dressed up in a suit and tie. At (*your/yours*), I wore comfortable clothes. Where did your
                        7.

brother and his wife go for (*their/theirs*) honeymoon?
                        8.

B: They had a very different honeymoon from (*our/ours*). (*Our/Ours*) honeymoon was a two-day
                                    9.   **10.**

trip to Chicago. (*Their/Theirs*) was a two-week trip to Hawaii.
            11.

A: I remember your wife made (*her/hers*) own dress. You saved a lot of money.
                    12.

B: Yes. But my sister-in-law, Gina, bought (*hers/his*). Sarah made her dress for under $100. But
                                13.

(*Gina/Gina's*) cost over $1,000.
    14.

A: The cost of a wedding isn't the most important thing. The most important thing is the

happiness that follows. My (*uncle's/uncle*) wedding cost over $30,000, but his marriage lasted
                        15.

only eight months.

EXERCISE 7 About You Discuss the answers to these questions with a partner.

1. What kind of clothes do a bride and groom wear in your native culture?

2. What kind of clothes do guests wear?

3. Do people use professional wedding planners in your country? Why or why not?

4.5 Questions with *Whose*

Whose + a noun asks a question about ownership or relationship.

Whose + Noun	Auxiliary Verb	Subject	Verb	Answer
Whose dress	did	the bride	borrow?	She borrowed her sister's dress.
Whose flowers	are	those?		They're the bride's flowers.
Whose last name	will	the bride	use?	She'll use her husband's last name.

Language Note:

Don't confuse *whose* with *who's*. *Who's* = *who is*.

      Who's that? That's the wedding planner.

      Whose mother is that? That's the bride's mother.

EXERCISE 8 Write a question with *whose*. The answer is given.

1. Whose flowers are these? _____

   They're the bride's flowers.

2. _____

   That's my father's car.

3. _____

   Those are the newlyweds' gifts.

4. _____

   She's wearing her sister's necklace.

5. _____

   They followed the wedding planner's advice.

6. _____

   They used their friend's house.

Economizing on a Wedding

🎧 **Read the following article. Pay special attention to the words in bold.**

CD 1
TR 23

The average cost of a wedding in the United States is $27,000. In the past, the bride's parents usually paid for the wedding. But since today's brides and grooms are older, they often pay for **it themselves**.

Here are some tips[5] from recently married people on how to economize on a wedding.

- "I always pictured **myself** in a beautiful white dress on my wedding day. But most dresses are over $1,000. I couldn't afford any of **them**. I found a great secondhand dress for $200. When my sister got married, she made her dress **herself** and spent only $100. When the guests saw **her** walk down the aisle, they said she looked beautiful.

- "We wanted professional invitations, but we decided to make **them ourselves**. We designed **them** on the computer."

- "I always wanted live music at my wedding, but professional musicians are expensive. My cousin plays piano, so I asked **him** to play for **us**. We used a DJ[6] for the dancing afterwards. We had to remind **ourselves** that the music wasn't the focus of the day— our marriage was."

- "Most couples want to get married in the summer. You can cut costs by having a wedding at a less popular time. A wedding in January is cheaper than a wedding in August. Ask **yourself** how important a summer wedding is."

---

5 *tip*: advice or useful information
6 *DJ (disk jockey)*: a person who plays recorded music

It is not good to economize on some things:

- "Don't try to save money by e-mailing invitations or thank-you cards. Guests are offended. You should send **them** by postal mail."

- "I asked a friend to take pictures at my wedding. When he showed **me** the pictures afterwards, I was very disappointed. Hire a professional photographer. You want to look at **yourselves** and guests for years to come."

The best way to economize is to invite only your closest relatives and friends.

COMPREHENSION CHECK Based on the reading, tell if the statement is true (**T**) or false (**F**).

1. Guests are offended if you make your own invitations.

2. The cost of a wedding is the same all through the year.

3. Guests expect to get a thank-you card by postal mail.

4.6 Object Pronouns

The object pronouns are *me, you, him, her, it, us,* and *them.*

Examples	Explanation
We made the invitations. We're going to send **them** out next month. I love the bride's dress. She borrowed **it** from her sister.	We use object pronouns after a verb.
We paid for the limousine service. We paid *for* **it** in advance. Did you see the photos? Are you happy *with* **them**?	An object pronoun can follow a preposition (*at, with, of, about, to, from, in,* etc.).
He invited **my wife and me** to the wedding. **My wife and I** went to the wedding.	Be careful with subjects and objects connected with *and*. After a verb, we use an object pronoun. Before a verb, we use a subject pronoun.

Language Notes:

1. An object can be direct or indirect.

   She invited **me** to the wedding. (A direct object receives the action of the verb.)

   He showed **me** the pictures. (An indirect object answers *to whom* or *for whom.*)

2. We can use *them* for plural people and things.

   The flowers are beautiful. Do you like **them**?

   The bridesmaids are beautiful. Let's take a picture of **them**.

3. Compare subject pronouns and object pronouns:

Subject Pronoun	Verb	Object Pronoun
You	love	me.
I	love	you.
She	loves	him.
He	loves	her.
We	love	it.
They	love	us.
We	love	them.

EXERCISE 9 Fill in the blanks with an object pronoun that corresponds to the underlined words.

1. In a traditional wedding, <u>the bride</u> doesn't arrive at the ceremony with the groom. He arrives

   before _____*her*_____ .

2. <u>The bride</u> wears <u>a veil</u>. The groom lifts _____ to kiss _____ .

3. <u>The groom</u> promises to love the bride, and the bride promises to love _____ .

4. Sometimes the bride and groom get <u>hotel rooms</u> for their guests. Do they pay for _____?

5. <u>We</u> sent a check to the bride and groom. They sent a note to thank _____ .

6. Did <u>you</u> receive the invitation? We want _____ to attend our wedding.

7. Yes. I received <u>the invitation</u>. I put _____ on my refrigerator.

8. You don't know <u>the groom's brothers</u>. Let me introduce you to _____ .

9. <u>I'm</u> going to the wedding. The bride sent _____ an invitation.

EXERCISE 10 Fill in the blanks with the correct subject pronoun, object pronoun, or possessive adjective.

A: How was your cousin Lisa's wedding last Saturday?

B: _____*It*_____ was great.
       _{1.}

A: How many guests were there?

B: About 200. I couldn't count _____ .
                                   _{2.}

A: Wow! That's a lot. It sounds like an expensive wedding. How did they pay for _____?
                                                                                     _{3.}

B: Lisa and Ron worked after _____ graduated from college and saved money.
                                 _{4.}

   _____ parents helped _____ too.
   _{5.}   _{6.}

A: Did Lisa wear a traditional white dress?

B: Yes. In fact, _____ wore _____ mother's wedding dress.
                     _{7.}   _{8.}

   She looked beautiful in _____ .
                           _{9.}

A: Where did _____ go on their honeymoon?
                 _{10.}

B: They went to Hawaii.

A: I hope _____'ll be happy. The wedding and honeymoon are important, but the
              _{11.}

   marriage that follows is what really counts.

B: I agree with _____ . But I'm sure they'll be happy. She loves _____
                                 12.   **13.**

and _____ loves _____ very much.
        14.   **15.**

A: Did you take pictures at the wedding?

B: Yes. Do you want to see _____ ? I have some on _____ cell phone.
                                    16.   **17.**

Here's a picture of Lisa and _____ .
                                 18.

A: Who's that older woman between the two of you?

B: That's _____ grandmother. We were so happy she could come to the wedding.
               19.

She lives in another state.

A: _____ grandmother looks so proud.
      20.

EXERCISE 11 Circle the correct words to complete each sentence.

1. (*I*/*I'm*) have a wonderful fiancé, Katya.
    a.

2. I love (*her*/*hers*) very much and she loves (*me*/*my*) too.
            a.   **b.**

3. (*I*/*I'm*) so happy because (*we*/*we're*) going to get married.
   a.   **b.**

4. (*Our*/*We're*) wedding will be in March.
    a.

5. My brother's wedding was small. (*Our*/*Ours*) is going to be big.
                                     a.

6. We invited all (*our*/*ours*) friends and relatives.
               a.

7. Some of (*them*/*they*) are coming from out of town.
          a.

8. (*They're*/*Their*) going to stay with relatives or in a hotel.
    a.

9. Katya has two sisters. (*Hers*/*Her*) sisters are going to be bridesmaids.
                       a.

10. (*Their*/*They're*) dresses are blue.
     a.

11. There's one problem: Katya's father. (*I*/*I'm*) don't like (*his*/*her*) father very much.
                                         a.   **b.**

12. I think (*he*/*he's*) doesn't like (*my*/*me*) either. (*He's*/*His*) very bossy.
          a.   **b.**   **c.**

13. But I like Katya's mother. (*Hers*/*Her*) mother is nice.
                       a.

14. The wedding will be in a church. The church has (*it's*/*its*) own reception hall. (*Its*/*It's*) going to be a
                                        a.   **b.**

beautiful wedding.

15. Katya and (*me*/*I*) are going to have our honeymoon in Hawaii. My parents gave Katya and (*me*/*I*)
              a.   **b.**

money for the honeymoon.

4.7 Reflexive Pronouns

We use a reflexive pronoun when the object refers to the subject of the sentence.

Examples	Explanation

She pictured **herself** in a beautiful white dress.
We tell **ourselves** that a wedding is very important.
They like to look at **themselves** in their wedding photos.
	A reflexive pronoun can be:
	  a direct object
	  an indirect object
	  the object of a preposition

She made the dress **all by herself.** They made the invitations **all by themselves.**	We add *(all) by* before a reflexive pronoun to mean "alone," "without help."
We enjoyed **ourselves** at the wedding. Help **yourself** to more cake. Make **yourself** at home.	We use reflexive pronouns in a few idiomatic expressions.

Subject	Verb	Reflexive Pronoun
I	see	myself.
You	see	yourself.
He	sees	himself.
She	sees	herself.
It	sees	itself.
We	see	ourselves.
You	see	yourselves.
They	see	themselves.

EXERCISE 12 Frank and Sylvia, a married couple, have problems balancing their relationship and other areas of their lives. Read each one's story and fill in the blanks with a reflexive pronoun.

Sylvia's Story:

Now that I'm married, I don't have time for _____*myself*_____ anymore. We used to
                                          1.

spend time with each other. Now that we have kids, we never have time for _____.
                                                      2.

We both work, but Frank doesn't help me with housework or with the kids. I have to do

everything all by _____. My husband thinks only of _____.
                     3.   4.

When he wants something, like a new cell phone or new software, he buys it. He never buys

me flowers or presents anymore. I tell _____ that he still loves me, but
                                         5.

sometimes I'm not so sure. Sometimes I think the problem is his fault, but sometimes I blame

_____.
     6.

Frank's Story:

Sylvia never has time for me anymore. We used to do things together. Now I have to do

everything by _____. If I want to go to a movie, she says that she's too busy or
                    7.

too tired or that the kids are sick. I rarely go to the movies, and if I do, I go by _____.
                                                                                     8.

It seems like all I do is work and pay bills. Other married people seem to enjoy

_____ more than we do. She says she wants me to help her with the
      9.

housework, but she really prefers to do everything _____ because she doesn't
                                                          10.

like the way I do things. She wants us to see a marriage counselor, but I don't like to tell other

people about my problems. I like to solve my problems _____.
                                                              11.

EXERCISE 13 Fill in the blanks with the correct pronoun or possessive form.

Frank and Sylvia used to do a lot of things together. _____They_____ went to movies,
                                                             1.

went out to restaurants, and took vacations together. But now _____ are always
                                                                        2.

too busy for each other. _____ have two children and spend most of
                                3.

_____ time taking care of _____. Frank and Sylvia bought a
      4.   **5.**

house recently and spend _____ free time taking care of _____.
                                6.   **7.**

It's an old house and needs a lot of work.

When Frank and Sylvia have a problem, _____ try to solve _____
                                               8.   **9.**

by _____. But sometimes Sylvia goes to _____ mother for advice.
       10.   **11.**

Frank never goes to _____ mother. He doesn't want to bother
                          12.

_____ with _____ problems. Frank often complains that Sylvia
      13.   **14.**

cares more about the kids and the house than about _____. Sylvia wants to go
                                                            15.

to a marriage counselor, but Frank doesn't want to go with _____. He always
                                                                   16.

says to Sylvia, "We don't need a marriage counselor. We can solve _____
                                                                           17.

problems by _____. You just need to pay more attention to _____.
                  18.   **19.**

If you want to see a counselor, you can go by _____. I'm not going." Sylvia feels
                                                    20.

very frustrated. She thinks that the marriage isn't going to get better by _____.
                                                                                21.

New Wedding Trends

CD 1
TR 24

Read the following article. Pay special attention to the words in bold.

Wedding traditions are changing. More and more young couples are choosing to create a unique wedding experience for themselves and for their guests. In traditional weddings, a clergyperson[7] faces the bride and groom and **reads them their vows**. The bride and groom simply say, "I do" in response to this question. But more and more couples today are writing their own vows and **saying them to each other** in their own words.

Churches, synagogues, and temples are still the most popular places for a wedding. But some couples are choosing to have a destination wedding—about one in four. They get married on the beach, on a mountaintop, or other unusual places. The bride and groom send their friends and relatives an invitation, but they know many won't attend because of the expense of traveling. They **tell their guests the date** at least three to four months in advance. Often they **send them "save-the-date" cards** so that their guests can make plans.

Another new trend in weddings is to create a wedding based on the couple's ethnic background. For example, in an African American wedding, some couples want to **show respect to their ancestors[8]** by jumping over a broom, a tradition from the time of slavery. The jumping of the broom symbolizes a new beginning by sweeping away the old and welcoming the new. Some African Americans use colorful clothing inspired by African costumes, rather than a white dress for the bride and a suit or tuxedo for the groom.

One thing stays the same. The newlyweds **send the guests thank-you cards** by mail to thank them for attending the wedding and for the gifts they gave.

An African American couple jumps over a broom.

---

7 *clergyperson*: a minister, rabbi, or other religious leader
8 *ancestor*: a grandparent, great-grandparent, great-great-grandparent, etc.

COMPREHENSION CHECK Based on the reading, tell if the statement is true (**T**) or false (**F**).

1. A destination wedding is more expensive for guests than a traditional wedding.

2. A destination wedding is more popular than a church wedding.

3. Jumping over a broom is part of some ethnic weddings.

4.8 Direct and Indirect Objects

Some verbs can have both a direct and an indirect object. The order of direct objects (DO) and indirect objects (IO) depends on the verb we use. With some verbs, it can also depend on whether we use a noun or a pronoun as the object.

With some verbs, pronouns affect word order.

Possible Word Orders	Verbs			
He gave his wife a present. (IO/DO) He gave a present to his wife. (DO to IO*) He gave it to his wife. (DO to IO) He gave her a present. (IO/DO). He gave a present to her. (DO to IO) He gave it to her. (DO to IO)	bring (e-)mail give	hand offer pay	read sell send	show tell write

Language Note:

*When the direct object is a noun, not a pronoun, we usually put the indirect object before the direct object. However, we sometimes put the direct object before the indirect object for emphasis or contrast.

> He didn't send you the invitation. He sent the invitation to me.

With some verbs, pronouns don't affect word order.

Word Order = DO to IO	Verbs			
He described the wedding to his friends. (DO to IO) He described it to them. (DO to IO) He described it to his friends. (DO to IO) He described the wedding to them. (DO to IO)	announce describe explain	introduce mention prove	recommend repeat report	speak suggest say

---

[9] For a more detailed list of verbs and the order of direct and indirect objects, see Appendix H.

EXERCISE 14 Fill in the blanks with the words given. Put them in the correct order. Add *to* if necessary. In some cases, more than one answer is possible.

A: How was your cousin's wedding? Can you describe _____it to me_____ ?
  <u>1. it/me</u>

B: It was beautiful. The bride read _____ and then the groom
  <u>2. a lovely poem/the groom</u>

   read _____ too.
  <u>3. a poem/her</u>

A: Did they get married in a church?

B: No. They got married in a beautiful garden. Why didn't you go? I thought they sent

   _____ .
  <u>4. an invitation/you</u>

A: They did. But I couldn't go. I wrote _____ and I explained
  <u>5. an e-mail/them</u>

   _____ . I had to take an important exam for college that day.
  <u>6. my problem/them</u>

   But I sent _____ .
  <u>7. a present/them</u>

B: I'm sure they'll appreciate it. It's too bad you couldn't go.

A: I'm sure I mentioned _____ a few weeks ago.
  <u>8. you/it</u>

B: You probably did, but I forgot.

A: Do you have pictures from the wedding?

B: I took a lot of pictures. I'll e-mail _____ tonight.
  <u>9. you/them</u>

A: Thanks.

4.9 *Say* and *Tell*

Say and *tell* have the same meaning, but we use them differently.

Examples	Explanation
She **said** her name.	We *say* something (Say + DO).
She **told** me her name.	We *tell* someone something (Tell + IO + DO).
She **said** her name to me.	We *say* something to someone (Say + DO to IO).
They **told** the musicians to start the music.	We *tell* someone to do something (Tell + IO *to* + verb).
She **said** (that) she wanted a big wedding.	We *say* (that) (Say + *that* + statement).
Tell the truth: do you love me?	We can use *tell the truth* or *tell a lie* without an indirect object.

EXERCISE 15 Fill in the blanks with the correct form of *say* or *tell*.

1. The bride _____ *said* _____, "I love you."

2. They _____ *told* _____ us the date of the wedding.

3. You _____ me the groom's name, but I forgot it.

4. _____ the truth: do you like the bride's dress?

5. The bride hates to _____ goodbye to her family.

6. During the ceremony, the bride and groom _____, "I do."

7. We _____ the band to play romantic music.

8. My neighbor wants to come to my wedding. I wasn't planning on inviting her, but I can't

   _____ no.

9. We _____ our daughter to economize on her wedding, but she _____

   that she wanted a fancy wedding.

EXERCISE 16 About You Discuss the answers to these questions with a partner.

1. Are wedding customs changing in your native culture? How?

2. In your native culture, what kind of vows do the bride and groom make to each other?

This couple climbed up Longs Peak in the Rocky Mountains on their wedding day.

QUESTIONS and ANSWERS
about American Weddings

CD 1
TR 25

Read the following questions and answers. Pay special attention to the words in bold.

Q: **Who pays** for the wedding?

A: Usually the bride and groom do, especially if they are working and earning money. In some cases, their parents help.

Q: **What's** a shower?

A: A shower is a party for the bride (sometimes the bride and groom) before the wedding. Guests give the couple gifts to help them start their new home. Typical gifts are cookware, linens,[10] and small kitchen appliances.

Q: **Who hosts**[11] the shower?

A: Usually the maid of honor hosts the shower.

Q: **When do** they **have** the shower?

A: Usually the shower is two to six weeks before the wedding.

Q: **How long does** it **take** to plan a wedding?

A: Most couples plan their wedding for seven to twelve months.

Q: **When do** the couples **send** invitations?

A: They usually send the invitations about eight weeks before the wedding.

Q: When guests come in from out of town, **who pays** for their hotel?

A: They pay for the hotel themselves. However, the groom pays for his groomsmen and the bride pays for her bridesmaids.

Q: **Whom does** the groom **choose** as his best man?

A: He usually chooses a brother or best friend. The groom chooses other close friends or male relatives as the groomsmen.

Q: **When do** the bride and groom **open** their gifts?

A: They open their gifts at home, not at the wedding.

Q: **How do** the guests **know** what the bride and groom need as gifts?

A: The bride and groom usually register for gifts at stores. They list the gift items they want and need for their new home. When the guests go to buy a gift, they check the registry in the store. However, money is the most popular gift.

Q: **How do** I **know** how much money to give?

A: Most guests spend about $100 on a gift. People who are closer to the bride or groom often spend more.

---

[10] *linens*: sheets, pillowcases, and towels
[11] *to host*: to invite and entertain guests

COMPREHENSION CHECK Based on the reading, tell if the statement is true (**T**) or false (**F**).

1. In most cases, the bride's parents pay for the wedding.

2. It takes about six weeks to plan for a wedding.

3. A registry in a store lets guests know what kind of gifts the bride and groom want.

4.10 Questions about the Subject

Statement	Question about the Subject
The groom **paid** for the rings.	Who **paid** for the wedding dress?
The bride **has** a white dress.	Who **has** a blue dress?
Some women **plan** the shower.	Which women **plan** the shower?
Some people **send** money.	How many people **send** money?
Someone's mother **cried** at the wedding.	Whose mother **cried** at the wedding?

Language Notes:

1. Questions about the subject do not include *do, does,* or *did.*

   For the simple present:
   - We use the *-s* form of the verb after *who.*
   - We use the *-s* form of the verb after *which* + singular noun.
   - We use the base form of the verb after *which* + plural noun.
   - We use the base form of the verb after *how many* + plural noun.

2. *What happened* is a subject question. We answer with a different verb.

   What happened after the wedding?

   Everyone **left**.

3. We often answer a subject question with a subject and an auxiliary verb.

   Who paid for the rings? The groom **did**.

   Who likes a simple wedding? I **do**.

4. Don't confuse *who's* (*who is*) and *whose.*

   Whose dresses are blue? The bridesmaids' dresses are blue.

   Who's that woman? She's the bride's grandmother.

EXERCISE 17 Read each statement. Then write a question with the words given. No answer is necessary.

1. Someone takes the bride to the groom. (*who*)

   Who takes the bride to the groom?

2. Someone holds the rings. (*who*)

   _____

3. Someone's car has a "just married" sign. (*whose car*)

   _____

continued

4. Some couples have a destination wedding. (*how many couples*)

_____

5. One woman has a camera. (*which woman*)

_____

6. Some guests stay at a hotel. (*which guests*)

_____

7. Many people give money. (*how many people*)

_____

4.11 Questions about the Complement

Statement	Question about the Complement
The groom **paid** a lot of money for the wedding.	How much **did** he **pay**?
The bride **has** a white dress.	What color dress **does** her mother **have**?
The bride **borrowed** her dress.	Whose dress **did** she **borrow**?
The bride and groom **chose** a restaurant for the wedding dinner.	Which restaurant **did** they **choose**?
The bride and groom **will go** on a honeymoon.	Where **will** they **go**?

Language Notes:

1. Questions about the complement include *do, does, did,* and other auxiliary verbs.
2. In a question about the object, *whom* is very formal. Informally, many people use *who.*

FORMAL: **Whom** did your brother marry?

INFORMAL: **Who** did your brother marry?

EXERCISE 18 Read each statement. Then write a question about the complement with the words given.

1. The wedding will be in a church. (*where*)

   Where will the wedding be?

2. I bought a nice gift. (*what*)

   _____

3. The bride's brother lives in another state. (*where*)

   _____

4. I'm going to spend a lot of money. (*how much*)

   _____

5. I received an invitation. (*when*)

_____

6. My brother needs to buy a new suit for the wedding. (*why*)

_____

7. They didn't invite our children. (*why*)

_____

EXERCISE 19 Read each statement. Then write a question with the words given. Some of the questions are about the subject. Some are about the complement.

1. The bride wears a white dress. (*what/the groom*)

_What does the groom wear?_____

2. The bride enters last. (*who/first*)

_Who enters first?_____

3. The bride throws the bouquet. (*when*)

_____

4. Some women try to catch the bouquet. (*which women*)

_____

5. The bride chooses women for bridesmaids. (*which women*)

_____

6. The band plays music. (*what kind of music*)

_____

7. Someone dances with the bride. (*who*)

_____

8. The guests give presents. (*what kind of presents*)

_____

9. Some people cry at the wedding. (*who*)

_____

10. There's a dinner after the ceremony. (*what/happen/after the dinner*)

_____

EXERCISE 20 Fill in the blanks to complete the questions in the conversation. Some of the questions are about the subject, and some are about the complement. In some cases, more than one answer is possible.

A: How do you have time to work, go to school, and take care of a family?

B: I don't have to do everything myself.

A: Who ___helps you___ ?

               1.

B: My husband helps me.

A: I usually cook in my house. Who _____ ?

                                 2.

B: Sometimes my husband cooks; sometimes I cook. We take turns.

A: I usually clean. Who _____ ?

                     3.

B: I usually clean the house.

A: How many _____ ?

                   4.

B: I have five children.

A: How many _____ ?

                   5.

B: Three children go to school. The younger ones stay home.

A: Do you send them to public school or private school?

B: One of my sons goes to private school.

A: Which son _____ ?

                    6.

B: The oldest does. He's in high school now.

A: It's hard to take care of so many children. How do you find the time to go to class?

B: As I said, my husband helps me a lot. And sometimes I use a babysitter.

A: I'm looking for a sitter. Who _____ ?

                         7.

B: I recommend our neighbor, Sasha. She's sixteen years old, and she's very good with our

children.

A: Maybe she's too busy to help me. How many families _____ ?

                                                8.

B: I think she works for only one other family. I'll give you her phone number. If she's not busy,

maybe she can work for you too.

EXERCISE 21 Fill in the blanks with *who, whom, who's,* or *whose.*

1. _____Who's_____ that woman over there?

   That's my mother-in-law.

2. _____ did you invite to the wedding?

   I invited all my friends and relatives.

3. _____ took pictures?

   My brother did. He borrowed a camera because his is broken.

4. _____ camera did he borrow?

   He borrowed my aunt's camera. She has a fantastic camera.

5. _____ your aunt?

   She's that woman over there.

EXERCISE 22 About You Find a partner. Use the questions to talk about weddings and marriages in your native cultures and countries.

1. Who pays for the wedding?
2. What happens at the wedding?
3. What happens after the wedding?
4. Do the guests bring gifts to the wedding?
5. What kind of gifts do they give?
6. Where do the bride and groom open the gifts?
7. How many people attend a wedding?
8. Where do people get married?
9. Do people dance at a wedding?
10. What color dress does the bride wear?
11. How long does a wedding last?
12. How do the bride and groom invite people? Do they send invitations?
13. Is there a shower before the wedding? Who hosts the shower? Who attends the shower?
14. Do the bride and groom send thank-you notes for the gifts?

SUMMARY OF LESSON 4

Pronouns and Possessive Forms

Subject Pronoun	Object Pronoun	Possessive Adjective	Possessive Pronoun	Reflexive Pronoun
I	me	my	mine	myself
you	you	your	yours	yourself
he	him	his	his	himself
she	her	her	hers	herself
it	it	its	—	itself
we	us	our	ours	ourselves
you	you	your	yours	yourselves
they	them	their	theirs	themselves
who	whom	whose	whose	—

Order of Direct and Indirect Objects

Example	Explanation
I sent my grandmother the date. I sent her the date. I sent the date to my grandmother. I sent the date to her. I sent it to my grandmother. I sent it to her.	Some verbs have two possible word orders (*bring, give, send, show, tell, write*). Pronouns can affect the word order.
They announced their engagement to their parents. They announced it to them.	Some verbs have one possible word order (*announce, describe, explain, say*). Pronouns don't affect the word order.

Possessive Form of Nouns

Singular Nouns	Plural Nouns	Inanimate Nouns
the **bride's** dress my **father's** house the **child's** toy the **man's** hat **Charles's** wife **today's** topic	the **bridesmaids'** dresses my **parents'** house the **children's** toys the **men's** hats	the door of the church the name of the hotel

Questions

About the Subject	About the Complement
Who **has** the rings? Which woman **wore** a red dress? How many people **came** to the wedding? What **happened** after the wedding? Who **will come** to the wedding?	Who(m) **do** you **know** at the wedding? Which women **did** you **meet**? How many people **did** they **invite**? What **did** they **serve** at the wedding? Who(m) **will** you **invite** to your wedding?

TEST/REVIEW

Circle the correct words to complete the conversation.

A: I know (*you*/*your*/*you're*) just got married. (*Tell*/*Say*/*Tell to*) me about (*you're*/*you*/*your*) wedding.
   1.   2.   3.

B: (*It's*/*It*/*Its*) was a small wedding. Sara wanted a big wedding, but a big wedding is so expensive.
   4.

   (*Hers*/*Her's*/*Her*) parents wanted to pay for (*it*/*its*/*it's*). (*Their*/*Their's*/*Theirs*) was a big wedding
   5.   6.   7.

   because they have a big family. But we don't have a lot of money. We wanted to pay for it

   (*ourself*/*ourselves*/*oneself*). We explained (*them the situation*/*the situation to them*/*the
   8.   9.

   situation them*). We showed (*them our budget*/*to them our budget*/*our budget them*), and they
                                                              10.

   didn't insist on a large wedding. We just invited (*our*/*ours*/*our's*) immediate families: parents,
                                                                    11.

   grandparents, sisters, brothers, aunts, and uncles.

A: How many people (*did attend*/*attended*/*did attended*) the wedding?
                              12.

B: Fifty. Unfortunately (*Sara's grandfather*/*grandfather Sara*/*grandfather of Sara*) didn't come.
                                        13.

A: Why not? What (*was happened*/*did happen*/*happened*) to (*him*/*his*/*he*)?
                                14.   15.

B: Nothing. (*His*/*Her*/*Her's*) grandfather lives in Peru. (*His*/*He*/*He's*) old and doesn't like to travel.
                  16.   17.

A: (*Your*/*You're*/*Yours*) grandparents are old too, aren't they? Did they come?
         18.

B: Yes, they did. (*Mines*/*Mine*/*My*) live nearby.
                        19.

A: Where (*you got*/*you get*/*did you get*) married?
                        20.

B: In a church. The (*name of the church*/*the church name*/*the church's name*) is St. John. We had a
                                    21.

   party afterwards at (*my uncle's house*/*house my uncle*/*my uncle house*). (*He*/*He's*/*His*) house is
                              22.   23.

   big. We even saved money on the wedding dress because Sara borrowed one.

A: (*Whose*/*Who's*/*Who*) dress (*did she borrow*/*she borrowed*/*borrowed she*)?
         24.   25.

B: She borrowed her cousin's dress. We saved money on photos too. My uncle took pictures, and

   he gave (*them us*/*us them*/*them to us*) on a disk. We printed (*they*/*them*/*its*) and made an album.
              26.   27.

   We went to Miami for our honeymoon. Sara's uncle has a home there. He let

   (*me and Sara*/*Sara and me*/*Sara and I*) use it. With the money we saved, we hope to buy a
              28.

   house soon.

A: (*You're*/*Your*/*You*) a wise man! When (*Lisa and I*/*me and Lisa*/*Lisa and me*) get married after
         29.   30.

   we graduate, I'd like to do the same thing. But I think Lisa won't agree. She wants a big wedding.

B: Who (*know*/*does know*/*knows*)? Start to talk to (*hers*/*her*/*she*) about it now.
            31.   32.

WRITING

PART 1 Editing Advice

1. Don't confuse contractions with possessive forms.

   You're
   ~~Your~~ late for the wedding. ~~Its~~ *It's* almost 6 o'clock.

   He's *His*   *They're*
   ~~His~~ married. ~~He's~~ wife is a doctor. ~~Their~~ from California.

2. Don't confuse *his* and *her*.

   her   *his*
   My sister loves ~~his~~ husband. My brother loves ~~her~~ wife.

3. Be careful to choose the right pronoun in compound subjects and objects.

   My mother and I
   ~~Me and my mother~~ planned the wedding.

   me
   My parents gave my husband and ~~I~~ $500.

4. Don't use an apostrophe to make a plural form.

   guests
   They invited many ~~guest's~~ to the wedding.

5. Don't use an auxiliary verb in a question about the subject.

   s
   Who ~~does~~ help the bride?

6. Put the apostrophe after the –*s* of a plural noun that ends in –*s*.

   parents'
   My ~~parent's~~ house is too small for the wedding.

7. Don't use –*s* in a possessive adjective. (A possessive adjective has no plural form.)

   Their~~s~~ parents live in Canada.

8. Use the correct word order with direct and indirect objects.

   their wedding customs to me
   They explained ~~me their wedding customs~~.

   it to them
   Do you have the wedding present? Please give ~~them it~~.

9. Don't confuse *say* and *tell*.

   told
   She ~~said~~ me about her wedding.

PART 2 Editing Practice

Some of the shaded words and phrases have mistakes. Find the mistakes and correct them. If the shaded words are correct, write C.

          C   *it's*

Sometimes we have an unrealistic view of marriage. We think that its all about love and
      1.   **2.**

nothing else. Some women especially think of the wedding as the bride's special day and don't
                                                3.

think about the marriage that follows.

     Me and my sister both wanted to get married. I got married when I was 27 years old. My
      4.   **5.**

husband was 30. We both had good careers. By the time I got married, many of my friends

were already married—and divorced. Some of they had small children.
                                     6.

My sister, Maya, got married right after high school. ~~Ours~~ [*her*] parents wanted her to wait,
                                                              7.   8.

but she didn't want to. She was so in love with ~~his~~ [*her*] boyfriend, Tony. My parent~~'~~s were against
                                                    9.   10.

it at first, and Tony's were too, but they gave ~~to~~ them permission to get married. ~~Mine~~ [*My*] sister
              11.   12.   13.

wanted to have a big wedding. But of course, Maya and Tony couldn't pay for it ~~themself~~ [*themselves.*]
                                                                                        14.

Mom and Dad ~~said~~ [*told*] them they would pay for the wedding, but it would have to be small.
              15.

      Maya and Tony really loved each other, but ~~there~~ [*their*] marriage didn't last more than three
                                                      16.

years. So what ~~did happen~~ [*happened*]? What ~~went~~ wrong? Maya and Tony didn't understand ~~they're~~ [*their*]
              17.   18.   19.

responsibilities as a married couple. They thought marriage would be love and romance.

My parents told ~~to~~ them that marriage includes bills, laundry, and children too. My father
              20.

said, "if you're going to stay in school, you have to budget not only ~~you're~~ [*your*] money but ~~you~~ [*your*] time
              21.   22.   23.

too." He also warned ~~they~~ [*them*], "If you have kids while you're still in school, ~~their~~ [*they're*] going to need
                      24.   25.   26.

your attention. ~~Whose~~ going to take care of them?" Tony and Maya soon had a baby girl. Then
              27.

they started to argue with each other about many thing~~'~~s [*things*].
                                                      28.

      Maya wants to stay in school but she can't. My mother can't help her because she works
                                                                              29.

full time. Tony loves ~~her~~ [*his*] daughter. ~~His~~ [*He's*] a good father and he works hard to support her, so
                      30.   31.

he can't finish college at this time. Their~~s~~ lives are so difficult now. I feel sorry for them. I'm
                                    32.   33.

happy my husband and ~~me~~ [*I*] established ourselves as responsible adults before marriage.
              34.   35.

      If you compare my sister and ~~I~~ [*me*], you can see a big difference in our lives. Her life is very
                                  36.

hard as a single mother with no career. ~~Its~~ [*It's*] too bad my sister didn't listen to our parent~~'~~s
                                          37.   38.

advice.

PART 3 Write About It

1. How is a typical wedding in your native culture different from a typical American wedding?
2. What are some problems most married people have today?

PART 4 Edit Your Writing

Read the Summary of Lesson 4 and the editing advice. Edit your writing from Part 3.

Thanksgiving, Pilgrims, and Native Americans

Destiny Buck, a Native American girl, proudly shows her horse.

Treat the Earth well: it was not given to you by your parents, it was loaned to you by your children. We do not inherit the Earth from our Ancestors, we borrow it from our Children.

—Ancient American Indian proverb

New York
Thanksgiving
Day Parade

THANKSGIVING

Read the following article. Pay special attention to the words in bold.

CD 1
TR 26

Thanksgiving is a very special American **holiday**. On the fourth Thursday in November, **Americans** come together with their **family** and **friends** to share a special meal and give thanks for all the good **things** in their **lives**. Typical **foods** on Thanksgiving are **turkey**, sweet **potatoes**, mashed **potatoes** and gravy, turkey **stuffing, cranberry sauce**, and pumpkin **pie** for dessert.

What is the **origin** of this great day? In 1620, a **group** of Pilgrims left England and came to America in search of religious **freedom**. There were 120 of them: **men**, **women**, and **children**. They started their new **life** in a deserted[1] American Indian **village** in what is now the **state** of Massachusetts. But **half** of them did not survive their first cold, hard **winter**. In the **spring**, two American **Indians**[2] found the **people** from England in very bad **condition**. They didn't have enough **food**, and they were in bad **health**. Squanto, an English-speaking American Indian, stayed with them for several **months** and taught them how to survive in this new **land**. He brought them deer **meat** and animal **skins**; he showed them how to grow **corn** and other **vegetables**; he showed them how to use **plants** as **medicine**; he explained how to use **fish** for **fertilizer**[3]—he taught

them many **skills** for **survival** in their new land. By the time their second **fall** arrived, the Pilgrims had enough food to get through their second winter. They were in better **health**. They decided to have a Thanksgiving **feast**[4] to celebrate their good **fortune**.[5] They invited Squanto and neighboring Indian **families** of the Wampanoag **tribe** to come to their **dinner**. The Pilgrims were surprised when ninety Indians showed up. The Pilgrims did not have enough food for so many people. Fortunately, the Indian **chief** sent some of his people to bring food to the **celebration**. They brought **deer, fish, beans, squash, cornbread, berries,** and wild **turkeys**. The feast lasted for three **days**. This was a short **time** of **peace** and **friendship** between the Indians and the Pilgrims.

Now on Thanksgiving, we eat some of the traditional **foods** from this **period** in American **history**.

---

1 *deserted*: empty of people
2 *American Indians*: the native people of America; American Indians are sometimes called Native Americans.
3 *fertilizer*: something put into the earth to help plants grow
4 *feast*: a large meal
5 *fortune*: luck

COMPREHENSION CHECK Based on the reading, tell if the statement is true (**T**) or false (**F**).

1. American Indians helped the Pilgrims through their first winter in America.

2. Squanto helped the Pilgrims learn about their new land.

3. The Pilgrims invited ninety American Indians for a feast of Thanksgiving.

5.1 Noun Plurals—Form

We use the plural to talk about more than one. Regular noun plurals add -s or -es.

Regular Noun Plurals				
Word Ending	**Example Noun**	**Plural Addition**	**Plural Form**	**Pronunciation**
Vowel	bee banana	+ s	bees bananas	/z/
ch sh x s	church dish box class	+ es	churches dishes boxes classes	/əz/
Voiceless consonants	snack month	+ s	snacks months	/s/
Voiced consonants	card pin	+ s	cards pins	/z/
Vowel + y	boy day	+ s	boys days	/z/
Consonant + y	lady story	y + ies	ladies stories	/z/
Vowel + o	video radio	+ s	videos radios	/z/
Consonant + o	potato hero	+ es	potatoes heroes	/z/
Exceptions: photos, pianos, solos, altos, sopranos, autos, tuxedos, avocados				
f or fe	leaf knife	f + ves	leaves knives	/z/
Exceptions: beliefs, chiefs, roofs, cliffs, chefs, and sheriffs				

continued

Irregular Noun Plurals			
Singular	Plural	Examples	Explanation
man woman tooth foot goose	men women teeth feet geese	The **women** cooked the dinner. The **men** washed the dishes.	Vowel change
sheep fish deer	sheep fish deer	There are many **fish** in the lake.	No change in word
child mouse person	children mice people	The **children** set the table. We invited a lot of **people** to dinner.	Different word form

Language Notes:

1. The plural of *person* can also be *persons*, but *people* is more common.

2. The pronunciation of *women* is /wɪmən/. We hear the difference between singular and plural in the first syllable.

EXERCISE 1 Fill in the blanks with the words you hear.

CD 1
TR 27

1. _____Airports_____ are often crowded right before Thanksgiving.
   a.

2. _____People_____ want to get home to their _____families_____.
   a.   b.

3. On Thanksgiving, people eat a very big _____dinner_____.
   a.

4. Before the big dinner, they often eat _____snacks_____, such as _____nuts_____ and potato
   a.   b.

   _____chips_____, while waiting for other _____guests_____ to arrive.
   c.   d.

5. The Thanksgiving meal usual includes turkey and sweet _____potatoes_____.
   a.

6. The typical Thanksgiving meal contains more than three thousand _____calories_____.
   a.

7. Many _____cities_____ have a parade on Thanksgiving morning. _____Thousands_____ of people
   a.   b.

   go to see the parade.

8. _____Children_____ like to watch the parade.
   a.

9. After the meal, it is a typical _____tradition_____ to watch professional football on TV.
   a.

10. Football is especially popular with the _____men_____.
    a.

EXERCISE 2 Write the plural form of each noun. If the plural ends in -s or -es, indicate if the pronunciation is /s/, /z/, or /əz/. If not, write Ø.

1. hour _____hours_____ ___/z/___
2. turkey _____ _____
3. cranberry ___Cranberries___ _____
4. potato ___potatoes___ _____
5. child _____ _____
6. family _____ _____
7. guest _____ _____
8. ship _____ _____
9. man _____ _____
10. woman _____ _____
11. apple _____ _____
12. peach _____ _____

13. spice _____ _____
14. pie _____ _____
15. knife _____ _____
16. deer _____ _____
17. watch _____ _____
18. tax _____ _____
19. pot _____ _____
20. goose _____ _____
21. dish _____ _____
22. month _____ _____
23. life _____ _____
24. plant _____ _____

EXERCISE 3 Fill in the blanks with the plural form of the words. You can use a word more than once.

A: Who prepares the Thanksgiving meal in your family?

B: As usual, the _____women_____ in my family do most of the cooking.
    1. woman

But the _____ help too. My husband usually makes the mashed
        2. man

_____ and gravy. I always prepare the turkey and stuffing. Even the
    3. potato

_____ help. Last year, my son and daughter made the cranberry sauce.
    4. child

A: Did they use fresh _____ ?
            5. cranberry

B: Yes, they did. They just boiled them with sugar and added fruit.

A: What kind of fruit did they use?

B: They used _____ .
            6. apple

A: What do you make for dessert?

continued

B: I don't make the dessert. I always invite my next-door _____. They bring several

_____. They buy them at a bakery.

        8. pie

A: It's nice when all the _____ help with the preparation.

        9. guest

B: I agree. I love Thanksgiving. The only thing I don't like is washing the _____

        10. dish

afterwards.

A: Same here. The _____ always say that they'll wash them later, but they're too

        11. man

busy watching the football game.

5.2 Using the Plural for Generalizations

Examples	Explanation
Football games last about three hours. **Sweet potatoes** are nutritious.	We can use the plural to make a generalization. We don't use the article, *the*, to make a generalization.

EXERCISE 4 About You Make a generalization about the following nouns. Talk about holiday traditions in your country or native culture. You may talk about family members, schools, businesses, etc. Discuss your answers with a partner.

1. children _For Chinese New Year, children get money in red envelopes._

2. men _____

3. women _____

4. children _____

5. grandparents _____

6. stores _____

7. schools _____

5.3 Special Cases of Singular and Plural

Examples	Explanation
The U.S. has more than 300 **million** people. **Millions** of people go shopping the day after Thanksgiving. My grandfather is in his **seventies**. He was born in the **1940s**.	We use the singular form for exact numbers. We use the plural form for inexact numbers. We use the plural form for an approximate age or year.
One of my **neighbors** brought a pie to our Thanksgiving dinner. One of the **men** helped with the dishes.	We use the plural form after the expression: one of (the, my, his, her, etc.).
Every **guest** brought something. Each **person** helped. We washed all the **dishes**.	We use a singular noun after every and each. We use a plural noun after all.
After dinner, the kids put on their **pajamas** and went to bed. We're wearing our best **clothes** today.	Some words have no singular form: pajamas, clothes, pants, slacks, (eye)glasses, scissors.
Let's watch the **news**. It's on after dinner. Let's not discuss **politics** during dinner. It's not a good subject.	Even though news and politics end in -s, they are singular.

EXERCISE 5 Fill in the blanks with the correct form of the word given.

1. Five _____men_____ watched the football game.
   <small>man</small>

2. One of the _____ helped make the cranberry sauce.
   <small>child</small>

3. Politics _____ not a good subject at the dinner table.
   <small>be</small>

4. Ten _____ people pass through the airports before Thanksgiving.
   <small>million</small>

5. _____ of people travel for Thanksgiving.
   <small>million</small>

6. Every _____ stayed to watch the game.
   <small>guest</small>

7. Thanksgiving is one of my favorite _____.
   <small>holiday</small>

8. _____ of people saw the parade.
   <small>thousand</small>

9. My grandmother came for Thanksgiving. She's in her _____.
   <small>eighty</small>

10. The children should go to bed. Their _____ are on the bed.
    <small>pajama</small>

11. English people started to come to America in the sixteen _____.
    <small>hundred</small>

12. One _____ twenty Pilgrims came in 1620.
    <small>hundred</small>

Cranberry Sauce

Read the following article. Pay special attention to the words in bold.

Cranberries are **a** very American **fruit**. They grow in the cooler regions of northeastern North America and are ready for harvest[6] in the fall. We see cranberry **juice** all year, but packages of fresh cranberries appear in **supermarkets** just before Thanksgiving.

American Indians introduced cranberries to the Pilgrims in 1621. The Indians used cranberries as a **food** and for different kinds of **medicines**. They also made **tea** from cranberries, and used it to add color to their **jewelry**.

Cranberries are very sour, so a recipe for cranberry sauce uses a lot of **sugar** or **honey**. You prepare cranberry sauce by boiling **water** with **sugar** and then adding the cranberries. You continue cooking them until the **skins** pop[7] open. Before serving, you cool the mixture in the refrigerator. Some people add pieces of **fruit**, such as **apples** or **pears**, to the cranberries. Some people sprinkle chopped **walnuts** on top. This is the perfect side dish to go with helpings of **turkey**.

---

6 *harvest*: a time for picking or gathering crops
7 *pop*: break, burst

Cranberries ready
for harvesting

COMPREHENSION CHECK Based on the reading, tell if the statement is true (**T**) or false (**F**).

1. Cranberries grow in all parts of the United States.

2. The Indians used cranberries for medicine.

3. The Pilgrims learned about cranberries from the American Indians.

5.4 Count and Noncount Nouns

A count noun is something we can count. It has a singular and plural form.

Examples	Explanation
We used one **apple** in the recipe. We used two **pears** in the recipe.	We use a count noun in the singular form or plural form. We can put *a, an,* or a number before a count noun.
Boil **water** and add **sugar**.	We use a noncount noun in the singular form only. We don't put *a, an,* or a number before a noncount noun.

There are several types of noncount nouns.

Group A: Nouns that have no distinct, separate parts. We look at the whole.			
milk	juice	bread	electricity
oil	yogurt	meat	lightning
water	pork	butter	thunder
coffee	honey	paper	cholesterol
tea	soup	air	blood

Group B: Nouns that have parts that are too small or insignificant to count.			
rice	hair	sand	salt
sugar	popcorn	grass	snow

Group C: Nouns that are classes or categories of things. The members of the category are not the same.	
money or cash (nickels, dimes, dollars)	mail (letters, packages, postcards, flyers)
furniture (chairs, tables, beds)	homework (essays, exercises, readings)
clothing (sweaters, pants, dresses)	jewelry (necklaces, bracelets, rings)
fruit (apples, peaches, pears)	produce (oranges, apples, corn)

Group D: Nouns that are abstractions.					
love	happiness	nutrition	patience	work	nature
truth	education	intelligence	poverty	health	help
beauty	advice	unemployment	music	fun	energy
luck/fortune	knowledge	pollution	art	information	friendship

Group E: Some fruits and vegetables are usually noncount nouns.					
broccoli	celery	lettuce	kale	asparagus	spinach
corn	squash	cauliflower	grapefruit	cabbage	celery

Language Note:

Count and *noncount* are grammatical terms, but they are not always logical. *Rice* and *beans* are both very small, but *rice* is a noncount noun and *bean* is a count noun.

EXERCISE 6 Fill in the blanks with a noncount noun from the box.

advice	snow	freedom ✓	friendship
health	work	corn	honey

1. The Pilgrims wanted to find _____freedom_____ in America.

2. They had poor _____health_____ during their first winter in America.

3. The American Indians gave the Pilgrims a lot of _____advice_____ about how to grow food.

4. Squanto taught them to plant _____corn_____.

5. The first winter was hard. It was cold and there was a lot of _____snow_____.

6. Learning American agriculture was hard _____work_____ for the Pilgrims.

7. In the beginning, there was _____friendship_____ between the Pilgrims and the American Indians.

8. Cranberries are very sour, so the Indians added _____honey_____.

5.5 Nouns That Can Be Both Count and Noncount

Some nouns can be noncount (NC) or count (C).

Examples	Explanation
(NC) **Life** in America was difficult. (C) The Pilgrims had difficult **lives**. (NC) The Pilgrims had a lot of **trouble** their first winter. (C) The American Indians' **troubles** began when the Europeans arrived. (NC) I like to spend **time** with my family on the holidays. (C) My neighbors invited me to their dinner many **times**. (NC) American Indians had **experience** with American winters. (C) The first winter for the Pilgrims was **a** bad **experience**.	The meaning or use of a noun determines whether it is count or noncount.
We put some **fruit** in the cranberry sauce. We prepare a lot of **food** for Thanksgiving. Oranges and lemons are citrus **fruits**. American Indians used cranberries as **a food** and as a dye.	When we talk about fruit or food in general, these words are noncount nouns. When we are referring to kinds or categories of food or fruit, these words are count nouns.
We ate some **pie** for dessert. We eat **turkey** on Thanksgiving. My friend brought three **pies** to the Thanksgiving dinner. One **turkey** is enough for the whole family.	When a noun refers to a part of the whole, it is a noncount noun. When a noun refers to the whole it is a count noun.

EXERCISE 7 Decide if each noun given is count or noncount. If it is a count noun, change it to the plural form. If it is a noncount noun, do not change it.

1. The _____Pilgrims_____ wanted _____freedom_____.
   a. Pilgrim   **b.** freedom

2. American Indians have a lot of respect for _____.
                                           a. nature

3. They love _____, _____, and _____.
               a. tree   **b.** bird   **c.** fish

4. Thanksgiving is a celebration of _____ and _____.
                                   a. peace   **b.** friendship

5. On Thanksgiving, Americans eat a lot of _____.
                                            a. food

6. Americans sometimes eat _____ for dessert.
                             a. pie

7. Squanto gave the Pilgrims a lot of _____ about planting _____ and other
                                  a. advice   **b.** corn

   _____. He had a lot of _____ about the land.
         c. vegetable   **d.** knowledge

8. The Pilgrims didn't have any _____ with American agriculture.
                                     a. experience

9. On the first Thanksgiving, American Indians brought _____, _____,
                                           a. meat   **b.** bean

   _____, and _____.
         c. bread   **d.** berry

10. The Pilgrims celebrated because they had a lot of good _____.
                                                a. fortune

11. American Indians use _____ for _____.
                         a. plant   **b.** medicine

12. I would like more _____ about American _____.
                        a. information   **b.** holiday

5.6 Units of Measure with Noncount Nouns

We don't usually put a number before a noncount noun. We use a unit of measure, which we can count—for example, two *cloves* of garlic.

By container	By portion	By measurement	By shape or whole piece	Other
a bottle of water	a slice (piece) of	an ounce of sugar	a loaf of bread	a piece of mail
a carton of milk	bread	a teaspoon of salt	an ear of corn	a piece of furniture
a jar of pickles	a piece of meat	a cup of oil	a piece of fruit	a piece of advice
a bag of flour	a piece of cake	a pound of meat	a head of lettuce	a piece of
a can of soda (pop)	a strip of bacon	a gallon of milk	a tube of toothpaste	information
a cup of coffee	a slice of pizza	a pint of cream	a bar of soap	a work of art
a glass of water	a piece of candy	a scoop of ice	a clove of garlic	a homework
a bowl of soup		cream	a stalk of celery	assignment
		a pinch of salt	a candy bar	a piece (sheet) of
				paper

Language Note:

We can use *a helping of* for almost any food.

    How many *helpings of turkey* did you have?

EXERCISE 8 Listen to this list of ingredients for turkey stuffing. Fill in the blanks with the unit of measure for each ingredient.

1. A half _____cup_____ of chopped onions

2. One _____stick_____ of butter

3. Two _____cloves_____ of garlic

4. Three _____stalks_____ of chopped celery

5. Four _____cups_____ of dry bread, cut into cubes

6. One quarter _____teaspoon_____ of salt

7. One _____tablespoon_____ of dry parsley

8. One _____cup_____ of hot chicken broth

EXERCISE 9 Fill in the blanks with a specific quantity or unit of measure + *of*. Answers may vary.

1. We bought three _____loaves of_____ bread for Thanksgiving.

2. Would you like a _____ water with dinner? There's a pitcher on

   the table. Help yourself.

3. You'll need a _____ butter to make the stuffing.

4. How many _____ garlic are in the stuffing?

5. After dinner, we served a _____ coffee to each guest.

6. Most guests ate a _____ pie after dinner.

7. Can I have your recipe for cranberry sauce? I need a pencil and a _____

   paper to write it down.

8. Would you like a _____ fruit after dinner? How about an apple or a tangerine?

9. I bought two _____ lettuce to make a salad.

10. Let me give you a _____ advice about Thanksgiving: There's a lot of food,

    but try to eat just a little of everything. If you eat too much, you won't feel good afterwards.

134 Lesson 5

EXERCISE 10 About You Find a partner. Talk about the food you eat on a holiday or special day. Describe the ingredients of this food.

5.7 A Lot Of, Much, Many

The choice of a quantity word sometimes depends on whether the noun is count (C) or noncount (NC).

	Examples	Explanation
Affirmative	(C) You needed **a lot of** cranberries for this recipe. (NC) We used **a lot of** sugar to make the cranberry sauce.	We can use *a lot of* with count and noncount nouns.
Affirmative	(C) I am thankful for **many** things. (NC) We eat **a lot of** food on Thanksgiving.	We use *many* with count nouns. We use *a lot of* with noncount nouns in affirmative statements. *Much* is rare in affirmative statements.
Negative	(C) The Pilgrims didn't have **many** skills in American agriculture. (NC) Today American Indians don't have **much** land.	We use *many* with count nouns. We use *much* with noncount nouns.
Negative	(C) The Pilgrims didn't have **a lot of** skills in American agriculture. (NC) Today American Indians don't have **a lot of** land.	We can use *a lot of* with both count and noncount nouns.
Question	(C) Did you invite **many** people for dinner? (NC) Did you eat **much** turkey?	We use *many* with count nouns. We use *much* with noncount nouns.
Question	(C) Did you invite **a lot of** guests for Thanksgiving? (NC) Did you eat **a lot of** turkey?	We can use *a lot of* with both count and noncount nouns.
Question	(C) **How many** hours did you cook the turkey? (NC) **How much** time did you spend on food preparation?	We use *how many* with count nouns. We use *how much* with noncount nouns.

Language Note:

When the noun is omitted (in the following sentence, *water*), we use *a lot*, not *a lot of*.

I usually drink **a lot of water**, but I didn't drink **a lot** today.

EXERCISE 11 Circle the correct words to complete this conversation. In some cases, more than one answer is correct. If so, circle both options.

A: Did you prepare (*a lot of*/*many*) food for Thanksgiving?
1.

B: No, I didn't prepare (*a lot*/*a lot of*). This year I didn't invite (*much*/*many*) people. I just invited
2.   3.

my immediate family.

A: How (*much*/*many*) people are there in your immediate family?
4.

B: Just seven. I bought a twelve-pound turkey. It was more than enough.

A: I don't know how to prepare a turkey. Is it (*a lot of*/*many*) work?
5.

B: Not really. But if it's frozen, it takes (*a lot of*/*much*) time to defrost it. Cooking it is easy.
6.

A: Did you make (*many*/*a lot of*) other dishes, like sweet potatoes and cranberry sauce?
7.

B: No. Each person in my family made something. That way I didn't have (*much*/*a lot of*) work.
8.

But we had (*many*/*a lot of*) work cleaning up.
9.

A: Have you thought about using paper plates? That way you won't have (*many*/*much*) work
10.

cleaning up.

B: I know (*many*/*much*) people do that, but I want my dinner to look elegant. For me, paper plates
11.

are for picnics.

The First Americans

Read the following article. Pay special attention to the words in bold.

Who were the first Americans? Long before Europeans came to America starting about 500 years ago, Indians inhabited[8] the Americas. We refer to these people as American Indians. Where did these people come from, and how did they get here?

Thousands of years ago, **there was** a land bridge connecting Eastern Siberia to Alaska. For many years, scientists believed that Siberians crossed this bridge about 15,000 years ago and spread out over the Americas.

In 1968, the skeleton of a young boy was found in Montana. Recently scientists tested the DNA[9] of this child's bones and learned that he lived 12,600 years ago. Scientists refer to his ancient Indian culture as Clovis culture, and to the boy as Clovis Boy. **Is there** a connection between Clovis Boy and Siberians? Definitely. Scientists compared the DNA from Clovis Boy with the DNA of a 24,000-year-old Siberian boy, and **there is** enough genetic[10] evidence to show that Clovis boy's ancestors were from Siberia.

But even more interesting is this: **There is** a genetic connection between Clovis Boy and about 80 percent of native North and South Americans today.

There were many tools and other objects buried with the boy. At that time, **there were** large mammals, such as mastodons, mammoths, horses, and camels in America. These early Americans used the tools to hunt these animals. These animals became extinct[11] in America, maybe because the Clovis people over-hunted.

Even though **there is** a lot to learn from this boy's bones, American Indians want to make sure that he is buried again in the same place. They see him as a connection to their ancestors. Shane Doyle, a member of the Crow tribe of Montana, was satisfied to find the connection of his people to Clovis Boy. But, says Doyle, "now it is time to put him back to rest again."

---

[8] *to inhabit*: to live in an area
[9] *DNA*: the genetic information in cells
[10] *genetic*: related to the traits that are transmitted from parents to offspring
[11] *extinct*: no longer in existence

Lucy, a fossil human skeleton dating back 3–4 million years, on display at the Cleveland Museum of Natural History in Ohio

Clovis tool

COMPREHENSION CHECK Based on the reading, tell if the statement is true (**T**) or false (**F**).

1. Most American Indians came to America from Siberia.

2. Clovis Boy is about 24,000 years old.

3. Most of today's American Indians are genetically connected to Clovis Boy.

5.8 *There* + a Form of *Be*

We use *there* + a form of *be* to introduce a subject into the conversation.

Examples	Explanation
There is a connection between Clovis Boy and today's American Indians. **There was peace** between the American Indians and the Pilgrims at first.	We use *there is/was* to introduce a singular noun.
There are American Indian tribes in Montana. **There were Indians** in America before the Europeans came.	We use *there are/were* to introduce a plural noun.

Were there any tools with Clovis Boy?
Yes, **there were.**
 	
Were there other people with Clovis Boy?
No, **there weren't.**
	For *yes/no* questions, we put *be* before *there*.
	For an affirmative short answer, we use
	    Yes, + *there* + form of *be*.
	For a negative short answer, we use
	    No, + *there* + form of *be* + *not*.

How many tools **were there** with him? There were more than 100. How much time **is there** between Thanksgiving and Christmas? There are about 28 days.	We often use *how many/how much* to ask a question with *there*. We put *be* before *there*.

Language Notes:

1. We can make a contraction with *there is: there's*. We don't make a contraction with *there are*.

2. If two nouns follow *there*, we use a singular verb if the first noun is singular. We use a plural verb if the first noun is plural.

    There **was** a skeleton and tools at the burial site.

    There **were** tools and a skeleton at the burial site.

3. After we introduce a noun with *there*, we can continue to speak of this noun with another pronoun (*they, it, she,* etc.).

    There is **information** in Clovis Boy's DNA.

    It's very important to scientists.

    There were **tools** with Clovis Boy.

    They give us information about his life.

4. For the future, we use *there* + *will be*.

    There **will be** a documentary about American Indians next week. **Will there be** a discussion after the movie? Yes, **there will.**

5. In *How many* questions with a location, we sometimes omit *there*.

    How many tools were (there) with Clovis Boy?

EXERCISE 12 Fill in the blanks with words you hear.

A: How many American Indians _____*are there*_____ in the U. S. today?
_{1.}

B: _____ about five million. But before the arrival of Europeans,
_{2.}

_____ many more.
_{3.}

A: How many _____ ?
_{4.}

B: _____ at least 12 million. Some historians think _____ up to
_{5.}   _{6.}

18 million.

A: On page 124, _____ an article about the first Thanksgiving.
_{7.}

_____ a beautiful story about peace. It says _____ friendship
_{8.}   _{9.}

between the Pilgrims and the American Indians.

B: Unfortunately, _____ didn't last. As more English people came to America,
_{10.}

_____ started to take the land away from the Indians. In 1830, President
_{11.}

Andrew Jackson sent American Indians away from their lands. They had to live on reservations.

A: What's a reservation?

B: _____ land given to the American Indians. American Indian children had to learn
_{12.}

English. Often _____ weren't allowed to speak their own language. As a result,
_{13.}

_____ very few American Indians today who speak the language of their
_{14.}

ancestors.

A: How many reservations _____ in the United States today?
_{15.}

B: _____ about 300.
_{16.}

EXERCISE 13 Fill in the blanks to complete each conversation. Use *there, is, are, was, were, it, they,* or a combination of these words. Use contractions wherever possible.

1. A: What's Siberia?

B: _____*It's*_____ a region of Russia.
_{a.}

A: How did people go from Siberia to Alaska thousands of years ago?

B: Today __*there is*__ water between these two places. But thousands of years ago, there
_{b.}

_____ a land connection.
_{c.}

continued

2. **A:** Where's Montana?

   B: _____ in the northwest of the United States.

   _{a.}

   A: _____ any reservations in Montana?

   _{b.}

   B: Yes, there _____ .

   _{c.}

3. **A:** How many tribes _____ in the U.S. today?

   _{a.}

   B: There _____ about 500 tribes in the U.S. today. Some, like the Navajo tribe in the

   _{b.}

   Southwest, are very big.

   A: How many people _____ in the Navajo tribe?

   _{c.}

   B: There are about 300,000 members.

4. **A:** _____ a very small tribe in California. It's the Cahuilla tribe.

   _{a.}

   B: How many members does _____ have?

   _{b.}

   A: In 2010, _____ had only eleven members.

   _{c.}

5. **A:** _____ a reservation in every state?

   _{a.}

   B: No, there _____ .

   _{b.}

   A: _____ any reservations in Illinois?

   _{c.}

   B: No, there _____ .

   _{d.}

6. **A:** Less than half of today's American Indians live on reservations.

   B: Why?

   A: _____ a lot of unemployment on many reservations. When American Indians

   _{a.}

   need jobs, _____ sometimes go to big cities.

   _{b.}

7. **A:** Did Europeans kill Indians?

   B: Yes, _____ did. Also, there _____ many deaths from diseases that

   _{a.}   _{b.}

   Europeans brought to America.

8. **A:** Will _____ another reading about American Indians in this lesson?

   _{a.}

   B: Yes, there will. _____ on page 142.

   _{b.}

5.9 Some, Any, A, No

Compare words used with count nouns (C) and noncount nouns (NC).

	Examples	Explanation
Affirmative	(C) There is **a** big reservation in the Southwest.	We use *a* or *an* with singular count nouns.
	(C) I put **some** apples in the cranberry sauce. (NC) I put **some** orange juice in the cranberry sauce.	We use *some* with both plural count nouns and noncount nouns.
Negative	(C) There are**n't any** American Indian reservations in Illinois. (C) There are **no** American Indian reservations in Illinois. (NC) There is**n't any information** about Clovis Boy's family. (NC) There is **no** information about Clovis Boy's family.	We use *not any* or *no* with both plural count nouns and noncount nouns.
Question	(C) Are there **any** nuts in the cranberry sauce? (NC) Is there **any** honey in the cranberry sauce?	We use *any* with both plural count nouns and noncount nouns.

Language Notes:

1. You will sometimes see *any* with a singular count noun.

   Which tribe should I write about? You can write about *any* tribe.

   Any, in this case, means "whichever you want." It doesn't matter which tribe.

2. Don't use a double negative.

   I don't have any information. (NOT: I don't have no information.)

EXERCISE 14 Fill in the blanks with *some, any, a, an,* or *no.*

1. **A:** There were _____ *some* _____ bones near Clovis Boy.

a.

   B: Were there _____ *any* _____ tools with him?

b.

2. **A:** Can you name _____ American Indian tribes?

a.

   B: Yes, I can name _____ tribes: the Navajo and the Crow.

b.

   A: Are there _____ Navajos in the Southwest today?

c.

   B: Yes, there are. There's _____ big Navajo reservation in the Southwest.

d.

3. **A:** I don't use sugar, so there's _____ sugar in this cranberry sauce.

a.

   B: Is there _____ honey?

b.

   A: Yes, there is. There's _____ fruit juice in it too. And there are _____

c.   d.

   pieces of apple too.

Navajo Code Talkers

Two Navajo code talkers relay orders over the radio using their native language in the early 1940s.

Read the following magazine article. Pay special attention to the words in bold.

American Indian languages are very complicated. There are many different languages and each one has **several** dialects.[12] One of these languages is the Navajo language. **Very few** non-Navajos can speak or understand it. One exception was Philip Johnston. Johnston was not an American Indian, but he grew up on the Navajo reservation and spoke the language fluently.

In World War II, the United States was at war with Japan. The Japanese were very skillful at breaking codes.[13] Johnston had an idea: to use Navajo Indians to create a code in their language.

In 1942, Johnston met with **several** American military men and explained his idea. At first, they weren't interested. Then Johnston met with Major James E. Jones of the Marines and spoke a **few** Navajo words to him. He convinced the major to give his idea a try.

The Marines recruited[14] twenty-nine speakers of Navajo to create a code based on their language. There weren't many military words in the Navajo language, so the Navajos had to develop words for these things. For example, a commanding general was a "war chief," a battleship was a "whale," and a submarine was an "iron fish."

In the first two days of code talking, more than eight hundred messages were sent without any errors.

About four hundred Navajos participated in the code program. During and after the war, they got **little** recognition for their great help in World War II. It wasn't until 1992 that the U.S. government honored the Navajo code talkers for their help in winning major battles of the war.

---

12 *dialect*: a regional variety of language
13 *code*: a system of hiding the real meaning of a message
14 *to recruit*: to look for and choose people to join the military

COMPREHENSION CHECK Based on the reading, tell if the statement is true (**T**) or false (**F**).

1. Philip Johnston learned the Navajo language as a child.

2. The Navajo language had many military words.

3. About eight hundred Navajos learned to use the code.

5.10 A Few, Several, A Little

	Examples	Explanation
Count	When Johnston spoke **a few** words of Navajo to Major Jones, the major was interested. The Navajo language has **several** dialects.	Use *a few* or *several* with count nouns.
Noncount	Johnston needed **a little** time to convince the major.	Use *a little* with noncount nouns.

EXERCISE 15 Choose the correct words to complete these sentences.

1. (*A few*/*A little*) American Indians came to help the Pilgrims in 1621.

2. They taught the Pilgrims (*a few*/*a little*) new skills for planting.

3. We read (*a little*/*several*) articles about American Indians.

4. Johnston met with (*several*/*a little*) military men.

5. He gave them (*a few*/*a little*) examples of the Navajo language.

6. (*A few*/*A little*) Navajo Indians developed a code.

7. It took (*a few*/*a little*) time to develop the code.

8. We now have (*a few*/*a little*) information about American Indians.

5.11 A Few vs. Few; A Little vs. Little

Examples	Explanation
We read **a few** articles about American Indians. **Few** non-Navajos could speak the Navajo language. **Very few** young American Indians speak the language of their ancestors.	*A few* means some or enough. *Few* and *very few* mean not enough; almost none.
There's **a little** turkey left over. Let's make a sandwich. The Navajo code talkers got **little** recognition for their help in World War II. The Pilgrims had **very little** food the first winter.	*A little* means some or enough. *Little* and *very little* mean not enough; almost none.

Language Note: Whether something is enough or not enough does not depend on the quantity. It depends on the perspective of the person.

EXERCISE 16 Fill in the blanks with *a little, very little, a few,* or *very few* in each conversation.

1. **A:** We read about American Indians in my ESL class. I'm starting to learn a _____a little_____

   about that topic. Did you know that Eskimos are American Indians too?

   B: Really? I know __very little__ about Eskimos. In fact, I know almost nothing.

   A: They live in Alaska, Canada, and Greenland. They make their houses out of ice.

   B: What do they eat? __Very few__ plants grow in the cold regions.

   A: They use a lot of sea animals for food. They eat whale, seal, and fish.

   B: I like to eat __a little__ fish, but I can't imagine eating it all the time. How do you

   know so much about Eskimos?

   A: I saw the movie *Eskimo*. I learned __a little__ about Eskimos from the movie.

   And I read __a few__ books. Do you want to borrow my books?

   B: No, thanks. I have __very little__ time for reading now. I have a lot of schoolwork.

2. **A:** Let's prepare the Thanksgiving dinner together. I always like to get __a little__

   help.

   B: I don't think I'm going to be much help. You know I have __very little__ experience

   in the kitchen.

   A: Don't worry. You can be my assistant. First, I need to put __a little__ oil on the turkey.

   B: There's __very little__ oil in the house. I don't think it's going to be enough.

   A: Don't worry. I have another bottle. Next, I need you to get the spices out of the cabinet for me. We're

   going to put __a few__ spices on the turkey. I also need __a little__ string to tie

   the legs. Then the turkey will be ready to go into the oven. Lastly, I need you to go to the store and get

   __a few__ things for me. Here's a list.

   B: Shopping! That's something I can do well.

   A: Why is it that in this family __very few__ men cook the turkey? I almost never see a man

   prepare the Thanksgiving dinner. In fact, __very few__ men even come into the kitchen unless

   they're hungry.

5.12 Too Much/Too Many vs. A Lot Of

Examples	Explanation
My friend left the reservation because there was **too much** unemployment. If we invite **too many** people to dinner, we won't have enough food. **A lot of** Navajo Indians live in the Southwest.	*Too much* and *too many* show an excessive quantity. A problem with the quantity is presented or implied. A *lot of* shows a large quantity. No problem is presented.
I feel sick. I ate **too much**.	We can put *too much* at the end of a verb phrase.

Language Note:

Sometimes we use *a lot* of in place of *too much/too many*.

> If we invite **a lot of** people to dinner, we won't have enough food.

EXERCISE 17 Fill in the blanks with *a lot of, too much,* or *too many*. In some cases, more than one answer is possible.

1. You put _____ too much _____ pepper in the potatoes, and they taste terrible.

2. On Thanksgiving Day, most people eat _____ too much _____ and don't feel well afterwards.

3. I'm so busy before Thanksgiving. I have no time to rest. I have _____ too many _____ things to do.

4. I love garlic. This recipe calls for _____ a lot of _____ garlic, so it's going to be delicious.

5. She's going to bake a cherry pie for Thanksgiving. She needs _____ a lot of _____ cherries.

6. I think I ate _____ too many _____ pieces of pie. Now I feel sick.

7. We had _____ too much _____ food at the Thanksgiving dinner. We had to throw away a lot.

8. There are _____ a lot of _____ American Indian languages.

9. The Navajo code talkers gave _____ a lot of _____ help during World War II.

10. The code talkers sent _____ a lot of _____ messages successfully.

SUMMARY OF LESSON 5

Words used before count and noncount nouns

Singular Count	Plural Count	Noncount
the apple	**the** apples	**the** sugar
an apple	**some** apples	**some** sugar
no apple	**no** apples	**no** sugar
	any apples *(with questions and negatives)*	**any** sugar *(with questions and negatives)*
	a lot of apples	**a lot of** sugar
	many apples	**much** sugar *(with questions and negatives)*
	a few apples	**a little** sugar
	two apples	**two** teaspoons of sugar
	several apples	
	How many apples?	**How much** sugar?

Sentences with *There*

Count	Noncount
There's one onion in the recipe.	**There is** some celery in the soup.
There are two carrots in the recipe.	**There isn't** any garlic in the soup.
Is there a potato in the recipe?	**Is there** any rice in the soup?
No, **there isn't.**	No, **there isn't.**
Are there any nuts in the recipe?	How much salt **is there** in the soup?
Yes, **there are.**	
How many nuts **are there** in the recipe?	

A Few/(Very) Few; A Little/(Very) Little

	Count	Noncount
some	**A few** people brought a pie to dinner.	Do you want **a little** sugar in your tea?
not enough	It's too bad that (**very**) **few** Navajos speak their language today.	The Navajo code talkers got (**very**) **little** recognition during World War II.

A Lot Of/Too Much/Too Many

Neutral (Count and Noncount)	Problematic (Count)	Problematic (Noncount)
I cooked **a lot** of potatoes. I put **a lot of** butter on the potatoes.	You put **too many** raisins in the stuffing. It's too sweet.	You put **too much** salt in the soup. I can't eat it.

TEST / REVIEW

Read this essay by an American Indian. Circle the correct words to complete it.

My name is Joseph Falling Snow. I'm (**an**/a/any) American Indian from a Sioux[15]
1.

reservation in South Dakota. There are (a little/little/**several**) Sioux reservations; I'm from the
2.

Pine Ridge reservation. I don't live in South Dakota anymore because I couldn't find (**a**/any/no)
3.

job. There's (a little/a few/**little**/few) work on my reservation. There's a lot of
4.

(**unemployment**/unemployments) there. (A poverty/**Poverty**) is a big problem on my reservation.
5.   **6.**

My uncle gave me (a/an/**some**/any) good (**advice**/advices). He told me to go to
7.   **8.**

(big city/**a big city**) to find (**a**/an/some/any) job. I decided to go to Minneapolis. There are
9.   **10.**

(much/**many**/any) job opportunities there. I had (**no**/not/any) trouble finding a job because I
11.   **12.**

have (**a lot of**/many/much) (experiences/**experience**) as a carpenter. The language of my tribe is
13.   **14.**

Lakota, but I know (any/a few/**very few**) words in my language. Most of the
15.

(**people**/person/peoples) on my reservation speak only English. (**A few**/Any/A little) older
16.   **17.**

people still speak our tribal language, but the language is dying out as the older people die.

(**A few**/A little/Few/Little) times a year, I go back to the reservation for a celebration,
18.

called a powwow. It gets very crowded at these times because (much/any/**a lot of**) people from
19.

our reservation and nearby reservations attend this celebration. We have

(much/too much/**a lot of**) fun. We dance to our (**music**/musics) and socialize with our
20.   **21.**

(friend/**friends**). We have (much/too much/**a lot of**) fun.
22.   **23.**

---

[15] *Sioux* is pronounced /su/.

WRITING

PART 1 Editing Advice

1. Some plural forms are irregular and don't take -s.

   There were a lot of childrens at the Thanksgiving dinner.

2. Use a singular noun and verb after *every*.

   Every tools tell us something about the Clovis people.

3. Use the plural form of the noun after *one of*.

   One of my neighbor made a pumpkin pie.

4. Don't use *a* or *an* before a plural noun.

   The code talkers had to create a new words.

5. Don't put *a* or *an* before a noncount noun.

   Clovis Boy's bones give us a useful information about the past.

6. A noncount noun is always singular.

   The American Indians gave the Pilgrims a lot of advices.

7. Use *there is* or *there are* to introduce a noun.

   There are
   Are a lot of Navajo Indians in the Southwest.

8. Don't use a specific noun after *there is/there are*.

   There's the Grand Canyon in Arizona.

9. Include *of* with a unit of measure.

   We used one cup sugar in the cranberry sauce.

10. Omit *of* after *a lot* when the noun is omitted.

    You ate a lot of turkey, but I didn't eat a lot of.

11. Use *a little/a few* to mean *some*. Use *(very) little/(very) few* to mean *not enough*.

    He went to a big city to find a job because there were a few jobs on the reservation.

12. Don't use *too much* or *too many* if the quantity doesn't present a problem.

    She loves to go back to the reservation because she has too many friends there.

13. Don't confuse *too* and *too much/too many*.

    The potatoes are too much salty. I can't eat them.

14. Don't use a double negative.

    The Navajo language doesn't have no word for "submarine."
    OR
    The Navajo language has no word for "submarine."

PART 2 Editing Practice

Some of the shaded words and phrases have mistakes. Find the mistakes and correct them. If the shaded words are correct, write C.

I love Thanksgiving. Every years, the whole family comes to our house for this holiday
                                       1.
C

and a few other holidays. But Thanksgiving is my favorite. There are a lot of childrens in my
2.   3.   4.

family and they love to see each other on Thanksgiving. They don't have many time to see
                                                                               5.

each other the rest of the year. It's so joyful to have too many children in the house few times
                                                          6.   7.

a year. There's a lot of noise when they're here, but we don't mind.
        8.   9.

We all bring some foods. One of my sister always makes a pumpkin pie. Her husband
                        10.   11.   12.

always makes a cookies in the shape of turkeys. My other sister makes cranberry sauce. She
              13.

uses a lot of sugars and sometimes it's too much sweet, but I never say anything. My brother
              14.   15.

doesn't like to cook, so he brings a lot fresh fruit. My cousin brings about 10 big bottles soda.
                                    16.   17.

I prepare the sweet potatoes. My mother always makes the turkey. It takes much time to cook
                      18.   19.

a big turkey.

We have a lot to prepare before Thanksgiving. My mother has very little time the week
            20.   21.

before because of her job. But I have a lot of because I don't have no homeworks that week. So
                                      22.   23.   24.

I clean the house. My father likes to help but he has very few experience in the kitchen, so my
                                                      25.

mother asks him to do the shopping. He doesn't have much experience shopping either, so she
                                                    26.

always gives him an advice about shopping with a list. But he always forgets to take the list
              27.

and buys too much. Last year he bought a fifty-pound bag of rice that we still haven't finished!
        28.

It's always fun to spend Thanksgiving with too many people. But there's one thing I don't
                                            29.   30.

like: are always a lot of dishes to wash afterwards.
      31.   32.

PART 3 Write About It

1. Write about a holiday celebration in your country. You may write about food, clothing, preparations, customs, etc. Use expressions of quantity.

2. Write about an ethnic minority in your native country or another country you know about. Where and how do these people live? Use expressions of quantity.

PART 4 Edit Your Writing

Reread the Summary of Lesson 5 and the editing advice. Edit your writing from Part 3.

A HEALTHY
PLANET,
A HEALTHY
BODY

A cyclist enjoys a quiet bike ride.

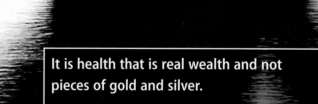

It is health that is real wealth and not pieces of gold and silver.

—Mahatma Gandhi

Feeding the Planet

A worker in a field of watermelons in California

Read the following article. Pay special attention to the words in bold.

CD 2
TR 2

Can you name some things that harm our environment? If you said cars, you're **right**. If you said smoke from **large** factories, well, that's a **big** part of the problem too. But maybe you didn't think of something in your **daily** life: your dinner. Agriculture, which produces your food, is more **harmful** to the environment than cars, trucks, trains, and airplanes combined. **Today's** farming uses our **water** supplies inefficiently.[1] Chemicals used on farms run into rivers and lakes and pollute[2] them. When **rain** forests and **grass**land are cleared for **farm** animals and crops, the result is often the extinction[3] of **wild**life.[4] **Farming** methods release harmful gases into the air. These gases are an **enormous** contributor to **global** warming.

By 2050, the **world** population will be nine billion, two billion more than it is today. Because of **population** growth, the problem of feeding so many people is **huge**. There will be a **growing** need for food all over the world. As countries such as China and India are becoming more **prosperous**,[5] there is an **increasing** demand for meat, eggs, and dairy.

How can we increase the amount of food and maintain a **healthy** planet? Here are some solutions.

1. It is **important** to stop cutting down forests for agriculture. This is very **destructive** to the environment.

2. We don't need to eat so much meat. Producing meat wastes **valuable** resources and contributes to **global** warming.

3. We need to stop wasting food. In **rich** countries, about 50 percent of food goes to trash. In **poor** countries, a lot of food is lost between the farmer and the market because storage and transportation are not **efficient.**

It won't be easy to make these changes, but if we don't try, the result will be terrible for **future** generations. All of us have to be **thoughtful** about the connection between the food on our plates, the farmers that produce it, and the effect on the planet. As we push our **shopping** carts down the aisles of our supermarkets, our **food** choices will decide our future.

---

1 *inefficiently:* in a way that is not productive or economical
2 *to pollute:* to contaminate, make impure or dirty
3 *extinction:* the state of no longer living or existing
4 *wildlife:* animals living in their natural setting
5 *prosperous:* wealthy

COMPREHENSION CHECK Based on the reading, tell if the statement is true (**T**) or false (**F**).

1. Agriculture can cause a lot of harm to the planet.

2. Rain forests cause a lot of harm to the planet.

3. If we eat less meat, this will be better for the planet.

6.1 Modifying a Noun

Examples	Explanation
Food is part of our **daily** life. We shouldn't waste **valuable** resources.	An adjective can modify or describe a noun. (*Daily* and *valuable* are adjectives.)
Population growth is a problem. Our **food** choices affect the environment.	A noun can modify or describe another noun. (*Population* and *food* are nouns.)

EXERCISE 1 Listen and fill in the blanks with the words you hear.

CD 2
TR 3

We know that it's _____important_____ to eat well and get _____enough_____ exercise.
     1.   2.

Health clubs are _____full_____ of people trying to get in shape. Sales of _____low_____-
     3.   4.

calorie foods show that Americans want to be _____thin_____. However, two-thirds of
     5.

_____American_____ adults are _____overweight_____. One in three American children is
     6.   7.

overweight. Weight is also becoming a _____national_____ problem as _____health_____ costs
     8.   9.

go up because of diseases related to obesity: _____heart_____ disease, stroke, diabetes, and
     10.

_____high_____ blood pressure.
     11.

What is the reason for this _____growing_____ problem? First, today's lifestyle does not
     12.

include enough _____physical_____ activity. When the U.S. was an _____agricultural_____
     13.   14.

society, farmers ate a _____big_____ meal, but they also worked hard in the fields.
     15.

_____Modern_____ technology removes _____hard, physical_____ activity from our
     16.   17.

_____daily_____ lives. Most trips are _____short_____, within _____walking_____
     18.   19.   20.

distance of home, but most Americans drive. Only 13 percent of schoolchildren walk or bike to a

school. Compare this to 48 percent in 1969. The _____average_____ American child spends
     21.

about thirty-five hours a week watching TV. Kids are not _____active_____ enough.
     22.

_____Today's_____ kids may be the first generation to have a shorter _____life_____
     23.   24.

expectancy than their parents.

6.2 Adjectives

Examples	Explanation
Rich countries waste food. **Large** factories cause pollution.	An adjective can come before a noun.
Farmers used to eat a **big, heavy** meal. We all want to have **active, healthy** kids.	Two adjectives can come before a noun. We separate the adjectives with a comma when we can change the order of the adjectives without changing the meaning.
We don't do **hard physical labor** any more. The **average American** child watches a lot of TV.	We don't use a comma if we can't reverse the order of the adjectives.
The problem is **huge.** Feeding 9 billion people seems almost **impossible.**	An adjective can come after *be, seem,* and the sense-perception verbs: *look, sound, smell, taste,* or *feel.*
It is **important** to protect the planet. It won't be **easy** to solve the problem.	An adjective can come after impersonal expressions beginning with *it.*
Are you **concerned** about the future? Scientists are **interested** in finding a solution.	Some *-ed* words are adjectives: *tired, worried, located, crowded, married, divorced, excited, disappointed, finished, frightened, filled,* and *concerned.*
We read an **interesting** article about farming. I learned **surprising** information about our food.	Some *-ing* words are adjectives: *interesting, amazing, surprising, exciting, boring, increasing,* and *growing.*
It is **extremely** important to find a solution. This is a **very** difficult problem.	*Very, so, quite,* and *extremely* can come before adjectives.
Is farming a problem? Yes, it is a huge **one.** Do you have any ideas about how to protect the planet? There are some good **ones** in the article.	After an adjective, we can substitute a singular noun with *one* and a plural noun with *ones.*

Language Notes:

1. Some conversational words that come before adjectives are: *pretty, sort of, kind of, really* and *real.*

    I was **kind of** surprised by the article.

    The food situation sounds **really** bad.

2. We don't make an adjective plural.

    a **big** farm   **big** farms

EXERCISE 2 Fill in blanks with one of the words from the box.

growing	tired	healthy	greasy	worried	sweet	high✓
important	ones	sick	one	rich	busy	valuable

1. Burgers and fries are _____high_____ in calories.

2. It is ___important___ to have a good diet.

3. Fries are cooked in oil. They are very ___greasy___.

4. If you don't eat a healthy diet, you can get ___sick___.

5. Some people eat a big breakfast. Others eat a small ___one___.

6. Are you ___worried___ about the future of the planet?

7. Children need to get enough sleep. It's not good to be ___tired___ in school.

8. Cookies are very ___sweet___.

9. Most Americans have ___busy___ lives and don't make the time to eat well.

10. Obesity is a ___growing___ problem. It is a bigger problem today than it was years ago.

11. We need to have a ___healthy___ body.

12. In ___rich___ countries, many people waste food. In poor ___countries___ ___ones___, there is not enough food.

13. We shouldn't waste ___valuable___ resources.

A green roof on an organic cooperative food store in Chicago, Illinois

EXERCISE 3 Circle the correct words to complete this conversation between a husband and his wife.

A: We're gaining weight. When we were younger, we used to be (*thin*/*thins*), but now that we're
1.

(*marry*/*married*), we're getting fat.
2.

B: Let's go jogging after work. There's a (*beautiful park*/*park beautiful*) where we can go.
3.

It's (*locate*/*located*) just a few blocks away from our apartment.
4.

A: But after work I'm always too (*tire*/*tired*). I just want to eat dinner and watch TV.
5.

B: It's not good to eat a big meal so late at night. In many countries, people eat a big meal during

the day and (*a small one*/*a small*) at night. If we do that, we have the rest of the day to burn off
6.

the calories.

A: I'm sure that's (*an idea very good*/*a very good idea*), but I don't have time to eat a big meal in
7.

the middle of the day.

B: We're always eating out in (*expensive*/*expensives*) restaurants. We should cook more at home.
8.

And we should go for a walk after dinner.

A: Good idea. Let's cook steaks tonight.

B: We need to eat less meat. Meat production is (*harm*/*harmful*) to the planet. It contributes to
9.

(*globe*/*global*) warming. I read (*an article very interesting*/*a very interesting article*) about it
10.   11.

today.

A: You're right. Let's eat fish tonight.

6.3 Noun Modifiers

Examples	Explanation
The **world** population is increasing. **Population** growth is a problem.	A noun can modify (describe) another noun. When two nouns come together, the second noun is more general than the first.
We use a **shopping** cart in a supermarket. **Farming** methods produce gas.	Sometimes a gerund (-ing word) describes a noun.
Potato chips have a lot of grease. My five-**year-old** son prefers candy to fruit.	The first noun is always singular. Potato chips are chips made from potatoes. A five-year-old son is a son who is five years old. When we use a number before the noun, we usually attach it to the noun with a hyphen.
Very few **schoolchildren** walk to school. Do you have a healthy **lifestyle**?	Sometimes we write the two nouns as one word. The noun modifier and the noun become a compound word.
Today's lifestyle doesn't include much physical activity. Everyone needs a good **night's** sleep.	Sometimes a possessive noun describes a noun, especially with time words.

Pronunciation Note:

When a noun describes a noun, the first noun usually receives the greater emphasis in speaking.

> I wear my **running** shoes when I go to the **health** club and use the **exercise** machines.

EXERCISE 4 Fill in the blanks with one of the words from the box.

rain	world	population✓	health	shopping
farm	walking	heart	food	

1. ___Population___ growth is a big problem.

2. The ___world___ population will be 9 billion in 2050.

3. When we shop at the supermarket, we need to make healthy ___food___ choices.

4. When we shop, we usually use a ___shopping___ cart.

5. Some people go to ___health___ clubs to exercise.

6. One result of a poor diet is ___heart___ disease.

7. Many children live within ___walking___ distance from their schools, but they go by bus or car.

8. Cows and pigs are ___farm___ animals.

9. Cutting down ___rain___ forests is harmful to the environment.

EXERCISE 5 Fill in the blanks to complete this conversation between a mother and her small son. Put the words given in the correct order. Remember to use the singular form for the first noun. Some answers are compound words.

A: We need a lot of things today. Let's take a ___shopping cart___ .
                                                  1. cart/shopping

B: Can I sit in the _____ ?
                           2. child/seat

A: You're much too big. You're a six-___year old___ boy.
                                     3. years/old

B: Mom, please buy me that cereal. It looks good. I saw it on a _____ .
                                                          4. commercial/TV

A: Let's read the ingredients on the _____ first. I want to see the
                                               5. cereal/box

_____ before we buy it. Let me put on my _____ .
                   6. content/sugar   7. glasses/eyes

Oh, dear. This cereal has twenty grams of sugar.

B: But I like sugar, Mom.

A: You know sugar is bad for your teeth. Remember what the dentist told you?

B: But I brush my teeth once a day.

A: I want you to use your _____ after every meal, not just once a day.
                                              8. teeth/brush

B: Mom, can we buy those _____ ?
                                       9. chips/potatoes

A: They have too much fat.

B: How about some soda?

A: You should drink more juice. How about some _____ ?
                                             10. juice/oranges

B: I don't like juice.

A: Let's get in the _____ and pay now. Maybe we should shop at the
                   11. line/check-out

_____ store next time.
                   12. food/health

EXERCISE 6 About You Make a list of things you usually have in your refrigerator. Compare your list to a partner's.

___orange juice, low-fat milk_____

_____

Get Healthy!

Read the following article. Pay special attention to the words in bold.

Experts in the United States have the following recommendations for living a healthier lifestyle:

1. Get active. Ride a bike or walk places instead of driving. Cars and other machines **greatly** reduce the need for physical activity. These machines help us move from place to place **easily** and **quickly** and work **efficiently**, but we don't use much physical energy.

2. Eat a **well**-balanced meal consisting of protein, grains, vegetables, and fruit. Some people just eat snacks all day. They eat a lot of junk food,[6] such as potato chips and soda.

3. Nutritionists recommend that families eat together. **Unfortunately**, many people often eat alone and **quickly**. If families eat their big meal together **slowly**, they can discuss the events of their day and enjoy their food and each other's company.

4. Take the soft drink and snack machines out of the schools and educate children **early** about nutrition and exercise. The typical teenager gets about 10 to 15 percent of his or her calories from soft drinks, which have no nutrition at all. Replace the food in the machines with water, juice, and healthy snacks.

5. Be careful of the food messages you hear from advertisers that say, "Eat this. Buy that." Technology allows advertisers to send us messages **constantly**. Many of these foods are high in fat and calories. Choose natural foods, such as fruits and nuts, instead of manufactured foods.

6. In addition to what individuals can do, communities need to build new housing more **carefully**. In many communities in the United States, it's hard to walk from place to place **easily** because there are no sidewalks. If we want people to get exercise in their communities, they need sidewalks. They also need bike paths so they can ride **safely**.

7. Change your diet. Eat meat **infrequently**. Twice a week is enough.

Parents need to set a good example so that their kids grow up in a **healthy way**.

---

[6] *junk food*: food that tastes good but is bad for your health

A woman jogs near Cannon Beach, Oregon.

COMPREHENSION CHECK Based on the reading, tell if the statement is true (**T**) or false (**F**).

1. Some schools sell unhealthy snacks in snack machines.

2. Protein is part of a well-balanced meal.

3. Most Americans eat with their families.

6.4 Adverbs

Examples	Explanation
Subject **Verb Phrase** **Adverb of Manner** You need to ride your bike **safely.** They ate lunch **quickly.** We should choose our food **carefully.**	An adverb of manner tells *how* or *in what way* the subject does something. We form most adverbs of manner by putting *–ly** at the end of an adjective. An adverb of manner usually follows the verb phrase.
Cars **greatly** reduce the need for physical activity. We **constantly** see ads on TV for food. I eat meat **infrequently.**	Other common *–ly* adverbs are: *eventually, annually, (in)frequently, certainly, greatly, suddenly, recently, directly, completely, generally, repeatedly, naturally, finally, probably, (un)fortunately, extremely, constantly.*
Do you eat **well**?	The adverb for *good* is *well.*
You should eat a **well**-balanced meal. We live in a **carefully** planned community.	An adverb can come before an adjective.
Adjective **Adverb** Farmers are **hard** workers. They work **hard.** He wants a **fast** meal. Don't eat so **fast.** We had a **late** dinner. We ate dinner **late.** He had an **early** lunch. He ate lunch **early.**	Some adjectives and adverbs have the same form: *hard, fast, early,* and *late.* (The *-ly* in *early* is not an adverb ending.)
She worked **hard** to prepare a good meal. Her son **hardly** ate anything.	*Hard* and *hardly* are both adverbs, but they have completely different meanings. *She worked* **hard** means she put a lot of effort into the work. *Hard* comes after the verb phrase. *He* **hardly** *ate anything* means he ate almost nothing. *Hardly* comes before the verb.
He came home **late** and missed dinner. **Lately**, he doesn't have time to eat a good meal. He doesn't get enough exercise **lately.**	*Late* and *lately* are both adverbs, but they have completely different meanings. *Late* means not on time. It comes after the verb phrase. *Lately* means recently. It comes at the beginning or end of the sentence.
She is a **friendly** person. She behaves **in a friendly manner.** He is a **lively** person. He dances **in a lively way.**	Some adjectives end in *-ly*: *lovely, lonely, friendly, lively,* and *ugly.* They have no adverb form. With these adjectives, we use an adverbial phrase (*in a* _____ *-ly way/manner*) to describe the action.

* For the spelling of *–ly* adverbs, see Appendix C.

We gain weight **very** easily. She cooks **extremely** well. He eats **so** fast. She exercises **really** hard. You eat **quite** slowly.	*Very, extremely, so, really,* and *quite* can come before an adverb. In conversation, people often shorten *really* to *real*: She exercises **real** hard.

EXERCISE 7 Fill in the blanks with an adverb from the box (or choose your own adverb). In some cases, more than one answer is possible.

cheaply	differently	constantly	poorly
briskly√	regularly	quickly	well

1. If you walk _____briskly_____ every day, you can lose weight.

2. TV gives us messages _____, telling us to buy more junk food.

3. Do you eat _____ or slowly?

4. You should exercise _____ if you want to stay healthy.

5. If you eat _____, you will not be healthy and strong.

6. If you eat _____, you will have no need to snack between meals.

7. In a fast-food restaurant, a family can eat _____. In another kind of restaurant, they have to spend a lot of money.

8. I used to eat a lot of junk food, but I changed. I eat _____ now. I eat fresh fruits and vegetables every day.

EXERCISE 8 About You Write the adverb form of the word given. Then check (√) the activities that you do in this way. Work with a partner. Make statements telling how you do these activities.

1. ___√___ shop _____carefully_____
                _{careful}
   I shop carefully. I always try to buy healthy food for my family. OR
   I don't shop carefully. I just buy a lot of frozen food.

2. _____ eat _____
               _{slow}

3. _____ walk _____
               _{fast}

4. _____ cook _____
               _{good}

continued

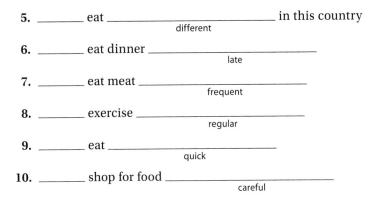

5. _____ eat _____ in this country
   different

6. _____ eat dinner _____
   late

7. _____ eat meat _____
   frequent

8. _____ exercise _____
   regular

9. _____ eat _____
   quick

10. _____ shop for food _____
    careful

6.5 Adjective vs. Adverb

An adjective describes a noun. An adverb describes a verb (phrase), an adjective, or another adverb.

Examples	Explanation
Jim is **serious** about good health. He takes his doctor's advice **seriously**.	*Serious* is an adjective. It describes a noun, *Jim*. *Seriously* is an adverb of manner. It tells how Jim takes his doctor's advice.
Your dinner looks **good**. The soup tastes **delicious**. You prepared it **carefully**. I tasted the soup **slowly** because it was hot.	We use an adjective, not an adverb, after the following verbs if we are describing the subject: *smell*, *sound*, *taste*, *look*, *seem*, *appear*, and *feel*. We use an adverb of manner if we are describing *how* the action (the verb phrase) is done.
The children got **hungry**. If you don't eat well, you can **get** sick.	We use an adjective, not an adverb, in expressions with *get*. Some expressions with *get* are *get hungry*, *get tired*, *get sick*, and *get rich*.
He's sick. He doesn't feel **well** today.	For health, we use *well*.
He's **extremely** healthy. He eats **extremely** well.	We use an adverb before an adjective or another adverb.
As usual, she cooked dinner.	We use the adjective, not the adverb, in the expression *as usual*.

Language Note:

In conversational English, people sometimes use *good* for health.

He's sick. He doesn't feel **good** today.

EXERCISE 9 Fill in the blanks with the correct form of the adjective or adverb given.

Last week I was invited to a potluck dinner at my math teacher's house. This is my first

month in the U.S., so I didn't know what "potluck" was. A _____*new*_____ friend of mine
                                                          1. new

told me that this is a dinner where each person brings some food. I wanted to make a

_____ impression, so I prepared my _____ dish from Mexico.
2. positive   **3. favorite**

I worked _____ hard to make it look and taste _____ .
         4. extreme   **5. good**

Most of the people at the dinner looked at my dish _____ . They didn't know
                                                    6. strange

what it was. They thought that Mexicans just eat tacos. They tasted my food

_____ , thinking that Mexicans make everything with hot peppers. But I didn't.
7. careful

I know that some people don't like _____ food. I prepared the meal
                                    8. spicy

_____ . As _____ , I put the hot sauce on the side.
9. thoughful   **10. usual**

A student from India brought Indian food. I was _____ to find out how
                                                 11. surprised

spicy Indian food is. The taste seemed very _____ to me, but I ate it anyway.
                                             12. strange

The party was great. I went home very _____ . I had to get up
                                       13. late

_____ the next morning, so I _____ slept at all that night.
14. early   **15. hard**

EXERCISE 10 About You Answer the questions. Discuss your answers with a partner.

1. When and where do you eat the big meal of the day?

_____

2. Do you eat differently compared to ten years ago? If so, how?

_____

3. Do you think people eat a healthy diet in your country? Why or why not?

_____

4. How much exercise do you get?

_____

A man is observed during an experiment in a research center sleep lab.

A Good Night's Sleep

CD 2
TR 5

Read the following article. Pay special attention to the words in bold.

Most people need seven to nine hours of sleep. But most Americans sleep less than seven hours a night. When people aren't **rested enough**, there may be a bad result. For example, if people drive when they're **too tired**, they can cause serious accidents on the road. According to the National Transportation Administration, sleepy drivers cause 100,000 accidents each year. Airplane safety also depends on well-rested pilots. An airplane crash in 2009 killed all the passengers. The National Transportation Safety Board concluded that the pilots were **too sleepy** to make good decisions.

Sleep is **very** important to our health. In experiments with rats, where the rats were not allowed to sleep, all of them were dead in about two weeks. More studies on sleep are needed, but scientists complain that they don't receive **enough money** for sleep research.

If sleep is so important, why don't we try to go to bed earlier and get at least eight hours of sleep? About 20 percent of Americans say that they don't get **enough sleep**. Are we **too busy**? Not always. Besides job and family responsibilities, Americans have a lot of other things that keep them out of bed.

Twenty-four-hour-a-day Internet and TV and all night supermarkets can take away from our sleep time.

What can we do to improve our sleep? Sleep experts have some recommendations:

- Don't nap during the day.
- Sleep in a dark room. **Too much light** in a room can harm sleep.
- Try not to have **too much stress** in your life.
- Don't get **too stimulated** before going to bed. Avoid activities such as watching TV or eating before bed.
- Go to bed at the same time every night.
- Avoid caffeine after lunchtime. If you drink **too much coffee** during the day, don't expect to get a good night's sleep.
- Exercise. Physical activity is **very good** for sleep. But if you exercise **too late** in the day, it will interfere with your sleep.

A good night's sleep is **very important,** so turn off the TV, shut down the computer, put away your devices, and sleep well.

COMPREHENSION CHECK Based on the reading, tell if the statement is true (**T**) or false (**F**).

1. Most people get seven to nine hours of sleep.

2. Scientists did sleep experiments with rats.

3. A lot of money goes into research for sleep experiments.

6.6 *Too, Too Much, Too Many,* and *Enough*

Examples	Explanation
The pilot was **too sleepy** to fly the airplane. You work **too hard** and don't relax.	We put *too* before adjectives and adverbs *Too* indicates a problem.
You spend **too much time** on the computer. You spend **too many hours** watching TV.	We put *too much* before a noncount noun. We put *too many* before a count noun.
He doesn't sleep well because he worries **too much.**	We put *too much* at the end of the verb phrase.
Five hours of sleep is not **good enough**. You worked **hard enough**. Get some rest now.	We put *enough* after adjectives and adverbs.
Some people don't get **enough exercise**. Do you get **enough hours** of sleep?	We put *enough* before noncount and count nouns.

Language Note:

An infinitive can follow a phrase with *too* and *enough*.

> I'm too tired **to drive**.
> I don't have enough time **to exercise**.

EXERCISE 11 Fill in the blanks with *too, too much, too many,* or *enough*.

1. Are Americans _____*too*_____ busy to get a good night's sleep?

2. Some people don't get _____ exercise, because of their busy lives.

3. It's hard to sleep if you exercise _____ late in the evening.

4. If you're _____ tired when you drive, you can cause an accident.

continued

5. Some people spend _____ time on the Internet. They should put away

   their electronic devices and go to bed.

6. If you drink _____ coffee, it can affect your sleep.

7. People drive everywhere. They don't walk _____.

8. Try not to eat _____ before you go to bed.

9. Children shouldn't drink so much soda, because it contains _____ sugar.

10. We need to think about the future. We need to make sure there is _____ food for the nine

    billion people on the planet in 2050.

11. Don't eat _____ meat. Try eating fish or chicken a few times a week.

EXERCISE 12 About You Discuss the answers to these questions with a partner.

1. How many hours do you sleep a night?

2. How many hours is enough for you?

6.7 *Too* and *Very*

Examples	Explanation
We ate dinner **very** late last night. We arrived at the theater **too late**. We missed the beginning of the movie. My grandmother is 85. She's **very** old, but she's in great health. The child is 6 years old. He's **too** old to sit in a shopping cart.	Don't confuse *very* and *too*. *Too* indicates a problem. The problem can be stated or implied. *Very* is a neutral word. It does not indicate a problem.

Language Note:

We can use *a little* before *too*.

  You woke up *a little too* late. You missed a great breakfast.

EXERCISE 13 Fill in the blanks with *too* or *very* in this conversation between a husband and his wife.

A: I enjoyed the dinner _____*very*_____ much.
                            1.

B: I'm glad you liked it. I worked _____*Very*_____ hard to prepare your favorite dishes.
                                   2.

A: Thanks! Everything was great. But the soup was a little _____*too*_____ salty.
                                                          3.

B: Oh. I thought you liked everything.

A: I did. Other than the salt, it was _____<u>very</u>_____ good. And I especially liked the potatoes.

           4.

B: I'm glad.

A: They were a little _____<u>too</u>_____ greasy, but I ate them anyway.

         5.

B: I'm afraid the meat was overcooked. I left it in the oven _____<u>too</u>_____ long.

         6.

A: Well, no one's perfect. I gave some to the dog.

B: What about the cake I made? Did you like that?

A: Yes. It was _____<u>very</u>_____ good. The only problem was it was _____<u>too</u>_____ small.

         7.   8.

    I was hoping to have another piece, but there was nothing left.

B: I thought you wanted to lose weight. You always say you're _____<u>too</u>_____ fat and need to

                                                          9.

    lose weight.

A: Fat? I'm not fat. I'm just right. But my clothes are _____<u>too</u>_____ small. When I washed

                                                         10.

    them, the water I used was _____<u>too</u>_____ hot and they shrank.

                                  11.

B: They didn't shrink. You gained weight.

EXERCISE 14 About You Write about some habits you wish to change to improve your health. Discuss your sentences with a partner.

1. <u>I don't get enough exercise.</u>

2. <u>I spend too much time online.</u>

3. _____

4. _____

5. _____

EXERCISE 15 About You Write about problems in the United States or your country. Discuss your sentences with a partner.

1. <u>We waste too much food in the U.S.</u>

2. _____

3. _____

4. _____

5. _____

SUMMARY OF LESSON 6

Adjectives and Adverbs

Adjectives	Adverbs
We had a **quick** lunch.	We ate **quickly**.
We had a **late** dinner.	We ate **late**.
She is a **good** cook.	She cooks **well**.
She looks **serious**.	She is looking at the label **seriously**.
As **usual**, he drank a cup of coffee.	He **usually** drinks coffee in the morning.

Adjective Modifiers and Noun Modifiers

Adjective Modifier	Noun Modifier
a **new** machine	an **exercise** machine
old shoes	**running** shoes
a **short** vacation	a two-**week** vacation
big problems	**today's** problems

Very/Too/Enough/Too Much/Too Many

Examples	Explanation
He's **very** healthy.	*very* + adjective
I slept **very** well.	*very* + adverb
I'm **too** sleepy.	*too* + adjective
It's **too** late to drive.	*too* + adverb
I'm rested **enough** to do my work.	verb + *enough*
Did you get **enough** sleep last night?	*enough* + noun
She doesn't eat ice cream because it has **too much** fat.	*too much* + noncount noun
She doesn't eat ice cream because it has **too many** calories.	*too many* + count noun
He loves coffee, but when he drinks **too much**, he can't sleep.	verb + *too much*

TEST/REVIEW

Choose the correct words to complete these sentences.

1. It's (too /*very*) important to get a good (night /*night's*) sleep.

2. Parents want their kids to eat (good /*well*).

3. We use a lot of resources to raise (*farm* / farms) animals.

4. Some farmers use chemicals to make cows grow (*fast* / fastly).

5. Farmers work very (*hard* / hardly).

6. If we use too (much /*many*) chemicals, we can harm the environment.

7. The (*world population* / population world) is increasing.

8. You seem (*sleepy* / sleepily). You shouldn't drive.

9. Did you get (sleep enough /*enough sleep*) last night?

10. I slept (good /*well*) last night.

11. I feel (*great* / greatly) today.

12. I took a two-(*hour* / hours) nap this afternoon.

13. Do you exercise (regular /*regularly*)?

14. Are you (*alert enough* / enough alert) to drive?

15. We ate dinner (*late* / lately) last night.

16. My grandfather's health is (too /*very*) good.

17. He's 75, but he looks like a 50-(*year* / years)-old man.

18. I'm always (very /*too*) tired to exercise after work.

19. Yesterday was an (extreme /*extremely*) hard day for me.

20. We like to go for a walk in the park near my house. It's (*very* / too) beautiful there.

21. Are you (*too* / too much) busy to exercise?

WRITING

PART 1 Editing Advice

1. Adjectives are always singular.

    People in poors countries don't eat a lot of meat.

2. Certain adjectives end with *-ed*.

    We're interest in taking care of the planet.
    (ed inserted above)

3. Put an adjective before the noun or after a linking verb, like *be*.

    She is a woman very healthy. *OR* The woman is very healthy.
    (very healthy woman written above "woman very healthy")

4. Use *one(s)* after an adjective to take the place of a noun.

    Do you prefer to sleep on a hard bed or a soft?
    (one inserted)

5. Put a specific noun before a general noun.

    We have to be careful about our supply water.
    (water supply written above)

6. A noun modifier is always singular.

    Don't eat so many potatoes chips.

7. An adverb of manner describes the action of a verb. An adjective describes a noun.

    I choose my food careful.
    (ly inserted)

    You seem seriously about exercise.

8. Don't put a *-ly* adverb of manner between the verb and the object.

    He read carefully the ingredients.
    (carefully inserted)

9. Adverbs of manner that don't end in *-ly* follow the verb phrase.

    He late came home.
    (late inserted)

10. *Too* indicates a problem. If there is no problem, use *very*.

    Your father is too healthy.
    (very written above too)

11. Don't use *too much* and *too many* before an adjective or adverb. Use *too*.

    She's too much tired to drive.

12. Put *enough* after the adjective.

    I'm enough rested to drive.
    (rested enough written above)

13. Don't confuse *hard* and *hardly*.

    I'm tired. I worked hardly all day.

    He's lazy. He hard worked at all.
    (ly inserted)

PART 2 Editing Practice

Some of the shaded words and phrases have mistakes. Find the mistakes and correct them. If the shaded words are correct, write C.

I exercise regularly and I eat very good most of the time. Luckily, I'm too healthy. I try to
1. *C* 2. *well* 3. *very*

eat a lot of fresh fruits and vegetables every day. I also eat a lot of wholes grains. I rarely eat
4. *X*

red meat. I eat fish or chicken. But I rarely eat chicken fried because it's too much greasy. Most
5. 6. *fried* 7. *much too*

mornings I have a glass of juice orange and cereal. For lunch, I have a small meal, usually a
8. *orange* 9.

tuna sandwich. For dinner, I like to eat a nice meal slowly. Most of the time, I cook dinner.
10. 11. *slow* / *X*

But on Fridays I have a three-hours biology course and I late get home, and I'm too much tire
12. 13. *get home late* 14. *much too* 15. *tired*

to cook. Then I'm not so carefully about what I eat. My roommate offers me food, but he eats
16.

very poorly. He often eats hamburgers and greasy fries from a fast-food place, or he brings
17. 18.

home a sausage pizza. He eats quickly his food, and he drinks a lot of sweets drinks. He
19. 20. *his food quickly* 21. *X*

thinks it's enough good, but I don't agree. When I eat with him, I don't eat so careful, and then
22. *good enough* 23. *carefully*

I don't feel well the next day. I think it's important to have a diet very healthy. I'm going to try
24. *good* 25. *very healthy diet*

hardly to have a better meal on Friday nights.
26.

PART 3 Write About It

1. Compare food in your native culture to food in the United States.

2. Describe your eating habits today with your eating habits in your native country.

PART 4 Edit Your Writing

Reread the Summary of Lesson 6 and the editing advice. Edit your writing from Part 3.

7 Time Words
The Past Continuous

Celebrity Cesar Millan (center)
during his citizenship ceremony

IMMIGRANTS AND REFUGEES

America was born as a nation of immigrants who have always contributed to its greatness.

—Charles B. Rangel

Immigrants arrive from Europe to Ellis Island in the early 1900s.

Ellis Island

Read the following article. Pay special attention to the words in bold.

In the 1800s, the United States experienced the largest human migration in the history of the world. As more and more immigrants came to the United States, it soon became clear that the original processing center was too small to handle such a large number. Ellis Island, in New York Harbor, was opened on January 1, 1892, as the new processing center. **When** the first passengers approached Ellis Island, they saw the new Statue of Liberty, which was only six years old.

The first person to enter Ellis Island was Annie Moore, a teenager from Ireland. **When** she got off the ship **after** traveling for twelve days with her two younger brothers, reporters were waiting to interview her. **After** she went through the registration process, an official gave her a ten dollar gold coin. That day, 700 immigrants passed through Ellis Island.

During the early 1900s, immigration continued to grow. The largest number of immigrants came **in** 1907. Approximately 1.25 million immigrants came through that year.

For sixty-two years, Ellis Island was the main door through which millions of immigrants entered

the United States. **From** the time it opened **in** 1892 **until** the time it closed **in** 1954, Ellis Island processed 12 million immigrants. Sometimes more than 10,000 people passed through the registry room in one 24-hour period. New arrivals often waited **for** many hours **while** inspectors checked to see if they met legal and medical standards. Most did not speak English, and they were tired, hungry, and confused. Two percent (250,000 people) did not meet the requirements to enter the U.S. and had to return to their countries.

After it closed down, Ellis Island remained abandoned[1] **until** 1965, when President Lyndon Johnson decided to restore[2] it as a monument. Restoration of Ellis Island was finished **by** 1990. Visitors to this monument could see the building as it looked **from** 1918 **to** 1920. Almost two million people visited the Ellis Island monument a year **until** a storm damaged the building in 2012. Luckily, the exhibits did not suffer damage.

Almost half of Americans are descendants of immigrants who passed through Ellis Island many years **ago.**

---

[1] *abandoned*: empty
[2] *to restore*: to make something look like it did when it was new

COMPREHENSION CHECK Based on the reading, tell if the statement is (**T**) true or (**F**) false.

1. Ellis Island was the first immigrant processing center in the United States.

2. On the day Annie Moore arrived from Ireland, 700 immigrants passed through Ellis Island.

3. Ellis Island processed 12 million immigrants in 1954.

7.1 Time Words

Time Word	Examples	Explanation
on	Ellis Island opened its doors on January 1, 1892.	We use *on* with a specific date or day.
in	Ellis Island opened **in** January. Ellis Island opened **in** 1892. **In** the early 1900s, many immigrants came to the U.S. My brother will come to the U.S. **in** two months.	We use *in* • with a month • with a year • with a group of years • to mean after a period of time
during	**During** the early 1900s, many immigrants came to the U.S. The building at Ellis Island suffered damage **during** a storm in 2012.	We use *during* with a period of time (*the 1900s, the month of May,* etc.). We use *during* with an event (*the storm, the trip, the movie,* etc.).
for	**For** 62 years, Ellis Island was the main entrance for immigrants to the U.S.	We use *for* with the quantity of years, months, weeks, days, etc.
by	**By** 1990, restoration of Ellis Island was complete.	We use *by* to mean *up to and including a specific time.*
from . . . . . .to . . .till . . .until	Ellis Island was open **from** 1892 **to** 1954. Ellis Island was open **from** 1892 **till** 1954. Ellis Island was open **from** 1892 **until** 1954.	We use *from* with the starting time. We use *to, till,* or *until* with the ending time.
while	**While** they were restoring Ellis Island, it was closed.	We use *while* to mean *during that time.*
when	**When** Ellis Island opened on January 1, 1892, 700 people passed through.	We use *when* to mean *at that time* or *starting at that time.*
while vs. during	New arrivals waited **while** inspectors checked their documents. New arrivals waited **during** the inspection.	We use *while* with a clause. (Clause = subject + verb) We use *during* with a noun (phrase).
until	Ellis Island remained closed **until** 1990.	We use *until* to mean *before that time and ending at that time.*
in vs. after	I will become a citizen **in** two months. The plane will arrive **after** 9 p.m. My brother will come to the U.S. **after** he gets his visa.	We use *in* to mean after a period of time. We use *after* with a date, time or action.
ago vs. before	She got married three years **ago**. She got married **before** she came to the U.S. **Before** 1892, there was a different processing center.	We use *ago* to mean *before now.* We use *before* with an event, a date, or a time.

EXERCISE 1 Listen to this article about the Immigration Act of 1965. Fill in the blanks with the words you hear.

_____Until_____ 1892, the United States did not restrict any group of foreigners from
 1.

coming as immigrants. But _____ 1924, Congress passed a law to limit
                                      2.

immigration. _____ 1924 _____ 1965, the United States had a
                    3.   4.

quota system. That means only a limited number of people could come from each country.

_____ all those years, this system discriminated against certain foreigners.
        5.

Northern and Western Europeans received preference over other nationalities. Asians, in

particular, were not welcome.

_____ the 1960s, Americans started to see the quota system as a form of
            6.

discrimination. _____ President Kennedy was in office, he gave a speech about
                          7.

immigration restrictions. He called this system "intolerable." Members of Congress invited

experts to give their opinions. _____ their discussions, they said that very little
                                          8.

would change as a result of changing the law. Congress passed a bill to eliminate the quota

system. When President Johnson signed the bill into law _____ October 3,
                                                                        9.

1965, he said, "It does not affect the lives of millions." But he was completely wrong.

_____ the first five years _____ the bill passed, immigration
          10.   11.

from Asian countries increased by 400%. _____ the 1950s, 6 percent of
                                                    12.

immigrants were Asian. _____ the 1990s, 31 percent of immigrants were from
                                13.

Asian countries. Other immigrants and political refugees started coming from Africa and

Latin America. _____ the end of the twentieth century, there was a great
                        14.

change in the American population.

When we see the diversity in the United States today, it is hard to imagine that many years

_____, certain groups of people were not allowed into the United States.
        15.

EXERCISE 2 Circle the correct time word to fill in the blanks.

1. I stayed in my country (until/by) I got a visa.

2. I applied for my visa (in/on) January.

3. I waited (for/from) January (till/at) June to get my visa.

4. I was very excited (*when*/*while*) I got my visa.

5. I got my visa five years (*before*/*ago*).

6. (*While*/*During*) my trip to the U.S., I couldn't sleep.

7. (*While*/*During*) I was on the airplane, I couldn't sleep.

8. I never thought about learning English (*by*/*until*) I applied for my visa.

9. I arrived in New York (*on*/*in*) July 4, 2014.

10. I was at the airport (*during*/*for*) three hours.

11. (*Until*/*By*) 3:30 p.m., I passed through immigration and customs and was ready to start my life in the U.S.

12. I hope my parents will come here (*in*/*after*) a few years.

13. I hope my parents will come here (*during*/*after*) they get their visa.

EXERCISE 3 Fill in the blanks with one of the time words from chart 7.1.

1. My grandfather came to the U.S. _____*when*_____ he was 36 years old.

2. My grandfather came to the U.S. many years _____.

3. He lived in Poland _____ 1911.

4. He arrived at Ellis Island _____ May of 1911.

5. He was alone and scared. He was nervous _____ he was in line.

6. In Poland, he didn't study English. He didn't speak a word of English _____ he started to

work in the U.S. Then he learned a little.

7. My grandmother was without her husband _____ 1911 _____ 1921.

8. My grandfather worked _____ ten years to save money to bring his wife and children to the

U.S. Finally, _____ 1921, he sent money to bring his family.

9. _____ the long trip, my aunt became sick.

10. My grandmother arrived with my mother and her siblings _____ August 13, 1921.

11. _____ the inspectors examined them, they decided to put my aunt in the hospital.

My grandmother was afraid the officials would send them back.

12. _____ the end of the week, my aunt was better.

13. _____ my aunt felt better, she passed the health inspection. They all took a train to Chicago

and started their new life there.

EXERCISE 4 About You Complete each statement about leaving your country. Share your answers with a partner.

1. I stayed in my country until *I won the diversity lottery.*

2. During my trip to the U.S., _____

3. I traveled for _____

4. While I was on the airplane, _____

5. I arrived on _____

6. When I arrived, _____

7. I never knew _____ until I came to the U.S.

7.2 *When* and *Whenever*

Examples	Explanation
When I went to New York a few years ago, I visited Ellis Island.	*When* means *at that time* or *after that time*.
Whenever I go to New York, I enjoy myself.	*Whenever* means *any time* or *every time*.

Language Note:

In the present, *when* and *whenever* are often interchangeable.

When/Whenever my grandfather tells me about his life, I find it very interesting.

EXERCISE 5 Add a main clause to complete each statement. Share your answers with a partner.

1. Whenever people travel by airplane, _____ *they have to pass through security.*

2. Whenever passengers pass through security, _____

3. Whenever passengers are on an airplane, _____

4. Whenever people fly to another country, _____

5. Whenever immigrants come to the U.S., _____

6. Whenever I'm on an airplane, _____

7. When I got my visa, _____

8. When I arrived in the U.S., _____

Henri and Bridget
Refugees from Rwanda

Read the following article. Pay special attention to the words in bold.

The United States is home to many of the world's refugees. In 2013, the United States took in more refugees than any other country in the world. In 2012, the United States took in almost 60,000 refugees. These are people who ran away from their countries because their lives were in danger.

Henri and Bridget and their children are refugees from Rwanda, Africa. Rwanda has two major tribes: the Hutus and the Tutsis. Henri is a Hutu and his wife, Bridget, is a Tutsi. Henri **was working** in a hospital in 1994 when he **heard** the news: someone killed the president of Rwanda. Soon after, violence began. Members of the Hutu tribe started killing members of the Tutsi tribe. Because the family was in danger, they ran from their country. First they ran to Congo. But their lives were in danger there. Then they ran to Zambia. While they **were living** in a Zambian refugee camp, they didn't have enough food, and

their children didn't go to school. They applied to the UNHCR (United Nations High Commissioner for Refugees) for permission to come to the United States. In 2004, they got permission.

When they **arrived** in Chicago, a volunteer from a refugee agency **was waiting** to meet them at the airport. She took them to their new apartment and helped them get settled. Volunteers helped them adapt to their new life: they enrolled their children in school and got medical attention for the family. At first everything was very strange for them, but little by little life became easier.

When they became American citizens, they decided to go back to Rwanda to search for their families. They didn't know if their family members were dead or alive. Fortunately, most of their relatives survived. They **were living** in a refugee camp in Congo. Henri and Bridget took them back to Rwanda, where they are living today.

The names of the people in this story have been changed to protect their identities.

Refugee Arrivals by Country of Nationality: Fiscal Years 2010 to 2012
(Ranked by 2012 country of nationality)

Country of nationality	2012		2011		2010	
	Number	Percent	Number	Percent	Number	Percent
Total..	58,179	100.0	56,384	100.0	73,293	100.0
Bhutan.....................................	15,070	25.9	14,999	26.6	12,363	16.9
Burma	14,160	24.3	16,972	30.1	16,693	22.8
Iraq...	12,163	20.9	9,388	16.7	18,016	24.6
Somalia	4,911	8.4	3,161	5.6	4,884	6.7
Cuba..	1,948	3.3	2,920	5.2	4,818	6.6
Congo, Democratic Republic................	1,863	3.2	977	1.7	3,174	4.3
Iran	1,758	3.0	2,032	3.6	3,543	4.8
Eritrea	1,346	2.3	2,032	3.6	2,570	3.5
Sudan......................................	1,077	1.9	334	0.6	558	0.8
Ethiopia...................................	620	1.1	560	1.0	668	0.9
All other countries, including unknown	3,263	5.6	3,009	5.3	6,006	8.2

Source: U.S.. Department of State, Bureau of Population, Refugees, and Migration (PRM), Worldwide Refugee Admissions Processing System (WRAPS).

COMPREHENSION CHECK Based on the reading, tell if the statement is (**T**) true or (**F**) false.

1. In 2012, the United States took in 60,000 refugees from Africa.

2. When Henri and Bridget were living in Rwanda, they applied to the UNHCR for permission to go to the United States.

3. Volunteers from a refugee agency helped them in the United States.

7.3 The Past Continuous³—Form

To form the past continuous, we use *was* or *were* + the present participle (*-ing* form of the verb).

Subject	Was/Were (+ *not*)	Present Participle	
I	was	reading	about refugees.
Henri	was	working	in a hospital.
You	were	asking	about Rwanda.
They	were not	living	in Rwanda.

Language Notes:

1. The contraction for *was not* is *wasn't*. The contraction for *were not* is *weren't*.

2. We can put an adverb between *was/were* and the present participle.

> He was **already** studying English at that time.

Compare statements, *yes/no* questions, short answers, and *wh-* questions.

Statement	Yes/No Question & Short Answer	Wh- Question
They **were living** in Zambia in 2003.	**Were** they **living** in a home? No, they **weren't**.	Where **were** they **living**?
They **weren't living** in their country.	**Were** they **living** in a refugee camp? Yes, they **were**.	Why **were** they **living** in a refugee camp? Why **weren't** they **living** in their country?
A volunteer **was helping** them in the U.S.	**Was** the volunteer **helping** them with English? Yes, she **was**.	Who else **was helping** them?

EXERCISE 6 Listen to the conversation. Fill in the blanks with the words you hear.

CD 2
TR 9

A: Before you came to the U.S., <u>were you living</u> with your parents?
　　　　　　　　　　　　　　　　　　1.

B: No, I _____ . I _____ at the university in another city.
　　　　　　2.　　　　　　**3.**

A: What _____ you _____ ?
　　　　　　　　4.　　　　　　**5.**

---

³ The past continuous is also called the past progressive.

B: I _____ to become a doctor, but a war broke out. I ran to a refugee
6.

camp in Kenya. While I _____ in the refugee camp, I tried to get
7.

information about my family back home, but I couldn't.

A: That's terrible. While you _____ in the refugee camp,
8.

_____ you _____ to come to the U.S.?
9.   10.

B: Of course, I _____ about it. I _____ English
11.   12.

with the hope of coming to the U.S. I didn't know if I would get permission. But finally the

United Nations gave me permission.

A: Who _____ for you at the airport when you arrived?
13.

B: A man from a refugee agency. When I arrived, he _____ a sign with my
14.

name on it. He could easily identify me because I _____ a name tag.
15.

A: Did you ever find your family?

B: Yes, I did. They _____ in a refugee camp in Zambia.
16.

EXERCISE 7 Fill in the blanks with the past continuous form of the verb given. In some cases, you just
need to complete the short answer.

1.

    A: I read an article about Annie Moore, the first immigrant to come to Ellis Island. Did you read it too?

    B: Yes. She ___was traveling___ to the U.S. with her younger brothers.
                  a. travel

    A: ___Were they traveling___ with their parents too?
              b. they/travel

    B: No, they ___weren't___ .
                    c.

    A: Why ___weren't they traveling___ with their parents?
              d. they/not/travel

    B: Their parents came to the U.S. first. They ___were waiting___ for their
                                        e. wait

    children at Ellis Island.

2.

    A: What ___were you doing___ at about nine o'clock last night?
              a. you/do

    ___Were you sleeping___ ? I called you and texted you, but you didn't answer.
              b. you/sleep

    B: I ___was watching___ a program on TV about immigration.
              c. watch

    I ___was taking___ notes because I want to write an essay about it.
            d. take

continued

3.

    A: My great-grandmother came through Ellis Island.

    B: _____Did_____ alone?
                         a. she/travel

    A: No, she _____. She was just a little girl. She
                                            b.

      _____Immigrated_____ to the U.S. with her parents and her brother. Her aunt
                      c. immigrate

      _____ in the U.S.
                   d. already/live

4.

    A: Where _____ when you heard about the assassination of the
                    a. you/live

      president?

    B: We _____ in Rwanda.
               b. live

    A: _____ ?
           c. you/work

    B: Yes, I _____ .
                 d.

    A: Where _____ ?
              e. you/work

    B: At a hospital. My wife was at home. She _____ care of the
                                          f. take

      children.

7.4 The Past Continuous with a Specific Time

Examples	Explanation
In 1993, Henri **was working** in a hospital.	We use the past continuous to show what was in progress at a specific time in the past.

EXERCISE 8 About You Find a partner. Tell your partner if the following things were happening in your life in January 2014.

1. go to school

   I was (not) going to school in January 2014.

2. work

3. go to school

4. study English

5. live in the U.S.

6. live with my parents

EXERCISE 9 About You Find a partner. Ask each other questions with *"What were you doing . . . ?"* at these times.

1. at six o'clock this morning

   A: What were you doing at six o'clock this morning?

   B: I was sleeping.

2. at ten o'clock last night

3. at four o'clock this morning

4. at five o'clock yesterday afternoon

5. at this time yesterday

6. at this time last year

7.5 The Past Continuous with a *When* Clause

Example	Explanation
Henri **was working** in a hospital **when** he **heard** the news. **When** Annie Moore **arrived** at Ellis Island in 1892, her parents **were waiting** for her.	We use the past continuous with the simple past in the same sentence to show the relationship of a longer past action to a shorter past action. We use *when* + the simple past in the clause with the shorter action. We use the past continuous in the clause with the longer action.

Language Note:

If the main clause precedes the time clause, do not separate the two clauses with a comma.
If the time clause precedes the main clause, separate the two clauses with a comma.

He was working in a hospital when he heard the news.
When he heard the news, he was working in a hospital.

EXERCISE 10 Use the past continuous for the longer action and the simple past for the shorter action.

1. She _____was traveling_____ to the U.S. when she _____met_____ her future husband.
   a. travel   **b.** meet

2. When I _____ at the airport, my uncle _____ for me.
   a. arrive   **b.** wait

3. Henri and Bridgett _____ in a refugee camp when they

   _____ permission to come to the U.S.
   b. get

4. I _____ a program on TV about immigration when I _____
   a. watch   **b.** fall

   asleep.

5. We _____ in the U.S. when a war _____ out in our country.
   a. live   **b.** break

6. My wife _____ care of the kids at home when we _____ the
   a. take   **b.** hear

   news about the president.

7. When the first ship _____ at Ellis Island in 1892, reporters
   a. arrive

   _____ to write about the arrival of the first immigrants there.
   b. wait

8. I _____ to the airport to pick up my aunt and uncle when I
   a. drive

   _____ a flat tire.
   b. have

EXERCISE 11 About You Discuss the answers to these questions with a partner.

1. Who was waiting for you when you arrived in the U.S.?

2. What were you thinking about when you arrived in the U.S.?

Albert Einstein
Refugee from Germany

Albert Einstein takes the oath during his citizenship ceremony.

🎧 **Read the following article. Pay special attention to the words in bold.**

CD 2
TR 10

Of the many refugees who came to the United States, one will always be remembered throughout the world: Albert Einstein. Einstein changed our understanding of the universe.

Einstein was born in Germany in 1879 to Jewish parents. When he graduated from college in Switzerland in 1900, he was planning to become a teacher of physics and math, but he couldn't find a job in those fields. Instead, he went to work in a patent[4] office as a technical expert from 1902 to 1909. **While** he **was working** at this job, he **studied** and **wrote** in his spare[5] time. In 1905, when he was only twenty-six years old, he published three papers about the basic structure of the universe. His theory of relativity explained the relationship of space and time. He returned to Germany to accept a research position at the University of Berlin. However, in 1920, **while** he **was lecturing** at the university, anti-Jewish groups often **interrupted** his lectures, saying they were "un-German."

In 1921, Einstein visited the United States for the first time. During his visit, he talked not only about his scientific theories, but also about world peace. **While** he **was traveling** outside the country in 1933, the Nazis **came** to power in Germany. They took his property, burned his books, and removed him from his university job.

The United States offered Einstein refugee status, and, in 1940, he became a U.S. citizen. He received many job offers from all over the world, but he decided to accept a position at Princeton University in New Jersey. He lived and worked there until he died in 1955.

---

[4] *patent*: a document that identifies the owner of a new invention. Only the person or company who has the patent can sell the invention.
[5] *spare*: free

COMPREHENSION CHECK Based on the reading, tell if the statement is (**T**) true or (**F**) false.

1. Einstein taught math and physics while he was living in Switzerland.

2. In 1933, Einstein returned to his university job in Germany.

3. Einstein developed his theory of relativity while he was living in the United States.

7.6 The Past Continuous with a *While* Clause

Examples	Explanation
While Einstein **was living** in Switzerland, he **developed** his theory of relativity. **While** Einstein **was traveling** outside of Germany, the Nazis **came** to power.	We use the past continuous with the simple past in the same sentence to show the relationship of a longer past action to a shorter past action. We use *while* + the past continuous in the clause with the longer action. We use the simple past in the clause with the shorter action.
Einstein was living in the U.S. **when** he **died.** **While** he **was living** in the U.S., he wrote many papers.	We use *when* + the simple past with the shorter action. We use *while* + the past continuous with the longer action.

Language Notes:

1. We can use *when* in place of *while* with a continuous action.

    While Einstein was living in Switzerland, he developed his theory.

    When Einstein was living in Switzerland, he developed his theory.

2. We cannot use *while* with an action that has no continuation.

    NOT: Einstein was living in the U.S. *while* he died.

3. The simple past form of *be* often has a continuous meaning.

    While Einstein **was** outside the country, the Nazis took his property.

4. Sometimes we use the past continuous in both clauses if the two actions occurred at about the same time.

    While Einstein **was working** at the patent office, he **was thinking** about his theory.

5. Sometimes we use the simple past in both clauses if the two actions occurred at about the same time.

    New arrivals **waited** at Ellis Island while inspectors **checked** their documents.

EXERCISE 12 Use the past continuous for the longer action and the simple past for the shorter action.

1. While I __was traveling__ to the U.S., I _____met_____ a nice man on the airplane.
   a. travel   b. meet

2. Einstein _____ about his theory of relativity while he _____
   a. write   b. work

   in a patent office.

3. While he _____, some people _____ his lectures.
   a. teach   b. interrupt

4. While I _____ the story about Einstein, I _____ to use my
   a. read   b. have

   dictionary to look up the word "patent."

5. While I ___was waiting___ for permission to come to the U.S., I _____ to
   a. wait   b. start
   study English.

6. While the teacher ___was talking___ about immigration, one of the students
   a. talk
   ___asked___ an interesting question.
   b. ask

7. I ___watched___ a movie on the airplane while I ___was traveling___ to the U.S.
   a. watch   b. travel

EXERCISE 13 Fill in the blanks with the simple past or the past continuous of the verb given to complete this conversation.

A: I ___was looking___ through some old boxes when I ___found___ this picture of you and
   1. look   2. find
Grandpa when you were young. How did you meet Grandpa?

B: One day I ___was walking___ in the park in my hometown in Poland when he
   3. walk
___stopped___ me to ask what time it was. We started to talk, and then he asked
   4. stop
me to go for a cup of coffee with him. We dated, but a few months later his family applied for the

green card lottery in the U.S. While we ___were dating___, they ___received___
   5. date   6. receive
a letter that gave them permission to immigrate to the U.S.

A: What happened next?

B: At first, I was worried that I'd never see your grandfather again. But he ___wrote___
   7. write
to me often and ___called___ me whenever he could. About a year later, he went
   8. call
back to Poland to visit me. While we ___were eating___ in a restaurant, he
   9. eat
___asked___ me to marry him.
   10. ask

A: Did you get married right away?

B: Yes. We got married a few weeks later, but then he had to return to the U.S. I couldn't go to the U.S.

with him. I had to wait several years.

A: That's awful. What did you do while you ___were waiting___?
   11. wait

B: I took English classes. Finally, I got permission to come. When I ___arrived___ at
   12. arrive
the airport, he ___was waiting___ with roses and balloons.
   13. wait

7.7 Simple Past vs. Past Continuous with *When*

Both the simple past and the past continuous can be used in a sentence that has a *when* clause. However, the time sequence is completely different.

Examples	Explanation
When Einstein **graduated** from college, he **tried** to get a job as a teacher. Einstein **came** to live in the U.S. **when** he **lost** his German citizenship.	If we use the simple past in both clauses, *when* means *after*.
When Einstein **entered** college, he **was living** in Switzerland. Einstein **was living** in the U.S. **when** he **died**.	If we use the simple past after *when* and the past continuous in the main clause, *when* means *at the same time*.

EXERCISE 14 Fill in the blanks with the simple past or the past continuous of the verb given.

1. Henri _____was living_____ in a refugee camp when he got his visa.

a. live

   When he got to the U.S., he _____needed_____ to find a job.

b. need

2. He _____ in a hospital when he heard the news about the president.

a. work

   When he _____ permission, he came to the United States.

b. get

3. When they arrived in the U.S., volunteers _____ them.

a. help

   When they arrived in the U.S., a volunteer _____ for them at the airport.

b. wait

4. They _____ in the U.S. when their fourth child was born.

a. live

   When their fourth child was born, they _____ to a bigger apartment.

b. move

5. When Henri learned enough English, he _____ to work in a hotel.

a. start

   He _____ in a hotel when his daughter was born.

b. work

6. Henri _____ morning English classes when he found a job.

a. take

   Henri _____ to night classes when he found a job.

b. change

7. When Einstein entered college, he _____ to become a teacher.

a. study

   When Einstein entered college, he _____ in Switzerland.

b. live

8. Einstein _____ a resident of the U.S. when he lost his German citizenship.

a. become

   Einstein _____ in the U.S. when he died.

b. live

7.8 Using the *-ing* Form After Time Words

When the main clause and the time clause have the same subject, we can delete the subject of the time clause and use a present participle (verb + *-ing*) after the time word.

Examples
Einstein left high school **before he finished** his studies.
Einstein left high school **before finishing** his studies.
After Einstein left high school, he studied mathematics and physics.
After leaving high school, Einstein studied mathematics and physics.

Language Note:

In the second set of examples above, notice that the subject (Einstein) becomes part of the main clause.

EXERCISE 15 Change these sentences. Use a present participle after the time word. Make any other necessary changes.

1. After ~~Einstein entered~~ entering the university, ~~he~~ Einstein developed his theory.

2. Einstein passed an exam before he entered the university.

3. He left high school before he received his diploma.

4. After Einstein developed his theory of relativity, he became famous.

5. He became interested in physics after he received books on science.

6. After Einstein came to the U.S., he got a job at Princeton.

7. Before they came to the U.S., Henri and Bridget lived in Zambia.

8. While the children were living in the refugee camp, they didn't go to school.

9. The parents were working while they were raising a family.

EXERCISE 16 About You With a partner, discuss your experience of immigration. Was the process difficult? How did you feel during the process?

SUMMARY OF LESSON 7

Time with Dates, Days, Time Periods, etc.

Time Word	Examples
from . . . to till until	**From** 1892 **to** 1954, Ellis Island was an immigrant processing center. **From** 1892 **till** 1954, Ellis Island was an immigrant processing center. **From** 1892 **until** 1954, Ellis Island was an immigrant processing center.
during	**During** that time, 12 million immigrants passed through Ellis Island.
for	New arrivals had to wait **for** many hours.
in	**In** 1905, Einstein wrote about relativity. **In** the early 1900s, immigration was high. I became a resident **in** March. He'll take his citizenship test **in** six months.
by	Restoration of Ellis Island was finished **by** 1990.
ago	One hundred years **ago**, new arrivals passed through Ellis Island.
on	We came to the U.S. **on** Wednesday.
until	Ellis Island remained closed **until** 1990.
after	**After** class, I saw a movie about immigration.
before	He became a citizen **before** his twentieth birthday.

Time Words with Clauses

Time Word	Examples
when	**When** my grandfather came to the U.S., he passed through Ellis Island. Henri was working in a hospital **when** he heard the news about the president.
while	**While** Einstein was traveling, the Nazis took his property in Germany.
whenever	**Whenever** you enter the U.S., you have to make a declaration of things you're bringing in.
until	Ellis Island remained closed **until** the restoration was complete.

Uses of the Past Continuous

Use	Examples
To describe a past action that was in progress at a specific moment	At 9:45 a.m., I **was driving** to the airport to pick up my brother. Where **were** you **living** in December, 2013?
With the simple past, to show the relationship of a longer past action to a shorter past action	Einstein **was living** in New Jersey when he died. While Einstein **was living** in Switzerland, he developed his theory of relativity.

TEST / REVIEW

Circle the correct words to complete each statement.

1. (*While* / *When*) Ellis Island opened (*on* / *in*) January 1, 1892, seven hundred immigrants passed through.

2. (*During* / *For*) the early 1900s, immigration was high.

3. Ellis Island closed as an immigrant processing center (*in* / *at*) 1954.

4. (*When* / *While*) Annie Moore arrived with her two brothers, her parents (*waited* / *were waiting*) for them.

5. (*While* / *For*) many years, immigrants from Asian countries weren't welcome.

6. The immigration law didn't change (*until* / *by*) 1965, (*when* / *while*) President Johnson (*signed* / *was signing*) a new law.

7. President Johnson started restoration of Ellis Island. It was finished (*until* / *by*) 1990.

8. (*While* / *Whenever*) people enter another country, they have to pass through customs.

9. (*During* / *While*) we were visiting New York last year, we (*decided* / *were deciding*) to see the Statue of Liberty.

10. You can visit the Statue of Liberty (*of* / *from*) 8:30 a.m. (*till* / *at*) 5 p.m.

11. Einstein died while he (*was living* / *lived*) in Princeton, New Jersey.

12. He lived in the U.S. (*for* / *during*) twenty-two years.

13. I came to the U.S. five years (*before* / *ago*).

14. When I (*arrived* / *was arriving*) in the U.S., I was so happy.

15. Before (*to come* / *coming*) to the U.S., I studied English.

16. I will become a citizen (*after* / *in*) five years.

WRITING

PART 1 Editing Advice

1. Put the subject before the verb in all clauses.

   my mother came

   When ~~came my mother~~ to the U.S., our family was so happy.

2. Use *when*, not *while,* if the action has no duration.

   When

   ~~While~~ she arrived, we were waiting for her.

3. Be careful to choose the correct time word.

   for

   She traveled ~~during~~ ten hours.

   on

   She arrived ~~in~~ May 2.

4. Don't confuse *before* and *ago.*

   ago

   I came to the U.S. three years ~~before~~.

5. After a time word, use an *-ing* form, not a base form.

   learning

   After ~~learn~~ English, she found a job.

6. Don't forget *be* and *–ing* with the past continuous.

   ing

   At 9:30 last night, I was watch ʌ a program about immigration.

   were

   They ʌ talking about famous immigrants on this program.

PART 2 Editing Practice

Some of the shaded words and phrases have mistakes. Find the mistakes and correct them. If the shaded words are correct, write C.

I left my country three years ago. But my husband didn't come with me. C
1.

He wanted to stay in our country during two more years until he *for*
2.   3.

finished college. While I got here, I started to study English right away.
4.

While I going to school, I worked in the school library.
5.   6.

My husband was plan to get a degree in engineering when a war broke
7.   8.   9.

out in our country. When started the war, he left the country quickly
10.

and went to a neighboring country. He was in a refugee camp during one
11.

year. While he was living in the camp, he started to study English. He applied
12.

for permission to come to the U.S. After wait for one year, he finally got
13.

permission. When he was getting here, we were so excited to see each other again.
14.   15.

He's learning English quickly. After he learns English well enough, he's

going to enter an engineering program. I know he'll be happy until he gets
16.

his engineering degree.

PART 3 Write About It

1. Write about a major historical event that took place in your country or in another part of the world. What was happening when this event took place? What happened afterwards? If you research your essay, provide your sources.

2. Write about an important event that took place in your life or in the life of a famous person.

PART 4 Edit Your Writing

Reread the Summary of Lesson 7 and the editing advice. Edit your writing from Part 3.

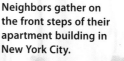

Neighbors gather on the front steps of their apartment building in New York City.

RULES and RECOMMENDATIONS

If you obey all the rules you miss all the fun.

—Katharine Hepburn

AN APARTMENT LEASE

A student packs her belongings before moving.

CD 2 TR 11

Read the following article. Pay special attention to the words in bold.

Do you live in an apartment? **Did** you **have to** sign a lease? **Could** you understand what you signed? A lease, or rental agreement, **can** be hard to read, but you **should** try to understand what you are signing.

Your lease is a legal agreement between the owner (landlord)[1] and you, the renter (tenant). A lease states the period of time for the rental, the amount of the rent, when the tenant **must** pay it, who pays for utilities,[2] and many rules the renter and the landlord **must** follow. Some leases contain the following rules:

- Pets **are not permitted**.

- Renters **may not** change the locks without the owner's permission.

- Renters **must** pay a late fee if they don't pay their rent on time.

The lease **might** even state how many overnight guests you **may** have and where you **can** or **cannot** park.

Many of the rules in the lease are for the benefit of the owner. The owner protects his or her property by requiring a security deposit. Usually a renter **has to** leave one to two months' rent as a deposit. The owner **can** use part or all of the money to repair damage the renter causes. However, the landlord **may not** keep the renter's money for normal wear and tear.[3]

There are also rules that protect the renter. For example, owners **must** provide heat during the winter months. In most cities, they **must** put a smoke detector in each apartment and in the halls. The owner **may not** raise the rent during the period of the lease.

When the landlord gives the renter the lease, it looks like an unchangeable document, but it isn't. Renters **don't have to** accept and sign the lease as is. If they don't agree to all the terms, they **can** ask for changes before they sign. For example, if you **would like** to have a pet, you **can** ask for permission by offering to pay a higher security deposit.

There **has to** be trust between the landlord and the renter. When looking for a new apartment, if you have a bad feeling about the landlord, you probably **ought to** look elsewhere.

---

[1] *landlord*: the owner of a rental property. If the owner is a woman, she is called "landlady."
[2] *utilities*: basic services such as water, electricity, or gas
[3] *normal wear and tear*: the normal use of an apartment

COMPREHENSION CHECK Based on the reading, tell if the statement is true (**T**) or false (**F**).

1. A renter cannot ask for changes to a lease.

2. The owner can use the security deposit to pay for a renter's damages.

3. The owner can raise the rent during the term of the lease.

8.1 Overview of Modals

The modal verbs are *can, could, should, would, may, might,* and *must.*

Examples	Explanation
A renter **must sign** a lease. A tenant **can ask** for changes before signing the lease.	The base form of the verb follows a modal. A modal never has an *-s* ending.
You **should not** pay your rent late. I **cannot** understand my lease.	To form the negative, we put *not* after the modal. The negative of *can* is written as one word: *cannot.* The contraction for *cannot* is *can't.*
If you don't trust the landlord, you **should probably look** for another apartment.	We can put an adverb between the modal and the main verb.

Observe these seven patterns with a modal:

AFFIRMATIVE STATEMENT:	We **can have** a cat in the apartment.
NEGATIVE STATEMENT:	We **can't have** a dog.
YES/NO QUESTION:	**Can** we **have** a bird?
SHORT ANSWER:	Yes, you **can**.
WH- QUESTION:	Why **can** we **have** a cat?
NEGATIVE *WH-* QUESTION:	Why **can't** we **have** a dog?
SUBJECT QUESTION:	Who **can have** a dog?

8.2 Phrasal Modals

Phrasal modals are expressions that are like modals in meaning.

Expressions	Examples
have to have got to be able to be supposed to be permitted to be allowed to ought to had better	He **has to** sign the lease. He **has got to** return the security deposit. He **is able to** pay the rent. I'm **supposed to** pay my rent by the first of the month. You **are not permitted to** park on the side of the building. You **are not allowed to** change the locks in your apartment. You **ought to** respect your neighbors. You **had better** read your lease carefully before signing it.

EXERCISE 1 Listen to these sentences about renting an apartment. Fill in the blanks with the words you hear.

1. When a lease is up for renewal, the owner _____*can*_____ offer the renter a new lease or he
   a.

   _____ ask the renter to leave.
        b.

2. The owner _____ notify the renter if he or she wants the renter to leave.
              a.

3. If you pay your rent late, you _____ have to pay a late fee.
                                  a.

4. If you want to make changes to the lease, you and the landlord _____ initial the changes.
                                                                    a.

5. What if you _____ move before the lease is up? What _____ you do?
                a.   b.

   You _____ inform the landlord as soon as possible.
           c.

6. _____ the landlord make you pay until the end of your lease? Yes, he _____.
        a.   b.

7. Some landlords _____ let you out of your lease by keeping your security deposit.
                   a.

   Or a landlord _____ make you pay until the end of your lease.
                  b.

8. The landlord _____ return your security deposit if there is no damage to the apartment.
                 a.

9. The landlord _____ obey the law. He _____ refuse to rent to a person
                 a.   b.

   because of sex, race, religion, nationality, or disability.

10. If the landlord doesn't keep his end of the agreement, you _____ need a lawyer.
                                                                a.

EXERCISE 2 Read each statement. Fill in the blanks to complete the question.

1. You should read the lease before you sign it. Why _____*should I*_____ read the lease before I sign it?

2. I can't have a dog. Why _____ a dog?

3. We must pay a security deposit. How much _____ ?

4. Someone must install a smoke detector. Who _____ a smoke detector?

5. The landlord must return the security deposit. When _____ it?

6. The landlord said I can pick up the key tomorrow. What time _____ the key?

8.3 Obligation/Necessity—*Must* and Phrasal Modals

Must	Phrasal Modal	Explanation
The landlord **must** provide smoke detectors.	The landlord **has to** provide smoke detectors.	We use *must* and *have to* for rules and obligations. *Must* is more formal than *have to*.
	I **'ve got to** call my landlord today. I **have to** tell him about a problem in my bathroom.	We use *have to* or *have got to* for personal obligations or necessities.
	At the end of my lease last June, I **had to** move. I **had to** find a bigger apartment.	*Must* has no past form. The past of both *must* and *have to* is *had to*.

Language Notes:

1. *Have got to* is usually contracted with a subject pronoun:

    I have got to = I've got to

    He has got to = He's got to

2. We don't use *have got to* for questions and negatives.

3. Many legal documents use *shall* for obligation.

    If the security deposit does not cover the cost of damages, the tenant shall pay additional costs to the owner.

Pronunciation Note: In informal speech, *have to* is often pronounced "hafta." *Has to* is often pronounced "hasta." *Got to* is often pronounced "gotta." Often *have* is omitted in speech before *got to*. In informal writing, people often write "gotta." (I gotta go now.)

EXERCISE 3 Fill in the blanks with one of the items from the box. Use the correct form of *have*.

have to notify	have to move	must put	must give ✓
have got to obey	have to sign	have to return	have got to clean

1. The landlord _____*must give*_____ you heat in cold weather.

2. You _____ the lease with a pen. A pencil is not acceptable.

3. The landlord _____ your security deposit if you leave your apartment

   in good condition.

4. The landlord _____ you if he wants you to leave at the end of your lease.

5. The landlord _____ a smoke detector in each apartment and in the hallways.

6. I _____ the rules of the lease.

7. My new apartment is dirty. I _____ it before I move in.

8. My old apartment was too expensive, so I _____ last month.

EXERCISE 4 About You Make a list of personal obligations you, your roommate, or your family members have in your apartment or house. Practice *have to* and *have got to*. Share your answers with a partner.

1. I've got to throw out the garbage twice a week.

2. My roommate has to clean the kitchen on the weekend.

3. _____

4. _____

5. _____

EXERCISE 5 About You Make a list of things you had to do last weekend. Share your answers with a partner.

1. I had to do my laundry.

2. _____

3. _____

4. _____

8.4 Permission/Prohibition—*May* and Phrasal Modals

May	Phrasal Modals	Explanation
The landlord **may** enter the apartment in case of emergency. The tenant **may not** leave items in the hallway.	The landlord **is permitted to** enter the apartment in case of emergency. The tenant **is not allowed** to leave items in the hallway.	We can use *may, be permitted to,* and *be allowed to* for permission or prohibition. We often see *may* in legal documents.

Language Notes:

1. *May not* and *must not* have the same meaning—prohibition.

   Tenants **may not** park behind the building.

   Tenants **must not** park behind the building.

2. Many legal documents use *shall* (*not*) for permission or prohibition.

   The tenant **shall not** change the locks without the owner's permission.

   The tenant **may not** leave personal items in the hallway.

EXERCISE 6 The rules for driving in the United States are somewhat different from state to state, but many are similar in most or all states. Fill in the blanks with one of the phrases from the box to complete each sentence.

aren't allowed to ride	must reduce	may not go	have to go
aren't permitted to hold	may drive	must have	must wear ✓
may not pass	have to get	may not park	may use

1. You _____ *must wear* _____ a seatbelt.

2. If you are from another state or another country, you _____ *may drive* _____ with a valid license. However, you _____ *have to get* _____ a license in the state where you're living (usually within ninety days).

3. You _____ *may not park* _____ in a disabled parking space unless your vehicle has a disabled license plate or a removable windshield card.

4. Bicycle riders _____ *aren't allowed to ride* _____ against traffic. They _____ *have to go* _____ in the same direction as traffic.

5. A driver _____ *must have* _____ insurance.

6. You _____ *may not pass* _____ on a hill or curve if you are not able to see the oncoming vehicles.

7. In many places, you _____ *are not permitted to hold* (aren't) a cell phone in your hand while driving. However, you _____ *may use* _____ a hands-free device.

8. Drivers _____ *must reduce* _____ their speed in a school zone during school hours.

9. When a school bus stops for children to get on or off, you _____ *may not go* _____ around it.

8.5 Expectation—*Be Supposed To*

Examples	Explanation
The landlord **is supposed to** give you a copy of the lease. When **am I supposed** to pay the rent? My friend **is supposed to** help me move.	*Be supposed to* expresses an expectation. We expect something because of • a law or a requirement • a personal obligation
We**'re not supposed to** have cats in my building, but my neighbor has one. I **was supposed to** pay my rent yesterday, but I forgot.	We use *be supposed to* when someone broke a rule or did not meet an expectation.

Pronunciation Note: We don't pronounce the *d* in *supposed to.*

EXERCISE 7 Finish these statements. Use *be supposed to* (present or past, affirmative or negative) and one of the verbs from the box.

use	paint	provide	pay✓	clean	take out
return	fix	replace	wash	have	

1. I _m supposed to pay_ my rent on the first of the month.

2. Pets are not permitted in my apartment. I _'m not supposed to have_ a pet.

3. In which months _is_ the landlord _supposed to provide_ heat?

4. The tenants _are supposed to clean_ the apartment before they move out.

5. My stove isn't working. My landlord _is supposed to fix_ it tomorrow.

6. We're going to move out next week. Our apartment is clean and in good condition. The landlord _is supposed to return_ our security deposit.

7. The janitor _is supposed to take out_ the garbage every day.

8. When we moved in, we _were supposed to use_ the back stairs, not the front stairs.

9. My smoke detector doesn't work. The landlord _is supposed to replace_ it.

10. My landlord _was supposed to paint_ the walls of my apartment last month, but he didn't do it. I'm still waiting.

11. My roommate _was supposed to wash_ the dishes last night, but she forgot.

8.6 Ability/Permission—*Can, Could,* and Phrasal Modals

Can/Could	Phrasal Modals	Explanation
I **can** clean the apartment by Friday. I **can't** understand the lease.	I **am able to** clean the apartment by Friday. I **am not able to** understand the lease.	Ability/ Inability
I **could** understand the first page of the lease. I **couldn't** understand the rest of lease.	I **was able to** understand the first page of the lease. I **wasn't able to** understand the rest of the lease.	Past Ability/ Inability
I **can** have a cat in my apartment. I **can't** have a dog.	I **am permitted to** have a cat. I **am not allowed to** have a dog.	Permission/ Prohibition
I **could** have a cat in my last apartment, but I **couldn't** have a dog.	I **was permitted to** have a cat in my last apartment, but I **wasn't allowed** to have a dog.	Past Permission/ Prohibition

Language Notes:

1. We also use *may* for permission. *May* is more formal than *can.*

2. A common expression with *can* is *can(not) afford.*

   I **can afford** a one-bedroom apartment. I **can't afford** a two-bedroom apartment.

Pronunciation Note: *Can* is not usually stressed in affirmative statements. In negative statements, *can't* is stressed but it is hard to hear the final *t*. So we must pay attention to the vowel sound and stress to hear the difference between *can* and *can't*.

I can "go." /kIn/   I "can't" go. /kænt/

In a short answer, we pronounce *can* as /kæn/.

Can you help me later?   Yes, I can. /kæn/

EXERCISE 8 Fill in the blanks with one of the words from the box below to complete this conversation.

can't carry	can give	can't do	couldn't reach
wasn't able to find	're not allowed to use✓	can you put	can cook
'm not allowed to leave	're not permitted to use	are you able to wash	can't afford

A: How do you like your new apartment?

B: The apartment is great. But I don't like some of the rules. For example,

we _'re not allowed to use_ the laundry room after 11 p.m. I work late, and I
.......................1.

can't do my laundry in the daytime.
..........2.

A: _Are you able to wash_ your clothes on Sundays?
.........3.

B: Yes, but that's when most people do their laundry. Also, I like to barbecue on the porch. But

we _'re not permitted to use_ a fire grill. We _can cook_ on a gas grill, but
.........4.   5.

I prefer a fire grill. Here's another problem. I use my bike every day, but

I _'m not allowed to leave_ it in the hallway. I'm on the third floor, and there's no elevator.
.........6.

I _can't carry_ my bike upstairs every day.
.........7.

A: _Can you put_ your bike in the basement?
.........8.

B: I don't know. I don't have a key to the basement. I called the landlord yesterday to ask him

about it, but I _couldn't reach_ him.
.........9.

A: Try again. Is your roommate happy with the apartment?

B: I don't have a roommate. I _wasn't able to find_ one. But the rent is high, and
.........10.

I _can't afford_ it on my own.
.........11.

A: I have a friend who's looking for a roommate. I _can give_ you his phone
.........12.

number.

B: Thanks.

SMOKE
Detectors

A firefighter stands on a ladder while fighting a fire at an apartment building.

CD 2
TR 13

Read the following article. Pay special attention to the words in bold.

Fire kills approximately 3,400 people each year, including about one hundred firefighters and over four hundred children under nine years old. Children set over 35,000 fires each year. Children have a natural curiosity about fire, so it's important to teach them that fire is a tool, not a toy. They must learn that they**'d better not** play with matches. You **should** keep matches and lighters locked up.

A smoke alarm greatly reduces your chances of being hurt in a fire. The primary job of a smoke alarm is to protect you while you're asleep. You **should** have a smoke alarm outside each bedroom and on each level of a home. You **ought to** have two emergency escape plans and practice escaping in the dark with your family. You **should** designate[4] a place to meet outside of the house. That way you can account for all family members.

A smoke alarm warns you of the danger. But when you hear it go off, you don't have much time. You**'d better** take action immediately. When you come to a closed door, you **should** check it with the back of your hand. If it feels hot, smoke or fire may be blocking your exit, so use your secondary escape route. Smoke harms people more than fire. If there is already smoke, you **should** crawl under it to exit the house. Call 9-1-1 from a neighbor's house. If a family member or a pet is missing, you **shouldn't** go back in. The fire department knows how to perform rescues safely.

A smoke alarm is only good if it's working properly. Replace the batteries at least once a year. You **should** use the test button each month to see if the alarm and batteries are working properly. A smoke alarm lasts about ten years. You **ought to** replace it even if it seems to be working.

About two out of three fire deaths happen in homes with no working smoke alarms. Most of these deaths can be prevented.

---

4 *to designate*: to point out, mark, or indicate

COMPREHENSION CHECK Based on the reading, tell if the statement is true (**T**) or false (**F**).

1. If a door feels hot, it can be dangerous to open it.

2. You should have a smoke alarm in every room of the house.

3. If you can't find all your family members or pets once you're outside, you should go back inside and look for them.

8.7 Advice—*Should, Ought To, Had Better*

Examples	Explanation
You **should** have a smoke alarm outside the bedrooms. You **shouldn't** go back into a burning building.	For advice, we use *should*. *Should* = It's a good idea. *Shouldn't* = It's a bad idea.
You **ought to** have two emergency escape plans.	*Ought to* means the same as *should*. We don't usually use *ought to* in questions and negatives.
When you hear the alarm, you **had better** take action immediately. We**'d better** leave quickly. The door feels hot. You**'d better not** open it.	When it is probable that something bad or unpleasant will happen, we use *had better (not)*. The contraction for *had* (in *had better*) is *'d*. I'd you'd he'd she'd we'd they'd

Language Note:

Must is for obligation or necessity, not for advice.

Compare:

Your landlord **must** give you a smoke detector. (obligation)

You **should** change the batteries once a year. (advice)

Pronunciation Note:

Native speakers often don't pronounce *had* or the *'d* in *had better*. You will hear people say,

You better get out of the house quickly; **you better** not try to save objects.

EXERCISE 9 Work with a partner. Take turns asking for and giving advice. Write your partner's advice on the line.

1. I'm going to move next week, and I hope to get my security deposit back.

   You should (or ought to) clean the apartment completely.

2. I just rented an apartment, but the rent is too high for me alone.

   _____

3. My upstairs neighbors make a lot of noise.

   _____

continued

4. I don't have enough batteries in the house for my smoke detectors.

_____

5. I want to paint the walls.

_____

6. My landlady doesn't provide enough heat in the winter.

_____

7. There is no smoke alarm near the bedroom.

_____

8. The landlord is going to raise the rent by 40 percent.

_____

EXERCISE 10 Fill in the blanks with one of the phrases from the box. Answers may vary.

ought to keep	shouldn't place	should pay✓	should unplug	'd better get out
shouldn't throw	should shut off	should never put	should always stay	

1. You _____ _should pay_ _____ attention to electrical cords in your house.

2. If the cord has an unusual smell or makes sparks, you _____ the

appliance immediately.

3. You _____ the cord of an appliance when not in use.

4. Most home fires occur in the kitchen while cooking. You _____ a fire

extinguisher near the cooking area.

5. You _____ a smoke detector near a stove. The smoke from cooking can

set it off unnecessarily.

6. You _____ in the kitchen while cooking.

7. If the room is filled with smoke, you _____ immediately. Don't wait!

8. If you use a microwave oven, you _____ anything with metal in it.

Metal can cause sparks and a fire.

9. You _____ compact fluorescent light (CFL) bulbs in the garbage when they

burn out. They contain mercury, which may be harmful. Find a place that disposes of them properly.

EXERCISE 11 Fill in the blanks with an appropriate verb (phrase) from the box to complete the conversation.

not wait	not use	take off✓	check	turn off
to have	get	have	to change	blow

A: I just moved into my first apartment, and my mother is so worried about me.

B: What is she worried about?

A: Everything. She tells me I'd better _____*take off*_____ my shoes when I enter the apartment
                                          1.

so my neighbors downstairs won't hear me walking around. She says I'd better

_____ the TV at 10 o'clock, or the neighbors won't be able to sleep. She also
        2.

tells me to check the batteries in my smoke detector once a month.

B: I agree that you should _____ them often, but once a month is excessive. They
                                      3.

say you ought _____ batteries twice a year.
                    4.

A: I only change my batteries when I hear the smoke detector beep.

B: You'd better _____ so long.
                          5.

A: Maybe you're right. My mother also says I ought _____ a fire extinguisher in
                                                              6.

the kitchen.

B: I read that that's a very good idea. Cooking is the major cause of home fires.

A: She thinks I'd better _____ candles in the house. But I like to use candles for
                                  7.

atmosphere when I'm having a party.

B: That's ok. But you should _____ them out immediately after the party.
                                        8.

A: And, of course, my mother says I shouldn't _____ any parties because I might
                                                          9.

disturb the neighbors.

B: I think your mother worries too much. She should _____ a hobby and let you live
                                                                10.

your own life. You're eighteen. You're an adult now.

8.8 Negatives of Modals

Examples	Explanation
Tenants **are not supposed** to leave bikes near the door, but someone always does it.	*Be not supposed to* shows that something is not acceptable by rule or custom.
Renters **must not** change the locks. Renters **may not** change the locks. Renters **cannot** change the locks. Renters **are not permitted to** change the locks. Renters **are not allowed to** change the locks.	*Must not, may not, cannot, be not allowed to,* and *be not permitted to* show prohibition.
I **cannot** reach the smoke detector. I **am not able to** reach the smoke detector.	*Cannot* and *be not able to* show inability.
You **shouldn't** go back into a burning building.	*Shouldn't* shows that something is not advisable.
Renters **don't have to** accept the lease as is. They can ask for changes.	*Don't have to* shows that something is not necessary. It often means that there is an option.
You **had better not** make noise at night. You can disturb your neighbors.	*Had better not* shows that a negative consequence can result.

Language Note:

Even though *have to* and *must* have basically the same meaning in the affirmative, in the negative they are completely different.

> You **must** sign the lease. = You **have to** sign the lease.

> The landlord **doesn't have to** renew the lease. (He has a choice.)

> He **must not** enter your apartment without your permission. (This is prohibited.)

EXERCISE 12 Circle the correct words to complete this list of advice on living in the United States. In some cases, both answers are possible, so circle both options.

1. Americans are generally on time for appointments. You (*can't*/*shouldn't*) keep people waiting.

2. You (*shouldn't*/*must not*) visit friends without an invitation. If someone says, "Let's get together sometime," wait for a specific invitation.

3. Americans don't like to wait in line but if they have to, they're usually courteous.

   You (*shouldn't*/*don't have to*) push to try to get ahead of someone.

4. Bribing[5] an official is against the law. You (*must not*/*don't have to*) offer a bribe if a police officer gives you a ticket or a government official turns down your application.

---

[5] *bribing*: the illegal act of offering money in exchange for something

5. When you buy new items in a store, you (*had better not/shouldn't*) try to negotiate the price. Prices in stores are fixed. However, a major exception is when buying a new car. You (*don't have to/must not*) pay the asking price. The price is negotiable.

6. You (*may not/must not*) drive without insurance in the U.S. You (*must/have to*) have insurance to protect the other car and driver. You (*don't have to/must not*) have insurance to protect your own car.

7. In most places, you (*may not/can't*) use a hand-held cell phone while driving.

8. A driver's license is often used for identification, but you (*must not/don't have to*) have a driver's license. You can get a state ID. A state ID looks like a driver's license, but you (*can't/aren't allowed to*) drive a car with it.

9. If you have a Social Security number, you (*shouldn't/can't*) give it to strangers over the phone. Someone can steal your identify and cause you a lot of problems.

10. Americans are very casual. If you're invited to an informal party at someone's house, you (*don't have to/may not*) dress up.

11. If you are invited to a party, you (*aren't supposed to/don't have to*) bring anything, but many guests will come with something to eat, such as a dessert, or something to drink. When you leave, you (*shouldn't/may not*) take that food or drink home. It's the custom to leave it there.

12. If you are invited to a formal wedding, you (*aren't supposed to/must not*) take children unless the invitation specifically invites them.

EXERCISE 13 Fill in the blanks with the negative of *have to, should, be supposed to, must, had better, can,* or *may* to complete the conversation between students (A) and their teacher (B). In some cases, more than one answer is possible.

A: Do I have to sit in a specific seat for the test?

B: No, you _____ don't have to _____ . You can choose any seat you want.
1.

A: Is it OK if I talk to another student during a test?

B: No. Absolutely not. You _____ talk to another student
2.

during a test.

A: Is it OK if I use my book?

B: Sorry. You _____ use your book.
3.

continued

A: What if I don't understand something on the test?

B: Please ask me if you have a question.

A: What happens if I'm late for the test? Will you let me in?

B: Of course I'll let you in. But you _____ come late. You'll need a

4.

lot of time for the test.

A: Do I have to bring my computer for the final test?

B: If you want to, you can. But you _____ bring it.

5.

There will be school computers you can use.

A: Do I have to write my final essay on the computer? Or can I use a pen and paper?

B: You can use whatever you want. You _____ use a computer.

6.

A: Do you have any advice on test-taking?

B: Yes. On the grammar section, if you see an item that is difficult for you, go on to the next item.

You _____ spend too much time on a difficult item, or you

7.

won't finish the test.

A: Can I bring coffee into the classroom?

B: The school has a rule about eating or drinking in the classroom. You

_____ bring food or drinks into the classroom.

8.

A: How long will we have for the test?

B: You'll have two hours. That's usually enough time. If you finish early, you

_____ stay. You can leave.

9.

Starting Life
IN A NEW COUNTRY

An immigrant shares this space with three other immigrants.

Read the following article. Pay special attention to the words in bold.

You're about to go to college in the United States. Or your family just moved to the United States. Your friends back home tell you, "It **must** be so exciting to live in a new country." But there are so many new rules and customs to learn. After the excitement wears off,[6] there are many questions you'll have and decisions you have to make.

Now you're here and you find yourself in situations that are completely new to you. You might ask yourself: "Should I buy a car or use public transportation? Should I get a roommate? If so, how and where? How do I find a doctor? Where do I get insurance? How do I find a job? When and where do I tip?" There **must** be hundreds of things you never thought about before.

Besides questions you have about life in the United States, you're probably discovering that many Americans are curious about you. Of course, they'll ask you where you're from. Keep in mind that they **might not** know much about your country. If you say Cambodia, for example, they **may** have no idea where this is. They **might not** have an understanding of the differences between Asians. If you say you're Asian, they might say, "Then you **must** be Chinese, right?" If you're Korean, Japanese, Vietnamese, or from any other country in Asia, these questions **might** seem silly. Be patient with Americans and gently explain where you're from and what language you speak. If you speak Spanish and come from Mexico or Guatemala, some Americans **might** say: "Oh, you're Spanish." People who say that **must not** know that "Spanish" refers only to the language or to people from Spain. If you're from Brazil, they **might** think you speak Spanish even though the language of Brazil is Portuguese.

Again, be patient. With time, you'll learn more about American behaviors, and others will learn more about you and your native culture.

---

[6] to wear off: to go away, little by little

COMPREHENSION CHECK Based on the reading, tell if the statement is (**T**) true or (**F**) false.

1. Americans are often curious about foreigners.

2. Some Americans think that all Asians are Chinese.

3. Everyone knows that *Spanish* refers to people from Spain.

8.9 Conclusions or Deductions—*Must*

Examples	Explanation
It **must** be so exciting to live in another country. You **must** find yourself in so many new situations. You're from Mexico? You **must** speak Spanish, then.	We often make a deduction or come to a conclusion using *must*. We think our assumption is probably true. (We may be wrong.)
I told a classmate that I'm from Brazil. He thinks I speak Spanish. He **must not** know much about Brazil.	For a negative deduction/conclusion, we use *must not*. We don't use a contraction.

Language Note:

Remember: We also use *must* to express necessity.

EXERCISE 14 Fill in the blanks with an appropriate verb phrase from the box to complete the conversation between two neighbors. You may use an answer more than once.

must spend	must have	must get	must not like
must know	must not be	must be	

A: Hi. My name's Alma. I live on the third floor. You _____ must be _____ new in this

1.

building.

B: I am. We just moved in last week. My name's Eva.

A: I noticed your last name on the mailbox. It's Gonzalez. Are you from Mexico?

B: No. Actually I'm from the Philippines.

A: I'm so sorry. You _____ must get _____ that mistake all the time. Are you going to

2.

school now?

B: Yes, I'm taking English classes at Washington College. I'm in Level 5.

A: You _____ must know _____ my husband, Hasan. He's also in the Level 5 class there.

3.

B: Oh, yes, I know him. I didn't know he lived in the same building. I never see him here. He

_____ must not be _____ home very much.

4.

A: He isn't. He has two jobs. By the way, I saw the movers carrying in a crib.

You ___must have___ a baby.
5.

B: We do. We have a ten-month-old son. He's sleeping now. Do you have any kids?

A: Yes. I have a sixteen-year-old-daughter and an eighteen-year-old son. I

___must spend___ half my time worrying about them. My daughter texts her
6.

friends all day.

B: Kids today ___must not like___ to talk much. They rely more on texting.
7.

A: You're right. Listen, I don't want to take up any more of your time. You

___must have___ a lot to do. I just wanted to bring you these cookies.
8.

B: That's very nice of you. They're still warm. They ___must be___ right out of
9.

the oven.

A: They are. Maybe we can talk some other time when you're all unpacked.

EXERCISE 15 Use *must* + base form to show Eva's conclusions about Alma's life when she is visiting Alma in her apartment. Answers may vary.

1. There is a bowl of food on the kitchen floor.

Alma's family must have a pet.

2. There is a nursing certificate on the wall with Alma's name on it.

_____

3. There are many different kinds of coffee on a kitchen shelf.

_____

4. There are a lot of classical music CDs.

_____

5. In Alma's bedroom, there's a sewing machine.

_____

6. There's a piano in the living room.

_____

7. On the kitchen calendar, there's an activity filled in for almost every day of the week.

_____

8.10 Possibility—*May/Might*

Examples	Explanation
Americans **might** ask you some strange questions. They **may** have little or no knowledge of your country.	*May* and *might* both have about the same meaning: possibility or uncertainty about the present.
They **may not** know much about your country. They **might not** know the difference between a Spanish person and a Spanish-speaking person.	For the negative, we use *may not* or *might not*. We don't use a contraction for these negatives.
I **may** get a roommate next semester. I **might** get a roommate next semester.	*May* and *might* can give a future meaning.

Language Notes:

1. *Maybe* is an adverb. It is one word. It usually comes at the beginning of the sentence and means *possibly* or *perhaps*. *May* and *might* are modals. They follow the subject and precede the verb.

   > **Maybe** he **is** Mexican. = He **may be** Mexican. = He **might be** Mexican.
   >
   > **Maybe** I **will get** a roommate next semester. = I **may get** a roommate next semester. = I **might get** a roommate next semester.

2. Remember, *must* shows a conclusion, an assumption, or a deduction.

   Compare:
   > You're from Mexico. You must speak Spanish. (assumption)
   > He speaks Spanish. He might be from Guatemala or Peru. (possibility)

EXERCISE 16 Take away *maybe* from each of the following sentences and rewrite the sentences using the modal given.

1. Maybe some questions seem silly to you. (*may*)

   Some questions may seem silly to you.

2. Maybe Americans don't know much about your country. (*may*)

   _____

3. Maybe you will become impatient with some questions. (*might*)

   _____

4. If you say you speak Spanish, maybe an American will say, "Oh, you're Spanish." (*may*)

   _____

5. Maybe you will be confused at times. (*may*)

   _____

6. Maybe Americans ask you some strange questions. (*might*)

_____

7. Maybe you will learn about Americans from their questions. (*might*)

_____

EXERCISE 17 Fill in the blanks with a verb to show possibilities. Answers may vary.

1. **A:** I'm going to move on Saturday. I'm going to need help. Can you help me?

   B: I'm not sure. I may _____ go _____ away this weekend.

                                    a.

2. **A:** My next-door neighbor's name is Terry Karson. I see her name on the doorbell but I never see her.

   B: Your neighbor may _____ be _____ a man. Terry is sometimes a man's name.

                                    a.

3. **A:** I need coins for the laundry room. Do you have any?

   B: Let me look. I might _____ have _____ some. No, I don't have any. Look in the laundry room.

                                          a.

   There might _____ be _____ a dollar-bill changer there.

                                b.

4. **A:** Do you know the landlord's address?

   B: No, I don't. Ask the manager. She might _have it_ ~~know it~~ .

                                                  a.

5. **A:** Do they allow cats in this building?

   B: I know they don't allow dogs, but they might _____ allow _____ cats.

                                                              a.

6. **A:** Are you going to stay in this apartment for another year?

   B: I'm not sure. I may _____ stay _____ . The landlord might _____ raise _____ the rent. If the rent

                              a.   **b.**

   goes up more than 25 percent, I'll move.

7. **A:** I have so much stuff in my closet. There's not enough room for my clothes.

   B: There might _____ be _____ lockers in the basement where you can store your things.

                                a.

   A: Really? I didn't know that.

   B: Let's look. I may _____ have _____ a key to the basement with me.

                                    b.

   A: That would be great.

8. **A:** When I tell people I'm from Korea, they ask me if I speak Chinese. I get so mad.

   B: Don't get mad. Be patient and teach them something. They may _____ learn _____ something

                                                                                  a.

   new from you.

At a **GARAGE SALE**

Read the following article. Pay special attention to the words in bold.

People often have a garage sale, a yard sale, or an apartment sale before they move. They **would like** to get rid of[7] things they don't want or need anymore. If you are the buyer, you can bargain[8] with the seller for less than the asking price. This should be a friendly, polite, direct conversation.

This is a conversation between a buyer and a seller that you might hear at a garage sale.

A: **May** I help you? I see you're looking at my microwave oven. **May** I answer any questions?

B: Yes. I'm interested in buying it, but I**'d like** to see how well it works.

A: It's in perfect working condition. **Would** you **like** to try it out right now?

B: Sure. **Could** you plug it in somewhere?

A: I have an outlet right here. **Why don't we** boil a cup of water so you can see how well it works?

(A few minutes later)

B: It seems to work well. **Would** you tell me why you're selling it, then?

A: We're moving next week. Our new apartment already has one.

B: How much do you want for it?

A: $40.

B: **Will** you take $30?

A: **Can** you wait a minute? I'll ask my wife.

(A few minutes later)

A: My wife says she'll let you have it for $35.

B: OK. **May** I write you a check?

A: I'm sorry. I**'d rather** have cash.

B: **Would** you hold it for me for an hour? I can go to the ATM and get cash.

A: **Could** you leave me a small deposit? Ten dollars, maybe?

B: Yes, I can.

A: Fine. I'll hold it for you.

People look at things for sale at a yard sale

---

7 *to get rid of*: to throw away or discard an unwanted item
8 *to bargain*: to negotiate for a lower price

COMPREHENSION CHECK Based on the reading, tell if the statement is (**T**) true or (**F**) false.

1. The buyer pays $40 for the microwave.

2. The buyer pays by cash.

3. The buyer has enough cash with him.

8.11 Using Modals for Politeness

Examples	Explanation
May **Can** **Could** } I write you a check?	We use *may, can,* or *could* + *I* to ask for permission.
Can **Could** **Will** **Would** } you plug it in?	We use *can, could, will,* or *would* + *you* to make a request.
Would you **like** to try out the microwave oven? Yes. I**'d like** to see if it works.	*Would like* has the same meaning as *want. Would like* is softer than *want.* The contraction for *would* after a pronoun is *'d.*
I **would rather** buy a used microwave **than** a new one. I**'d rather** not spend a lot of money. **Would** you **rather** pay with cash **or** by check? I**'d rather** pay by check.	*Would rather* shows a preference of choices. We use *than* in statements. We use *or* in questions. The second choice can be omitted if it's obvious. The contraction for *would* after a pronoun is *'d.* The negative is *would rather not.*
Why don't you go to the ATM to get cash? **Why don't we** boil a cup of water?	We can use a negative question to offer a polite suggestion.
May I help you? **Can** I help you?	In a shopping situation, the salesperson often uses these questions.

Language Notes:

1. When asking for permission, some English speakers think it is more polite to use *may* or *could* rather than *can.*

2. When making a request, some English speakers think it is more polite to use *could* or *would* rather than *can* and *will.*

EXERCISE 18 Make the language of this conversation between a buyer and seller more polite or softer by using modals and other polite expressions in place of the underlined words. Answers may vary.

A: <u>What do you want?</u> *May I help you?*
           1.

B: I'm interested in that lamp. <u>Show it to me</u>. Does it work?
                                    2.

A: I'll go and get a light bulb. <u>Wait a minute</u>.
                                     3.

B: <u>Let's plug it in.</u>
         4.

(*A few minutes later*)

A: Good idea. You see? It works fine.

B: How much do you want for it?

A: I have two of them. They're $10 each. I <u>prefer to sell</u> them together.
                                               5.

B: <u>Give them both to me for $15.</u>
              6.

A: I'll sell them to you for $17.

B: Great. How about this TV? Does it work?

A: <u>Try it out.</u>
          7.

B: It seems fine. <u>I want to take</u> the TV and the two lamps. <u>I'll write you a check.</u>
                        8.   9.

A: <u>I prefer to have cash.</u>
          10.

B: I only have five dollars on me.

A: OK. I'll take a check. <u>Show me some identification.</u>
                                           11.

B: Here's my driver's license.

A: That's fine. Just write the check to James Kucinski.

B: <u>Spell your name for me.</u>
            12.

A: K-U-C-I-N-S-K-I.

EXERCISE 19 About You Work with a partner. Use *would rather* to ask and answer questions.

1. own a house / a condominium

    A: Would you rather own a house or a condominium?

    B: I'd rather own a condominium (than a house).

2. live in the U.S. / in another country

3. own a condominium / rent an apartment

4. have young neighbors / old neighbors

5. have wood floors / carpeted floors

6. live in the center of the city / in a suburb

7. drive to work / take public transportation

SUMMARY OF LESSON 8

Modals

Modal	Examples	Explanation
can	I **can** stay in this apartment until March. I **can** carry my bicycle up to my apartment. **Can** I write you a check? **Can** you plug in the microwave, please? You **can't** paint the walls without the landlord's permission.	Permission Ability/Possibility Asking permission Request Prohibition
should	You **should** change the batteries in the smoke detector. You **shouldn't** leave matches in the reach of small children.	A good idea A bad idea
may	**May** I borrow your pen? You **may** leave the room. The tenant **may not** leave things in the hallway. I **may** move next month. The landlord **may** have an extra key.	Asking permission Giving permission Prohibition Future possibility Present possibility
might	I **might** move next month. The landlord **might** have an extra key.	Future possibility Present possibility
must	The landlord **must** install smoke detectors. The tenant **must not** change the locks. The new neighbors have a crib. They **must** have a baby.	Necessity—Formal Prohibition—Formal Conclusion/Deduction
would	**Would** you help me move?	Request
would like	I **would like** to buy your used TV.	Want
would rather	I **would rather** have a roommate than live alone.	Preference
could	In my last apartment, I **couldn't** have a pet. In my country, I **could** attend college for free. **Could** you help me move? **Could** I borrow your car?	Past permission Past ability Request Asking permission

Phrasal Modals

Phrasal Modals	Examples	Explanation
have to	She **has to** find a roommate. I **had to** move last month.	Necessity Past necessity
have got to	She **has got to** sign the lease. I've **got to** pay my rent tomorrow.	Necessity
not have to	You **don't have to** pay with cash. You can pay by check.	Lack of necessity
had better	You **had better** get permission before changing the locks.	Warning
be supposed to	We **are not supposed to** have a dog here. I **was supposed to** pay my rent by the fifth of the month, but I forgot.	Expectation by rule or custom Past: reporting an unmet expectation
be able to	I **am able to** carry my bike to my apartment. Everyone **was able to** get out of the apartment during the fire.	Ability Past ability
be permitted to be allowed to	We **are not permitted/allowed to** park here overnight. In my last apartment, I **was not permitted/allowed to** leave my bike in the hallway.	Permission Past permission
ought to	You **ought to** change the batteries in your smoke detector.	A good idea

TEST / REVIEW

Circle the correct expression to complete the conversation.

A: I'm moving on Saturday. (**Could**/May) you help me?
1.

B: I (should/**would**) like to help you, but I have a bad back. I went to my doctor last week, and she
2.

told me that I (**shouldn't**/don't have to) lift anything heavy for a while. (**Can**/Would) I help you
3.   4.

any other way besides lifting things?

A: Yes. I don't have enough boxes. (Should/**Would**) you help me find some?
5.

B: Sure. I (**have to**/must) go shopping this afternoon. I'll pick up some boxes while I'm at the
6.

supermarket.

A: Boxes can be heavy. You (would/**had**) better not lift them yourself.
7.

B: Don't worry. I'll have someone put them in my car for me.

A: Thanks. I don't have a free minute. I (**couldn't go**/can't go) to class all last week. There's so
8.

much to do.

B: I know what you mean. You (might/**must**) be tired.
9.

A: I am. I have another favor to ask. (**Can**/Would) I borrow your van on Saturday?
10.

B: I (should/**have to**) work on Saturday. How about Sunday? I (must not/**don't have to**) work on
11.   12.

Sunday.

A: Sunday's too late. I (**'ve got to**/should) move out on Saturday. The new tenants are moving
13.

in on Sunday morning.

B: Oh, I see. My brother has a van too. He (**has to**/should) work Saturday, but only for half a day.
14.

He (must/**might**) be able to let you use his van.
15.

A: Thanks. (**Could**/May) you ask him for me? I'd appreciate it.
16.

B: Sure. I (should/**can**) ask him later this evening. Why are you moving? You have a great
17.

apartment.

A: We (**'d rather**/'d better) live in the suburbs. And I want to have a dog.
18.

I (shouldn't/**'m not supposed to**) have a dog in my present apartment. But my new landlord says
19.

I (might/**can**) have one.
20.

WRITING

PART 1 Editing Advice

1. After a modal, use the base form.

   You must ~~to~~ pay your rent on time.

2. A modal has no –*s* form.

   He can~~s~~ carry his bike upstairs.

3. Don't forget *to* after *be permitted, be allowed, be supposed, be able* and *ought*.

   We're not permitted _{to} leave a bicycle in the hallway.

   I don't like my apartment. I ought _{to} look for a new one.

4. Don't forget *be* before *permitted to, allowed to, supposed to,* and *able to*.

   I _{am} not supposed to have a pet in my apartment.

5. Use the correct word order in a question.

   What ~~I should~~ _{should I} do in case of fire?

6. Don't use *can* for past. Use *could* + a base form.

   I ~~can't found~~ _{couldn't find} a roommate, so I live alone.

7. Don't forget *would* before *rather*.

   I _{would} rather live with my parents than live alone.

8. Don't forget *had* before *better*.

   You _{had} better not park here. You can get a ticket.

9. Don't forget *have* before *got to*.

   I _{'ve} got to change the batteries in the smoke detectors.

10. Don't use *maybe* before a verb.

   I ~~maybe will~~ _{may} move next month.

11. Use *not* for negative modals.

   I don't like garage sales. I'd rather ~~don't~~ _{not} buy used things.

PART 2 Editing Practice

Some of the shaded words and phrases have mistakes. Find the mistakes and correct them. If the shaded words are correct, write *C*.

   I am renting an apartment, and I would like to give _C you some advice. First, before you
   _{1.}

move in, you should ~~to~~ take pictures of the empty apartment, keep a copy of the pictures
      _{2.}

for yourself, and e-mail a copy to the landlord. The pictures will show the condition of the

apartment before you moved in, so the landlord can't to blame you for damages you didn't do.
3.

Test everything, like light switches, toilets, and faucets. You maybe will find that something
4.

isn't working properly. Make a list of these things. You better show this list to the landlord
5.

immediately. He should fix these things before you move in. If not, he ought give you a credit
6.   7.

on your rent so that you can fix them yourself, if you rather do it that way.
8.

You can finding checklists online. You can search for "rental condition checklist." This list
9.   10.

may help you identify many common problems.
11.

Second, you got to take your lease seriously. If the lease says "no pets," that means no
12.

pets. If you not allowed to have a pet, it's for a good reason. A pet cans cause damage.
13.   14.

Dogs make noise too, so this rule protects other tenants. If you are not supposed use the
15.

laundry room during certain hours, this might be because of the noise.
16.

Third, before you sign a lease, you should try to find out something about the landlord,
17.

the neighbors, and the neighborhood. How you can do that? You can waiting outside the
18.   19.

building during a busy late afternoon or on a weekend and talk to the tenants walking in

and out. Interview them. Are they happy? Are there any problems? What should you know
20.

before signing the lease? In my last apartment, I didn't do this. I was surprised to find that I

couldn't park my car on the street overnight, so I must to park far away. This is not the fault of
21.   22.

the landlord or the lease, but this was inconvenient for me. I'd rather don't have this situation
23.

again. Find out what you can before signing a lease for a place where you may don't be happy.
24.

PART 3 Write About It

1. Compare apartment life in the United States with apartment life in another country.

2. Compare driving rules in the United States with driving rules in another country.

PART 4 Edit Your Writing

Reread the Summary of Lesson 8 and the editing advice. Edit your writing from Part 3.

A virtual-reality system developed at
the University of Illinois at Chicago

VIRTUAL COMMUNITIES

> Technology is nothing. What's important is that you have a faith in people, that they're basically good and smart, and if you give them tools, they'll do wonderful things with them.
>
> —Steve Jobs

Google

Sergey Brin

Read the following article. Pay special attention to the words in bold.

How many times **have** you **wanted** a quick answer to something and **gone** to your computer to google it? The word "google" **has become** synonymous[1] with search. Since its start in 1998, Google **has been** one of the most popular search engines. It **has grown** from a research project of two college students to a business that now employs approximately fifty thousand people.

Google's founders, Larry Page and Sergey Brin, **have known** each other since 1995, when they were graduate students[2] in computer science at Stanford University in California. They realized that Internet search was an important field and began working to make searching easier. Both Page and Brin left their studies at Stanford to work on their project and **have** never **returned** to finish their degrees. In 2014, when they were 41 years old, Forbes Magazine listed Page's and Brin's net worth at about $30 billion each.

Larry Page

Brin was born in Russia, but he **has lived** in the United States since he was five. His father was a mathematician in Russia. Page, whose parents were computer experts, **has been** interested in computers since he was six years old.

When Google started in 1998, it did ten thousand searches a day. Today it does three billion a day in forty languages. It indexes[3] thirty trillion Web pages.

How is Google different from other search engines? **Have** you ever **noticed** how many ads there are on other search engines? News, sports scores, links for shopping, and more fill other search engines. Brin and Page wanted a clean home page. They believed that people come to the Internet to search for information, not to see unwanted data. The success of Google over its competitors **has proven** that this is true.

Over the years, Google **has added** other features to its Web site: Google Images, Google Drive, Google Calendar, Google Earth, and more. But one thing **hasn't changed**: the clean opening page that Google offers its users.

---

[1] *synonomous*: the same meaning as
[2] *graduate student*: a student who studies for a higher degree such as a Master's or Doctorate
[3] *to index*: to sort, categorize, and organize information

COMPREHENSION CHECK Based on the reading, tell if the statement is true (**T**) or false (**F**).

1. Larry Page and Sergey Brin have known each other since they were children.

2. Larry Page has been interested in computers since he was a child.

3. Brin and Page have finished their college degrees.

9.1 The Present Perfect—Forms

We form the present perfect with the auxiliary verb *have* or *has* plus the past participle.

Subject	*Have/Has* (+ *not*)	Past Participle		Explanation
I	**have**	**used**	Google.	We use *have* with the subjects *I, you, we, they*, a plural subject, or *there* + a plural subject.
You	**have not**	**heard of**	Larry Page.	
We	**have**	**read**	about Sergey Brin.	
Brin and Page	**have**	**become**	billionaires.	
There	**have**	**been**	many changes in computers.	
Brin	**has**	**lived**	in the U.S. most of his life.	We use *has* with the subjects *he, she, it*, a singular subject, or *there* + a singular subject.
Google	**has not**	**used**	ads on its opening page.	
There	**has**	**been**	a lot of interest in search.	

Language Notes:

1. The contraction for *have not* is *haven't*. The contraction for *has not* is *hasn't*.

    I **haven't used** other search engines.

    He **hasn't used** them either.

2. We can contract most subject pronouns with *have* or *has*: *I've, you've, we've, they've, he's, she's, it's*.

    I**'ve used Google** many times.

    He**'s found** the information he needs.

3. We can contract *there* + *is*.

    There's been advancement in technology.

4. We can contract most singular nouns with *has*.

    Brin**'s been** in the U.S. most of his life.

5. We don't make a contraction with *has* if the noun ends in *s, se, ce, ge, z, ze, sh, ch*, or *x*.

    Page **has** made a lot of money. (no contraction for *Page has*)

6. The apostrophe + *s* can mean *has* or *is*. The verb form following the contraction will tell you what the contraction means.

    He**'s worked** with computers. (*He's = He has*)

    He**'s working** with computers. (*He's = He is*)

continued

Compare statements, *yes/no* questions, short answers, and *wh-* questions.

Statement	Yes/No Question and Short Answer	Wh- Question
Brin **has been** interested in search for a long time.	**Has** Page **been** interested in search for a long time? Yes, he **has**.	How long **has** he **been interested** in search?
You **have used** Google many times.	**Have** you **used** other search engines? No, I **haven't**.	Why **haven't** you **used** other search engines?
Some things **have changed**.	**Has** the clean home page **changed**? No, it **hasn't**.	What **has changed**?

EXERCISE 1 Fill in the blanks with the words you hear.

CD 2
TR 17

The Internet _____has made_____ it easy to get information. But it _____

                    1.   **2.**

also _____ easy for cybercriminals, people who commit crimes through the

        3.

Internet, to steal your personal data. About 18 percent of adult Internet users

_____ victims of online crime.

              4.

   Cybercriminals steal important information such as Social Security numbers or credit

card numbers. According to a Consumer Report survey, 62 percent of responders

_____ nothing to protect their online privacy.

            5.

_____ you ever _____ to a coffee shop and

      6.   **7.**

_____ the Wi-Fi there? If so, other customers can easily gain access to your

      8.

private information. _____ you _____ about that? Also,

                              9.   **10.**

the cloud seems like a good place to store data, but it _____ it easy for

                                                                    11.

criminals to steal information.

   Without knowing it, it is possible that you _____ ordinary thieves

                                                      12.

too much information. _____ you ever _____ news about an

                              13.   **14.**

upcoming trip on a social media site? _____ you _____ where

                                              15.   **16.**

you're going on your next vacation, when you're leaving, and how long you'll be gone?

   Then you _____ also _____ thieves know when your house

                  17.   **18.**

will be empty.

In addition to stealing private information from your computer, hackers—people who

illegally get into computer systems—_____ into bank websites and

          19.

_____ large amounts of money. In 2014, for example, a hacker stole $100 million

   20.

from bank accounts. Hackers _____ information from government

           21.

sites too.

     Since the beginning of the Internet, security _____ a problem.

                                          22.

_____ you ever _____ a victim?

   23.   24.

EXERCISE 2 Write the base form and the simple past form for each past participle in the chart. If the simple past and the past participle are the same, write S. If they are different, write D.

Base Form	Simple Past Form	Past Participle	Same (S) or Different (D)
want	wanted	wanted	S
be	was/were	been	D
		grown	
		known	
		stolen	
		returned	
		become	
		noticed	
		added	
		changed	
		made	
		had	
		gone	
		done	
		thought	
		told	
		let	
		broken	
		gotten	
		lived	

9.2 The Past Participle

Base Form	Simple Past Form	Past Participle	Explanation
work wonder change	worked wondered changed	worked wondered changed	The past participle is the same as the simple past form for all regular verbs.
hear make let	heard made let	heard made let	For some irregular verbs, the past participle is the same as the simple past form.
break grow go	broke grew went	broken grown gone	For other irregular verbs, the simple past and the past participle are different.

For the following verbs, the past form and past participle are different.[4]

Base Form	Past Form	Past Participle
become	became	become
come	came	come
run	ran	run
blow	blew	blown
draw	drew	drawn
fly	flew	flown
grow	grew	grown
know	knew	known
throw	threw	thrown
tear	tore	torn
wear	wore	worn
break	broke	broken
choose	chose	chosen
freeze	froze	frozen
speak	spoke	spoken
steal	stole	stolen
begin	began	begun
drink	drank	drunk
ring	rang	rung
sing	sang	sung
sink	sank	sunk
swim	swam	swum

Base Form	Past Form	Past Participle
bite	bit	bitten
drive	drove	driven
ride	rode	ridden
rise	rose	risen
write	wrote	written
be	was/were	been
eat	ate	eaten
fall	fell	fallen
forgive	forgave	forgiven
give	gave	given
mistake	mistook	mistaken
see	saw	seen
shake	shook	shaken
take	took	taken
do	did	done
forget	forgot	forgotten
get	got	gotten
go	went	gone
lie	lay	lain
prove	proved	proven (or proved)
show	showed	shown (or showed)

---

4 For an alphabetical list of irregular past participles, see Appendix B

EXERCISE 3 Write the past participle of these verbs.

1. eat _____eaten_____
2. go _____
3. see _____
4. look _____
5. study _____
6. bring _____
7. take _____
8. say _____
9. be _____
10. find _____

11. give _____
12. leave _____
13. live _____
14. know _____
15. like _____
16. fall _____
17. feel _____
18. come _____
19. break _____
20. wear _____

21. choose_____
22. grow _____
23. drive _____
24. write _____
25. put _____
26. begin _____
27. want _____
28. get _____
29. fly _____
30. drink _____

EXERCISE 4 Fill in the blanks with the present perfect form of a verb from the box. You can use one verb more than once. Make a contraction with *have* or *has* where possible.

do	read	know	use	be
finish	go	have	steal	

1. I 've read _____ several articles about Internet security.

2. You _____ Wi-Fi in coffee shops.

3. _____ you _____ anything to protect personal information?

4. _____ your friend _____ careful with Wi-Fi at coffee shops?

5. Larry Page _____ Sergey Brin since they were students at Stanford University.

6. _____ they _____ college? No. They left college to start Google.

7. It _____ easy for hackers to steal information.

8. Some hackers _____ a lot of money.

9. Some hackers _____ to jail for stealing money online.

10. _____ your computer ever _____ a virus?

EXERCISE 5 Use the words in parentheses to write a question about each statement.

1. Google has changed the way people search. (*how*)

   How has Google changed the way people search?

2. I have used several search engines. (*which ones*)

   _____

3. Brin and Page haven't finished their college degree. (*why*)

   _____

4. They have made a lot of money. (*how much*)

   _____

5. Brin has been in the U.S. for many years. (*how long*)

   _____

6. You haven't been careful about Internet security in coffee shops. (*why*)

   _____

7. Internet security has become a big problem. (*why*)

   _____

8. Hackers have stolen money from banks. (*how much*)

   _____

9. You have bought anti-virus software. (*what kind*)

   _____

9.3 The Present Perfect with an Adverb

Subject	Has/Have (+ not)	Adverb	Past Participle		Explanation
Page and Brin	**have**	never	**finished**	their college degree.	We can put an adverb between the auxiliary verb (*have/has*) and the past participle.
Internet security	**has**	often	**been**	a problem.	
I	**haven't**	always	**been**	careful in a coffee shop.	
You	**have**	probably	**used**	Wi-Fi in a coffee shop.	

Language Note:

The adverb *already* can come between the auxiliary verb and the main verb or after the verb phrase.

They have **already** become billionaires.

They have become billionaires **already**.

EXERCISE 6 Add the word in parentheses to each sentence.

1. You have used your laptop in a coffee shop. (*probably*)

   You have probably used your laptop in a coffee shop.

2. I have installed an anti-virus program. (*already*)

   _____

3. We have heard of Larry Page. (*never*)

   _____

4. Page and Brin have been interested in search technology. (*always*)

   _____

5. You have used Google. (*probably*)

   _____

6. Brin hasn't finished his college degree. (*even*)

   _____

7. I have read the article about Internet security. (*already*)

   _____

The organization Mattresses for Congo uses online crowdfunding to purchase and deliver new mattresses to hospitals in the Democratic Republic of Congo.

CROWDFUNDING

🎧 Read the following article. Pay special attention to the words in bold.

CD 2
TR 18

Have you ever **had** an idea for a business but no way to fund it? **Have** you **asked** relatives and friends for money to help you? If you **have done** these things, you know it isn't easy to get people interested in investing in your dream. After getting money from relatives and friends, it's hard to find more people willing to invest. Lately people **have found** a different way to raise cash: through crowdfunding. Crowdfunding is a method of "collecting small amounts of money from a lot of different people, usually by using the Internet." While the idea **has been** around for possibly hundreds of years, the word "crowdfunding" **has** only **existed** since 2006.

Crowdfunding websites, which started to appear on the Internet in 2010, **have helped** individuals raise billions of dollars worldwide. So how does it work? A person demonstrates his idea in a short video and states his financial goal and the time frame for raising money. Usually the first investors are family and friends. Little by little strangers become interested and donate money.

Not all crowdfunding plans are for profit. Some people **have used** crowdfunding websites that are specifically for philanthropic[5] projects. These sites **have attracted** people who want to make the world a better place. One crowdfunding project is called "Mattresses for Congo." The creators' goal was to raise fifty thousand dollars to purchase hospital mattresses in remote[6] areas of Congo. They not only reached their goal; they exceeded[7] it. They **have begun** to explore how they can do something similar in other countries.

If you want more information, just google "crowdfunding" and you will find a number of different sites specializing in different types of projects.

---

5 *philanthropic*: intended to help others
6 *remote*: located far from the main population
7 *to exceed*: to go beyond what is intended or expected

COMPREHENSION CHECK Based on the reading, tell if the statement is true (**T**) or false (**F**).

1. Sometimes strangers help fund a crowdfunding project.

2. The idea of crowdfunding is old, but it has become easier to do with the Internet.

3. The "Mattresses for Congo" project didn't reach its financial goal.

9.4 The Present Perfect—Overview of Uses

Examples	Explanation
People **have used** crowdfunding on the Internet since 2010. Google **has been** in existence for over 20 years.	We use the present perfect to show that an action or state started in the past and continues to the present.
I **have used** my laptop in coffee shops many times. How many articles about crowdfunding **have** you **read**?	We use the present perfect to show that an action repeated during a period of time that started in the past and includes the present.
Have you ever **asked** relatives for money?	We use the present perfect to show that an action occurred at an indefinite time in the past.

EXERCISE 7 Tell if the sentences show continuation from past to present (**C**), repetition from past to present (**R**), or an indefinite time in the past (**I**).

1. Larry Page has been interested in computers since he was a child. _____C_____

2. How many e-mails have you received today? _____

3. I've had my laptop for one year. _____

4. The word "crowdfunding" has been in existence since 2006. _____

5. Internet security has become a big problem. _____

6. Has your computer ever had a virus? _____

7. My cousin has used crowdfunding two times. _____

8. Have you ever used your laptop in a coffee shop? _____

9.5 The Present Perfect with Continuation from Past to Present

We use the present perfect to show that an action or state started in the past and continues to the present.

NOW

PAST ←————————————————————————→ FUTURE

I **have had** my laptop for two months.

Examples	Explanation
Crowdfunding **has been** around **for about ten years.**	We use *for* + an amount of time: *for two months, for three years, for a long time,* etc.
Crowdfunding sites **have been** on the Internet **since 2006.**	We use *since* with a date, month, year, etc., to show when the action began.
I **have been** interested in computers (**ever**) **since I was** a child.	We use *since* or *ever since* with the beginning of a continuous action or state. The verb in the *since* clause is simple past.
How long have you had your computer?	We use *how long* to ask about the amount of time from the past to the present.
I **have always dreamed** of starting a business.	We use the present perfect with *always* to show that an action or state began in the past and continues to the present.
I **have never heard** of crowdfunding.	We use the present perfect with *never* to show that something has not occurred any time before now.

EXERCISE 8 Fill in the blanks with the words from the box. You may use an item more than once.

've been interested	ever since	've always wanted
how long	for	has never used
graduated	has	've had
since	was	has been
had	have	have been

1. I've been interested in computers _____*since*_____ I _____*was*_____ in high school.

2. I _____ to start my own business. Maybe now I can do it with crowdfunding.

3. The word "crowdfunding" _____ existed _____ 2006.

4. I _____ in crowdfunding _____ I read the article on page 234.

5. Crowdfunding websites _____ around _____ over ten years.

6. My grandmother _____ a computer. She doesn't like computers.

7. I _____ my tablet _____ three months.

8. _____ _____ you _____ your tablet?

9. I've had my laptop ever since I _____ from high school.

10. _____ 1998, Google _____ one of the most popular search engines.

EXERCISE 9 About You Write true statements using the present perfect form of the verbs given and *for, since, always,* or *never.* If possible, write about technology. Share your sentences with a partner.

1. (*have*)   I've had my smart phone since March. _____

2. (*like*)   _____

3. (*be*)   _____

4. (*want*)   _____

5. (*know*)   _____

6. (*have*)   _____

EXERCISE 10 Fill in the blanks with the present perfect and other missing words to complete this conversation. Use context clues to help you.

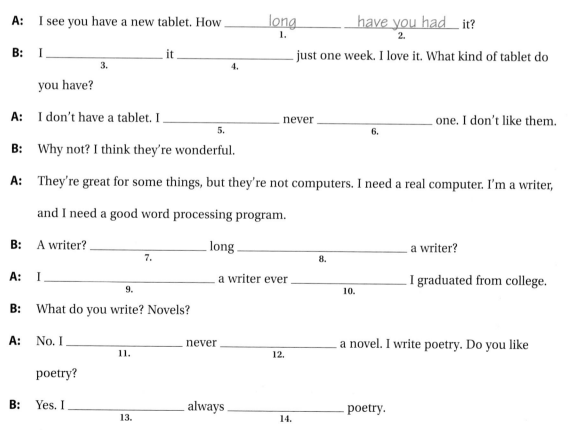

A: I see you have a new tablet. How _____long_____ ___have you had___ it?
                                             1.   2.

B: I _____ it _____ just one week. I love it. What kind of tablet do
                3.   4.
       you have?

A: I don't have a tablet. I _____ never _____ one. I don't like them.
                                       5.   6.

B: Why not? I think they're wonderful.

A: They're great for some things, but they're not computers. I need a real computer. I'm a writer,

       and I need a good word processing program.

B: A writer? _____ long _____ a writer?
                         7.   8.

A: I _____ a writer ever _____ I graduated from college.
                9.   10.

B: What do you write? Novels?

A: No. I _____ never _____ a novel. I write poetry. Do you like
                   11.   12.
       poetry?

B: Yes. I _____ always _____ poetry.
                   13.   14.

A: I'll give you a copy of my latest book.

9.6 The Simple Past, The Present Perfect, The Simple Present

Examples	Explanation
Sergey Brin **came** to the U.S. in 1979. Brin **has been** in the U.S. since 1979. Brin **lives** in California.	We use the simple past with an action that is completely past. We use the present perfect to connect the past to the present. We use the simple present to refer only to the present.
When **did** you **learn** about crowdfunding? How long **have** you **known** about crowdfunding?	We use *when* to ask about the past. We use *how long* to ask about the connection of past to present.

EXERCISE 11 Fill in the blanks with the present perfect or the simple present form of the verb given. Include any other words you see.

A: I _____*have*_____ a great idea for a business but no way of funding it.
    1. have

B: What about crowdfunding?

A: I _____ of it. What is it?
    2. never hear

B: It's a way of getting money from friends, relatives, and strangers. Look it up online and you'll

    find a lot of crowdfunding websites.

A: This is terrific! How _____ about it?
    3. you/know

B: I _____ about it ever since I _____ an article
    4. know   5. read

    about it a few years ago.

A: So it _____ around for a long time?
    6. be

B: The idea _____ around for a long time but on the Internet only since
    7. be

    2010. A friend of mine _____ it last year to start a small business. In a
    8. use

    short time, he _____ $25,000.
    9. collect

A: Wow! I _____ so happy you told me about it. I'm going to look it up right now.
    10. be

EXERCISE 12 Circle the correct word to complete this conversation between a teacher (A) and students (B) and (C).

A: I (*like*/*have liked*) to know about my students' lives. Let's start with Bernard. Where are you
_____1.

from?

B: I'm from Rwanda.

A: Maybe some of the other students (*never hear*/*have never heard*) of Rwanda. Let's google it so
_____2.

everyone can see where it is in Africa. OK. Here it is. (*Have you been*/*Are you*) in the U.S. for a
_____3.

long time?

B: No, (*I'm not*/*I haven't*).
_____4.

A: How long (*are you*/*have you been*) in the U.S.?
_____5.

B: I (*came*/*have come*) to the U.S. in 2014.
_____6.

A: Thanks, Bernard. What about you, Carlos? Where are you from?

C: I'm from Puerto Rico.

A: Can you tell us a little about your country?

C: Puerto Rico isn't a country. It (*'s*/*'s been*) a territory of the United States. Puerto Ricans
_____7.

(*are*/*have been*) American citizens.
_____8.

A: Let's google "Puerto Rico." When (*did Puerto Rico become*/*has Puerto Rico become*) a territory
_____9.

of the U.S.?

C: In 1898. Puerto Rico used to belong to Spain. The U.S. (*fought*/*has fought*) a war with Spain
_____10.

and the U.S. (*won*/*has won*).
_____11.

A: Thank you for this information. Please tell the class what language you speak in Puerto Rico.

C: We speak Spanish, but I (*'ve had*/*had*) English lessons since I was in high school.
_____12.

A: Thanks, Carlos.

Khan Academy

Salman Khan records one of his tutorials for the Khan Academy.

🎧 Read the following article. Pay special attention to the words in bold.

CD 2
TR 19

Have you ever **had** trouble keeping up with a class? **Have** you **been** bored because your class moves too slowly for you? Either way, learning in a group can sometimes be frustrating.

Khan Academy, created by Salman Khan in 2006, **has** quickly **become** the largest "school" in the world. Students learn at their own pace online with short videos. With over five thousand lectures in many different subjects, it **has attracted** about ten million students a month, from kindergarten through high school. Amazingly, Khan **has** never **charged** any money for his videos. They are available to anyone anywhere in the world with a computer and an Internet connection.

Salman Khan didn't start out to create a revolution in instruction. In 2004, his niece asked him for help in math. He started to create math videos for her to view online. Then he decided to make his videos available to anyone who wanted to get math help. One day he received an e-mail from a stranger who improved his math grade by using his videos. The email said, "You **have changed** my life and the lives of everyone in my family."

Khan's life **has changed** too. In 2009, he quit his job and started making more instructional videos. At first he focused on math, but over the past few years, he **has added** many other subjects, including history, science, and art. Volunteers **have helped** translate his videos into at least twenty-five different languages. Khan **has** personally **created** over three thousand videos.

At first Khan had no funding for his project. Since he started to appear on TV, he **has attracted** financial support from many people, including Bill Gates. So far he **has raised** almost twenty million dollars.

Many teachers **have started** to use Khan's lectures to supplement[8] their classroom instruction. Because most of today's students are digital natives, it is not surprising that Khan Academy **has become** so popular with today's students.

---

8 *to supplement*: to add to

COMPREHENSION CHECK Based on the reading, tell if the statement is true (**T**) or false (**F**).

1. Khan Academy is available only in the United States.

2. Khan Academy is for elementary and high school students.

3. Salman Khan has created many of the videos himself.

9.7 The Present Perfect with Repetition from Past to Present

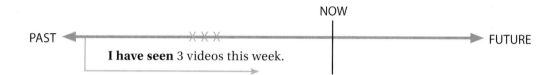

NOW

PAST ← ✗ ✗ ✗ → FUTURE

I have seen 3 videos this week.

Examples	Explanation
Khan **has appeared** on TV many times. Up to now, Khan Academy **has created** over five thousand videos. I **have watched** ten math videos on Khan Academy so far.	We use the present perfect to talk about repetition in a time period that includes the present. We expect more repetition. Adding the words *so far* and *up to now* indicate that we are counting up to the present moment.
How many times **has** Khan **been** on TV? How much money **has** he **charged** for his videos? He **hasn't charged** any money **at all** for his videos.	We can ask a question about repetition from past to present with *how much* and *how many*. To indicate zero times, we can use a negative verb + *at all*.

Language Note:

We use the present perfect in a time period that is open. There is a possibility of more repetition.

We use the simple past with a time period that is finished or closed: *2004, 50 years ago, last week*, etc. There is no possibility of more repetition.

COMPARE:

Khan **has made** over 3,000 videos so far. (possibility for more videos)

Khan **has added** new subjects over the years. (possibility for adding new subjects)

Khan **made** a few videos in 2004 for his niece. (2004 ends the time period)

My grandmother **took** several computer courses in her life. She died two years ago. (Grandmother's death ends possibility for more repetition.)

EXERCISE 13 Fill in the blanks with the present perfect form of one of the verbs from the box.

| add | read | help√ | not charge | translate | use | attract | have | appear | be |

1. Salman Khan _____*has helped*_____ a lot of students improve their math skills.

2. Khan Academy _____ millions of students.

3. So far Khan _____ any money for his instructional videos.

4. Khan started with math, but he _____ many other subjects.

5. Volunteers _____ Khan's lectures into about twenty-five different languages so far.

6. Khan _____ on many TV programs.

7. How many times _____ you _____ instructional videos?

8. How many articles about the Internet _____ we _____ so far?

9. Google _____ billions of searches since 1998.

EXERCISE 14 Fill in the blanks with the simple past or the present perfect form of the verb given.

1. In 2012, a popular news magazine _____*chose*_____ Salman Khan as one of the 100 most
   choose

   influential people of that year.

2. He _____*has been*_____ on the cover of several magazines.
   be

3. Several news programs _____ Salman Khan over the past few years.
   interview

4. Khan _____ Khan Academy in 2006.
   start

5. Sergey Brin and Larry Page _____ each other in college in 1995.
   meet

6. So far they _____ Google's clean home page.
   not change

7. I _____ my laptop in coffee shops many times.
   use

8. Yesterday I _____ to a coffee shop to work on my laptop.
   go

9. My cousin is using crowdfunding to fund his project. So far he _____
   receive

   80 percent of his financial goal.

EXERCISE 15 Fill in the blanks with the simple past or the present perfect form of the verb given. Use contractions wherever possible.

A: Do you have any hobbies?

B: Yes. I love to read.

A: How many books _have you read_ this year?
1. you/read

B: I _____ about twenty books so far this year. Last month I _____ on
2. read   **3.** go

vacation for two weeks and I _____ ten books while I _____ at the
4. read   **5.** be

beach.

A: How _____ so many books on your vacation? They're heavy.
6. you/carry

B: I _____ only one: my tablet. Before I left on my trip, I _____ about
7. carry   **8.** download

twenty-five books.

A: Are book downloads expensive?

B: I pay about $10 a book. But I _____ much more than that on print
9. spend

books over the years. My public library _____ about 5,000 books
10. make

available for download so far, and those are free. Every month they add new electronic books.

A: I _____ to download books from my library. I don't know if they have
11. never/try

electronic books.

B: I'm sure they do. Most libraries do these days.

9.8 The Present Perfect with an Indefinite Time in the Past

We often use the present perfect with an indefinite time in the past.

Examples	Explanation
A: Have you **ever heard** of Khan Academy? **B:** Yes, I **have**. **A: Have** you **ever seen** Khan's history videos? **B:** No, I never **have**. But I**'ve used** several of his math videos this semester.	We use the present perfect with *ever* to ask a question about any time from past to present. We can answer an *ever* question with the present perfect when there is no reference to time. The time is indefinite or repeated in an open time frame.
A: I know your brother is using crowdfunding to raise money. **Has** he **raised** enough money **yet** for his project? **B:** No, **not yet**. But he **has already raised** over $5,000.	We use the present perfect in a question with *yet* to ask about an expected action. We use *yet* with questions and negative statements. We use *already* with affirmative statements.
A stranger wrote to Salman Khan, "You **have changed** my life." Khan Academy **has become** the largest "school" in the world.	We can use the present perfect to talk about the past without any reference to time when the time is not important, not known, or imprecise. Using the present perfect, rather than the simple past, shows that the past is relevant to a present situation or discussion.

EXERCISE 16 Fill in the blanks to complete each conversation using the correct form of the verb and *yet* or *already*.

1. **A:** <u>Has your grandmother bought</u> a computer _____<u>yet</u>_____ ?
   a. your grandmother/buy   b.

   B: No, not _____<u>yet</u>_____ . She _____ to several stores _____ ,
   c.   d. go   e.

   but she _____ _____ . She needs me to help her.
   f. not/ decide   g.

2. **A:** The teacher gave us an assignment to write about crowdfunding. _____ it
   a. you/do

   _____ ?
   b.

   B: No, not _____ . But I _____ several articles about it.
   c.   d. read

   I _____ what to write about _____ .
   e. not/decide   f.

3. **A:** I just bought a new computer. My daughter helped me.

   B: _____ an anti-virus program for you _____ ?
   a. your daughter/install   b.

   A: Yes. She _____ _____ .
   c.   d.

4. **A:** I just read the article about Khan Academy. _____ it _____ ?
   a. you/read   b.

   B: Yes, I _____ .
   c.

   A: I know Salman Khan _____ mostly math videos. _____
   d. make   e. he/make

   any other kind of videos _____ ?
   f.

   B: Yes. He _____ videos in many subjects. And volunteers _____
   g. create   h. translate

   them into many different languages.

   A: My language is Urdu. _____ videos into my language _____ ?
   i. they/translate   j.

   B: Yes, they _____ .
   k.

5. A: I have trouble with math. I can't keep up with the teacher.

B: _____ the teacher for help?

            a. you/ask

A: Yes, I _____. But she only has time once a week. I need help after every class.

         b.

B: _____ Khan Academy _____?

       c. you/try   **d.**

A: No. Where's Khan Academy? Is it in this city?

B: It's not a physical location. It's on the Internet.

A: I've _____ looked for help on the Internet, but it wasn't very good.

         e.

B: But you _____ Khan Academy _____. Try it.

        f. not/try   **g.**

I'm sure you'll get the help you need.

EXERCISE 17 About You Find a partner. Use *Have you ever* + the past participle of the verb given to ask questions. Answer with: *Yes, I have; No, I haven't;* or *No, I never have.*

1. (*study*) computer programming

    A: Have you ever studied computer programming?

    B: No, I never have.

2. (*google*) your own name

3. (*use*) the Web to look for a person you haven't seen in a long time

4. (*add*) hardware to your computer

5. (*download*) music from the Internet

6. (*use*) a search engine in your native language

7. (*send*) photos by e-mail

8. (*buy*) something online

9. (*pay*) someone to fix your computer

10. (*edit*) photos on your computer

11. (*take*) a selfie with your cell phone

12. (*see*) the movie *The Social Network*

13. (*hear*) of Mark Zuckerberg

9.9 The Present Perfect vs. The Simple Past

Examples	Explanation
A: You were talking about getting a new computer. **Have** you **gotten** one **yet**? **B:** Yes. I **got** a new one last week. **A: Have** you **seen** any of Khan's videos? **B:** Yes. I **saw** one this morning. **A: Have** you **ever taken** a chemistry class? **B:** Yes. Last semester I **took** Chemistry 101.	We can answer a present perfect question with the simple past and a definite time. Some definite times expressions are: • *last week, month, year, semester* • *in 2008* • *two weeks ago* • *when I was 18 years old*
How long **have** you **had** your computer? When **did** you **buy** your computer?	For a question with *how long* that connects the past to the present, we the use present perfect. For a question with *when* about a specific time before now, we use the past.

EXERCISE 18 Fill in the blanks with the correct form of the verb given and any other words you see.

1. **A:** <u>Have you ever sent</u> money to help pay for a crowdfunding project?
     a. you/ever/send

   B: No, I _____. But last week my sister _____ a project that she's
     b.   c. see

   interested in, so she _____ money to help fund it.
     d. send

2. **A:** I need money for a new project I'm working on.

   B: _____ your friends for money?
     a. you/ever/ask

   A: No, I never _____. I don't like to borrow money from friends. Last year a friend
     b.

   of mine _____ money from me and never paid me back.
     c. borrow

   B: _____ it to him?
     d. you/ever/mention

   A: No, I _____. I don't like to talk to friends about money.
     e.

   B: _____ of crowdfunding?
     f. you/ever/hear

   A: Yes, I _____. But I don't know how to use it.
     g.

3. **A:** You asked me for a suggestion for math help, and I told you about Khan Academy.

   _____ it yet?
     a. you/try

   B: Yes. Thanks for your suggestion. I _____ for it immediately.
     b. look

   A: _____ you?
     c. help

B: Oh, yes. I _____ d. get an A on my last calculus test. How long _____ e. you/know about Khan Academy?

A: For about a year. My cousin _____ f. tell me about it.

4. **A:** _____ a. you/ever/hear of Sergey Brin and Larry Page?

B: No, I never _____ b. . Who are they?

A: They're the creators of Google.

B: When _____ c. they/create Google?

A: They _____ d. work on it when they _____ e. be in college. They _____ f. put it on the Internet in 1998.

B: "Sergey" sounds like a Russian name.

A: He is Russian. He _____ g. come to the U.S. when he _____ h. be a child.

5. **A:** _____ a. your computer/ever/get a virus?

B: Yes, it _____ b. . Yesterday someone _____ c. use my e-mail to send a message to everyone in my address book. I don't know how that happened.

A: _____ d. you/ever/use your laptop or tablet in a coffee shop to connect to the Internet?

B: Yes, I _____ e. . In fact, I _____ f. go to a coffee shop a few days ago to use the Wi-Fi there.

A: Maybe someone in the coffee shop _____ g. steal your personal information.

B: Is that possible?

A: Yes, it is. Actually, it's not uncommon. I sent you an article about Internet security. _____ h. you/read it yet?

B: No, I _____ i. . I _____ j. have time.

A: I suggest you read it.

Technology: Genealogy and the Genographic Project

Read the following article. Pay special attention to the words in bold.

CD 2
TR 20

Genealogy[9] is one of the most popular hobbies in the United States. The percentage of Americans interested in family history **has been increasing** steadily. This increase has to do with the ease of searching on the Internet.

Cyndi Howells quit her job in 1992 and **has been working** on her family tree ever since. To help other family historians, she created a website called Cyndi's List. Over the years, this site **has been growing**.

Although the Internet has made research easier, it is only the beginning for serious family historians. Genealogists[10] still need to go to libraries to find public records, such as the U.S. Census. Since 1790, the U.S. Census Bureau **has been conducting** a census every ten years.

But genealogy research on the Internet and in libraries can only go back a couple of hundred years. Then it stops. In the past, that meant the end of one's family search. But since the beginning of the twenty-first century, serious family historians **have been using** genetics to trace their backgrounds. This technology shows the relationship between people, going back thousands of years.

In 2005, National Geographic started the Genographic Project. Since then, it **has been collecting** and **analyzing** DNA[11] from people all over the world. Dr. Spencer Wells, founder of the project, **has been using** this information to understand how we are all related to each other.

How does this project work? People get a DNA kit, put in a bit of saliva, and send it back. Dr. Wells has concluded that all humans alive today descended from early humans who lived in Eastern Africa around two hundred thousand years ago. Dr. Wells **has been studying** human migration[12] from Africa to other parts of the world. Dr. Wells thinks that by understanding who we are and where we came from, we will have a better sense of where we are going.

---

[9] *genealogy*: the study of family history
[10] *genealogist*: family historian
[11] *DNA*: the molecules that carry genetic information and define the traits of a person, plant, or animal
[12] *migration*: movement from one place to another, usually in large groups

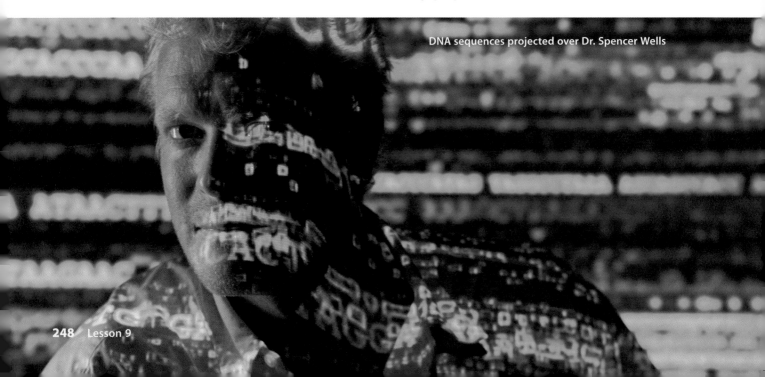

DNA sequences projected over Dr. Spencer Wells

COMPREHENSION CHECK Based on the reading, tell if the statement is true (**T**) or false (**F**).

1. Library and Internet research for genealogy can help us find family information from thousands of years ago.

2. DNA analysis can show us the relationship of people all over the world.

3. The U.S. Census provides family historians with useful information.

9.10 The Present Perfect Continuous[13]—Forms

Subject	Have/Has+ not)	been	Present Participle	
Cyndi Howells	has	been	working	on her family history since 1992.
The Genographic Project	has	been	analyzing	information since 2005.
Family historians	have	been	using	DNA to trace their backgrounds.
The U.S. Census Bureau	hasn't	been	keeping	detailed records for more than 150 years.

Observe statements, *yes/no* questions, short answers, and *wh-* questions.

Statement	Yes/No Question & Short Answer	Wh- Question
Dr. Wells **has been studying** DNA for several years.	**Has** he **been studying** the DNA of people all over the world? Yes, he **has**.	How long **has** he **been studying** human DNA?
You **have been thinking** about researching your family history.	**Have** you **been thinking** about DNA testing? No, I **haven't**.	Why **haven't** you **been thinking** about DNA testing?
Cyndi Howells **has been working** on her family history.	**Have** you **been working** on your family history? No, I **haven't**.	Who **has been working** on your family history?

EXERCISE 19 Fill in the blanks with the words you hear.

CD 2
TR 21

The U.S. Census ___has been collecting___ information every ten years since 1790.
        1.

Family historians _____ advantage of census records to trace
                              2.

their family history. What is the difference between the early census and the census today?

In 1790, when the population was less than 4 million, the government wanted to find out

how many men were eligible for military service, so census workers didn't even count

children. In more recent years, the government _____ this
                                                          3.

information to give citizens representation in Congress and to decide how to use federal

money for schools, hospitals, roads, and more.

---

[13] The present perfect continuous is sometimes called the present perfect progressive.

At first the census results were available to everyone. In modern times, the government

_____ the privacy of individuals. Census information is not available until
　　　4.

72 years later. Genealogists were excited when the 1940 census information became available

in 2012.

Since 1950, the government _____ computers to compile census data,
　　　　　　　　　　　　　　　　　5.

making the information available much faster.

Before 1960, census takers went door to door. Since 1960, the government

_____ census forms to people through the U.S. mail.
　　　6.

For many years, the census forms were only in English. In recent years, the U.S.

government _____ census forms available in several languages besides English.
　　　　　　　　7.

The government found that it needed data between the ten-year intervals. Since 2005, the

census bureau _____ information every year from a sample of Americans. Each
　　　　　　　　8.

year, 3.5 million households receive a questionnaire.

EXERCISE 20 Fill in the blanks with the present perfect continuous form of the verb given. Include
any other words you see.

1. How long _has Cyndi been managing_ a genealogy website?
　　　　　　　Cyndi/manage

2. Interest in genealogy _____.
　　　　　　　　　　　　　grow

3. Cyndi Howells _____ on her family history since 1992.
　　　　　　　　　　work

4. Cyndi _____ all over the U.S. to genealogy groups.
　　　　　　lecture

5. The number of genealogy websites _____.
　　　　　　　　　　　　　　　　increase

6. How long _____ records?
　　　　　U.S. Census Bureau/keep

7. How _____ information?
　　U.S. Census Bureau/collect

8. _____ on a family tree? Yes, I _____.
　　　　you/work

9. Family historians _____ the Internet to do family research since the 1990s.
　　　　　　　　　　　use

10. How long _____ human DNA?
　　　　　　Dr. Wells/study

9.11 The Present Perfect Continuous—Use

We use the present perfect continuous to show that an action started in the past and continues to the present.

Examples	Explanation
The U.S. Census **has been collecting** information **for** over 200 years.	We use *for* with the amount of time.
Cyndi's Web site **has been helping** family historians **since** 1996.	We use *since* with the beginning time.
Cyndi **has been working** full-time on her website **since** she **quit** her job.	We use the simple past in the *since*-clause.
I **have been studying** my family history since 2010. OR I **have studied** my family history since 2010.	With some verbs (*live, work, study, teach,* and *wear*), we can use either the present perfect or the present perfect continuous with actions that began in the past and continue to the present. The meaning is the same.
My father is working on our family tree right now. He **has been working** on it since 9 a.m.	If an action is still happening, we use the present perfect continuous, not the present perfect.
I **have been** interested in genealogy for ten years. She **has wanted** to learn about her family history since she was in high school.	We do not use the continuous form with nonaction verbs, such as *be, like, want, have, know, remember, see.* For a complete list of nonaction verbs, see chart **2.5**.
I **have been thinking** *about* sending my DNA for anaylsis. I **have** always **thought** *that* genealogy is an interesting hobby.	*Think* can be an action or nonaction verb, depending on its meaning. *Think about* = action verb *Think that* = nonaction verb
Some people **have had** a lot of success in locating information. We **have been having** a hard time locating information about our ancestors.	*Have* is usually a nonaction verb. However, *have* is an action verb in these expressions: *have experience, have a hard time, have a good time, have difficulty,* and *have trouble.*
My family **lives** in the U.S. My family **came** to the U.S. in 2005. My family **has been living** in the U.S. since 2005.	We use the simple present when the action refers only to the present. We use the simple past when the action is completely past. We use the present perfect continuous tense that the action started in the past and continues to the present.

Language Note:

We do not use the continuous form with *always* and *never*.

> I have always loved technology.
> I have never studied my family history.

EXERCISE 21 Fill in the blanks to complete the conversations.

1. **A:** _____Are_____ you studying your family history?
    a.

   B: Yes, I _____.
    b.

   A: How long _____ your family history?
    c.

   B: _____ about five years.
    d.

2. **A:** _____ Spencer Wells working on the Genographic Project?
    a.

   B: Yes, he _____.
    b.

   A: _____ long _____ he been _____ on this project?
    c.   d.   e.

   B: _____ 2005.
    f.

3. **A:** Are you working on your family history?

   B: Yes, I _____.
    a.

   A: How long _____ you _____ on your family history?
    b.   c.

   B: I _____ on it _____ about ten years.
    d.   e.

4. **A:** Is your sister using your computer now?

   B: Yes, she _____.
    a.

   A: _____ long _____ it?
    b.   c.

   B: _____ she woke up this morning!
    d.

5. **A:** _____ the U.S. Census Bureau collect information about Americans?
    a.

   B: Yes, it _____.
    b.

   A: How _____ the U.S. Census Bureau _____
    c.   d.

   information about Americans?

   B: For _____.
    e.

6. **A:** _____ your grandparents live in the U.S.?
    a.

   B: Yes, they _____.
    b.

   A: How _____ in the U.S.?
    c.

   B: Since they _____ born.
    d.

EXERCISE 22 About You Write true statements using the present perfect with the words given and *for* or *since*. Share your sentences with a partner.

1. work   My brother has been working as an engineer for six years.

2. study   _____

3. live   _____

4. use   _____

5. try   _____

EXERCISE 23 Fill in the blanks with the correct form of the verb given. Use the present perfect, present perfect continuous, or the simple past. Fill in any other missing words.

A: Hi. My name is Ana. I'm from Guatemala.

B: Hi, Ana. My name is Jimmy. My family is from Cuba. How __long have you been living__ here?
      1. you/live

A: I _____ here for about six months. What about you?
      2. only/be

B: I _____ born in the U.S. My family _____ Cuba in 1962.
      3. be   **4.** leave

   Lately I _____ to trace my family history.
      5. try

A: Me too. I've been _____ on a family tree _____ many years.
      6. work   **7.**

B: When _____?
      8. you/start

A: I _____ when I _____ sixteen years old. Over the years,
      9. start   **10.** be

   I _____ a lot of interesting information about my family. Some
      11. find

   of my ancestors were Mayans and some were from Spain and France.

B: Where _____ all that information?
      12. you/find

A: There's a wonderful site called Cyndi's List. I _____ it _____
      13. use   **14.**

   around 2001. Last summer I _____ to Spain, to look for information there.
      15. go

B: How many ancestors _____ so far?
      16. you/find

A: So far I _____ about fifty in four generations. I'm still looking.
      17. find

B: _____ of the Genographic Project?
      18. you/ever/hear

A: No, I _____. What is it?
      19.

B: It connects people from all over the world, back thousands of years.

SUMMARY OF LESSON 9

Compare the Present Perfect and the Simple Past.

Present Perfect	Simple Past
The action of the sentence began in the past and includes the present.	The action of the sentence is completely past.
Sergey Brin **has been** in the U.S. since 1979.	Sergey Brin **came** to the U.S. in 1979.
Khan's videos **have been** available for many years.	Khan **created** his first math videos in 2004.
I've always **wanted** to learn more about my family's history.	When I was a child, I always **wanted** to spend time with my grandparents.
How long **have** you **been** interested in genealogy?	When **did** you **start** your family tree?

Present Perfect	Simple Past
Repetition from past to present	Repetition in a past time period
Khan Academy **has created** over 5,000 videos so far.	Khan **created** several videos for his niece in 2004.

Present Perfect	Simple Past
The action took place at an indefinite time between the past and the present.	The action took place at a definite time in the past.
Have you ever **used** Cyndi's list?	**Did** you **use** the 1940 census in 2012?
My brother **has raised** $5,000 on a crowdfunding site already.	He **put** his project on crowdfunding site six months ago.
I'm interested in the DNA project. I've **received** my kit, but I **haven't sent** the sample back yet.	My friend **sent** her DNA sample to the Genographic Project last month.

Compare the Present Perfect and the Present Perfect Continuous.

Present Perfect	Present Perfect Continuous
A continuous action (nonaction verbs) I **have been** interested in genealogy for five years.	A continuous action (action verbs) I've **been working** on my family tree for five years.
A repeated action Cyndi Howell's Web site **has won** several awards.	A nonstop action The U.S. Census Bureau **has been keeping** records since the 1880s.
Question with *how many/how much* How many times **has** Khan **been** on the cover of a magazine? How much time **has** he **spent** on Khan Academy?	Question with *how long* How long **has** Khan **been living** in Boston?
An action that is at an indefinite time, completely in the past Many teachers **have started** to use Khan lectures in their classrooms.	An action that started in the past and is still happening Dr. Wells **has been collecting** DNA for several years.

TEST / REVIEW

Fill in the blanks with the simple past, the present perfect, or the present perfect continuous form of the verbs given. Include any other words you see. In some cases, more than one answer is possible.

A: What do you do for a living?

B: I _____*work*_____ as a programmer. I __*'ve been working*__ as a programmer for five
                1. work   2. work

    years. But my job is boring.

A: _____ about changing jobs?
                      3. you/think/ever

B: Yes. Since I _____ a child, I _____ to be
                   4. be   5. always/want

    to be an actor. When I was in college, I _____ in a few plays.
                                          6. be

    But since I _____ , I _____ time to act.
                 7. graduate   8. not/have

    What about you?

A: I _____ in computer security.
                9. work

B: How long _____ that?
                  10. you/do

A: For about six years.

B: I _____ the field of computer security is very important.
            11. think

A: Yes, it is. But lately I _____ the computer for other things too. My hobby
                       12. use

    is genealogy. I _____ on my family tree for about a year. Last
                    13. work

    month I _____ information about my father's ancestors. My grandfather
            14. find

    _____ with us now, and he likes to tell us about his past. He
                15. live

    _____ born in Italy, but he _____ here when he was very young,
          16. be   17. come

    so he _____ here most of his life. He _____
                18. live   19. not/remember

    much about Italy. I _____ any information about my mother's
                20. not/find

    ancestors yet.

WRITING

PART 1 Editing Advice

1. Don't confuse the *-ing* form and the past participle.

   taking
   I've been ~~taken~~ a course in genealogy.

   given
   My parents have ~~giving~~ me family photos.

2. Use the present perfect, not the simple present or present continuous, to describe an action or state that started in the past and continues to the present.

   had
   He ~~has~~ his laptop for two years. ^

   have you been
   How long ~~are you~~ studying math? ^

3. Use *for*, not *since*, with the amount of time.

   for
   I've been interested in my family's history ~~since~~ three years.

4. Use the simple past, not the present perfect, with a specific past time.

   studied
   He ~~has studied~~ algebra when he was in high school.

   did   study
   When ~~have~~ you ~~studied~~ algebra?

5. Use the simple past, not the present perfect, in a *since* clause.

   put
   He has collected $5,000 since he ~~has put~~ his project on a crowdfunding site.

6. Use the correct word order with adverbs.

   never studied   *ever heard*
   I have ~~studied never~~ my family history. Have you ~~heard ever~~ of Dr. Spencer Wells?

7. Use the correct word order in questions.

   has your family
   How long ~~your family has~~ been in this country?

8. Use *yet* for negative statements; use *already* for affirmative statements.

   yet
   I haven't taken advanced algebra ~~already~~.

9. Don't forget the verb *have* in the present perfect (continuous).

   have
   I been studying my family history for two years. ^

10. Don't forget the *-ed* of the past participle.

    ed
    He's watch a math video several times. ^

11. Use the present perfect, not the present perfect continuous, with *always, never, yet, already, ever,* a repeated action, or a nonaction verb.

    collected
    Dr. Wells has ~~been collecting~~ about 700,000 DNA samples so far.

    become
    Genealogy has ~~been becoming~~ very popular.

12. Don't use *time* after *how long*.

    How long ~~time~~ have you had your computer?

PART 2 Editing Practice

Some of the shaded words and phrases have mistakes. Find the mistakes and correct them. If the shaded words are correct, write C.

How many changes ~~you have~~ *have you* made since you came *C* to the U.S.? For our journal, our
1.   2.

teacher asked us to answer this question. I have come to the U.S. two and a half years ago.
3.

Things have change a lot for me since I've come to the U.S. Here are some of the changes:
4.   5.

First, since the past two years, I am studying to be a software engineer. I knew a little
6.   7.   8.

about this subject before I came here, but my knowledge has improve a lot. I started to work
9.   10.   11.

part-time in a computer company three months ago. Since I have started my job, I haven't have
12.   13.   14.

much time for fun.

Second, I have a driver's permit, and I'm learning how to drive. I haven't took the driver's
15.

test yet because I'm not ready. I haven't practiced enough already.
16.   17.   18.

Third, I've been eaten a lot of different foods like hamburgers and pizza. I never ate those
19.   20.

in my country. Unfortunately, I been gaining weight.
21.

Fourth, I've gone to several museums in this city. But I've taken never a trip to another
22.   23.

American city. I'd like to visit New York, but I haven't saved enough money yet.
24.   25.

Fifth, I've been living in three apartments so far. In my country, I lived in the same house
26.   27.

with my family all my life.

One thing that bothers me is this: I've answered the following questions about a thousand
28.

times so far: "Where do you come from?" and "How long time you have been in the U.S.?"
29.   30.

I'm getting tired of always answering the same question. But in general, I been happy since I
31.

came to the U.S.
32.

PART 3 Write About It

1. Write about new technology that you've started using recently. How has that made your life different?
2. Write about several changes in technology in recent years. How has recent technology changed the way we do things?

PART 4 Edit Your Writing

Reread the Summary of Lesson 9 and the editing advice. Edit your writing from Part 3.

JOBS

Engineers work at night on a city building project.

Choose a job you love, and you will never have to work a day in your life.

—Confucius

FINDING A JOB

Read the following article. Pay special attention to the words in bold.

Finding a job in the United States takes time and effort. Here are some tips[1] to help you:

- Write a good résumé. Include only relevant[2] experience. Describe your accomplishments.[3] Avoid **including** unnecessary information. Consider **asking** a friend to read your résumé to check it for grammar and spelling mistakes.

- Find out about available jobs. One way is by **looking** in the newspaper or on the Internet. Another way is by **networking.** Networking means **exchanging** information with anyone you know who might know of a job. These people might be able to give you insider information about a company, such as who is in charge of **hiring** and what it is like to work at their company. You can find out about a job before it is even advertised. The *Wall Street Journal* reports that 94 percent of people who succeed in finding a job say that networking was a big help.

- Practice the interview. The more prepared you are, the more relaxed you will feel and the more you will convey[4] confidence. If you are worried about **saying** or **doing** the wrong thing, practice will help.

- Learn something about the company by **going** to the company's website.

---

1 *tip*: useful information
2 *relevant*: closely connected
3 *accomplishment*: a difficult thing done well
4 *to convey*: to communicate

- Arrive at least fifteen minutes before the scheduled time of your interview. **Feeling** relaxed is important. **Arriving** on time or just a few minutes before the interview doesn't give you time to relax.

- Use professional behavior during the interview. Avoid **chewing** gum. Turn off your cell phone completely.

- Avoid **saying** anything negative about your current job or employer.

- One question might be, "Tell me something about yourself." Instead of **talking** about your personal life, focus on your skills and work experience. Answer each question concisely.[5] Avoid **giving** long answers.

- At the end of the interview, offer a firm handshake. **Thanking** the interviewer by letter a few days later is a good idea.

Some people send out hundreds of résumés and go on dozens of interviews before finding a job. **Looking** for a job isn't something you do just once or twice in your lifetime.

---

[5] *concisely*: using few words to communicate

COMPREHENSION CHECK Based on the reading, tell if the statement is true (**T**) or false (**F**).

1. Networking means getting information from the Internet.

2. The interviewer might ask you to describe your weaknesses.

3. If the interviewer says, "Tell me something about yourself," you should talk about your family.

10.1 Gerunds—An Overview

A gerund is the *–ing* form of a verb.

Examples	Explanation
Finding a job is hard.	A gerund (phrase) can be the subject of a sentence.
I recommend **talking** to a job counselor.	A gerund (phrase) can be the object of the verb.
Are you thinking about **changing** careers?	A gerund (phrase) can be the object of a preposition.
I'm worried about **not writing** a good résumé.	We put *not* in front of a gerund to make it negative.

Language Notes:

1. A gerund phrase is a gerund + a noun or noun phrase
   - *finding* a job
   - *exchanging* information
   - *preparing* for a job interview

2. For an example of a résumé, see Appendix N.

EXERCISE 1 Listen to these tips on how to be more successful at your job. Fill in the blanks with the words you hear.

You care ____about keeping____ your job. You may not be aware _____ things that
1.   2.

can make your supervisor think less of you. So here are a few tips:

- Avoid _____ about things you have to do. If you dislike _____
3.   4.

  on a project, keep it to yourself. Don't say, "It's not my job." Even if you don't like _____
                                                               5.

  it, do it anyway _____.
                          6.

- Practice _____ positive words to show confidence and a good attitude.
                      7.

  _____ "It's not fair" makes you sound like a small child.
                  8.

- Get used _____ strong words. Instead _____ "I think I
                      9.   10.

  can do the job," simply say "I can do the job. When do you need the work done?" Most people don't

  know how they sound. Consider _____ a friend listen to the way you talk. Or
                                        11.

  try _____ yourself and analyzing what you say.
          12.

- Don't point out your weaknesses. "I'm not good _____ reports" sounds bad.
                                        13.

  Instead say, "I want to do a good job. I'd like to work with someone who can help me learn to write

  better reports."

- _____ a coworker that you don't like a supervisor is not a good idea. You
          14.

  never know what this person might say to the supervisor.

- If you're interested _____ more tips on good job behavior, there are books
                      15.

  and online sources that can give you more information.

10.2 Gerunds as Subjects

Examples	Explanation
Using positive words conveys confidence. **Not dressing** appropriately gives a bad impression.	We can use a gerund or gerund phrase as the subject of the sentence.
Exchanging ideas with friends **is** helpful. **Visiting** company websites **pays** off.	A gerund subject takes a singular verb.

262 Lesson 10

EXERCISE 2 Use the gerund form of one of the verbs from the box to complete each sentence.

wear	feel	know	get✓	network	prepare	select

1. _____*Getting*_____ a good night's sleep will help you feel rested and alert for an interview.

2. _____ with other people will improve your chances of finding a job.

3. _____ your clothes the night before the interview gives you more time

   in the morning.

4. _____ a good résumé is very important. Some people use a résumé service.

5. _____ something about the company will help you make a good impression.

6. Not _____ serious clothes to the interview will give a very bad impression.

7. _____ relaxed before an interview is important.

EXERCISE 3 About You Fill in the blanks with the gerund form of the verb given. Then tell if this behavior is or isn't common in a work situation in your country.

1. ____*Socializing*____ with the boss (*is*/*isn't*) common.
   socialize

2. _____ the boss by his or her first name (*is*/*isn't*) acceptable.
   call

3. _____ with coworkers (*is*/*isn't*) common.
   socialize

4. _____ on time (*is*/*isn't*) very important.
   arrive

5. _____ a personal computer at a job (*is*/*isn't*) common.
   use

6. _____ jeans to the office (*is*/*isn't*) acceptable.
   wear

7. _____ a long lunch break (*is*/*isn't*) the custom.
   take

8. _____ from home (*is*/*isn't*) common.
   work

9. _____ coffee or tea while working (*is*/*isn't*) acceptable.
   drink

EXERCISE 4 About You In preparing for an interview, it is good to think about the following questions. Answer these questions. Give a lot of thought to your answers and compare them with a partner's answers. An example is given for each item.

1. What are your strengths?

   Working well with others; learning quickly; thinking fast in difficult situations

2. What are some of your weaknesses?

   _____

3. List your accomplishments and achievements. (They can be achievements in jobs, sports, school, etc.)

   _____

4. What are your short-term goals?

   _____

5. What are your long-term goals?

   _____

6. What are some things you like in a job situation? (personalities, tasks, environments, types of work)

   _____

7. What are some things you dislike? (personalities, tasks, environments, types of work)

   _____

EXERCISE 5 Work with a partner to write sentences about behaviors during an interview that would hurt your chances of getting a job.

1. *Chewing gum during the interview looks bad.*

2. _____

3. _____

4. _____

5. _____

6. _____

10.3 Gerunds as Objects

Examples	Explanation
Do you **enjoy working** on a team? **Avoid complaining** about your supervisor.	A gerund (phrase) can be the object of many verbs.
I **went shopping** for work clothes last weekend. After work, I like to **go swimming**.	We use *go* + gerund in expressions of recreational activities.

A gerund (phrase) can follow these verbs:

admit	dislike	love	quit
appreciate	enjoy	mind	recommend
avoid	finish	miss	start
begin	hate	postpone	stop
consider	imagine	practice	suggest
continue	keep (on)	prefer	
discuss	like	put off	

We use *go* + gerund in the following expressions:

go boating	go camping	go fishing	go hunting
go jogging	go shopping	go skating	go swimming
go bowling	go dancing	go hiking	go skiing

Language Notes:

1. *I mind* means that something bothers me. *I don't mind* means that something is OK with me; it doesn't bother me.

    Do you **mind wearing** a suit to work? No, I don't **mind**.

2. *Put off* means postpone.

    Don't **put off writing** your résumé. Do it now.

EXERCISE 6 Use the gerund form of a verb from the box to complete each conversation.

answer	shop	find	say	get	be	do ✓
work	wear	go	act	discuss	talk	read

1. **A:** I want to quit my boring job. I dislike _____*doing*_____ the same thing every day.

a.

   B: I suggest _____ another job before you quit. I can't imagine _____

b.   c.

   without a job.

2. **A:** Interviewing for a job scares me. I hate _____ about my strengths.

a.

   B: Have you considered _____ help from a job counselor? You can practice

b.

   _____ common interview questions. I have a good book about job hunting.

c.

   When I finish _____ it, you can borrow it.

d.

continued

3. **A:** I have to wear a suit for my new job.

   B: I dislike _____ anything but jeans.
   _{a.}

   A: Me too. I have to go _____ for some new clothes. Can you help me pick something out?
   _{b.}

   B: Sorry. I don't have time. I suggest ___going___ to a store and asking the salesperson to help you.
   _{c.}

4. **A:** I really like my job.

   B: What do you like about it?

   A: I enjoy ___working___ on a team. The people on my team are smart and exciting. I like
   _{a.}

   ___discussing___ how to do a project with them.
   _{b.}

5. **A:** My boss always asks me to do something that isn't my job. Sometimes I have to tell her, "It's not fair."

   B: Stop ___saying___ "It's not fair" and just do it. Quit ___acting___ like a small child.
   _{a.}   _{b.}

EXERCISE 7 About You Use the words below to make statements about yourself regarding jobs. Share your answers with a partner.

1. I hate _getting up every morning at 5 for my job._____

2. I enjoy _____

3. I don't mind _____

4. I've considered _____

5. I can't imagine _____

6. I avoid _____

7. I began _____

EXERCISE 8 About You Make a list of suggestions and recommendations for someone looking for a job or about to go on a job interview. Discuss your list with a partner.

1. _I recommend getting a good night's sleep the night before the interview._____

2. _____

3. _____

4. _____

5. _____

6. _____

10.4 Preposition + Gerund

A gerund can follow certain verb + preposition or adjective + preposition combinations.

Common Verb + Preposition Combinations		Examples
verb + *about*	care about complain about dream about forget about know about talk about think about worry about	My sister **dreams about becoming** an engineer.
verb + *to*	look forward to object to	I **look forward to getting** a job and **saving** money.
verb + *on*	depend on insist on plan on	I **plan on going** to a career counselor.
verb + *in*	believe in succeed in	My father **succeeded in finding** a good job.
verb + object + *from*	stop + . . . + from	No one can **stop** you **from following** your dream.
Common Adjective + Preposition Combinations		Examples
adjective + *of*	afraid of capable of guilty of proud of tired of	I'm **afraid of losing** my job.
adjective + *about*	concerned about excited about upset about worried about sad about	He is **upset about not getting** the job.
adjective + *for*	responsible for famous for	Who is **responsible for hiring** in this company?
adjective + *to* + object + *for*	grateful to . . . for	I'm **grateful to** you **for helping** me find a job.
adjective + *at*	good at successful at	I'm not very **good at writing** a résumé.
adjective + *to*	accustomed to used to	I'm not **accustomed to talking** about my strengths.
adjective + *in*	interested in successful in	Are you **interested in getting** a better job?

Language Notes:

1. In general, you can use a gerund after any preposition.

   What is your method *of* **preparing** for an interview?

   It's hard to do well at an interview *without* **practicing**.

2. For a list of verbs and adjectives followed by a preposition, see Appendix G.

EXERCISE 9 Fill in the blanks with a preposition and the gerund form of a verb from the box.

talk	do	work✓	complain	get	help
be	practice✓	tell	hear	go✓	connect

1. **A:** I plan _____on going_____ to India for a year to work in a clinic as a physician assistant.
   a.

   B: That's great. You've talked a lot _about helping_ other people. This is your chance.
   b.

   A: When I get back, I'd like to go to medical school, but it's so expensive. I'm worried __about ...telling__
   c.

   not _getting_ financial aid.
   d.

   B: With your experience in India, you're a good candidate for financial aid.

2. **A:** I have an interview next week. I'm afraid _about_ not _doing_ well.
   a.   **b.**

   B: Have you thought _about practicing_ for the interview?
   c.

   A: No, I haven't. I don't know how to do that.

   B: I have a friend who has a lot of experience with job interviews. Are you interested _in talking_
   d.

   with her? She can give you good tips. I can set up a meeting for you.

   (*A few weeks later...*)

   A: I'm grateful to you _for connecting me_ with your friend. She helped me a lot.
   e.

3. **A:** Some people complain _about working_ long hours. But I don't even have a job.
   a.

   I'm upset _about being_ unemployed for so long.
   b.

   B: How long have you been unemployed?

   A: For almost six months. I'm worried _about telling_ the interviewer about my long
   c.

   unemployment. It might hurt my chances of getting a job.

4. **A:** A coworker of mine always insists _on complaining_ about the boss. She hates the boss.
   a.

   B: Tell her you're not interested _in hearing_ her complaints.
   b.

EXERCISE 10 About You Fill in the blanks with a preposition + gerund or noun phrase to complete each statement about jobs. Share your answers with a partner.

1. I'm afraid _of losing my job._

2. I'm not accustomed _____

3. Coworkers often talk _____

4. After work, I'm (not) interested _____

5. I worry _____

6. I'm proud _____

7. I'm not used _____

8. On Fridays, most workers look forward _____

EXERCISE 11 Fill in the blanks with the gerund form of the verb given. Some of the blanks need a preposition before the gerund. If so, add the preposition.

A: I need to find a job. I've had ten interviews, but so far no job.

B: Have you thought _about practicing_ for the interview? You can practice _____
   1. practice   **2.** answer

   questions that the interviewer might ask you. Many interviewers ask the same general

   questions. For example, the interviewer will probably ask you to name your strengths.

A: I dislike _____ about myself.
   3. talk

B: But it's necessary. And she'll probably ask you to name your weaknesses too.

A: What should I say? I'm afraid _____ the truth about my weaknesses.
   4. tell

B: There's a way to make your answer sound positive. For example, "I'm a perfectionist. I worry

   _____ in a project with mistakes. But I plan _____
   5. turn   **6.** be

   careful so that I meet deadlines."

A: Wow! That sounds more like a strength than a weakness.

B: That's the idea. Here's another possible question: "Do you mind _____ overtime
   7. stay

   to finish a project?"

A: Will I have to work overtime? I'll have to get a babysitter for my son.

B: Don't complain _____ a babysitter. Don't mention personal problems.
   8. get

A: It feels like I'm never going to find a job. I'm tired _____.
   9. look

B: Be patient. If you keep _____ , you'll succeed _____ a job.
   10. try   **11.** find

   I suggest _____ a book that gives you sample interview questions.
   12. get

A: Thanks so much. I'm grateful to you _____ me so much help.
   13. give

Employees cheer just before opening a store during a busy holiday shopping weekend.

EMPLOYMENT ENGAGEMENT

CD 2
TR 24

Read the following article. Pay special attention to the words in bold.

Do you like **to go** to work? Or are you glad **to leave** at the end of the day? If you have a full time job, you probably spend most of your waking hours at work. It would be nice **to spend** that time in a pleasant atmosphere, right?

According to a survey, 70 percent of Americans are not happy at work. They often feel job burnout: physical and mental stress. Some of them can't wait **to get** home, but they often take their stress home with them to their families.

When workers are happy, they do a better job and the company gains from this. What makes workers happy? The answer is "employee engagement." Researchers have been studying what makes a worker feel engaged. Engaged employees are enthusiastic about their work. Researchers have found that it takes a combination of things **to build** an engaged workforce:

1. Employees need **to feel** that the boss appreciates their work.

2. Workers need **to take** breaks during the day. When people work continuously, they feel worse physically. More work is not necessarily better work. Some experts believe that workers need a break every ninety minutes. Some companies have fitness facilities and nap rooms for their employees.

3. Workers want **to be** able to focus on one thing at a time. Too often managers want them **to do** several things at once. The result is workers get stressed out and their work suffers.

4. Workers want **to feel** that they are doing something meaningful. They want **to be** excited about what they're doing.

Employers need **to choose** a job candidate who fits the company's mission.[6] A worker who doesn't fit in is likely[7] **to quit**. It takes time and costs money **to train** a new employee. So it's important for a company **to hire** the right people and **make** the work atmosphere fun and meaningful.

---

6 *mission*: purpose
7 *is likely*: is probably going to

COMPREHENSION CHECK Based on the reading, tell if the statement is true (**T**) or false (**F**).

1. One way to promote employee engagement is for the employer to show the employee appreciation.

2. The majority of Americans are happy to go to work.

3. It is expensive for a company to train a new employee.

10.5 Infinitives—An Overview

An infinitive is *to* + the base form of a verb.

Examples	Explanation
Are you happy **to go** to work? I need **to take** a break. It's important **to hire** the right people for the job.	We can use an infinitive after certain adjectives. We can use an infinitive after certain verbs. We can use an infinitive after expressions beginning with *it*.
They decided **not to hire** me.	To make an infinitive negative, we put *not* before the infinitive.

Language Note:

When we connect two infinitives with *and*, we usually omit *to* after *and*.

He wants **to take** a break and **rest**.

EXERCISE 12 Fill in the blanks with the words you hear.

CD 2
TR 25

It's important ___to write___ a good, clear résumé. It's only necessary
                1.

_____ your most recent and related work. Employers are busy people.
     2.

Don't expect them _____ long résumés.
                     3.

You need _____ your abilities in your résumé. Employers expect you
             4.

_____ action verbs _____ your experience. Don't begin your
    5.   **6.**

sentences with "I." Use past-tense verbs such as: *managed, designed, created,* and *developed.*

It's not enough _____ you improved something. Be specific. How did you
              7.

improve it?

Before making copies of your résumé, it's important _____ the grammar
                   8.

and spelling. Employers want _____ if you have good communication skills.
              9.

Ask a friend or teacher _____ your résumé and check for mistakes.
           10.

continued

It isn't necessary _____ references. If the employer wants you

_____ references, he or she will ask you _____ so during or

after the interview.

Don't include personal information such as marital status, age, race, family information,

or hobbies.

Be honest in your résumé. Employers can check your information. No one wants

_____ a liar.

10.6 Infinitives after Expressions with *It*

Examples	Explanation
It's important **to write** a good résumé. It isn't necessary **to include** all your experience. It's a good idea **to practice** before an interview.	An infinitive phrase can follow certain expressions beginning with *it*.
It's important *for managers* **to show** appreciation. It was hard *for me* **to leave** my last job.	We use *for* + a noun or object pronoun to make a statement that is true of a specific person or people.
It takes patience **to find** a job. It took *me* three weeks **to finish** my project.	We can use an infinitive after *take* + *time*, *patience*, or *money*. We can add an object before the infinitive.
It costs a lot of money **to train** a new worker. It cost *me* **$100 to use a résumé service**.	We can use an infinitive after *cost* + (object) + money.
It's important **to do** a good job. **Doing** a good job is important.	There is no difference in meaning between an infinitive after an *it* expression and a gerund subject.

We often use an infinitive after *it* + *be* + these words:

dangerous	expensive	a good/bad idea	impossible/possible
difficult	fun	hard	necessary
easy	a good/bad experience	important	a pleasure

EXERCISE 13 Fill in the blanks with the infinitive form of a verb from the box.

practice	check	have✓	describe	write	include	dress

1. It's necessary _____ to have _____ a Social Security card.

2. When you write a résumé, it isn't necessary _____ all your previous experience.

   Choose only the most recent and related experience.

3. It's important _____ your spelling and grammar before sending a résumé.

4. It's important _____ your past work experience in detail, using words

like *managed, designed, supervised,* and *built.*

5. It takes time _____ a good résumé.

6. It's a good idea _____ interview questions before going to an interview.

7. It's important _____ your best when you go to an interview, so choose

your clothes carefully.

EXERCISE 14 Complete each statement with an infinitive phrase to talk about work. You can add an object, if you like.

1. It's easy _to get information about a company online._ _____

2. It's necessary _for me to work overtime once a month._ _____

3. It's important _____

4. It's impossible _____

5. It's possible _____

6. It's necessary _____

7. It isn't a good idea _____

8. It's hard _____

10.7 Infinitives after Adjectives

Examples	Explanation
Are you **available to work** overtime? A happy worker is **likely to stay** with the company.	An infinitive (phrase) can follow certain adjectives.

An infinitive can follow these adjectives:				
afraid	glad	lucky	proud	sorry
available	happy	prepared	ready	surprised

Language Note:

Afraid and *proud* can be followed by an infinitive too.

I'm afraid **of talking** about my weaknesses. = I'm afraid **to talk** about my weaknesses.

He's proud **of being** a college graduate. = He's proud **to be** a college graduate.

EXERCISE 15 Complete the conversation with the appropriate infinitive form of a verb from the box.

help	talk	show	go✓	have	answer	wait	say

A: I have my first interview tomorrow. I'm afraid _____ *to go* _____ alone. Would you go
                                         1.

with me?

B: I'd be happy _____ in the car. But nobody can go with you to an interview.
                              2.

You have to do it alone. It sounds like you're not ready _____ a job interview.
                                                    3.

You should see a job counselor and get some practice before you have an interview.

A: I don't have time. Maybe you can help me.

B: I'd be happy _____ you. We can go over some basic questions. Here's one
                              4.

question you should be ready _____: Why are you leaving your present job?
                                         5.

A: I'm afraid _____ anything about my present job. I don't like my supervisor.
                          6.

B: Never say that! I'd be happy _____ you a few good websites that will give you
                              7.

typical questions and good answers.

A: Thanks. I'm glad you were available _____ to me this afternoon. I feel a little
                                          8.

better now.

10.8 Infinitives after Verbs

Examples	Explanation
I need **to find** a better job. I want **to make** more money.	An infinitive (phrase) can follow certain verbs.

We can follow these verbs with an infinitive:					
agree	decide	learn	remember	begin*	love*
attempt	expect	need	try	continue*	prefer*
begin	forget	plan	want	hate*	start*
choose	hope	promise	would like	like*	

Language Notes:

1. A gerund can also follow these verbs* with little or no difference in meaning. See **10.3**.

    I love **to work** with children. = I love **working** with children.

2. *Plan on* + gerund is the same as *plan* + infinitive.

    I plan **on seeing** a counselor. = I plan **to see** a counselor.

3. Remember that in some expressions, *to* is part of a verb phrase, not part of an infinitive.

    I look forward **to starting** my new job. (verb + *to* + gerund)

    I need **to write** a résumé. (verb + infinitive)

EXERCISE 16 Fill in the blanks with the infinitive form of a verb from the box.

feel	take	go	ask	find	sleep✓
work	get	be	hear	have	

A: How's your new job?

B: I really like it. It's a great company. We can take a break every two hours. And we even have a nap room. Sometimes people need _____*to sleep*_____ for a few minutes.

1.

A: I've never heard of a nap room. I would like _____ a nap in the middle

2.

of the day. I usually start _____ tired around 2 p.m. but I have to keep

3.

working. How's your boss?

B: She's wonderful. She includes us on company decisions. Employees want

_____ like their opinion is important, don't you think?

4.

A: Yes, I do.

B: It's fun for me _____ to work. After six months on the job, we can

5.

choose _____ from home too. But I prefer _____

6.   7.

with my team members at the office.

A: You're lucky _____ such a good job. My job is terrible.

8.

B: I'm sorry _____ that.

9.

A: I need _____ a new job. Do you know if your company is hiring?

10.

B: I don't know. But I promise _____ on Monday morning.

11.

EXERCISE 17 About You Work with a partner who has a job. Use the phrases to ask a question. Your partner will answer.

1. afraid/give your boss your opinion

   A: Are you afraid to give your boss your opinion?

   B: Yes, I am. OR No, I'm not.

2. like/go to work every day

3. plan/stay at your job for a long time

4. expect/make a lot of money

5. need/work at home

6. hope/get a better position within the company

continued

7. like/socialize with your coworkers

8. try/keep up with changes in technology

9. want/work overtime

10. hate/get up in the morning to go to work

10.9 Objects before Infinitives

Examples	Explanation
I **want my boss to appreciate** my work. My boss **expects me to work** overtime.	We can use an object noun or pronoun between some verbs and an infinitive.

We can use an object between these verbs and an infinitive:			
advise	expect	need	want
allow	help	permit	would like
ask	invite	tell	

Language Note:

We can follow *help* by either an object + base form or an object + infinitive.

He helped me **find** a job.

He helped me *to* **find** a job.

EXERCISE 18 Fill in the blanks with pronouns and infinitives to complete the conversation.

A: I want to quit my job.

B: Why?

A: I don't like my supervisor. He expects ___me to work___ at night and on weekends.

                  1. work

B: But you get extra pay for that, don't you?

A: No. I asked _____ me a raise, but he said the company can't afford it.

                  2. give

B: Is that the only problem?

A: No. My coworkers and I like to go out for lunch. But he doesn't want _____ out.

                                                3. go

He expects _____ in the company cafeteria.

                  4. eat

B: That's awful. He should permit _____ wherever you want to.

                                    5. eat

A: That's what I think. I also have a problem with my team manager. She never gives anyone a

compliment. When I do a good job, I expect _____ something nice. But she

                                                        6. say

only says something when we make a mistake.

10.10 Infinitives to Show Purpose

Examples	Explanation
You can use the Internet **in order to find** job information. I need a car **in order to get** to work.	We use *in order to* + verb to show purpose.
You can use the Internet **to find** job information. I need a car **to get** to work.	*To* is the short form of *in order to*.

Language Notes:

1. The purpose phrase can come before the main clause. If so, we often use a comma after the purpose phrase.

> I need a car **to get** to work.

> **To get** to work, I need a car.

EXERCISE 19 Fill in the blanks with an infinitive to show purpose. Answers will vary.

1. I bought the Sunday newspaper _(in order) to look for_ a job.

2. I called the company _____ an appointment.

3. She wants to work overtime _____ more money.

4. You can use a résumé writing service _____ your résumé.

5. My job is in a distant suburb. I need a car _____ to work.

6. In the U.S., you need experience _____ a job, and you need a

   job _____ experience.

7. You need to practice _____ well on an interview.

8. You should ask someone to read your résumé for you _____

   sure you didn't make any mistakes in grammar or spelling.

9. You should try networking _____ your chances of finding a job.

10.11 Infinitive or Gerund after a Verb

Examples	Explanation
I started **looking** for a job a month ago. I started **to look** for a job a month ago.	We can follow these verbs with either a gerund or an infinitive with almost no difference in meaning: *begin, continue, like, love, prefer, start.*
I was sleepy, so I **stopped (in order) to get** a cup of coffee. I **stopped driving** to work. Now I take public transportation.	Following *stop* with a gerund or infinitive affects the meaning. *Stop* + infinitive means stop one activity in order to start something different. *Stop* + gerund means quit.
I **used to be** a teacher. Now I work in a hotel. I'm **not used to talking** about my strengths, but that's what you have to do to find a job. At first it was hard for me, but I finally **got used to** working at night.	*Used to* + base form tells about a past habit or custom. This habit or custom has been discontinued. *Be used to* + gerund, noun, or pronoun means *be accustomed to.* Something is or was familiar to a person. *Get used to* + gerund, noun, or pronoun means *become accustomed to.*

Language Notes:

1. The negative of *used to* + base form is *didn't use to.* (We remove the *d*.)

   I **didn't use to** drive to work.

2. The negative of *be* + *used to* + gerund, noun, or pronoun is *isn't/aren't/wasn't/weren't used to.* (We do not remove the *d*.)

   I'm not used to working on Saturdays.

3. The negative of *get/got used to* is usually *can't/couldn't get used to.*

   He **can't get used to** working the second at night.

EXERCISE 20 Circle the correct words to complete this story. In some cases, both choices are possible. If that's the case, circle both choices.

I was tired of driving to the office every day, so I started (**to use/using**) public
1.

transportation. But I was still wasting two hours a day. So my boss agreed to let me work from

home a few days a week. At first I had some difficulty. I (**wasn't used to being**/didn't use to be)
2.

alone all day, so I felt a bit lonely.

I had to get used to (stick/**sticking**) to a schedule. Every time the phone rang, I stopped
3.

(**to answer**/answering) it. Because I had a lot of work to do, I had to find a way to deal with
4.

personal phone calls. I decided to stop (to answer/**answering**) the phone completely until I
5.

was finished with my day's work. Now I return calls only in the evening.

I had the same problem with e-mail and text messages. I usually prefer

(**to answer/answering**) an e-mail or text as soon as it comes in. But I was losing concentration.
6.

Now I stop (**to work/working**) every two hours, get a little exercise, answer my personal
7.

e-mails and texts, and then get back to work.

Now (I used to work/**I'm used to working**) at home. I save time by not traveling, I save
8.

money on gas or public transportation, and I love (to set/**setting**) my own schedule.
9.

SUMMARY OF LESSON 10

Gerunds

Examples	Use of Gerunds
Working all day is hard.	As the subject of the sentence
I don't enjoy **working** as a taxi driver.	After certain verbs
I **go shopping** after work.	In many idiomatic expressions with *go*
I'm worried about **losing** my job.	After prepositions

Infinitives

Examples	Use of Infinitives
I need **to find** a new job.	After certain verbs
My boss wants me **to work** overtime.	After an object
I'm ready **to quit**.	After certain adjectives
It's important **to have** some free time.	After certain expressions beginning with *it*
I work (in order) **to support** my family.	To show purpose

Gerund or Infinitive—No Difference in Meaning

Gerund	Infinitive
I like **working** with computers. She began **working** at 8:30.	I like **to work** with computers. She began **to work** at 8:30.
Writing a good résumé is important.	It's important **to write** a good résumé.

Gerund or Infinitive—Difference in Meaning

Examples	Uses
I **used to work** at night. Now I work in the day.	Past habit
I'm **used to working** at night. It's not a problem for me.	Customary activity
I stopped **to make** a personal phone call.	Stop in order to do something else
Stop **making** personal phone calls at work. The boss won't like it.	Quit completely

TEST / REVIEW

Fill in the blanks with the gerund or infinitive form of the verb given. In some cases, both a gerund and an infinitive are possible. Add a preposition where needed.

A: Hi, Molly. I haven't seen you in ages. What's going on in your life?

B: I've made many changes. First, I quit _____ *working* _____ in a factory. I disliked
1. work

_____ ~~to do~~ *doing* _____ the same thing every day. And I wasn't used
2. do

_____ *to standing* _____ on my feet all day. My boss often wanted me
3. stand

_____ *to work* _____ overtime on Saturdays. I need _____ *to be* _____ with my
4. work   5. be

children on Saturdays.

A: So what do you plan _____ *to do* _____ ?
6. do

B: I've started _____ *taking* *to take* _____ some general courses at the community college.
7. take

A: What career are you planning?

B: I'm not sure. I'm interested _____ *in working* _____ with children. Maybe I'll become a
8. work

teacher's aide. I've also thought _____ *of working* _____ in a day-care center. I care
9. work

_____ *about helping* _____ people.
10. help

A: It's important _____ *to have* _____ a job that you like. So you're starting a whole new
11. have

career.

B: It's not new, really. Before I came to the U.S., I used _____ *to be* _____ a kindergarten
12. be

teacher. But my English wasn't so good when I came here, so I found a job in a factory. I look

forward _____ *to going* _____ back to my former profession.
13. go

A: How did you learn English so fast?

B: By _____ *talking* _____ with people at work and _____ *watching* _____ TV.
14. talk   15. watch

But it hasn't been easy for me _____ *to understand* _____ English. I studied formal English
16. understand

in my country, but here I have to get used _____ *to saying* _____ things like "gonna"
17. say

and "wanna." I've had to make a lot of changes.

A: Let's get together some time and talk some more.

B: I'd love to. Maybe we can go _____ *shopping* _____ together sometime.
18. shop

WRITING

PART 1 Editing Advice

1. Use a gerund after a preposition.

   getting
   He succeeded in ~~to get~~ a good job.

2. Use the correct preposition.

   on
   She insisted ~~in~~ helping me with my résumé.

3. Use a gerund after certain verbs.

   ing
   I enjoy ~~to~~ work ∧ with children.

4. Use an infinitive after certain verbs.

   to
   I decided ∧ quit my job.

5. Use a gerund, not a base form, as a subject.

   Finding
   ~~Find~~ a good job is important.

6. Don't forget to include *it* before certain adjectives.

   It's
   ~~Is~~ important to find a good job.

7. Don't use the past form after *to*.

   see
   I decided to ~~saw~~ a job counselor.

8. After *want, expect, need, advise*, and *ask*, use an object pronoun, not a subject pronoun, before the infinitive. Don't use *that* as a connector.

   me to
   He wants ~~that I~~ check the spelling on his résumé.

9. Use *for*, not *to*, when introducing an object after impersonal expressions beginning with *it*. Use the object pronoun after *for*.

   for them
   It's important ~~to they~~ to finish their project on time.

10. Use *to* + base form, not *for*, to show purpose.

    to
    I called the company ~~for~~ make an appointment.

11. Don't put *be* before *used to* for the habitual past.

    I ~~am~~ used to work in an office. Now I work in a hospital.

12. Don't use the *-ing* form after *used to* for the habitual past.

    She used to work~~ing~~ on Saturdays, but now she has Saturdays off.

13. Don't forget the *d* in *used to*.

    d
    I use ∧ to drive to work. Now I take public transportation.

PART 2 Editing Practice

Some of the shaded words and phrases have mistakes. Find the mistakes and correct them. If the shaded words are correct, write C.

I'm planning [to] be a nurse. I'd love to be a doctor, but I don't want [to] be in school for so many
 1.   2.   3.

years. My mother is a doctor, and she wanted [me to] that I study medicine too. I know that you're
                                              4.

never too old to learn something new, but I'm thirty-five years old, and start something new [starting/to start]
                                                                                          5.

at my age is not easy. [Studying] Study medicine takes too long. It would take me eight years [to] become
                        6.   7.

a doctor. I went to my college counselor to get advice [C]. She advised me [to] take biology and
                                                      8.   9.

chemistry this semester as well as English and math. It's hard [for] to me to take so many courses,
                                                               10.

but I have no choice.

In my country, [I used to] I'm used to work in a nursing home. I enjoyed [helping] to help older people, but
                11.   12.

I didn't make enough money. When I decided [to come] to came to the U.S., I had to think about my
                                            13.

future. People say that [it is] is not hard to find a job [C] as a nurse in the U.S. It's important for me to [C]
                        14.   15.   16.

be in a profession where I can help people. I can do that more quickly by going [C] into a nursing
                                                                               17.

program.

PART 3 Write About It

1. Write about the differences between working in the U.S. and working in another country. You may write about coworkers, salary, vacation time, relationships with superiors, punctuality, or another topic about work that interests you.

2. Write about your current job or a job you had in the past. Tell what you like(d) or don't (didn't) like about that job.

PART 4 Edit Your Writing

Reread the Summary of Lesson 10 and the editing advice. Edit your writing from Part 3.

11
Adjective Clauses

Participants of the Millennial Trains Project 2014 ride from Chicago to New York City.

MAKING CONNECTIONS
WITH FRIENDS

Many people will walk in and out of
your life, but only true friends will leave
footprints in your heart.

—Eleanor Roosevelt

Reconnecting
with Old Friends

Members of a 1964 class gather for a photo during their 50th high school reunion.

🎧
CD 3
TR 2
Reading the following article. Pay special attention to the words in bold.

Estimates show that Americans move about 11.7 times in their lifetimes. As a result, they often lose touch with old friends. Usually, during their twenties and thirties, people are too busy building their careers and starting their families to think much about the past. However, as people get older, they often start to wonder about the best friend **they had in high school**, the soldier **with whom they served in the military**, or the person **who lived next door** when they were growing up.

Before the Internet, finding an old friend required going to libraries to search through old phone books of different cities. It was hard work, and you needed a lot of luck. It was especially hard to find women **who changed their names when they got married**.

Then came the Web, **which made it possible to find someone in seconds.** There are several sites **where** alumni[1] of a specific high school can include themselves according to the year **they graduated**. Married women list themselves by their maiden names[2] so that others can find them easily.

Another way **that people make connections with old friends** is through class reunions. Often people come from out of town for a reunion, **which can last for a whole weekend**: Friday evening in the high school **that they attended**, Saturday evening for a dinner in a restaurant or hotel, and a Sunday brunch. They remember the time **when they were young** and exchange information about what they are doing today. They sometimes bring their high school yearbooks, **which have pictures of the graduates**, other students, and school activities.

It takes some effort to connect with old friends. Looking back at fond memories, renewing old friendships, making new friends, and even starting a new romance with an old love can be the reward.

---

[1] *alumni*: graduates or former students of a school
[2] *maiden name*: a woman's family name before she marries

COMPREHENSION CHECK Based on the reading, tell if the statement is true (**T**) or false (**F**).

1. Because Americans move a lot in their lifetimes, they sometimes lose touch with friends.

2. Women usually list their maiden names on a high school website.

3. A yearbook is a book that shows the people who attended the reunion.

11.1 Adjective Clauses—Overview

Examples	Explanation
It is sometimes hard to find married women **who have changed their last names.** What is the name of the high school **that you attended**?	An adjective clause is a group of words that contains a subject and verb. It describes or identifies the noun before it (*women, high school*).

Language Notes:

1. *Who, whom, that, which, whose, where,* and *when* mark the beginning of an adjective clause. Sometimes an adjective clause begins with no marker.

    I have a lot of friends **who moved away after we graduated.**

    The friends **I had in high school** are married now. (no marker)

2. Some adjective clauses are set apart from the rest of the sentence with commas.

    I like to look at my yearbook, **which has pictures of my classmates.**

3. An adjective clause can identify any noun in a sentence.

    Von Steuben High School, **which is located in Chicago,** is a science academy.

    I attended Von Steuben High School, **which is located in Chicago**.

4. Compare adjectives and adjective clauses. An adjective precedes a noun. An adjective clause follows a noun.

    I attended a **big** high school.

    I attended a high school **that has over 5,000 students**.

EXERCISE 1 Fill in the blanks with the words you hear.

Why do so many Americans lose touch with old friends _____*that*_____ they had

1.

when they were younger? One reason is mobility. The average American will probably move

11.7 times in his or her lifetime. Even though the number of people _____ move

2.

to a different state has gone down considerably since the 1950s, _____

3.

3.5 percent of households moved from state to state, there are still a lot of people

_____ move across state lines.

4.

continued

Some people move to states _____ the climate is better. The states
5.

_____ are losing the most population are in cold climates: New York, Illinois,
6.

New Jersey, and Connecticut. One exception to this is North Dakota, _____ has
7.

very cold winter weather. It has a growing oil industry and low unemployment, so it attracts

young people who are looking for jobs. However, older people usually want to live in states

_____ have a good climate.
8.

Some cities, such as San Francisco, attract high-paid professionals, _____
9.

drive up the cost of living. This makes it hard to attract lower-paid workers, such as

construction workers, _____ skills are just as important but _____
10.   11.

don't earn enough to live in San Francisco.

Washington, DC, is another place _____ attracts new residents. From 2011
12.

to 2012, Washington acquired 6,000 new people. Most of these were young professionals

_____ were looking for work.
13.

11.2 Relative Pronouns as Subjects

A relative pronoun can be the subject of the adjective clause.

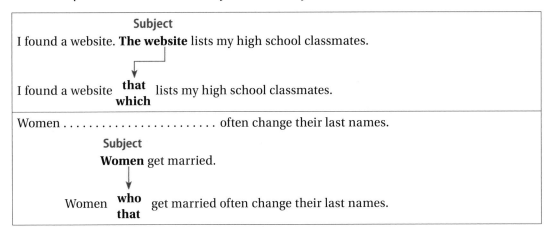

Language Notes:

1. The relative pronouns *who, that,* and *which* can be the subject of the adjective clause.
   Use *who* or *that* for people. Use *that* or *which* for things.

2. The verb in the adjective clause must agree in number with its subject.

   A **woman** who **gets** married usually changes her name.

   Women who **get** married usually change their names.

Punctuation Note:

When the noun is unique, we set the adjective clause apart from the rest of the sentence with commas. We use only *who* and *which*; we don't use *that*.

Compare:

I want to move to a state **that has low unemployment.** (no comma)

I want to move to North Dakota**, which has low unemployment.** (North Dakota is unique.)

EXERCISE 2 Fill in the blanks with a phrase from the box.

who have moved	that allows	who plan ✓	who live	who have changed
who plays	that is convenient	that was popular	that will cover	
that is different	who can create	who have died	who graduated	

Planning a reunion takes time and effort. People _____*who plan*_____ a reunion start at
                                                    1.

least a year in advance. They form a committee of about ten people. Each committee member

has a task _____ from the tasks of other committee members. For
                        2.

example, one committe member needs to calculate a budget for the reunion activities. The

reunion committee will charge an amount of money _____ the cost
                                                              3.

of attending the various activities. Another committee member is in charge of locating

classmates. This is the hardest part, so all members of the committee help. To find classmates,

the committee uses phone books, word of mouth, social media sites, and other websites to

search. It is especially hard to find women _____ their names. The
                                                        4.

committee has to find classmates _____ nearby and classmates
                                            5.

_____ away. Sadly, sometimes they even find some classmates
            6.

_____ .
            7.

The committee chooses someone _____ a reunion website. A
                                            8.

reunion website is something _____ classmates to read about each
                                        9.

others' lives.

The committee tries to set a date _____ for most people. Most
                                                10.

reunions are in the summer. The committee hopes to find about 50 percent of the people

_____ with their class, but 25 percent is a more realistic number.
            11.

continued

At the reunion dinner, there's often a DJ. This is a person _____

_____
12.

recorded music. The DJ uses music _____ when the students were in

_____
13.

high school.

EXERCISE 3 About You Fill in the blanks with *who* or *that* + a form of the verb given. Then complete the statement. Answers will vary.

1. most of the students _who graduated_ from my high school
   graduate
   Most of the students who graduated from my high school went to college.

2. friends ___who moved___ to another state
   move
   I have several friends who moved to a different state.

3. a classmate of mine _____ in life
   succeed

4. a social media site _____ photos of my friends
   have

5. the music _____ popular when I was in high school
   be

6. a person _____ next door to me when I was growing up
   live

7. classmates _____ to college
   go

8. a teacher _____ me
   inspire

11.3 Relative Pronouns as Objects

The relative pronoun can be the object of the adjective clause.

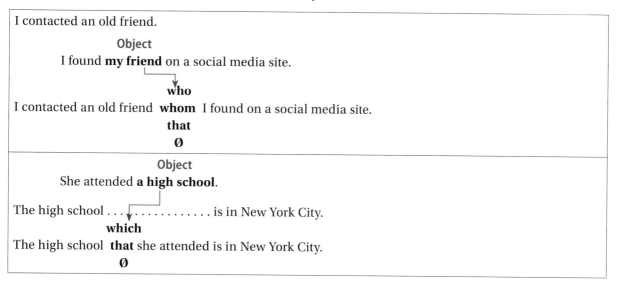

I contacted an old friend.

Object
I found **my friend** on a social media site.

who
I contacted an old friend **whom** I found on a social media site.
that
Ø

Object
She attended **a high school**.

The high school . . . . is in New York City.
which
The high school **that** she attended is in New York City.
Ø

Language Notes:

1. The relative pronouns *who(m), that,* and *which* can be the object of the adjective clause. In conversation, we usually omit the relative pronoun when it is the object of the adjective clause.

   I contacted an old friend I found on a social media site.

   The high school she attended is in New York City.

2. *Whom* is more formal than *who* when it is the object of the adjective clause. However, the relative pronoun is usually omitted altogether in conversation.

   I reconnected with an old friend **who(m)** I saw at the reunion.

   I reconnected with an old friend I saw at the reunion.

Punctuation Note:

When the noun is unique, we set the adjective clause apart from the rest of the sentence with commas. We use only *who* and *which*; we don't use *that.*

Compare:

The high school **(that) she attended** is very small. (no comma)

Taft High School, **which I attended from 1998-2002,** is very small. (Taft High School is unique.)

EXERCISE 4 Underline the adjective clause in each sentence.

1. I've lost touch with some of the friends <u>I had in high school</u>.

2. The high school I attended is in another city.

3. The teachers I had in high school are all old now.

4. We didn't have to buy the textbooks we used in high school.

continued

5. My best friend married a man she met in college.

6. The friends I've made in this country don't know much about my country.

7. At the reunion, she saw a guy she dated in high school.

EXERCISE 5 Fill in the blanks with a phrase from the box to complete the conversation between a mother and her teenage daughter.

she hasn't seen	I had ✓	she put	she wrote
she married	I have for them	they attended	we had
I made	you take	they graduated	

A: I'd like to contact an old friend _____I had_____ in high school. I wish I could find her. I'll
_____
1.

never forget the good times _____ back then. When we graduated, we said
_____
2.

we'd always stay in touch. But then we went to different colleges.

B: Didn't you keep in touch by e-mail?

A: When I was in college, e-mail didn't exist. At first we wrote letters. But little by little we wrote

less and less until, eventually, we stopped writing. I still have the letters

_____ to me in a box in the basement.
3.

B: Why don't you write to the address on the letters?

A: That wouldn't work. The address _____ on the letters was of the college
4.

town where she lived. I don't know what happened to her after she left college.

B: Have you tried calling her parents?

A: The phone number _____ is now disconnected. Maybe her parents
5.

have died.

B: Why don't you try one of those classmates websites? There are websites with names of students

categorized by the high school _____ and the dates
6.

_____ .
7.

A: But my friend probably got married. I don't know the last name of the man

_____ .
8.

B: That's not a problem. You can search for her by her maiden name on these sites.

A: If I find her, she'll probably think I'm crazy for contacting her almost twenty-five years later.

B: I'm sure she'll be happy to receive communication from a good friend

_____ in years. When I graduate from high school, I'm never going to lose
    9.

contact with the friends _____. We'll always stay in touch.
                         10.

A: That's what you think. But as time passes your lives go in different directions, and you

lose touch.

B: But today we have all kinds of social media.

A: Well, that's a help. Even so, the direction _____ in life is different from the
                                                11.

direction your friends choose.

EXERCISE 6 Fill in the blanks with appropriate words to complete the conversation. Answers may
vary. You may use both subject and object relative pronouns. Remember: You can omit an object
relative pronoun.

A: I'm lonely. I have a lot of friends in my native country, but I don't have enough friends here.

The friends _(that) I have there_ send me e-mail and photos all the time, but that's not
            1.

enough. I need to make new friends here.

B: Haven't you met any people here?

A: Of course. But the people _____ here don't share my interests. I like
                                2.

reading, meditating, and going for quiet walks. Americans seem to like parties, TV, sports,

movies, and going to restaurants.

B: You're never going to meet people with the interests _____. Your interests
                                                          3.

don't include other people. You need some interests _____ other people,
                                                     4.

like tennis or dancing, to mention just a few.

A: The activities _____ cost money, and I don't have much.
                     5.

B: There are many parks in this city _____ free tennis courts. If you like to
                                        6.

dance, I know of a park district near here _____ free dance classes. In fact,
                                           7.

there are a lot of things _____ in this city. I can give you a list, if you want.
                          8.

A: Thanks. I appreciate the suggestions _____ me.
                                            9.

B: Tomorrow I'll e-mail you a list of interesting activities. I'm sure you'll find something

_____ on that list.
        10.

EXERCISE 7 `About You` Use the words given to write a sentence. Discuss your answers with a partner.

1. the high school I attended

   The high school I attended was very small.

   OR

   I can show you a picture of the high school I attended.

2. the kids I knew in high school

   _____

3. the teachers I had in high school

   _____

4. the subject I liked best in high school

   _____

5. the way I stay in touch with old friends

   _____

6. the best friend I had in high school

   _____

7. the social media I use

   _____

8. the friends I had when I was a child

   _____

9. the activities I liked in high school

   _____

MAKING CONNECTIONS
USING Meetup

Members of a Meetup group gathering at a park to watch birds

🎧 **Read the following article. Pay special attention to the words in bold.**

CD 3
TR 4

Would you like to meet people **whose** interests are the same as yours? Maybe you like to knit and would like to meet with other knitters. Or maybe you're interested in the theater and want to find people **with whom** you can attend a play. A website called Meetup lets you do that. Unlike most social networking groups, **whose** members communicate with each other online, Meetup members actually meet each other in person. Most Meetup members want to get together just for fun: to play chess, discuss books, ride their bikes, practice French, etc. Some Meetups are support groups: people get together with others who have the same problem. For example, there are Meetups of people who have lost a spouse, or parents **whose** children have a serious disease. Other Meetup groups are for the purpose of career networking. As of 2014, there were about 16 million Meetup members in almost 200 countries.

Meetup was the brainchild[3] of Scott Heiferman, **whose** idea for creating these communities came as a result of the September 11, 2001 attacks in the United States. Heiferman stated that the manner **in which** the people of New York City came together in the aftermath[4] of that traumatic[5] event inspired him. He wanted to make it easy for people to connect with strangers in their own community. He created Meetup in 2002.

Meetup connects people online so that they can meet offline. Anyone can start a Meetup. Meetup believes that "people can change their personal world, or the whole world, by organizing themselves into groups that are powerful enough to make a difference."

---

[3] *brainchild*: an important idea or project of a person
[4] *aftermath*: the result of a tragic event
[5] *traumatic*: psychologically harmful

COMPREHENSION CHECK Based on the reading, tell if the statement is true (**T**) or false (**F**).

1. Meetup members first make contact online.

2. All Meetup groups are for the purpose of having fun together.

3. Scott Heiferman got his idea for Meetup after the tragedy of September 11, 2001.

11.4 Relative Pronouns as Objects of Prepositions

A relative pronoun can be the object of a preposition.

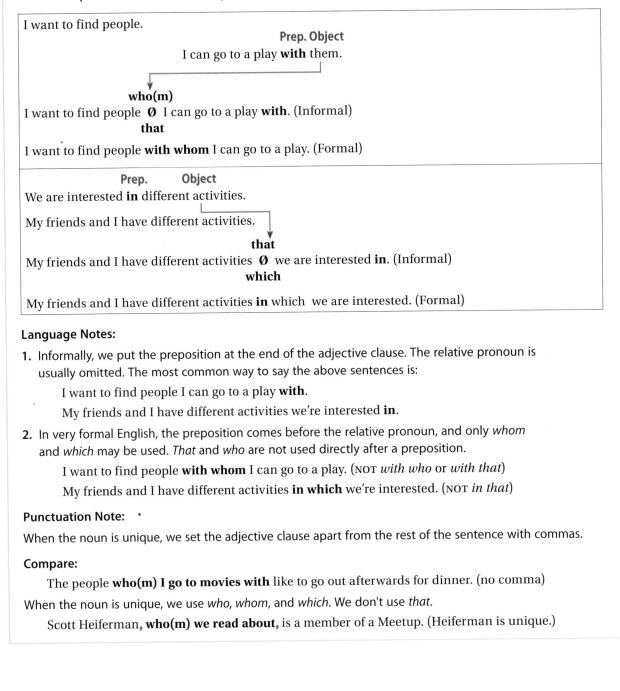

Language Notes:

1. Informally, we put the preposition at the end of the adjective clause. The relative pronoun is usually omitted. The most common way to say the above sentences is:

   I want to find people I can go to a play **with**.

   My friends and I have different activities we're interested **in**.

2. In very formal English, the preposition comes before the relative pronoun, and only *whom* and *which* may be used. *That* and *who* are not used directly after a preposition.

   I want to find people **with whom** I can go to a play. (NOT *with who* or *with that*)

   My friends and I have different activities **in which** we're interested. (NOT *in that*)

Punctuation Note:

When the noun is unique, we set the adjective clause apart from the rest of the sentence with commas.

Compare:

The people **who(m) I go to movies with** like to go out afterwards for dinner. (no comma)

When the noun is unique, we use *who*, *whom*, and *which*. We don't use *that*.

Scott Heiferman, **who(m) we read about,** is a member of a Meetup. (Heiferman is unique.)

EXERCISE 8 Change these sentences to make them more informal.

1. I'd like to find people with whom I can go hiking.

   I'd like to find people I can go hiking with.

2. A woman with whom I work started a Meetup for young Hispanic professionals.

3. Scott Heiferman, about whom we read, is a member of a parents' Meetup.

4. He pays attention to the Meetups for which people are signing up.

5. People want to get together with others with whom they share a common interest.

6. The office in which Scott works is located in New York City.

EXERCISE 9 Change the sentences to formal English.

1. What is the name of the high school you graduated from?

   What is the name of the high school from which you graduated?

2. He found a friend that he served in the military with.

3. I can't find the friend I was looking for.

4. The high school she graduated from was torn down.

5. Do you remember the teacher I was talking about?

6. In high school, the activities I was interested in were baseball and band.

11.5 *Whose* + Noun

Whose is the possessive form of *who*. It represents *his, her, its, their,* or the possessive form of the noun.

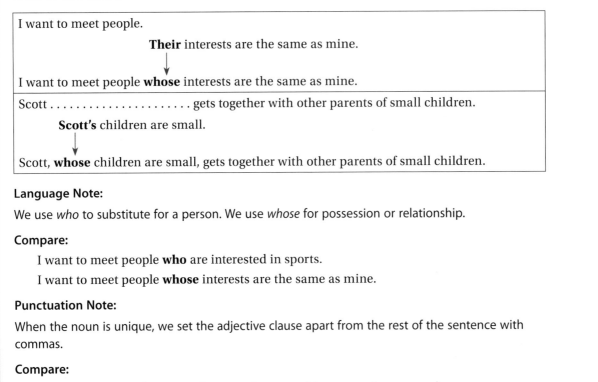

I want to meet people.
Their interests are the same as mine.
↓
I want to meet people **whose** interests are the same as mine.
Scott . . . . gets together with other parents of small children.
Scott's children are small.
↓
Scott, **whose** children are small, gets together with other parents of small children.

Language Note:

We use *who* to substitute for a person. We use *whose* for possession or relationship.

Compare:

I want to meet people **who** are interested in sports.

I want to meet people **whose** interests are the same as mine.

Punctuation Note:

When the noun is unique, we set the adjective clause apart from the rest of the sentence with commas.

Compare:

I go to a Meetup **whose members are interested in sports**. (no comma)

Heiferman, **whose office is in New York,** created Meetup after September 11th. (Heiferman is unique.)

EXERCISE 10 Fill in the blanks with *whose* + a word from the box.

jobs	last name	inspiration
family	interests ✓	members

1. Do you want to meet people ____whose interests____ are the same as yours?

2. I joined a French Meetup _____ speak French very well.

3. People _____ keep them busy don't always have the time or energy

   to get together with friends.

4. I lost touch with an old friend _____ moved to another state.

5. I'm looking for a woman _____ used to be Carter. She changed it when she got married.

6. Scott Heiferman, _____ came from the way people came together after the 9/11 tragedy, started Meetup in 2002.

EXERCISE 11 Some people were asked what kind of friends they'd like to meet. Fill in the blanks with a response, using the words given.

1. I'd like to meet people ___*whose values are the same as mine*___.
   Their values are the same as mine.

2. My math group is a club _____.
   I found it through Meetup.

3. I'd like to find a friend _____.
   I can trust that friend.

4. I don't want to be with people _____.
   They don't take life seriously.

5. I want to meet people _____.
   They like to play soccer.

6. I joined a Spanish Meetup _____.
   Its members speak Spanish very well.

7. We meet in a coffee shop _____.
   It isn't crowded in the morning.

8. I go to a book club Meetup _____.
   It meets at my local library.

9. There's a Meetup for divorced people _____.
   They have children.

10. I go to a Meetup for parents _____.
    Their children are deaf.

11. The Meetup _____ has about fifty members.
    I go to it.

12. The person _____ is a nice woman I met
    I play tennis with her.
    at a Meetup.

13. People _____ interest me.
    Their political views are similar to mine.

14. Neighbors _____ have a lot in common
    The neighbors have small children.
    with me.

Mark Zuckerberg AND Facebook

🎧
CD 3
TR 5

Read the following article. Pay special attention to the words in bold.

Mark Zuckerberg, the creator of Facebook, changed the way we connect with friends. He started his social network in 2004, **when** he was a student at Harvard University. He realized that busy students wanted to be able to know about their friends' activities and thoughts. Within one month of starting Facebook, half of the undergraduate students at Harvard had signed up. He originally created the network just for Harvard students. Then he expanded Facebook to include other colleges in the Boston area. By the end of 2004, Facebook had one million users. In 2014, **when** Facebook was ten years old, it had over a billion users. And Zuckerberg had a net worth[6] of almost 30 billion dollars—by the time he was thirty years old!

When did Zuckerberg first have the idea of networking on the Internet? Zuckerberg became interested in computers when he was very young. He created his first network in 1996, **when** he was only twelve years old. He wanted to create a computer messaging system for his father's dental practice. With young Mark's system, his father could know when a patient arrived in the waiting room. Members of his family also used his network to communicate with each other. His family called it Zucknet.

At the end of his second year of college, Zuckerberg traveled to California, **where** he met with investors who had heard about his social network. The investors offered him half a million dollars to develop his site. Zuckerberg dropped out of Harvard to run Facebook from Silicon Valley,[7] which is the center of the technology industry.

Today there are many other social networking sites for sharing ideas and photos, but none has had as great an impact as Facebook.

---

6   *net worth*: the value of all a person's property, money, etc. minus what he or she owes to others
7   *Silicon Valley*: an area near San Francisco that is home to many of the world's largest technology companies

Mark Zuckerberg

700 M   700 M   1.4 B

COMPREHENSION CHECK Based on the reading, tell if the statement is true (**T**) or false (**F**).

1. Mark Zuckerberg created his first network for his father's business.

2. Zuckerberg created Facebook after graduating from college.

3. Zuckerberg developed Facebook with his own money.

11.6 Adjective Clauses with *Where* and *When*

Some adjective clauses begin with relative adverbs, *where* and *when*.

Examples	Explanation
Zuckerberg started Facebook at Harvard, **where he was a student.** Students need to find a quiet place **where they can study.**	*Where* means "in that place."
Do you remember a time **(when) there were no social media sites?** Zuckerberg created his first networking site in 1996, **when he was only 12 years old.**	*When* means "at that time."

Punctuation Note:

When the noun is unique, we set the adjective clause apart from the rest of the sentence with commas.

Compare:

> I visited a website **where I found the names of my classmates.** (No comma)
> I visited Facebook, **where I found one of my old high school friends.** (Facebook is a unique website.)
> I remember the year **(when) I graduated from high school.** (No comma)
> Zuckerberg started Facebook in 2004, **when he was a student at Harvard.** (2004 is a unique year.)

We can omit *when* in a sentence with no comma. We cannot omit *where*.

EXERCISE 12 Fill in the blanks with a phrase from the box to complete the conversation between a son and his father.

where you could buy	when kids were friends	where we used to meet	I saw
when we didn't have	when there was a war	where you met ✓	

A: Do you remember the place _____*where you met*_____ Mom?
1.

B: We met in high school. I'll never forget the day _____ your mother for the first
2.

time. She was such a pretty girl.

A: Did you go to the same school?

B: Yes. We were in a typing class together. She was sitting at the typewriter next to mine.

A: Dad, what's a typewriter?

continued

B: There was a time _____ computers. We had to type our

papers on typewriters.

A: That's so weird. Did you start dating right away?

B: No. We were friends. There was a time _____ before they

started dating. Near our school, there was a soda shop _____.
                                                                                    5.

A: What's a soda shop, Dad?

B: It's a store _____ milk shakes, sodas, and hamburgers.
                                    6.

We used to sit there after school drinking one soda with two straws.

A: That doesn't seem too romantic to me. So did you get married as soon as you graduated from

high school?

B: No. I graduated from high school at a time _____ going on
                                                                  7.

in this country. Mom went to college and I went into the army. Then, when I got out of the

army, I started college. We got married after I graduated.

EXERCISE 13 Fill in the blanks with *who, whom, that, which, when, where, whose,* or *Ø* for no word. In
some cases, more than one answer is possible.

A: I'm getting married in two months.

B: Congratulations. Are you marrying the woman _____*(whom)*_____ you met at Mark's
                                                                        1.

party last year?

A: Oh, no. I broke up with that woman a long time ago. I'm going to marry a woman

_____ I met at a Meetup about ten months ago. She's the woman
                2.

_____ I introduced you to last week.
                3.

B: Oh, I remember. What's your fiancée's name? I forgot.

A: Sarah Liston.

B: I know someone _____ last name is Liston. I wonder if they're from the
                                            4.

same family.

A: I doubt it. Sarah comes from Canada.

B: At what kind of Meetup did you meet her? Was it a singles' Meetup?

A: Oh, no. It was a Meetup for people _____ like to dine out.
5.

B: How many people are in your group?

A: It's a large group—maybe twenty-five people. So we have to meet at a time

_____ the restaurant isn't crowded because we need a lot of tables.
6.

B: I'd like to join this Meetup. When are you going to meet next?

A: In about three weeks. I'll send you an e-mail _____ has information
7.

about our group and its members. It has the name of the restaurant

_____ we're going to meet and the time _____
8.   9.

we're going to get together.

EXERCISE 14 About You Use the words given to form an adjective clause. Then tell a partner if you agree or disagree. Give your reasons.

1. My friends are people __(whom) I can trust with all my secrets__ .
I can trust them with all my secrets.

2. A good friend is a person _____ almost every day.
I see him.

3. A good friend is a person _____ .
She would lend me money.

4. A good friend is a person _____ .
He knows everything about me.

5. Most of my friends are people _____ .
Their political views are similar to mine.

6. Most of my friends are people _____ .
They speak my native language.

7. It is hard for me to be friends with a person _____ .
His religious beliefs are different from mine.

8. It is hard for me to be friends with a person _____ .
The person lives far away.

9. It's important for me to have friends _____ .
Their interests are the same as mine.

10. This school is a place _____ .
I can make many new friends easily at this school.

11. Childhood is the only time in one's life _____ .
It is easy to make friends at this time.

SUMMARY OF LESSON 11

Adjective Clauses with:

Relative Pronoun as Subject
I lost touch with a friend **who/that moved to Alaska**.
A high school **that/which has a strong science program** attracts good students.
Mark Zuckerberg, **who created Facebook**, is a billionaire.
North Dakota, **which has cold winters**, has attracted people looking for jobs.

Relative Pronoun as Object
I have a new friend **who/whom/that/Ø I met at a Meetup**.
The high school **that/which/Ø I attended** is not very big.
My wife, **who/whom I met at a math Meetup**, is a teacher.
My tenth high school reunion, **which I attended last year**, was at a hotel.

Relative Pronoun as Object of Preposition	
Formal:	Some of the friends **with whom I went to high school** moved away.
Informal:	Some of the friends **who(m)/that/Ø I went to high school with** moved away.
Formal:	The Meetup **about which I told you** meets at a neighborhood café.
Informal:	The Meetup **that/which/Ø I told you about** meets at a neighborhood café.

Relative Pronoun for Possession
I have a friend **whose brother lives in Japan**.
Scott Heiferman, **whose inspiration came from the aftermath of 9/11**, created Meetup to bring people together.

Relative Adverb for Place
I like to visit the city **where I went** to college.
Boston, **where I went to college,** is cold in the winter.

Relative Adverb for Time
My friends and I get together in a café at a time **when/Ø it isn't crowded**.
We get together on Monday at 4 o'clock, **when the café isn't crowded.**

TEST/REVIEW

Fill in the blanks with *who, whom, that, which, whose, where, when,* or *Ø.* In some cases, more than one answer is possible.

1. I'm still friends with the people ___who or whom or that or Ø___ I met in high school.

2. The high school _____ I attended is in Poland.

3. Most of the people with _____ I went to high school still live in our hometown.

4. Childhood is the time _____ it's easiest to make friends.

5. There are some teachers _____ names I've forgotten.

6. A coffee shop near my house is the place _____ my chess Meetup gets together.

7. I use several social networking sites _____ allow me to exchange information

   with my friends.

8. Mark Zuckerberg, _____ created his first network when he was a child, has

   become a billionaire.

9. Zuckerberg started Facebook in 2004, _____ he was twenty years old.

10. Silicon Valley, _____ is the center of technology, is in California.

11. The high school from _____ I graduated has around 5,000 students.

12. My sister married Mark Peters, _____ she met at a Meetup.

WRITING

PART 1 Editing Advice

1. Use *who* or *that* to introduce a person. Use *that* or *which* to introduce a thing.

    The states ~~what~~ *that* are losing the most population are in cold climates.

    I have many friends ~~which~~ *who* go to Meetups.

2. If the relative pronoun is the subject of the adjective clause, don't omit it.

    She started a group ∧ *that* now has 100 members.

3. Use *whose* to substitute for a possessive form.

    Zuckerberg, ~~his~~ *whose* father was a dentist, created a network for his father's business.

4. If the relative pronoun is used as the object of the adjective clause, don't put an object after the verb of the adjective clause.

    There are a lot of interesting Meetups that I found ~~them~~.

5. Use subject-verb agreement in the adjective clause.

    I have a friend who live∧ *s* in Madrid.

6. Put a noun before an adjective clause.

    A person who
    ~~Who~~ has a few good friends is lucky.

7. Use *where*, not *that*, to mean "in a place."

    She moved to North Dakota, ~~that~~ *where* she found a good job.

8. Use *whom* and *which*, not *who* and *that*, if the preposition precedes the relative pronoun.

    He found a group in ~~that~~ *which* he's interested.

    I've never met the person about ~~who~~ *whom* you are talking.

9. Use the correct word order in an adjective clause (subject before verb).

    The first network that ~~created Zuckerberg~~ *Zuckerberg created* was for his father's business.

10. Don't confuse *whose* (possessive form) and *who's* (*who is*).

    A woman ~~whose~~ *who's* in my science Meetup teaches biology at a high school.

PART 2 Editing Practice

Some of the shaded words and phrases have mistakes. Find the mistakes and correct them. If the shaded words are correct, write C.

        C

I would like to find one of the friends that I had in college. I found a website that I can

                     1.   *where*

                                                 2.

look for old friends. My friend, whose name is Linda Gast, got married shortly after we

                           3.

graduated. The man which she married is Bart Reed. I tried googling the names "Linda

                  4.

Gast" and "Linda Reed" but I had no luck. I found a woman with who she shared a room in

                                                    5.

college, and she gave me a phone number. The phone number that gave me her roommate

                                     6.   **7.**

is not in service anymore. I called a man what used to be her neighbor, but he said that she

                               8.

moved away a long time ago. The last reunion that I attended it was four years ago, but she

                                 9.   **10.**

wasn't there. The people were our friends in high school didn't know anything about her. I

                 11.

looked in the phone book and found some people their name is the same as hers, but they

                                         12.

weren't the right people. I went back to the high school that we were students, but they had no

                                       13.

information about her.

    Because of the Internet, now is a time when it's easier than ever to find people. But

                                          14.

my search, which have taken me almost five years, has produced no result. Recently I met

        15.   **16.**

someone whose a friend of her brother, and he told me that Linda's now living in South

             17.

America. He's going to try to find Linda's current address. Looking for Linda is hard but I'm

determined to find her. Who tries hard enough usually succeeds.

               18.

PART 3 Write About It

1. Write a short composition comparing the friendships you have today with the friendships you had when you were younger.

2. Write a short composition comparing social relationships in your country with social relationships in the United States.

PART 4 Edit Your Writing

Reread the Summary of Lesson 11 and the editing advice. Edit your writing from Part 3.

SPORTS AND ATHLETES

A runner in the Marathon des Sables,
a foot race considered one of the
toughest races in the world

Obstacles don't have to stop you. If you run into a wall, don't turn around and give up. Figure out how to climb it, go through it, or work around it.

—Michael Jordan

Gregg Treinish
Extreme Athlete and Conservationist

Read the following article. Pay special attention to the words in bold.

Gregg Treinish is an adventurer who turned his love of physical challenges into something more.

In 2004, Treinish hiked the Appalachian Trail, one of **the longest** footpaths in the world, measuring about 2,180 miles (3,508 km) in length. This path follows through fourteen states from Maine to Georgia. Maryland and West Virginia are **the easiest** states to hike. New Hampshire and Maine are **the most difficult**. While Treinish was hiking one of **the hardest** parts, he kept slipping and cutting his legs on the sharp rock. In frustration,[1] he picked up a rock and threw it at a tree. "I felt like **the lowest** person on earth," he said. He knew he wanted to do something more, but he didn't know what that was.

Then, starting in 2006, he and his friend, Deia Schlosberg, spent two years hiking 7,800 miles from Ecuador to Tierra del Fuego, following along the Andes Mountains, **the longest** mountain chain in the world. When they arrived, they commented that Tierra del Fuego was one of **the most spectacular** places on Earth.

In 2008, National Geographic named Gregg Treinish Adventurer of the Year. But he wasn't fulfilled.[2] He felt his **biggest** challenge was in his mind. He began asking himself: Is it enough to hike **the longest, most difficult** trails? Am I doing anything to help the world? How can I turn my adventures into something more beneficial to the world?

Treinish had an idea: He thought that scientists might need information from hard-to-reach places where only **the bravest** adventurers go. And he was right. Scientists want data, samples, and photographs from **the most remote** places on earth—places that they can't go to themselves. Treinish founded Adventurers and Scientists for Conservation (ASC) to connect scientists with extreme adventurers. Now, when athletes go to these unusual places, they can do something to benefit the world by collecting information for scientists. Several thousand adventurers have collected data with ASC.

ASC mountain climbers have discovered Earth's **highest** known plant life on Mount Everest and have brought back samples for researchers to study. These samples help farmers learn to grow crops in extreme conditions.

For Treinish, connecting science and outdoor adventure is **the most satisfying** kind of adventure. "Adventurers tell me these chances to give back have changed their whole perspective.[3] Now, being **the strongest** or summiting **the coolest** peak[4] isn't what's important. Trying to contribute and make a difference is what matters. And there's so much more we can do."

---

[1] *frustration*: a feeling of disappointment or anger at not being able to accomplish something
[2] *fulfilled*: satisfied
[3] *perspective*: a way of seeing things; point of view
[4] *to summit a peak*: to reach the top of a mountain

COMPREHENSION CHECK Based on the reading, tell if the statement is true (**T**) or false (**F**).

1. Gregg Treinish hiked along the Andes Mountains alone.

2. The difficulty of the Appalachian Trail changes as a hiker goes from state to state.

3. Gregg's goal is to connect adventurers with each other.

12.1 The Superlative Form of Adjectives and Adverbs[5]

	Simple	Superlative
One-syllable adjectives and adverbs	long big	the longest the biggest
Two-syllable adjectives that end in *y*	easy happy	the easiest the happiest
Other two-syllable adjectives	remote extreme	the most remote the most extreme
Some two-syllable adjectives have two forms.	simple common	the simplest the most simple the commonest the most common
Adjectives with three or more syllables	spectacular difficult	the most spectacular the most difficult
-ly adverbs	quickly directly	the most quickly the most directly
Irregular superlatives	good/well bad/badly far	the best the worst the farthest
Quantity words	little few	the least the fewest
	a lot much many	the most

Language Notes:

1. Other two-syllable adjectives that have two forms are:

    handsome, quiet, gentle, narrow, clever, friendly, angry, polite, stupid

2. Adjectives that are past participles use *the most*.

    tired—the most tired

    fulfilled—the most fulfilled

    worried—the most worried

---

[5] For spelling rules for superlatives, see Appendix M.

EXERCISE 1 Listen to this conversation about Emma Gatewood, another amazing athlete.
Fill in the blanks with the words you hear.

A: I just read an article about one of _the most interesting_ athletes.
1.

B: Was it about Michael Phelps? He's _____ swimmer in the world.
2.

A: No. It was about a woman.

B: Was it Missy Franklin? She was _____ female swimmer at the 2012
3.

Olympics. I liked her _____ of all the female swimmers in 2012.
4.

A: No. This woman was never at the Olympics. Her name was Emma Gatewood. She was the first

woman to hike the Appalachian Trail solo—at the age of 67! People often called her "Grandma

Gatewood." She believed that hikers should carry _____ equipment
5.

possible. She wasn't interested in taking _____ equipment for her
6.

hike. She took a homemade bag and carried a blanket, a raincoat, and a shower curtain.

B: A shower curtain? What for?

A: She used it to make a tent.

B: That's _____ thing I've ever heard.
7.

A: She believed in doing things _____ way possible.
8.

B: And _____ way possible too. What about food?
9.

A: She carried some dried food, but she did _____ she could to find
10.

wild food.

B: She was quite a woman!

A: She hiked the Appalachian Trail again at the age of 75. At that time she was

_____ woman to hike the trail.

11.

B: I've read stories of several athletes, but I like her story _____.

12.

She inspires me _____ .

13.

A: Me too. She's one of _____ athletes I've ever read about.

14.

EXERCISE 2 Review the spelling rules for superlative forms in Appendix M. Write the superlative of each word.

1. fat   _the fattest_

2. important   _the most important_

3. interesting _____

4. good   _____

5. responsible _____

6. thin   _____

7. carefully   _____

8. bad   _____

9. famous   _____

10. lucky   _____

11. simple   _____

12. extreme   _____

13. far   _____

14. bored   _____

12.2 Superlatives—Use

Examples	Explanation
The Andes is **the longest** mountain chain in the world. What is **the most difficult** part of the Appalachian Trail?	We use the superlative form to point out the number one item(s) of a group of three or more.
Treinish hiked **some of the most difficult** trails. Gatewood was **one of the most remarkable** hikers.	We often say "one/some of the" before a superlative form. The noun that follows is plural.
Mt. Everest is **the highest** mountain **in the world**. The Appalachian Trail is not **the longest** trail **in the United States**.	We often put a prepositional phrase after a superlative phrase: *in the world, of all time, in the U.S.,* etc.
The north part of the Appalachian Trail is **the least challenging**.	You can use *the least* to make a superlative.
What is the most spectacular place **(that) you've ever seen?**	An adjective clause with the present perfect and *ever* often completes a superlative statement.
In 2012, **the fastest swimmer** in the world was Michael Phelps. Michael Phelps won **the most medals** at the 2012 Olympics.	A superlative form can precede any noun in the sentence.
Grandma Gatewood inspires me **the most**. I like her story **the best**.	A superlative form can follow the verb (phrase).

continued

Language Notes:

1. Use *the* before a superlative form. Omit *the* if there is a possessive form before a superlative.

    What was **your most challenging** adventure? (NOT: *your the* most challenging)

2. When the verb *be* connects a noun to a superlative adjective + noun, there are two possible word orders:

    Football is the most popular sport in the U.S.

    The most popular sport in the U.S. is football.

EXERCISE 3 Write the superlative form of the word given.

1. At age 15, Michael Phelps was ___the youngest___ American male swimmer in 68 years to make
   _{young}

   an Olympic team.

2. At the 2008 Olympics, he broke a record set in 1972, making him _____ swimmer
   _{fast}

   ever for that event.

3. Many people think Michael Phelps was _____ athlete at the 2012 Olympics.
   _{exciting}

4. A popular sports magazine named Phelps _____ sportsman of the year in 2008.
   _{good}

5. At the 2012 Olympics in London, he was _____ swimmer.
   _{successful}

6. He won _____ medals at the 2012 Olympics.
   _{a lot}

7. Will anyone take his place? Or will he always be _____ swimmer of all time?
   _{great}

EXERCISE 4 About You Give your opinion. Write a superlative sentence about each of the following items. Then compare your answers to a partner's.

1. popular athlete in my country

   Manny Pacquiao is one of the most popular athletes in my country.

2. boring sport

   _____

3. interesting sport

   _____

4. good athlete

   _____

5. bad thing about (*name a sport*)

   _____

6. popular athlete in my country

_____

7. easy sport for children

_____

8. challenging sport

_____

9. dangerous adventure

_____

EXERCISE 5 About You Use the words to write superlative sentences about your experiences. Use the present perfect form with *ever* after the superlative. Share your answers with a partner.

1. long/distance/walk

My hike through the Alps was the longest distance I've ever walked.

2. interesting/sporting event/see

_____

3. dangerous/thing/do

_____

4. difficult/sport/play

_____

5. good/athlete/see

_____

6. challenging/thing/do

_____

Americans' Attitude Toward Soccer

Read the following article. Pay special attention to the words in bold.

Almost everyone in the world calls it "football." Americans call it soccer. Whatever you call it, it is by far the most popular sport in the world. In many countries, top international soccer players are as well-known as rock stars or actors—but not in the United States.

In 1999, when the Women's World Cup was played in the United States, there was **more excitement** about soccer than ever before. It seemed as if the United States might start to become **more interested** in this international sport. But in 2014, when the World Cup was held in Brazil, only seven percent of Americans had plans to watch it. Eighty-six percent of Americans said they knew nothing or only a little about the World Cup. Two-thirds of Americans said they didn't know that Brazil was the host nation.

Some statistics show that interest in soccer is **higher** than before. Certainly, during the World Cup, there is a **larger** audience for soccer than at other times. But soccer is still much **less popular** in the United States than in the rest of the world.

Experts believe that to increase interest in soccer, professional teams have to produce **better** players—and they have to capture kids' interest at a **younger** age. Many American parents enroll their kids in soccer programs because they consider soccer **safer** than other sports, such as football or hockey. Between 1990 and 2010, the number of young players doubled. While **more** American kids are playing soccer than ever before, European and Latin American youth soccer programs are **more demanding**. Youngsters there who show talent in soccer are encouraged to go into even **more rigorous**[6] training.

European and Latin American young athletes dream of becoming the next Lionel Messi. American kids want to grow up to be the next Lebron James. Will this change? Only time will tell.

---

[6] *rigorous*: difficult; having high standards

U.S. player Lauren Holiday moments before scoring a goal against Japan during the Women's World Cup 2015.

COMPREHENSION CHECK Based on the reading, tell if the statement is true (**T**) or false (**F**).

1. American soccer players are as well-known as movie stars.

2. Interest in soccer is slowly increasing in the United States.

3. Most Americans watch soccer during the World Cup.

12.3 Comparative Forms of Adjectives and Adverbs[7]

	Simple	Comparative
One-syllable adjectives and adverbs	high large	higher larger
Two-syllable adjectives that end in *y*	easy happy	easier happier
Other two-syllable adjectives	remote extreme	more remote more extreme
Some two-syllable adjectives have two forms	simple common	simpler more simple commoner more common
Adjectives with three or more syllables	popular demanding	more popular more demanding
-ly adverbs	quickly directly	more quickly more directly
Irregular comparatives	good/well bad/badly far	better worse farther
Quantity words	little few	less fewer
	a lot much many	more

Language Notes:

1. Other two-syllable adjectives that have two forms are:

   handsome, quiet, gentle, narrow, clever, friendly, angry, polite, stupid

2. Adjectives that are past participles use *more*.

   tired—more tired

   fulfilled—more fulfilled

   worried—more worried

3. We use *than* before the second item of comparison.

   Football is more popular **than** soccer in the U.S.

---

7 For spelling rules for comparatives, see Appendix M.

🎧
CD 3
TR 9
EXERCISE 6 Listen to the following article. Fill in the blanks with the words you hear.

What are the differences between college sports and professional sports? Of course,

professional athletes are ___more experienced than___ college athletes, but college athletes
                              1.

are _____ and sometimes _____ . The ticket
              2.   **3.**

prices are _____ for professional sports _____ they are
                    4.   **5.**

for college sports. In professional sports, athletes make a lot of money, but college athletes

don't. So college athletes are _____ about the sport
                                              6.

_____ they are about the financial gain.
          7.

In college baseball, players use aluminum bats; in professional baseball, players use

wooden bats. Fans like the sound the wooden bat makes _____ the
                                                                  8.

sound of the aluminum bat. The baseball stadium for professional baseball is

_____ than the baseball stadium for college baseball.
          9.

Some fans think that college basketball is _____ professional
                                                          10.

basketball. The atmosphere of college basketball is _____ because college
                                                                11.

students cheer on their favorite team _____ after a score. The fans of
                                                  12.

professional basketball are _____ the fans of college basketball.
                                      13.

College basketball is _____ either college baseball or football.
                                14.

The fans are _____ to the action. College football has a
                    15.

_____ crowd if the home team is good that year.
          16.

In professional sports, fans are sometimes _____ in their favorite
                                                          17.

players _____ the whole team. In college sports, the team gets
              18.

_____ than the individual players.
          19.

Which do you think is _____ ?
                                20.

EXERCISE 7 Review the spelling rules of comparative forms in Appendix M. Write the comparative form of each word.

1. fat   _____fatter_____   4. low   _____

2. important   _____more important_____   5. beautifully   _____

3. exciting   _____   6. good   _____

7. remarkable	_____	12. surprised	_____
8. athletic	_____	13. high	_____
9. bad	_____	14. large	_____
10. rigorous	_____	15. far	_____
11. challenging	_____	16. enthusiastically	_____

12.4 Comparatives—Use

Examples	Explanation
Basketball is **livelier than** baseball. Soccer is **more popular than** boxing.	We use the comparative form to show the difference between two people or things.
European children train **more rigorously** in soccer **than** American children.	We use *than* before the second item of comparison.
Soccer is **less popular than** football in the U.S.	We can use *less* to make a comparison.
College athletes have **less experience than** professional athletes. Soccer players have **fewer injuries** than football players.	We can put *more, less, fewer, better, worse,* and other comparative forms before a noun. We use *less* with noncount nouns; we use *fewer* with count nouns.
My sister **likes soccer more** than I do. You **play basketball better** than your brother does.	We can put *more, less, better, worse,* and other comparative forms after a verb (phrase).
Interest in soccer is **much lower** in the U.S. than it is in other countries. I like soccer **a little better** than I like baseball.	*Much* or *a little* can come before a comparative form.
The more they practice, **the better** they play. **The older** you are, **the harder** it is to learn a new sport.	We can use two comparisons in one sentence to show cause and result.

Language Notes:

1. Omit *than* if the second item of comparison is not included.

    Basketball is popular in the U.S., but football is **more popular**.

2. When a pronoun follows *than*, the correct form is the subject pronoun (*he, she, I,* etc.). Usually an auxiliary verb follows (*is, do, did, can,* etc.). Informally, many Americans use the object pronoun (*him, her, me,* etc.) after *than* without an auxiliary verb.

    FORMAL: You are taller than **I am**.   FORMAL: I can play soccer better than **he can**.

    INFORMAL: You are taller than **me**.   INFORMAL: I can play soccer better than **him**.

EXERCISE 8 Circle the correct words to complete each statement.

1. Professional athletes make (much more/more much) money than college athletes.

2. A basketball player is (more tall/taller) than a gymnast.

3. A baseball game has (little/less) action than a soccer game.

continued

4. Football players use (*more padding/padding more*) than soccer players.

5. Football players are (*much/more*) heavier than soccer players.

6. A football team has (*much/more*) players than a baseball team.

7. Americans are (*enthusiastic less/less enthusiastic*) about soccer than Europeans.

8. Michael Phelps (*faster swims/swims faster*) than other swimmers.

9. Who plays (*better/more better*), college athletes or professional athletes?

10. College baseball has (*fewer/less*) fans than college basketball.

11. I think football is exciting, but soccer is (*more exciting/more exciting than*).

EXERCISE 9 Fill in the blank with the comparative of a word from the box. Include *than* when necessary.

easily	tall	strong	slow	popular√	active	large	good

1. In the U.S., basketball is _____ more popular than _____ soccer.

2. Basketball players are usually _____ football players.

3. A golf game (18 holes) takes about 3 or 4 hours. It is much _____ most

   other sports.

4. A soccer ball is _____ a tennis ball.

5. Children learn sports _____ adults.

6. People who lift weights are _____ people who don't.

7. Soccer players are always moving. Soccer players are _____ baseball players.

8. Professional athletes are usually _____ college athletes.

EXERCISE 10 Use the information in the chart to write sentences that compare these two female Olympic swimmers. Answers may vary.

	Missy Franklin	Natalie Coughlin
year born	1995	1982
height	6 feet 1 inches tall	5 feet 8 inches tall
weight	165 pounds	139 pounds
education	didn't finish college	graduated from college
age when she started to swim competitively	7	6
participation in Olympic Games	competed in Olympics in 2012	competed in Olympics in 2004, 2008, 2012
competed in number of events in 2012	7	4

1. <u>Missy is younger than Nancy. OR Nancy is older than Missy.</u>

2. _____

3. _____

4. _____

5. _____

6. _____

7. _____

Missy Franklin

EXERCISE 11 About You Compare yourself to a family member or friend. Share your answers with a partner.

1. interested in baseball

   <u>My brother is more interested in baseball than I am.</u>

2. tall

   _____

3. strong

   _____

continued

4. athletic

_____

5. competitive

_____

6. enthusiastic about sports

_____

7. a good swimmer

_____

8. knowledgeable about soccer

_____

EXERCISE 12 Fill in the blanks with the comparative or superlative form of the word given. Include _than_ or _the_ when necessary.

1. In the U.S., baseball is ___more popular than___ soccer.

popular

2. Baseball is one of ___the most popular___ sports in the U.S.

popular

3. A tennis ball is _____ a baseball.

soft

4. An athlete who wins the gold medal is _____ athlete in his or her sport.

good

5. Who is _____ basketball player in the world?

tall

6. I am _____ in baseball _____ in basketball.

interested

7. In my opinion, soccer is _____ sport in the world.

exciting

8. Weightlifters are _____ golfers.

muscular

9. Soccer is a _____ sport _____ baseball.

fast

10. A basketball team has _____ players _____ a

few

    baseball team.

11. My friend and I both jog. I run _____ my friend.

far

12. Who's a _____ soccer player—you or your brother?

good

13. In golf, the player who has _____ scores wins.

low

14. European soccer players are _____ American soccer players.

well-known

An Amazing Athlete

Erik Weihenmayer
on Mount Everest

🎧 **Read the following article. Pay special attention to the words in bold.**

CD 3
TR 10

Erik Weihenmayer is **as tough as** any mountain climber. In 2001, he made his way to the top of the highest mountain in the world—Mount Everest—at the age of 33. But Erik is different from other mountain climbers in one important way—he is completely blind. He is the only blind person to reach the top of the tallest mountain.

Erik was an athletic child who lost his vision in his early teens. At first he refused to use a cane or learn braille,[8] insisting he could do **as well as** any teenager. But he finally came to accept his disability. He couldn't play **the same** sports **as** he used to. He would never be able to play basketball or catch a football again. At sixteen, he became interested in rock climbing. Rock climbing led to mountain climbing, the greatest challenge of his life.

The members of his climbing team say that Erik isn't different from a sighted climber. He has **as much training as** the others. He is **as strong as** the rest. He **is like** any other climber: flexible, mentally tough, and able to tolerate physical pain.

Climbing Mount Everest was a challenge for every climber on Erik's team. The reaction to the mountain air for Erik was **the same as** it was for his teammates: lack of oxygen causes the heart to beat more slowly than usual, and the brain does not function **as clearly as** normal. To climb Mount Everest is an achievement for any athlete. Erik Weihenmayer showed that his disability wasn't **as important as** his ability.

---

[8] *braille*: a system of reading and writing for the blind that uses raised dots for letters, numbers, and symbols
[9] *accommodation*: a change so that people can work together

COMPREHENSION CHECK Based on the reading, tell if the statement is true (**T**) or false (**F**).

1. When Erik became blind, he continued to participate in sports.

2. Erik doesn't have as much training as his teammates.

3. At the highest altitudes, the brain functions as clearly as normal.

12.5 As . . . As

Examples	Explanation
Erik is **as strong as** his teammates. At high altitudes, the brain doesn't function **as clearly as** normal.	We can show that two things are equal or unequal in some way by using: *(not) as* + adjective/adverb + *as*
Skiing is not **as difficult as** mountain climbing.	When we make a comparison of unequal items, we put the lesser item first.

Language Note:

Omit the second *as* if the second item of comparison is omitted.

Baseball is popular in the U.S. Soccer is not **as popular**.

EXERCISE 13 Fill in the blanks with a word from the box and *as . . . as*.

strong	well	dangerous✓	clearly	prepared

1. Rock climbing is not _____ *as dangerous as* _____ mountain climbing.

2. At high altitudes, you can't think _____ you can at lower altitudes.

3. Erik trained well, and he was _____ his teammates.

4. When Erik became blind, he wanted to do _____ any other teenager.

5. Erik is _____ other climbers.

EXERCISE 14 Change these comparative sentences to sentences using *not as . . . as*.

1. Europeans are more interested in soccer than Americans.

   Americans are not as interested in soccer as Europeans.

2. Soccer is more popular in Latin America than it is in the U.S.

   _____

3. Football is more dangerous than soccer for children.

_____

4. Missy Franklin is younger than Natalie Coughlin.

_____

5. Missy Franklin is taller than Natalie Coughlin.

_____

6. Professional European soccer players are more famous than professional American soccer players.

_____

EXERCISE 15 About You Compare yourself to another person. (Or compare two people you know.) Use the following words and *as . . . as.* You may add a comparative statement if there is inequality. Discuss your answers with a partner.

1. athletic

I'm not as athletic as my uncle. He's much more athletic than I am.

2. interested in basketball

_____

3. good at sports

_____

4. walk fast

_____

5. strong

_____

6. excited about soccer

_____

7. muscular

_____

12.6 As Many/Much . . . As

Examples	Explanation

Soccer players don't usually have **as many injuries as** football players.
Erik had **as much training as** his teammates.
	We can show that two things are equal or unequal in quantity by using:
	    (*not*) *as many* + count noun + *as*
	    (*not*) *as much* + noncount noun + *as*

I don't play soccer **as much as** I used to.	We can use *as much as* after a verb phrase.

EXERCISE 16 Fill in the blanks with *as much/many...as*.

1. Does Gregg Treinish get _____as much_____ satisfaction from extreme sports _____as_____ he

   used to?

2. Nancy Coughlin didn't win _____ medals in the 2012 Olympics _____

   she did in the 2008 Olympics.

3. You don't hear about Michael Jordan _____ you used to.

4. Grandma Gatewood didn't carry _____ equipment on the Appalachian Trail

   _____ other hikers.

5. She didn't spend _____ money on equipment _____ other hikers.

6. Michael Phelps didn't win _____ gold medals in 2012 _____ he did in 2008.

7. American soccer teams don't win _____ games at the World Cup _____

   European teams.

8. Americans don't show _____ interest in soccer _____ Latin Americans.

9. Americans don't know _____ about soccer _____ Europeans.

EXERCISE 17 About You Fill in information about yourself. Then find a partner and compare your answers.

Example: I don't spend as much time in nature as my partner does.

	Not at all	Occasionally	Frequently
1. I spend time in nature.	○	●	○
2. I exercise.	○	○	○
3. I read sports magazines.	○	○	○
4. I attend sporting events.	○	○	○
5. I watch basketball games.	○	○	○
6. I watch soccer on TV.	○	○	○

EXERCISE 18 About You Compare yourself today to the way you were five years ago. Use *as . . . as*, *as much/many . . . as*, or a comparative form. Share your answers with a partner.

1. thin

   I'm not as thin as I was five years ago.   OR I'm heavier than I was five years ago.

2. strong

   _____

3. physically fit

   _____

4. interested in sports

   _____

5. exercise

   _____

6. have time to relax

   _____

7. watch sports programs on TV

   _____

12.7 The Same . . . As

We can show that two things are equal or not with *the same . . . (as)*

Examples	Explanation
Pattern A: Erik had **the same ability as** his teammates.	**Pattern A:** Noun 1 + verb + *the same* noun *as* + Noun 2.
Pattern B: Erik and his teammates had **the same ability**.	**Pattern B:** Noun 1 and Noun 2 + verb + *the same* noun.

Language Note: We can make statements of equality or inequality with many types of nouns, such as *size*, *shape*, *color*, *value*, *religion*, *age*, *height*, or *nationality*.

COMPARE:

He is **the same height as** his teammate. (*height* = noun)

He is **as tall as** his teammate. (*tall* = adjective)

Missy **isn't the same age as** Natalie. (*age* = noun)

Missy **isn't as old as** Natalie. (*old* = adjective)

EXERCISE 19 Use the words to make statements with (not) the same (. . . as).

1. a golf ball/a tennis ball (*size*)

   A golf ball isn't the same size as a tennis ball.

2. a basketball team/a soccer team (*number of players*)

   A basketball team and a soccer team don't have the same number of players.

3. a soccer ball/a football (*shape*)

   _____

4. a soccer player/a basketball player (*height*)

   _____

5. a college athlete/a professional athlete (*experience*)

   _____

6. a hardball/a softball (*size*)

   _____

7. football players/soccer players (*uniforms*)

   _____

EXERCISE 20 Use the information in the chart to compare two Olympic swimmers. Use two methods of comparison.

Michael Phelps	Ryan Lochte
born 1985	born 1984
won 22 medals in the 2012 Olympics	won 11 medals in the 2012 Olympics
6 feet 4 inches tall	6 feet 2 inches tall
194 pounds	194 pounds
received bachelor's degree	received bachelor's degree
started swimming at age 7	started swimming at age 5
participated in 2004, 2008, 2012 Olympics	participated in 2008 and 2012 Olympics

1. Ryan is older than Michael.

   Ryan and Michael weren't born in the same year.

2. _____

   _____

3. _____

_____

4. _____

_____

5. _____

_____

6. _____

_____

7. _____

_____

Ryan Lochte and
Michael Phelps

FOOTBALL AND SOCCER

🎧
CD 3
TR 11
Read the following article. Pay special attention to the words in bold.

It may seem strange that Americans give the name "football" to a game played mostly by throwing and carrying a ball with one's hands. Speakers of a language other than English usually refer to this sport as *American football*, but in the United States, it's simply *football*.

Many of the rules in soccer and football are the same. In both games, there are eleven players on each side, and a team scores its points by getting the ball past the goal of the other team. The playing fields for both teams **are** also very much **alike**.

When the action begins, the two games look very different. In addition to using their feet, soccer players are allowed to hit the ball with their heads. In football, the only person allowed to touch the ball with his feet is a special player known as the kicker. Also, in football,

tackling[10] the player who has the ball is not only allowed but encouraged, whereas[11] tackling in soccer will get the tackler thrown out of the game.

Football players and soccer players don't **dress alike** or even **look alike** in many ways. Since blocking and tackling are a big part of American football, the players are often very large and muscular and wear heavy padding and helmets. Soccer players, on the other hand, are usually thinner and wear shorts and polo shirts. This gives them more freedom of movement so that they can show off the fancy footwork that makes soccer such a popular game around the world.

---

10 *tackling*: knocking a player carrying the ball to the ground
11 *whereas*: in contrast to

COMPREHENSION CHECK Based on the reading, tell if the statement is true (**T**) or false (**F**).

1. A soccer team and a football team don't have the same number of players.

2. It is common to see tackling in a football game.

3. Football players need padding to protect their bodies.

12.8 Showing Similarity with *Like* and *Alike*

We can show that two things are similar (or not) with *like* and *alike*.

Examples	Explanation
Pattern A: A soccer player **looks like** a rugby player. A soccer player **doesn't look like** a football player.	**Pattern A:** Noun 1 + verb + *like* + Noun 2
Pattern B: A soccer player and a rugby player **look alike**. A soccer player and a football player **don't look alike**.	**Pattern B:** Noun 1 and Noun 2 + verb + *alike*
Pattern A: He **is like** his brother in some ways. They both love soccer. He **is not like** his sister. They have different interests.	**Pattern A:** Noun 1 + *be like* + Noun 2
Pattern B: He and his brother **are alike** in some ways. He and his sister **are not alike**.	**Pattern B:** Noun 1 and Noun 2 + *be alike*

Language Notes:

1. We use the sense perception verbs (*look, sound, smell, taste, feel,* and *seem*) with *like* and *alike* to show an outward similarity or difference.

2. We can use other verbs with *like/alike: act, sing, dress, think,* etc.

   A soccer player doesn't **dress like** a football player.

   A soccer player and a football player **don't dress alike**.

3. We use *be like/be alike* to show an inward similarity or difference.
   Compare:

   Erik **looks like** an athlete. He's tall and strong. (*look like* = an outward similarity)

   Erik **is like** his teammates. He's a strong climber. (*be like* = an inward similarity)

EXERCISE 21 Fill in the blanks with an item from the box. You can use some items more than once.

are alike	is like	don't look like	look like	aren't alike
dress alike	think alike	look alike	am not like	sound like

1. **A:** You're so tall. You _____look like_____ a basketball player.
   a.

   B: Everyone who sees me says the same thing.

2. **A:** _____ wrestling _____ boxing?
   a.   b.

   B: In some ways, they _____ because they fight in a ring. But in many ways they're different.
   c.

3. **A:** My brother and I _____ in some ways.
   a.

   B: How?

   A: We're both very athletic.

4. **A:** Soccer players _____ football players at all.
   a.

   B: Football players are much bigger. And they wear completely different uniforms.

5. **A:** The swimming competition and the diving competition at the Olympics are very different.

   B: You're right. They _____ at all.
   a.

6. **A:** You _____ your brother.
   a.

   B: Everybody says that. We both talk about our favorite soccer team all the time.

7. **A:** My nieces are identical twins. They _____. Here's a picture of them.
   a.

   B: Oh, how cute. They're wearing the same outfit.

   A: Yes. They like to _____. But they _____ in all ways. One loves sports.
   b.   c.

   The other doesn't.

8. **A:** I have a great idea. Let's take the day off and go to a baseball game.

   B: I had the exact same idea. You and I _____.
   a.

9. **A:** My sister is a great swimmer.

   B: What about you?

   A: When it comes to swimming, I _____ my sister at all. I'm afraid of the water.
   a.

   B: But you _____ in some ways. You're both interested in mountain climbing.
   b.

EXERCISE 22 [About You] Compare yourself to someone in your family or compare two members of your family using the following words. Share your answers with a partner.

1. look like <u>I don't look like my mother. She's tall. I'm very short.</u>

2. be like _____

3. be alike _____

4. look like _____

5. think alike _____

6. dress like _____

7. act like _____

EXERCISE 23 Fill in the blanks in the conversation. Use different methods of comparison from this lesson. Use context clues to help you.

A: I heard that you have a twin brother. Do you and your brother look _____<u>alike</u>_____?
1.

B: No. He _____ look _____ me at all.
2. 3.

A: But you're twins.

B: We're fraternal twins. That's different from identical twins. We're not even _____
4.

height. He's not _____ I am. He's 5'8". I'm 6'2".
5.

A: But you're _____ in some ways, aren't you?
6.

B: No. We're completely different. I'm athletic, and I'm on the high school football team, but David

hates sports. He's a much _____ student than I am. He gets all A's. He's more
7.

_____ our mother, who loves to read and learn new things, and I _____
8. 9.

our father, who's athletic and loves to build things. Also, I'm outgoing, but he's very shy. And we

don't dress _____ at all. He likes to wear neat, conservative clothes, but I prefer
10.

torn jeans and T-shirts. There's only one similarity: over the phone, people don't know if it's my

brother or me. We sound _____.
11.

SUMMARY OF LESSON 12

Simple, Comparative, and Superlative Forms

SHORT WORDS
Jacob is **tall**.   Mark is **taller than** Jacob.   Bart is **the tallest** member of the basketball team.

LONG WORDS
Basketball is **popular** in the U.S.   Basketball is **more popular than** soccer in the U.S.   Soccer is **the most popular** sport in the world.

Comparisons with *as . . . as* and *the same . . . as*

Soccer players aren't **as tall as** basketball players.   Soccer players aren't **the same height as** basketball players.   Soccer players and basketball players aren't **the same height.**
I didn't swim **as many minutes as** you did.   I didn't spend **as much time** in the pool **as** you did.   I don't work out **as much as** you do.

Comparisons with *Like* and *Alike*

She**'s like** her mother. They're both interested in sports.   She and her mother **are alike**. They're both interested in sports.   She **looks like** her mother. They're both tall and strong.   She and her mother **look alike**. They're both tall and strong.

TEST / REVIEW

Fill in the blanks to complete the conversation. In some cases, answers may vary.

A: It's football season, and my husband doesn't pay as _____much_____ attention to me
1.

_____as_____ he does to his football games. Many women have _____
2.   3.

problem _____ I do. They call us "football widows" because we lose our
4.

husbands during football season.

B: Your husband sounds _____ my husband. I feel _____ a widow,
5.   6.

too. Most men act _____ during football season. My husband isn't _____
7.   8.

interested in me as he is in watching TV. He looks _____ a robot in front of the TV.
9.

When I complain, he tells me to sit down and join him. But I don't like football.

A: I think soccer is much _____ than football. My favorite team
10.

is the Chicago Fire.

B: In my opinion, they're not _____ good _____ the Los Angeles
11.   12.

Galaxy. I think the Galaxy is much _____. But
13.

_____ teams are from Europe and Latin America.
14.

A: Exactly! Soccer is _____ sport in the world. It's only in the
15.

U.S. that it isn't very popular. Even during the World Cup, Americans don't pay

_____ attention to the games as Europeans and Latin Americans.
16.

B: It's crazy! I think the action in soccer is _____ the action in football. And
17.

it's _____ fun to watch soccer players. Football players look
18.

_____ big monsters with their helmets and padding.
19.

B: Did you watch the World Cup in 2014? The _____ game was between Germany
20.

and Argentina. I mentioned Lionel Messi to my husband, and he said "Who's that"? I said,

"He's _____ player in the world."
21.

A: I love Messi. He's a strong player. But Cristiano Ronaldo is even _____.
22.

B: Well, let's do our favorite sport: shopping. We can spend _____ time
23.

shopping _____ they do in front of the TV.
24.

A: You and I think _____. We're football widows, so our husbands can be
25.

"shopping widowers."

WRITING

PART 1 Editing Advice

1. Don't use *more* and *-er* together.

   He plays baseball ~~more~~ better than his brother.

2. Use *than* before the second item of comparison.

   Soccer is more exciting ~~that~~ *than* baseball.

3. Use *the* before a superlative form.

   Mt. Everest is ^*the* tallest mountain in the world.

4. Use a plural noun in the phrase "one of the [superlative] [nouns]."

   Lionel Messi is one of the best soccer player^*s* in the world.

5. Use the correct word order.

   I ~~more like sports~~ *like sports more* than you do.

   I have ~~interest more~~ *more interest* than you do in sports.

6. Use *be like* for inward similarity. Use *look like* for an outward similarity.

   He is ~~look~~ like his brother. They are both talented athletes.

   He ~~is~~ ^*s* look like his brother. They are both tall and muscular.

7. Use the correct negative for *be like, look like, sound like, feel like*, etc.

   He ~~isn't~~ *doesn't* look like an athlete. He's not in good shape.

8. Use *the same* before nouns.

   A baseball isn't ~~the same~~ *as* big as a volleyball.

9. Use *as* before adjectives and adverbs.

   A baseball isn't the same ~~big~~ *size* as a volleyball.

10. With equality and inequality, use *as* with the second item.

    A football isn't the same shape ~~than~~ *as* a soccer ball.

11. Don't confuse *more* and *most*.

    Tierra del Fuego is the ~~more~~ *most* spectacular place he has ever seen.

PART 2 Editing Practice

Some of the shaded words and phrases have mistakes. Find the mistakes and correct them. If the shaded words are correct, write *C*.

                              most   *C*

Soccer is the ~~more~~ popular sport in the world. It is more popular than football, baseball,
                 1.   **2.**

and basketball combined. I know Americans prefer football, but for me soccer is much more
                                                                    3.

interesting that football. In fact, I think soccer is the more exciting sport in the world. There
     4.   **5.**

are some good American teams, but they aren't as good as some of the European teams.
                                    6.

I think Italy has one of the best team.
                   7.   **8.**

    The name "football" is confusing. "Football" is sounds like a game where you use your
                                          9.

feet, but football players carry the ball. A football and a soccer ball don't look alike at all. A
                                                10.

soccer ball is round, but a football isn't. The game of football isn't look like the game of soccer
                                              11.

at all. These sports are completely different. The players are different too. Soccer players are

not the same big as football players. There is just one similarity: a soccer team has the same
        12.   **13.**

number of players as a football team.
             14.

    I especially like Cristiano Ronaldo. In my opinion, he is one of the best player in the
                                                15.

world. I love to watch soccer, but I like to play it even more. When I lived in my country,

I played more better because I more practiced. I played every weekend. But here I don't have
          16.   **17.**

time as much as before. I watch it on TV but it isn't as much fun as playing it.
     18.   **19.**

PART 3 Write About It

1. Write an essay that compares two athletes from the same sport. If you don't follow sports, compare two famous people from the same field (politics, movies, art, etc.). If you use information from an outside source, please attach that source to your essay.

2. Write an essay about a person who made an amazing accomplishment. You can write about a famous person or a person you know. If you use information from an outside source, please attach that source to your essay.

PART 4 Edit Your Writing

Reread the Summary of Lesson 12 and the editing advice. Edit your writing from Part 3.

13

Passive Voice and Active Voice

THE LAW

Lady Justice is an international symbol of the law.

The minute you read something that you can't understand, you can almost be sure that it was drawn up by a lawyer.

—Will Rogers

The Supreme Court

CD 3
TR 12

Read the following article. Pay special attention to the words in bold.

You have probably heard of the Supreme Court of the United States. Why **was** this court **created**, how **are** the justices **selected**, and how is it different from other courts?

The Supreme Court **was created** by the U.S. Constitution to balance the power of the president and Congress. It has nine justices,[1] one of whom is the Chief Justice. The president nominates a justice, but he doesn't have the final say. His choice has to **be confirmed**[2] by the Senate. Supreme Court justices **are** not **appointed** for a fixed number of years. According to the Constitution, they "shall hold their offices during good behavior." This usually means they serve for life or until they retire. Until 1981, all the justices were male. Then Sandra Day O'Connor, who **was nominated** by President Ronald Reagan, became the first female justice.

About 10,000 cases **are filed** every year, but the Supreme Court hears only about seventy-five to eighty cases. The Supreme Court hears cases that **are appealed**[3] from lower courts when these courts are not able to resolve a conflict. No new evidence[4] **is presented** and no witnesses **are heard**. Attorneys[5] present their case in writing and orally. The judges listen to each side, review the evidence that **was presented** in the lower courts, and meet privately to decide the case. A simple majority of five justices is all that **is needed** to decide a case.

Once a case **is heard** on the Supreme Court, it **cannot be heard** in any other court. The justices' decision is final.

---

1 *justice*: a judge in a court of law
2 *confirmed*: formally accepted
3 *appealed*: brought from a lower court to a higher court for review
4 *evidence*: words or objects that support the truth of something
5 *attorney*: a lawyer

U.S. Supreme Court Building,
Washington, DC

COMPREHENSION CHECK Based on the reading, tell if the statement is true (**T**) or false (**F**).

1. The president has the final word in selecting a Supreme Court justice.

2. To decide a case, all the justices must agree.

3. A Supreme Court justice can serve for life.

13.1 Active and Passive Voice—Overview

Examples			Explanation
Subject Reagan	**Verb** **chose**	**Object** O'Connor.	Some sentences are in the **active voice**. The subject performs the action of the verb.
Subject O'Connor	**Verb** *be* past participle **was chosen**	**by Agent** by Reagan.	Some sentences are in the **passive voice.** The subject receives the action of the verb. To form the passive voice, we use *be* + the past participle of the verb. Some passive sentences have an agent. The agent is in the *by* phrase.
O'Connor **was chosen** in 1981. About 10,000 cases **are filed** with the Supreme Court every year.			Many passive sentences don't mention an agent.

EXERCISE 1 Listen to the article about a famous case. Fill in the blanks with the words you hear.

CD 3
TR 13

One of the most famous cases heard in the Supreme Court _____is known_____
                                                                        1.

as Brown versus The Board of Education. According to an 1879 Kansas law, elementary

schools _____ to segregate children—separate them according to
              2.

race. Black and white children _____ to different schools. School
                                          3.

boards said that all children _____ "separate but equal" education.
                                    4.

In the early 1950s, when black parents tried to enroll their children in a neighborhood

school in Topeka, Kansas, they _____ . Oliver Brown was one of the
                                        5.

parents. Brown's daughter _____ to walk six blocks to a school bus
                                6.

stop to ride a bus to her segregated school.

continued

The Topeka school board _____ in court. The District Court ruled
                                                    7.
in favor of segregated education. Then a group of black parents challenged this "separate but

equal" law and took their case to the Supreme Court in 1953. The Supreme Court ruled that

children _____ by segregation. All nine justices agreed that
                        8.
segregation was unconstitutional.

All schools in the United States _____ by the Supreme Court's
                                                9.
decision. All schools _____ to admit black children.
                             10.

13.2 The Passive Voice—Form

To form the passive voice, we use *be* + the past participle of the verb.

	Active	Passive
Simple Present	The Constitution **protects** Americans.	Americans **are protected** by the Constitution.
Future	The judge **will make** a decision. The judge **is going to make** a decision.	A decision **will be made** soon. A decision **is going to be made** soon.
Simple Past	Parents **challenged** the school board.	The school board **was challenged** in 1953.
Present Perfect	The court **has heard** the case.	The case **has been heard** by the court.
Infinitive	The court **has to make** a decision.	A decision **has to be made** by the court.
Modal	They **should change** the law.	The law **should be changed**.

Language Notes:

1. The tense of the sentence is shown by the verb *be*. The past participle of the main verb is used with every tense.

2. An adverb can be placed between the auxiliary verb and the main verb.

   The attorneys **are** *often* **asked** questions.

3. When the agent is included after a passive verb, we use *by* + noun or object pronoun.

   I was helped **by the attorneys.**   My sister was helped **by them** too.

4. If two verbs in the passive voice are connected with *and,* we don't repeat the verb *be*.

   All schools **were affected** and **required** to admit black children.

5. Some active verbs have two objects: a direct object and an indirect object. When this is the case, the passive sentence can begin with either object. If the direct object becomes the subject of the passive sentence, *to* is used before the indirect object.

   Active: They **gave** the child permission.

   Passive: The child **was given** permission.   Permission **was given** <u>to</u> the child.

EXERCISE 2 Change each sentence to passive voice. Use the same tense. Do not include the agent.

1. They **take** a vote. _A vote is taken._

2. They **made** a decision. _____

3. They **will take** a vote. _____

4. They **are going to change** the law. _____

5. We **have paid** the attorneys. _____

6. We **must find** a good lawyer. _____

7. They **need to write** a report. _____

EXERCISE 3 Underline the verb. Then write *A* if the sentence is active or *P* if the sentence is passive.

1. The justices <u>discussed</u> the case in private. _____A_____

2. A decision <u>was made</u> to change the law. _____P_____

3. Sandra Day O'Connor became the first female justice on the Supreme Court. _____

4. About seventy-five cases are heard in the Supreme Court each year. _____

5. Some laws need to be changed. _____

6. The justices sometimes interrupt the attorneys. _____

7. Some justices will retire soon. _____

8. In many court cases, witnesses are brought in. _____

9. In criminal court, witnesses are questioned. _____

10. Schools in Kansas separated African American children from other children. _____

11. The first African American justice was appointed to the Supreme Court in 1967. _____

12. Things have changed a lot in the last 60 years. _____

Members of a jury taking the oath

JURY DUTY

CD 3
TR 14

Read the following article. Pay special attention to the words in bold.

All Americans **are protected** by the Constitution. No one person can decide if a person is guilty of a crime. Every citizen has the right to a trial by jury. When a person **is charged** with a crime, he **is considered** innocent until the jury decides he is guilty.

Most American citizens **are chosen** for jury duty at some time in their lives. How **are** jurors **chosen**? The court gets the names of citizens from lists of taxpayers, licensed drivers, and voters. Many people **are called** to the courthouse for the selection of a jury. From this large group, a limited number of people **is chosen**. Alternates[6] are also chosen. The lawyers and the judge ask each person questions to see if the person is going to be fair. If the person has made any judgment about the case before hearing the facts presented in the trial, he **is** not **selected**. If the person doesn't understand enough English, he **is** not **selected**. The court needs jurors who can understand the facts and be open-minded. When the final jury selection **is made**, the jurors must promise to be fair in deciding the case.

Sometimes a trial goes on for several days or more. Jurors **are** not **permitted** to talk with family members and friends about the case. In some cases, jurors **are** not **permitted** to go home until the case is over. They stay in a hotel and **are** not **permitted** to watch TV or read newspapers that give information about the case.

After the jurors hear the case, they have to make a decision. They go to a separate room and talk about what they heard and saw in the courtroom. When they are finished discussing the case, they take a vote.

Jurors **are paid** for their work. They receive a small amount of money per day. Employers must give a worker permission to take off work to be on a jury. Jury duty **is considered** a very serious responsibility.

---

6 *alternate*: a person who takes the place of a juror who cannot serve for some reason, such as illness

COMPREHENSION CHECK Based on the reading, tell if the statement is true (**T**) or false (**F**).

1. Only American citizens are selected for a jury in the U.S.

2. People with limited English are often not selected for jury duty.

3. Jurors receive a small amount of money for serving.

13.3 Passive Voice—Use

Examples	Explanation
Laws **should be obeyed.** The jurors **will be paid** at the end of the day. A man **was charged** with a crime.	The passive voice is often used without an agent when: • the action is done by people in general. • the agent is not known or not important. • the agent is obvious.
Active: The lawyers **presented** the case yesterday. **Passive:** The case **was presented** in two hours. **Active:** The judge and the lawyers **choose** twelve people. **Passive:** People who don't understand English **are not chosen.**	The passive voice is used to shift the emphasis from the agent to the receiver of the action.
A Supreme Court justice **is nominated** by the president.	The passive voice is sometimes used with an agent.
It **is considered** the responsibility of every citizen to serve on a jury.	Often the passive voice is used after *it* when talking about general beliefs, findings, and discoveries.

Language Note:

Informally, *they* is often used as the subject in an active sentence when the subject is not a specific person. Compare:

> *They* **give** you instructions in court. (Informal)
> You **are given** instructions in court. (Formal)

EXERCISE 4 Fill in the blanks with the passive voice of the verb given. Use the simple present.

1. Jurors _____are chosen_____ from lists.

choose

2. Only people over eighteen years old _____ for jury duty.

select

3. A questionnaire _____ out and _____.

fill   *return*

4. Many people _____ to the courthouse.

call

5. Not everyone _____ .

choose

6. The jurors _____ a lot of questions.

ask

7. Jurors _____ time for lunch.

permit

8. Jurors _____ a paycheck at the end of the day for their work.

give

EXERCISE 5 Fill in the blanks with the passive voice of the verb given. Use the simple past.

1. I _____was sent_____ a letter.
   _{send}

2. I _____ to go to the courthouse on Fifth Street.
   _{tell}

3. My name _____ .
   _{call}

4. I _____ a form to fill out.
   _{give}

5. A video about jury duty _____ on a large TV.
   _{show}

6. The jurors _____ to the third floor of the building.
   _{take}

7. I _____ a lot of questions by the lawyers.
   _{ask}

8. I _____ for the jury.
   _{choose}

EXERCISE 6 Fill in the blanks with the passive voice of the verb given. Use the present perfect.

1. The jurors _____have been given_____ a lot of information.
   _{give}

2. Many books _____ about the courts.
   _{write}

3. Many movies _____ about criminal trials.
   _{make}

4. Many people _____ for jury duty.
   _{choose}

5. Your name _____ for jury duty.
   _{select}

6. The check _____ with the clerk.
   _{leave}

7. The check _____ in an envelope.
   _{put}

8. A notice about jury duty _____ to your house.
   _{send}

EXERCISE 7 Fill in the blanks with the passive voice of the verb given. Use the future.

1. You _____will be taken_____ to a courtroom.
   _{take}

2. You _____ to stand up when the judge enters the room.
   _{tell}

3. Each of you _____ a lot of questions.
   _{ask}

4. The lawyers _____ .
   _{introduce}

5. Information about the case _____ to you.
   _{present}

6. Twelve of you _____ .
   _{select}

7. Besides the twelve jurors, two alternates _____ .
   _{choose}

8. All of you _____ .
   _{pay}

EXERCISE 8 Fill in the blanks with the passive voice for each of the underlined verbs.

1. The jury <u>took</u> a vote. The vote _____ *was taken* _____ after three hours.

2. The lawyers <u>asked</u> a lot of questions. The questions _____ in order to find facts.

3. The court <u>will pay</u> us. We _____ $20 a day.

4. They <u>told</u> us to wait. We _____ to wait on the second floor.

5. They <u>gave</u> us instructions. We _____ instructions about the law.

6. People <u>pay</u> for the services of a lawyer. Lawyers _____ a lot of money for their services.

7. You <u>should use</u> a pen to fill out the form. A pen _____ for all legal documents.

8. They <u>showed</u> us a film about the court system. We _____ the film before we went into the courtroom.

9. Someone <u>needs to tell</u> us what to do. We _____ how the jury system works.

10. Many people <u>consider</u> Brown v. the Board of Education a very important case.

    It _____ an important step toward the end of inequalities.

13.4 Negatives and Questions with the Passive Voice

Compare statements, *yes/no* questions, short answers, and *wh-* questions.

AFFIRMATIVE STATEMENT:	They **are permitted** to talk to other jurors.
NEGATIVE STATEMENT:	They **aren't permitted** to talk to family members.
YES/NO QUESTION:	**Are** they **permitted** to eat in the courtroom?
SHORT ANSWER:	No, they **aren't**.
WH- QUESTION:	What **are** they **permitted** to do in the courtroom?
NEGATIVE WH- QUESTION:	Why **aren't** they **permitted** to talk to family members?
SUBJECT QUESTION:	Who **is permitted** in the courtroom?

EXERCISE 9 Write *A* if the sentence is active. Write *P* if the sentence is passive.

1. Did you go to court last week? _____ *A* _____

2. Which courtroom were you sent to? _____

3. The jurors didn't agree with each other. _____

4. Jurors aren't paid a lot of money. _____

5. I haven't been selected for a jury. _____

continued

6. Some jurors won't be needed. _____

7. How many questions did the lawyers ask you? _____

8. Did you receive a letter for jury duty? _____

9. How are justices selected for the Supreme Court? _____

10. Which justice will resign next? _____

11. A witness must not lie in court. _____

12. How was the case decided? _____

EXERCISE 10 Fill in the blanks with the negative form of the underlined verbs.

1. I <u>was selected</u> for jury duty last year. I _____ *wasn't selected* _____ this year.

2. The jurors <u>are paid</u>. They _____ a lot of money.

3. Twelve people <u>were chosen</u>. People who don't understand English well _____ .

4. We <u>are allowed</u> to eat in the waiting room. We _____ to eat in the courtroom.

5. We <u>were told</u> to keep an open mind. We _____ how to vote.

6. We <u>have been given</u> instructions. We _____ our checks yet.

EXERCISE 11 Change the statements to questions using the words given.

1. The jurors are paid. (*how much*)

   <u>How much are the jurors paid?</u> _____

2. The jurors are given a lunch break. (*when*)

   _____

3. I wasn't chosen for the jury. (*why*)

   _____

4. You were given information about the case. (*what kind of information*)

   _____

5. A film will be shown. (*when*)

   _____

6. Several jurors have been sent home. (*which jurors*)

   _____

Unusual Lawsuits

CD 3
TR 15

Read the following article. Pay special attention to the words in bold.

When a person **is injured** or **harmed**, it is the court's job to determine who is at fault. Most court cases never **make** the news. But a few of them **appear** in the newspapers, online, and on the evening news because they are so unusual.

In 1992, a seventy-nine-year-old woman in New Mexico **sued**[7] a fast-food restaurant for burns she suffered after spilling hot coffee on herself while driving. At first the woman **asked** for $11,000 to cover her medical expenses. When the restaurant **refused**, the case **went** to court and the woman **was awarded** nearly $3 million.

In 2002, a group of teenagers **sued** several fast-food chains for serving food that **made** them fat. The case **was thrown** out of court. According to Congressman Ric Keller, Americans have to "get away from this new culture where people always **try** to play the victim and **blame** others for their problems." Mr. Keller, who is overweight and **eats** at fast-food chains from time to time, **said** that suing "the food industry **is** not **going to make** a single individual any skinnier. It **will** only **make** the trial attorneys' bank accounts fatter." The court system **is designed** to protect us, but it's up to us to make sure that trials **remain** serious.

In June 2004, an Indiana woman **sued** a cell phone company for causing an auto accident in which she **was involved**. The court **decided** that the manufacturer of a cell phone **cannot be held** responsible for an auto accident involving a driver using its product. In March 2000, a teenage girl in Virginia **was struck** and **killed** by a driver conducting business on a cell phone. The girl's family **sued** the driver's employer for $30 million for wrongful death. They **said** that it was the company's fault because employees **are expected** to conduct business while driving. The family **lost** its case.

We **are protected** by the law, but as individuals, we **need** to take personal responsibility too.

---

[7] *to sue*: to claim in court that a person's legal rights have been violated

COMPREHENSION CHECK Based on the reading, tell if the statement is true (**T**) or false (**F**).

1. Congressman Keller believes that fast-food restaurants should be held responsible for making people fat.

2. According to a 2004 Indiana case, a cell phone company is not responsible when an accident is caused by a driver talking on a cell phone.

3. In 1992, a New Mexico woman won $11,000 from a fast-food company when she burned herself with hot coffee.

13.5 Transitive and Intransitive Verbs

Transitive verbs have an object. Intransitive verbs have no object.

Examples	Explanation
(A) A driver using a cell phone **caused** the accident. (P) The accident **was caused** by a driver using a cell phone.	Transitive verbs have an active (A) and a passive (P) form.
(A) The judge **gave** us instructions. (P) We **were given** instructions in the morning.	The active voice is more common than the passive voice when there is a specific agent.
The woman **went** to court. The accident **happened** in Virginia. The teenager **died.** The case **seems** strange to me. The coffee **felt** hot.	Intransitive verbs don't have a passive form. Some intransitive verbs are: *arrive, be, become, come, complain, depend, die, fall, go, grow (in a natural way), happen, laugh, leave (a place), occur, rain, recover (from an illness), remain, run, sleep, stay, work* and the sense perception verbs: *appear, feel, look, seem, smell, sound, taste.*

Language Notes:

1. Even though *have* and *want* are followed by an object, these verbs are not usually used in the passive voice.

    Sam **has** a new cell phone. (NOT: *A new cell phone is had by Sam.*)

    She **wants** a new car. (NOT: *A new car is wanted by her.*)

2. Some verbs can be used both as transitive verbs and intransitive verbs.

    The child **grows** fast. (intransitive)

    Farmers **grow** corn. Corn **is grown** in Illinois. (transitive)

EXERCISE 12 Find and underline the main verb in each sentence. Then identify which sentences can be changed to the passive voice and change those sentences. If no change is possible, write *no change* or *NC* on the line.

1. The woman <u>became</u> angry.

   NC

2. The woman <u>sued</u> the cell phone company.

   The cell phone company was sued by the woman.

3. The driver used a cell phone.

   _____ .

4. Can we hold the driver responsible?

   _____ .

5. Laws protect us.

   _____ .

6. How did the accident happen?

   _____ .

7. Some court cases seem silly.

   _____ .

8. The Supreme Court has decided important cases.

   _____ .

9. The Constitution protects people.

   _____ .

10. Jurors should arrive on time to court.

   _____ .

11. I fell asleep in court.

   _____ .

EXERCISE 13 Circle the correct words to complete each sentence.

1. Congressman Keller (*eats*/*is eaten*) fast food.

2. A driver (*spilled*/*was spilled*) hot coffee.

3. What (*happened*/*was happened*) when she spilled the coffee?

4. The woman (*awarded*/*was awarded*) $3 million in a lawsuit.

5. Some unusual cases (*have filed*/*have been filed*) in court.

6. People (*shouldn't blame*/*should be blamed*) a company for their own irresponsible behavior.

7. A hands-free phone system (*should use*/*should be used*) when driving.

8. Fast food (*eats*/*is eaten*) by a lot of teenagers.

9. How many people (*die*/*are died*) in car accidents each year?

10. Five justices (*need*/*are needed*) to decide a case in the Supreme Court.

11. Parents (*became*/*were become*) angry about school segregation.

12. This case (*knows*/*is known*) as Brown vs. the Board of Education.

13. All U.S. schools (*affected*/*were affected*) by the court ruling.

EXERCISE 14 Circle the correct verb to complete the conversation.

A: Why weren't you at work last week? Were you sick?

B: No. I (*chose*/*was chosen*) to be on a jury.
　　　　　　　　　　　　1.

A: How was it?

B: It was very interesting. A man (*arrested*/*was arrested*) for fighting with a police officer. The jury
　　　　　　　　　　　　　　　　　　　　　　2.
selection was interesting too. But it took half a day to choose twelve people.

A: Why?

B: The judge and lawyers (*interviewed*/*were interviewed*) more than fifty people.
　　　　　　　　　　　　　　　　　　3.

A: Why so many people?

B: Well, several people (*didn't understand*/*weren't understood*) the judge's questions.
　　　　　　　　　　　　　　　　　　　　4.
And a woman (*told*/*was told*) the judge that she was very sick. She (*gave*/*was given*)
　　　　　　　　　　　5.　　　　　　　　　　　　　　　　　　　　　　6.
permission to leave. I don't know why the other people (*didn't choose*/*weren't chosen*).
　　　　　　　　　　　　　　　　　　　　　　　　　　　　　　7.

A: How long did it take the jurors to make a decision?

B: About two hours. One of the jurors (*didn't agree/wasn't agreed*) with the other eleven jurors. We
8.

(*talked/were talked*) about the evidence until she changed her mind.
9.

A: (*Did you pay/Were you paid*) for the days you missed work?
10.

B: Of course. Employers have to pay. That's the law.

A: Now that you've done it once, you won't have to do it again. Right?

B: No, that's not true. This was the second time I (*choose/was chosen*).
11.

EXERCISE 15 About You Work with a partner. Use the sentences in the chart to ask and answer
questions about the legal system in a country you know about.

Country: _____

	Yes	No
1. People are treated fairly in court.		
2. Citizens are selected to be on a jury.		
3. People are represented by lawyers in court.		
4. Lawyers make a lot of money.		
5. Famous trials are shown on TV.		
6. Punishment is severe for certain crimes.		
7. The death penalty is used in some cases.		
8. The laws are generally fair.		
9. The country has a Supreme Court.		

SUMMARY OF LESSON 13

Active and Passive Voice—Forms

Active	Passive
Sam **drove** the car.	The car **was driven** (by Sam).
Sam **didn't drive** the car.	The car **wasn't driven** (by Sam).
Sam **will drive** the car.	The car **will be driven** (by Sam).
Sam **has driven** the car.	The car **has been driven** (by Sam).
Sam often **drives** the car.	The car **is** often **driven** (by Sam).
Sam **should drive** the car.	The car **should be driven** (by Sam).
Sam **needs to drive** the car.	The car **needs to be driven** (by Sam).
Did Sam **drive** the car?	**Was** the car **driven** (by Sam)?
When **did** Sam **drive** the car?	When **was** the car **driven** (by Sam)?
Why **didn't** Sam **drive** the car?	Why **wasn't** the car **driven** (by Sam)?

The Active Voice—Use

Examples	Explanation
I **hired** an attorney. The attorney **prepared** the evidence. She **will present** the evidence in court.	In most cases, when either the active or passive can be used, we use the active voice.
The accident **happened** last month. She **went** to court.	When the verb is intransitive (it has no object), the active voice must be used. There is no choice.

The Passive Voice—Use

Examples	Explanation
I **was chosen** for jury duty.	The agent is not known or is not important.
The criminal **was taken** to jail.	The agent is obvious.
Jury duty **is considered** a responsibility of every citizen.	The agent is everybody or people in general.
The court paid me. I **was paid** at the end of the day.	The emphasis is shifted from the agent to the receiver of the action.
It **was discovered** that many accidents are the result of driver distraction.	We begin with *it* when talking about general beliefs and findings.
Accidents **are caused** by distracted drivers.	The emphasis is on the receiver of the action more than on the agent. (In this case, the agent is included in a *by* phrase.)

TEST / REVIEW

Fill in the blanks with the active or passive voice of the verb given.

In many countries, laws _have been passed_ that prohibit drivers from using cell
                                   1. present perfect: *pass*

phones while driving. In a few countries, such as Japan, both hand-held and hands-free cell

phone use _____ . In the U.S., the law _____ on the
                2. present perfect: *ban*   **3.** simple present: *depend*

place where you _____ .
                4. simple present: *live*

States _____ to become tougher on drivers who use cell phones. In
                5. present perfect: *start*

New York, for example, the use of hand-held cell phones while driving

_____ but the use of hands-free devices _____ .
        6. simple present: *prohibit*   **7.** simple present: *permit*

A driver who _____ this law can be fined $50 for a first offense, $50–200
              8. simple present: *not/obey*

for a second offense, and $50–400 after that. In addition, a driver _____
                                                        9. can/lose

his or her license for two to six months. In Alaska, the fine for using a hand-held device while

driving is $10,000. A driver _____ to jail for up to one year. Texting while
                        10. can/even/send

driving _____ an even greater problem. Drivers _____
        11. present perfect: *become*   **12.** simple present: *need*

to look away from the road in order to text. The risk of causing an accident while texting is

twenty-three times higher than it is while driving without this distraction. In 2011, 21,000

people _____ in cell phone related crashes.
                13. simple past: *injure*

But the problem of driver distraction is not only a result of cell phones and texting.

According to one study, it _____ that 80 percent of accidents
                        14. simple past: *find*

_____ by drivers who are not paying attention. This study
        15. simple present: *cause*

_____ that drivers _____ by many things: eating,
        16. simple past: *determine*   **17.** simple present: *distract*

putting on makeup, reading, reaching for things, and changing stations on the radio.

Over 3,000 people _____ in 2010 as a result of driver distraction. It is
                        18. simple past: *kill*

clear that all drivers _____ to give driving their full attention.
        19. simple present: *need*

WRITING

PART 1 Editing Advice

1. Never use *do, does,* or *did* to form the passive voice.

   wasn't found
   The criminal ~~didn't find~~.

   were
   Where ~~did~~ the jurors taken?

2. Don't use the passive voice with *happen, die, become, sleep, work, live, fall, seem,* or other intransitive verbs.

   The accident ~~was~~ happened three weeks ago.

3. Don't confuse the *-ing* form with the past participle.

   taken
   The criminal was ~~taking~~ to jail.

4. Don't forget the *-ed* ending for a regular past participle.

   ed
   My cousin was select to be on a jury.
                    ^

5. Don't forget to use *be* with a passive sentence.

   was
   The evidence presented in court.
               ^

6. Use the correct word order with adverbs.

   never selected
   I was ~~selected never~~ to be on a jury.

PART 2 Editing Practice

Some of the shaded words and phrases have mistakes. Find the mistakes and correct them. If the shaded words are correct, write C.

didn't   C
   I ~~wasn't~~ come to class last week. My classmates wanted to know if I was sick. I explained
      1.   **2.**

that I had jury duty. Only citizens of the U.S. can serve on a jury, so my friends were surprised.
         3.   **4.**

But I was become a citizen six months ago. Last month I was received a letter in the mail
       5.   **6.**

telling me I had to report for duty. I'm still an ESL student and my English is far from perfect,

but I was selected. I was ask a lot of questions, and I answered them without a problem. Many
       7.   **8.**   **9.**

people were rejected, and I don't know why, but I chosen.
       10.   **11.**

   The case was about a traffic accident. Here's what was happened: A man hit a woman's
                                                    12.   **13.**

car and was left the scene of the accident. Her car was badly damage. Luckily, the woman
        14.   **15.**

didn't injured. The woman saw the driver's license plate and wrote down the number. She
16.   **17.**   **18.**

also was taken a picture of the car with her cell phone as the driver was leaving. She called
     19.

the police. The police caught him. He was driven without a license. They also determined
    20.   21.
that the man was texting while driving. My friends asked me, "How was that determined?
          22.   23.
The police checked the phone records and was found that at the exact time of the accident, he
                                             24.
was texting. The case lasted for two days. All the jurors were agreed that the man was guilty.
              25.   26.
The man was given a $500 fine. His driver's license was suspended for one year.
         27.   28.
    I think a lot of accidents are cause by people talking on the phone or texting while
                              29.
driving. According to the law, we're not permit to text and drive. But in some places you can
                                  30.
talk on the phone and drive. I hope the law will be changed and that talking on a cell phone
                                       31.
will be against the law too.
  32.

PART 3 Write About It

1. Write about an experience you have had with the court system in the U.S. or your native country.

2. Write about a famous court case that you know of. Do you agree with the decision of the jury?
   (If you research your topic, attach a copy of your sources.)

PART 4 Edit Your Writing

Reread the Summary of Lesson 13 and the editing advice. Edit your writing from Part 3.

MONEY

This design of the $100 bill was created by artist Brian Thompson.

Making money isn't hard in itself. What's hard is to earn it doing something worth devoting your life to.

—Carlos Ruiz Zafón

Millennials and Money

Read the following article. Pay special attention to the words in bold.

You've probably been hearing a lot about millennials these days. What, exactly, is **a millennial? A millennial** is **a person** born approximately between 1980 and 2000. This is **the** largest group of Americans, 78 million. Right now **millennials** make up 25 percent of **the workforce.**[1] By 2020, they will be **the majority** of **the workforce** and **the** largest **group** of consumers, so **marketers** are especially interested in this group and their spending habits.

Millennials' attitudes towards **money** and spending are different from those of their parents, **the "boomers"** (born between 1946 and 1964), or "Generation Xers," (born between 1965 and 1980). First, they often shop online, where they can compare **prices, products,** and **vendors.** They are more influenced by **the opinions** of other consumers than by **the recommendation** of family and friends. Second, they prefer to rent **things** rather than own them; they prefer movie and music **subscriptions** rather than **ownership** of DVDs or CDs. They get their music and movies on their smartphones, tablets, or computers. A significant number of them don't even own **a television.** Third, they like to spend their money on life experiences, such as **entertainment, restaurants,** and **travel** rather than on **goods.** They often have **the attitude** of "YOLO": You Only Live Once. They want to experience all **life** has to offer. Generally, they are optimistic[2] about **the future.**

What influences these attitudes? At **the end** of 2007, the United States went into a deep economic recession.[3] **The** average **salary** for a person just out of college in 2013 was $34,500. This was **the** lowest starting **salary** for a college graduate since 1998. And recent college graduates have been entering **the** job **market** with huge college **debt.**[4] As a result, millennials have learned to be careful with **money.** They are getting married later than previous **generations,** and many don't believe in spending a lot of **money** on **an** expensive **wedding.** They often use **public transportation** and **bicycles** for short **trips** or use car-sharing **services.** They prefer to rent **an apartment** rather than buy **a house** because they don't want large financial **commitments.**

American **millennials** spend $600 billion **dollars** a year. **Marketers** need to understand **the mentality** and **habits** of millennnials if they wish to attract their dollars.

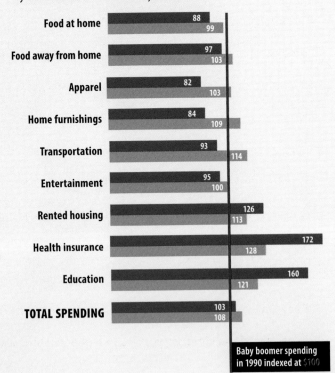

Spending on Major Categories
by Millennials & Gen X vs. Baby Boomers

Category	Millennials in 2010	Generation X in 2000
Food at home	88	99
Food away from home	97	103
Apparel	82	103
Home furnishings	84	109
Transportation	93	114
Entertainment	95	100
Rented housing	126	113
Health insurance	172	128
Education	160	121
TOTAL SPENDING	103	108

Baby boomer spending in 1990 indexed at $100

■ Millennials in 2010
■ Generation X in 2000

---

1 *workforce:* all workers employed in a specific area
2 *optimistic:* believing that good things will happen
3 *recession:* a time when economic activity is not strong
4 *debt:* an amount of money owed

Lesson 14

COMPREHENSION CHECK Based on the reading, tell if the statement is true (**T**) or false (**F**).

1. Millennials make their buying decisions mostly on recommendations from friends.

2. Millenials buy a lot of CDs and DVDs.

3. Millennials make up the largest portion of Americans today.

14.1 Articles—An Overview

Examples	Explanation
Do you want **an** expensive wedding? **A** college graduate wants to find **a** good job.	The indefinite articles *a* and *an* are used before a noun to refer to non-specific things and people (singular only).
Many people use **the** Internet to shop online. **The** boomers were born between 1946 and 1964.	The definite article *the* is used before a noun to refer to specific things and people (singular or plural).
Marketers are interested in **millennials**. **Ownership** of DVDs does not interest **millennials**.	A noun can be used without an article to refer to non-specific things and people.

EXERCISE 1 Listen to the following story. Fill in the blanks with the article you hear. If you don't hear an article, fill in the blank with Ø.

_____Ø_____ Millennials are _____the_____ first generation in American
　　1.　　　　　　　　　　　　　　　2.

history to have _____a_____ lower standard of living than their parents. Millennials
　　　　　　　　3.

looking for _____a_____ job in 2010 faced _____an_____ unemployment rate of
　　　　　　　4.　　　　　　　　　　　　5.

almost 10 percent. _____The_____ average debt for _____a_____ millennial
　　　　　　　　　　6.　　　　　　　　　　　　7.

college graduate in 2013 was approximately $30,000. In _____a_____ recent book,
　　　　　　　　　　　　　　　　　　　　　　　　　　8.

called _____The_____ *Next America,* _____Ø_____ author, Paul Taylor, describes
　　　　　9.　　　　　　　　　　　　10.

_____the_____ economic changes we will see as boomers retire.
　　11.

　　Millennials are not only different from their parents' generation in spending. They are

_____the_____ first generation to grow up with _____Ø_____ technology.
　　12.　　　　　　　　　　　　　　　　　13.

_____The_____ amount of time it takes _____a_____ product to reach a 50
　　14.　　　　　　　　　　　　　　15.

percent adoption by _____Ø_____ consumers has become much shorter. It took
　　　　　　　　　16.

thirty-one years for radio to reach 50 percent of consumers; television twenty-eight years;

home computers eighteen years; smartphones three and a half years. Consumers have

adopted _____Ø_____ smartphones ten times faster than they adopted
　　　　　17.

_____Ø_____ computers.
　18.

continued

Millennials also have _____ ⌀ _____ different values from their parents. In 2013, 26
                                 19.

percent of millennials between eighteen and thirty-two were married. In 1980, forty-eight

percent of _____ ⌀ _____ boomers in this age group were married. Millennials value
                        20.

_____ ⌀ _____ fun and _____ ⌀ _____ discovery. Boomers value _____ ⌀ _____
            21.   **22.**   **23.**

family and _____ ⌀ _____ practicality.
                        24.

14.2 Making Generalizations

Examples	Explanation
Smart phones are more popular than **flip phones**. **A smart phone** is more popular than **a flip phone**.	We can make a generalization about a count subject in two ways: no article + plural noun OR *a* or *an* + singular noun
Fun is important for young people. **Ownership** is not important for millennials.	We don't use an article to make a generalization about a noncount subject.
Millennials like **movies**. Millennials value **discovery**.	To make a generalization about an object, count or noncount, we don't use an article. We use the plural form for count nouns. Noncount nouns are always singular.

EXERCISE 2 Match the subject on the left with the verb phrase on the right.

1. A shopper   are expensive.

2. TVs   is short. You only live once (Y.O.L.O.).

3. Kids   is often directed at millennials.

4. Parents   wants to get a good price.

5. Advertising   often buy toys for their children.

6. Parents often tell kids that   like to give gifts to their grandchildren.

7. Grandparents   money doesn't grow on trees.

8. A child   needs to learn about money.

9. Life   want to have toys.

EXERCISE 3 Complete the sentence to make a generalization about the subject given. You may work
with a partner.

1. Millennials _have different values from their parents._

2. A college graduate _____

3. Consumers _____

4. Life for older Americans _____

5. Good jobs _____

6. A wedding _____

7. Technology _____

8. Marketers _____

9. Boomers _____

10. DVDs _____

11. Money _____

EXERCISE 4 About You Put a check (✓) next to the statements that are generally true in your country. Discuss your answers with a partner.

_____ 1. A bank is a safe place to keep your money.

_____ 2. Doctors make a lot of money.

_____ 3. Teenagers have part-time jobs.

_____ 4. Children work.

_____ 5. Teachers earn a good salary.

_____ 6. A government official makes a lot of money.

_____ 7. Businesses are closed on Sundays.

14.3 Classifying or Defining the Subject

Examples	Explanation
A millennial is **a** person born between 1980 and 2000. "Recession" is **an** economic term.	We classify or define a singular count noun like this: Singular noun + *is* + *a(n)* + (adjective) + noun.
Boomers are **Americans** born between 1946 and 1964. CDs are compact **discs**.	We classify or define a plural count noun like this: Plural noun + *are* + (adjective) + noun.
What's a millennial? **What** are boomers?	We can ask for a definition with *what*.

Language Note:

We can also use *the* in a definition if the noun is specific.

> *The Next America* is **the** name of a book.

> A salary is **the** amount of money you get from working at your job.

EXERCISE 5 In the left column, fill in the blank with the verb and an article if needed. Then match the subject on the left with the definition or classification on the right.

1. Y.O.L.O. _____ is an _____   person born between 1946 and 1964.

2. A boomer _____   owed money.

3. A recession _____   book about the future of the U.S.

4. Debt _____   abbreviation.

5. A vendor _____   kids between the ages of thirteen and nineteen.

6. *The Next America* _____   a person or company that sells something.

7. Paul Taylor _____   a time when the economy isn't strong.

8. Teenagers _____   the man who wrote *The Next America*.

EXERCISE 6 Define or classify the subject given. You may work with a partner.

1. A CD _____ is a disk that contains digital music. _____

2. A quarter _____

3. A dime _____

4. A credit card _____

5. A debit card _____

6. A diamond _____

7. Silver and gold _____

8. Marketers _____

9. Consumers _____

10. A bank _____

11. A wallet _____

Kids and Money

CD 3 TR 18

Read the following article. Pay special attention to the words in bold.

Kids like to spend money. With part-time jobs, **an** allowance[5] from their parents, gifts from grandparents and others, and no bills to pay, kids have **the** most disposable income[6] of any part of American society. According to **a** 2012 statistic, teens between fifteen and seventeen have over $2,000 a year to spend. Their spending behavior was not affected by **the** recession that started in 2007. While some teens think about saving their money, about 21 percent say they don't save **any** money at all.

The average American child gets **an** allowance of $780 a year. In ninety percent of American homes, kids are expected to do some chores[7] in exchange for their allowance. In many cases, this is no more than one hour **a** week. What does an allowance teach a child about money? Many experts believe **the** answer is nothing!

Parents need to talk to kids about money early. When is the best time? **The** earlier **the** better, according to experts. Even pre-school children can learn about money. For example, they can learn that you need money to buy things and that you earn money by working. They can learn that there is **a** difference between **the** things you want and **the** things you need. Between six and ten, children can learn to make choices and to compare prices. Between eleven and thirteen, they can learn that they should save ten cents of every dollar they receive. Between fourteen and eighteen, they should start to compare **the** cost of different colleges.

Warren Buffet is one of **the** most famous billionaires in **the** world. He says that **the** age at which parents teach their kids good financial habits will determine how successful the child will be later in life. Buffet taught his children **the** value of learning from experience. He allowed them to succeed and fail on their own. He did not help them financially if they got in **any** trouble. Interestingly, he is not planning on leaving his grown children **a** large inheritance[8]. He said, "I want to give my kids just enough so that they would feel that they could do anything, but not so much that they would feel like doing nothing."

---

5 *allowance*: money children get from their parents for everyday expenses
6 *disposable income*: money a person can spend after expenses
7 *chore*: a household job, such as washing the dishes
8 *inheritance*: money a person receives from someone who died

COMPREHENSION CHECK Based on the reading, tell if the statement is true (**T**) or false (**F**).

1. Many experts believe that giving children an allowance teaches them the value of money.

2. Most kids who get an allowance are expected to do several hours a week of chores.

3. Warren Buffet plans to leave his children the majority of his wealth.

14.4 Non-Specific Nouns

Examples	Explanation
She has **a** job. She gets **an** allowance.	We use *a* or *an* to introduce a singular non-specific count noun. The noun doesn't refer to anything specific or definite.
He has to do (**some**) chores. He doesn't have (**any**) chores on weekdays. Does he have (**any**) chores on Sunday?	We use *some* or *any* to introduce a plural non-specific count noun. *Some* and *any* can be omitted.
He needs (**some**) money. He doesn't have (**any**) cash. Is there (**any**) money in your checking account?	We use *some* and *any* to introduce a non-specific noncount noun.

Language Notes:

1. Both *some* and *any* can be used in questions with plural nouns and noncount nouns.

   Do you have **some** money? Do you have **any** quarters?

2. *Some* and *any* can be omitted.

   Do you have money? Do you have quarters?

EXERCISE 7 Fill in the blanks with *a, an, some, any,* or *Ø* (for no article) to complete the conversation between a son (A) and his mother (B). In some cases, more than one answer is possible.

A: Mom, I want to get _____*a*_____ job.
                               1.

B: But you're only sixteen years old.

A: I'm old enough to work. I need to make _____ money.
                                                  2.

B: Grandma and Grandpa always give you _____*Ø*_____ money for your birthday. And we
                                            3.

give you _____*Ø*_____ fifteen dollars a week. Isn't that enough money for you?
         4.

A: It's not even enough to take _____*a*_____ girl to _____*a*_____ movie.
                                   5.   **6.**

B: What are you going to do about school? You won't have _____*any*_____ time to study.
                                                             7.

A: You know I'm _____*a*_____ good student. I'm sure I won't have _____*any*_____
                   8.   **9.**

problems working part-time. We don't have _____*any* (*Ø*)_____ homework on weekends.
                                           10.

B: I'm worried about your grades falling. Maybe we should raise your allowance. Then you won't

have to work.

A: I want to have my own money. I want to buy _____*some*_____ new clothes.
11.

And I'm going to save _____*some*_____ money each week. Then I can buy
12.

_____*a*_____ car someday.
13.

B: Why do you want a car? You have _____*a*_____ bike.
14.

A: Bikes are great for exercise, but if my job is far away, I'll need a car for transportation.

B: So, you need _____*a*_____ job to buy _____*a*_____ car, and you need
15.   16.

_____*a*_____ car to get to work.
17.

A: Yes. My friends work, and they're good students. I'm not _____*a*_____ baby anymore.
18.

I really want to work.

14.5 Specific Nouns

We use *the* to refer to specific objects and people (singular or plural).

Examples	Explanation
The reading on page 365 is about kids and money. **The pictures** in this lesson are related to money. What did you do with **the money** I gave you?	We use *the* with a specific noun. A noun is specific if it is defined in the phrase or clause after the noun.
The first reading in this lesson is about millennials and money. When is **the right** time to talk to kids about money?	We use *the* when there is only one of something. We usually use *the* with the following words: *first, second, next, last, only, same, back, front,* and *right*.
Where's **the teacher**? I have a question about **the reading** on kids and money.	We use *the* when there is a shared experience. Students in the same class talk about *the* teacher, *the* textbook, *the* homework, *the* board.
Teenagers should put some of their savings in **the bank**. They want money to go to **the** movies with their friends.	We use *the* with certain familiar places and people: the bank the beach the bus the zoo the post office the train the park the doctor the movies the store the hospital
Warren Buffet is one of **the richest** people in the world. What's **the best** way to teach kids about money?	We use *the* before a superlative form.
Millennials often use **the Internet** to shop.	We use *the* before a unique noun.
You have **an allowance**. You can use **the allowance** to go out with your friends. There is **some money** on the table. You can use **the money** to go to the movies.	After a non-specific noun is introduced with *a/an/some/any,* we use the definite article to refer to a specific example of this noun.

continued

Language Notes:

1. We often use *the* before two comparatives when they appear together.

   When should you teach kids about money? **The** earlier **the** better.

   The younger the child is, **the** simpler your explanation should be.

2. We don't use *the* to make a generalization. Compare:

   Life today is very different from **life** forty years ago. (*Life* is general.)

   The life of my grandparents is different from my life. (*The life* is specific.)

3. When we introduce a noun with *there + be*, we use the indefinite article. We can refer to the noun again with *the*.

   There was **a recession** in 2007. **The recession** affected a lot of people.

EXERCISE 8 Fill in the blanks with *a* or *the*.

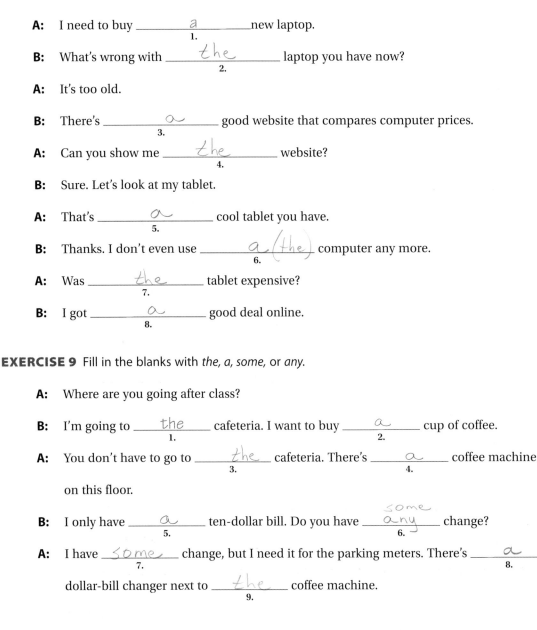

A: I need to buy _____a_____ new laptop.
1.

B: What's wrong with _____the_____ laptop you have now?
2.

A: It's too old.

B: There's _____a_____ good website that compares computer prices.
3.

A: Can you show me _____the_____ website?
4.

B: Sure. Let's look at my tablet.

A: That's _____a_____ cool tablet you have.
5.

B: Thanks. I don't even use _____a (the)_____ computer any more.
6.

A: Was _____the_____ tablet expensive?
7.

B: I got _____a_____ good deal online.
8.

EXERCISE 9 Fill in the blanks with *the, a, some,* or *any*.

A: Where are you going after class?

B: I'm going to ___the___ cafeteria. I want to buy ___a___ cup of coffee.
1.   2.

A: You don't have to go to ___the___ cafeteria. There's ___a___ coffee machine
3.   4.

on this floor.

B: I only have ___a___ ten-dollar bill. Do you have ___any / some___ change?
5.   6.

A: I have ___some___ change, but I need it for the parking meters. There's ___a___
7.   8.

dollar-bill changer next to ___the___ coffee machine.
9.

B: Uh-oh. ___The___ coffee machine is out of order. I guess I'll have to go to ___the___
_{10.}   _{11.}

cafeteria after all. Do you want to go with me?

A: Sorry. I don't have ___any___ time.
                                 _{12.}

EXERCISE 10 Fill in the blanks with *the, a, an, any, some* or Ø for no article. In some cases, more than one answer is possible.

1. **A:** Mom, I need to buy ___some___ new jeans.
                                                  a.

   B: There are ___some___ jeans are on this rack. Which ones do you like?
                                          b.

   A: I love these. Don't you?

   B: But they're torn.

   A: That's ___the___ style these days.
                                      c.

   B: I'll never understand ___Ø___ kids. In my day, ___Ø___ torn clothes
                                    d.   **e.**

   meant you were poor.

   A: That's silly.

   B: I think ___Ø___ life was better back then.
                                      f.

   A: You always compare your childhood with today's kids, but ___Ø___ times have
                                                              g.

   changed. So, what did you decide about ___the___ jeans? Can I buy them? I have
                                                              h.

   enough money from ___the___ job I had last summer.
                                            i.

   B: I suppose so. Go try them on. ___The___ dressing room is over there.
                                                           j.

2. **A:** Where are you going?

   B: To ___the___ bank. I want to deposit ___a___ check, and I need to get
                      a.   **b.**

   ___some___ cash. There's ___an___ ATM at ___the___
    c.   **d.**   **e.**

   supermarket on ___the___ corner.
                                      f.

   A: I'll go with you.

   (At the ATM)

   B: Oh, no. Look. ___The___ ATM is out of order.
                                      g.

   A: Don't worry. There's ___an___ ATM on ___the___ next corner.
                                          h.   **i.**

   B: That ATM doesn't belong to my bank. If I use it, I'll have to pay ___a___ fee.
                                                                          j.

continued

A: How much is ___the___ fee?
                   k.

B: It's usually $3.00 or $3.50. That's a lot of money to me. ___The___ more I save,
                                                                                         l.

___the___ more I have to spend on ___the___ things I want.
m.   **n.**

3. A: I'm going to ___the___ post office. I need to buy ___some___ stamps.
                     a.   **b.**

B: I'll go with you. I want to mail ___a___ package to my parents.
                                          c.

A: What's in ___the___ package?
                     d.

B: ___A___ coat for my sister, and ___∅___ money for my mother.
           e.   **f.**

A: You should never send ___∅___ money by mail. You should buy
                                          g.

___a___ money order at ___the___ bank.
           h.   **i.**

B: How much does it cost?

A: Well, if you have ___an___ account in ___the___ bank, it's usually free.
                                   j.   **k.**

If not, you'll probably have to pay ___a___ fee.
                                         l.

14.6 Specific or Non-Specific Nouns with Quantity Words

Examples	Explanation
All children like toys. **Most** American homes have a television. **Few** people are billionaires.	We use *all, most, many, some, (a) few,* and *(a) little* before non-specific nouns.
All of the readings in this lesson are about money. **Very few of the** people in my country are rich. None of the readings **gives** information about how to make money.	We use *all of the, most of the, many of the, some of the, (a) few of the, (a) little of the,* and *none of the* before specific nouns.

Language Notes:

1. After *all, of* is often omitted.

   All the readings in this lesson are about money.

2. After *none of the* + plural noun, a singular verb is correct. However, a plural verb is often used in less formal speech or writing.

3. Delete *the* when there is a possessive form.

   He spent **all of his money** on a new car.

4. Remember, *few* and *little* without *a* mean not enough. We often put *very* before these words to emphasize that the quantity is not enough.

EXERCISE 11 About You Fill in the blanks with *all, most, some,* or *(very) few* to make a general statement about your country or another country you know about. Discuss your answers with a partner.

1. _____ *Some* _____ people have a car.

2. _____ schools have computers.

3. _____ teachers have a good salary.

4. _____ people use credit cards.

5. _____ kids get an allowance.

6. _____ parents buy a lot of toys for their children.

7. _____ college graduates can find a good job.

8. _____ people have a checking account.

9. _____ grandparents give their grandchildren a lot of gifts.

EXERCISE 12 About You Fill in the blanks with a quantity word to make a statement about specific nouns. If you use *none*, change the verb to the singular form.

1. _____ *A few of the* _____ students in this class are boomers.

2. _____ people I know are millennials.

3. _____ my friends shop online.

4. _____ students in this class have a job.

5. _____ people I know have a smart phone.

6. _____ older people in my family use technology.

7. _____ kids in my family use technology.

8. _____ computers at this school are new.

Billionaires

Bill and Melinda Gates

🎧 CD 3 TR 19 **Read the following article. Pay special attention to the words in bold.**

It's hard to imagine having over a billion dollars. Only about 1,600 people in the world are billionaires. The United States leads the world with the largest number. In 2013, the United States had over 400 billionaires. **Another** area of the world that produces a large number is Asia, with close to 400.

As hard as it is to imagine having over a billion dollars, try to imagine accumulating[9] this wealth before the age of forty! In 2014, a financial website, *Bankrate.com*, listed the ten youngest billionaires in the world. The richest, Mark Zuckerberg, the founder of Facebook, had a net worth of $33 billion in 2014. But he's not the only one to get rich from Facebook. **Another** person who became a billionaire from Facebook is Dustin Moskovitz. While **other** billionaires prefer to live a life of luxury, Moskovitz rides his bike to work and flies commercial airlines. Both Zuckerberg and Moskovitz have signed The Giving Pledge, which Warren Buffet and **another** famous billionaire, Bill Gates started. The Giving Pledge has gotten the commitment[10] of Zuckerberg, Moskovitz, and **others** to give the majority of their wealth to philanthropy[11] while they're still alive.

The second richest person on *Bankrate's* list in 2014 was Yang Huiyan, from China. She made her money in real estate. She also inherited money from her father. She's the only woman on the list. All **the others** are men.

Some of the billionaires on the list became rich mainly by inheriting family money. One of these is Fahd Hariri of Lebanon. He and his five siblings inherited their father's wealth when their father, the Prime Minister of Lebanon, was assassinated[12] in 2005. Hariri now owns a furniture company, which supplies furniture to **other** wealthy people, mostly in Saudi Arabia.

Another billionaire who inherited his money is German prince Albert von Thurn und Taxis, who first joined a billionaire list at the age of eight but officially inherited his fortune when he turned eighteen.

If we think about inheriting this large amount of money, we might think of what a nice life we can have. On **the other** hand, we might think, "Would easy money kill our motivation?"

---

[9] *to accumulate*: to gather together
[10] *commitment*: a promise
[11] *philanthropy*: the practice of giving money to people in need
[12] *to assassinate*: to kill

COMPREHENSION CHECK Based on the reading, tell if the statement is true (**T**) or false (**F**).

1. The richest person on *Bankrate's* list is a woman.

2. All of the people on the list inherited money from their family.

3. The youngest billionaire was a German prince, who was a billionaire by the time he was eight years old.

14.7 *Another and Other*

The use of *other* and *another* depends on whether a noun is singular or plural, specific or non-specific.

The other + a singular noun is definite. It means the only one remaining.

One person in the photo is Bill Gates. _____

The other person is Melinda Gates. _____

The other + a plural noun is definite. It means all the remaining ones.

One billionaire on the list is a woman. _____

All **the other** billionaires are men. _____

Another + a singular noun is indefinite. It means one of several.

One billionaire is Mark Zuckerberg. _____

Another billionaire is Dustin Moskovitz. _____

Other + a plural noun is indefinite. It means some, but not all of the remaining ones.

Some billionaires are from the United States. _____

Other billionaires are from Asia. _____

EXERCISE 13 Circle the correct words to complete this conversation.

A: Last month I went to the doctor, and she sent me to get an X-ray. I got a bill and paid it, but

then I got (another/the other) bill. Can you help me figure this out?
1.

B: Let's see. Well, one bill is from the doctor. (*The other/Another*) bill is from the X-ray lab.
2.

continued

A: This is crazy.

B: I know, right? Wait for your insurance to pay. After your insurance pays, they'll send you

(*another/other*) bill that shows the amount you have to pay.
    3.

A: There are two phone numbers. Which one should I call for information?

B: The first number is for telephone service. (*The other/Another*) number is a fax number.
                                                            4.

A: How do I pay?

B: There are two methods of payment: One method is by check. (*Other/The other*) method is by
                                                                    5.

credit card.

A: I hate paying bills. Every month I get a gas bill, a cell phone bill, an electricity bill, a cable bill,

and (*other/another*) bills. This is so confusing.
    6.

B: Some people send a check, but (*other/another*) people set up direct payment. Call the electric
                                                       7.

company and all (*other/the other*) companies to see if you can set up an automatic payment
                                                  8.

from your checking account. That way you don't have to think about bills every month.

14.8 More about Another and Other

Examples	Explanation
One young billionaire is Mark Zuckerberg. **Another billionaire** is Dustin Muskovitz. **Another one** is Dustin Muskovitz. **Another** is Dustin Muskovitz.	After *another* or *the other*, we can substitute a singular noun with *one*. We can also omit *one*.
One billionaire is a woman. **The other billionaires** are men. **The other ones** are men. **The others** are men.	After *other* or *the other*, we can substitute a plural noun with *ones*. We can also omit *ones*. If we omit it, we use *others*, not *other*.
This ten-dollar bill is torn. Please give me **another** one.	*Another* is sometimes used to mean a different one, or one more.

Language Note:

We omit *the* when we use a possessive form.

> I have two bank accounts. One account is a checking account. **My other** account is a savings account. (NOT: *my the other*)

EXERCISE 14 Fill in the blanks with *the other, another, the others,* or *other* to complete the conversation between a grandson (A) and his grandfather (B).

A: I want to buy ___*another*___ pair of sneakers.
    1.

B: You already have about six pairs of sneakers. I bought you a new pair for your last birthday.

A: The new pair is fine, but all _____ are too small for me. You know I'm
    2.

growing very fast, so I threw them away.

B: Why did you throw them away? _____ boys in your neighborhood
    3.

could use them.

A: They wouldn't like them. They're out of style.

B: You kids are so wasteful today. What's wrong with the sneakers I bought you last month? If they

fit you, why do you need _____ pair?
    4.

A: Everybody in my class at school has red sneakers with the laces tied backward.

B: Do you always have to have what all _____ kids in school have? Can't
    5.

you think for yourself?

A: Didn't you ask your parents for stuff when you were in middle school?

B: My parents were poor, and my two brothers and I worked to help them. When we outgrew our

clothes, we gave them to _____ families nearby. And our neighbors
    6.

gave us the things that their children outgrew. One neighbor had two sons. One son was a year

older than me. _____ one was two years younger. So we were
    7.

constantly passing clothes back and forth. We never threw things out. We didn't waste our

parents' money. My oldest brother worked in a factory and gave all his salary to our parents. My

_____ brother and I helped our father in his business. My dad didn't
    8.

give us a salary. It was our duty to help him.

A: You don't understand how important it is to look like all _____ kids.
    9.

B: I guess I don't. I'm old-fashioned. Every generation has _____ way of
    10.

looking at things.

14.9 Definite and Indefinite Pronouns

Examples	Explanation
A: Did you read **the article** about **the billionaires**? **B:** Yes, I read **it** yesterday. Five of **them** are Americans.	We use definite pronouns *him, her, them*, and *it* to refer to specific count nouns.
I'm going to buy a laptop. I need **one** to take notes in class.	We use the indefinite pronoun *one* to refer to a non-specific singular count noun.
Noncount: My son asked me for money. I didn't give him **any**. Do you think I should give him **some**? **Count:** I told him not to buy video games, but he bought **some**. I wanted him to buy books, but he didn't buy **any**.	With noncount nouns and plural count nouns, we refer to a non-specific noun as follows: • *some* for affirmative statements • *any* for negative statements • *some* or *any* for questions.

Language Notes:

1. We often use *any* and *some* before *more*.

    Son: I don't have enough money. I need **some more**.

    Dad: I'm not going to give you **any more**.

2. We can start with a non-specific noun, but when referring to it specifically, we use a definite pronoun.

    I have **some questions** about one of the billionaires. Can you answer **them** for me?

EXERCISE 15 Fill in the blanks with *one* or *it* to complete the conversation between a mother (A) and her teenage daughter (B).

A: I have a brochure from the state university. Do you want to look at ___it___ with me?
1.

B: I don't know, Mom. I don't know if I want to go to college when I graduate.

A: Why not? We've been planning for _____ since the day you were born.
2.

B: College is not for everyone. I want to be an artist.

A: Artists don't make any money! You can be _____ and still go to college. Please choose a
3.

more practical career, like teaching.

B: I'm not really interested in a college degree.

A: But it's good to have _____ anyway.
4.

B: I don't know why. In college, I'll have to study general courses, too, like math and biology. You

know I hate math. I'm not good at _____.
5.

A: Maybe we should look at art schools. There's one downtown. Do you want to visit _____?
6.

B: We can probably find information about _____ online.
7.

A: (*Looking at the art website*) This school sounds great. Let's call and ask for an application.

B: I'm sure you can get _____ online.
    8.

A: Oh, yes. Here it is. Let's print a copy of _____.
    9.

B: You can fill _____ out online and submit _____ electronically.
    10.   11.

EXERCISE 16 Fill in the blanks with *one, some, any, it, a, an, the,* or Ø (for no article) to complete the conversation between a teenager and her mother. In some cases, more than one answer is possible.

A: Can I have fifteen dollars? I want to buy _____*a*_____ poster of my favorite singer.
    1.

B: I gave you _____ money last week. What did you do with _____?
    2.   3.

A: I spent _____ on a movie.
    4.

B: No, you can't have _____ more money until next week. Besides, why do you want a
    5.

    poster? You already have _____ of your favorite singer in your room.
    6.

A: I took _____ down. I don't even like her anymore.
    7.

B: What happened to all _____ money Grandpa gave you for your birthday?
    8.

A: I don't have _____ money any more. I spent _____.
    9.   10.

B: You have to learn that _____ money doesn't grow on trees. If you want me to give you
    11.

    _____, you'll have to work for it. You can start by cleaning your room.
    12.

A: But I cleaned _____ two weeks ago.
    13.

B: That was two weeks ago. It's dirty again.

A: I don't have _____ time. I have to meet my friends.
    14.

B: You can't go out. You need to do your homework.

A: I don't have _____. Please let me have fifteen dollars.
    15.

B: When I was your age, I had _____ job.
    16.

A: I wanted to get a job last summer, but I couldn't find _____.
    17.

B: You didn't try hard enough. When I worked, I gave my parents half of _____ money I
    18.

    earned. You kids today have _____ easy life.
    19.

A: Why do _____ parents always say that to _____ kids?
    20.   21.

B: Because it's true. It's time you learn that _____ life is hard.
    22.

SUMMARY OF LESSON 14

Articles

Indefinite

	Count—Singular	Count—Plural	Noncount
General	*A/An*	*Ø Article*	*Ø Article*
	A child likes toys.	**Children** like toys. I love **children**.	**Money** can't buy happiness. Everyone needs **money**.
Non-Specific	*A/An*	*Some/Any*	*Some/Any*
	I bought **a toy**.	I bought **some toys**. I didn't buy **any games**. Did you buy **any games**?	I spent **some money**. I didn't buy **any candy**. Do you have **any time?**
Classification/Definition	*A/An*	*Ø Article*	
	"Recession" is **an economic term**.	Teenagers are **young adults**.	

Definite

	Count—Singular	Count—Plural	Noncount
Specific	**The reading** on page 365 is about kids and money.	**The pictures** in this lesson are about money.	**The information** about millennials is interesting.
Unique	**The Internet** is a great tool.	**The Hawaiian Islands** are beautiful.	

Other/Another

	Specific	Non-Specific
Singular	the other book the other one the other my other book	another book another one another
Plural	the other books the other ones the others my other books	other books other ones others

Indefinite Pronouns

We use *one/some/any* to substitute for non-specific nouns.

Singular Count	I need a quarter. Do you have **one**?
Plural Count	I need some pennies. You have **some**.
Noncount	I don't have any change. Do you have **any**?

TEST / REVIEW

Circle the correct words to complete the conversation. (Ø means no article is needed.)

A: I bought my daughter (*a*/*the*/*some*) new doll for her birthday. Now she's asking me to buy her
   1.

   (*the other*/*another*/*other*) one. There's nothing wrong with (*a*/*the*/*Ø*) doll I bought her last
      2.   **3.**

   month. She just got bored with it.

B: That's how (*Ø*/*the*/*a*) kids are. They don't understand (*a*/*the*/*Ø*) value of money.
            4.   **5.**

A: You're right. They think that (*a*/*the*/*Ø*) money grows on trees.
                              6.

B: I suppose it's our fault. We have to set (*Ø*/*a*/*the*) good example. On the one hand, we tell them
                                    7.

   to be careful about money. On (*the other*/*other*/*another*) hand, we buy a lot of things we don't
                              8.

   really need. We use (*a*/*the*/*Ø*) credit cards instead of (*a*/*the*/*Ø*) cash and worry about paying
              9.   **10.**

   (*a*/*the*/*Ø*) bill later.
      11.

A: I suppose you're right. Last month we bought (*the*/*a*/*Ø*) new TV.
                                          12.

B: I thought you bought (*it*/*one*) last year.
                  13.

A: We did. But we were at the appliance store last month looking for (*the*/*a*/*Ø*) new dishwasher
                                                        14.

   when we saw a much bigger, better TV. We decided to get (*it*/*one*).
                                          15.

B: What did you do with (*the other*/*another*/*other*) TV?
                     16.

A: We put (*it*/*one*) in (*the*/*a*/*Ø*) basement. I suppose we didn't really need
        17.   **18.**

   (*other*/*any other*/*another*) one.
         19.

B: Last weekend my husband bought (*a*/*some*/*the*) new phone. He said (*a*/*the*/*Ø*) new one has
                              20.   **21.**

   better apps than (*another*/*other*/*the other*) one. And it has better games. He got tired of
               22.

   (*another*/*the others*/*the other*) games.
         23.

A: Our kids are imitating us. We need to make (*some*/*any*/*the*) changes in our own behavior. I'm
                                    24.

   going to start (*a*/*the*/*Ø*) budget tonight. I'm going to start saving (*a*/*any*/*some*) money each
          25.   **26.**

   month.

B: Do you need (*a*/*any*/*the*) help with it? There's (*a*/*the*/*Ø*) course at the community college on
            27.   **28.**

   how to manage your money. Do you want to take it with me?

A: That's (*a*/*Ø*/*the*) good idea. How much does it cost?
         29.

B: I'm not sure. Some courses are $50 a course. (*Others*/*Other*/*Another*) courses are $100 a credit
                                             30.

   hour. We should take it no matter what it costs.

WRITING

PART 1 Editing Advice

1. Choose the correct article or Ø for no article.

   Warren Buffet is ^a^ famous billionaire.

   What is ^the^ first job you had?

   You should save ~~a~~ money for college.

2. Use *the* after a quantity word when the noun is specific.

   I spent most of ^the^ money my grandparents gave me.

3. Use a plural count noun after a quantity expression.

   A few of my friend^s^ have a part-time job.

4. *Another* is always singular.

   Some teenagers save their money. ~~Another~~ *Other* teenagers spend it without thinking about their future.

5. *A* and *an* are always singular.

   Mark Zuckerberg and Warren Buffet are ~~a~~ billionaires.

6. Use *a* or *an* for a definition or a classification of a singular count noun.

   A millennial is ^a^ person born between 1980 and 2000.

7. Don't use the definite article with a possessive form.

   I have use two cards for my purchases. One is my credit card. My ~~the~~ other card is a debit card.

8. Don't use *the* to make a general statement about a noun.

   ~~The~~ ^M^ money doesn't buy happiness.

   ~~The~~ ^C^ children like toys.

9. Use an indefinite pronoun to substitute for a non-specific noun.

   I have a checking account. Do you have ~~it~~ *one*?

10. Before a plural noun or pronoun, use *other*, not *others*.

    Some billionaires are from the U.S. ~~Others~~ Other billionaires are from Asia.

PART 2 Editing Practice

Some of the shaded words and phrases have mistakes. Find the mistakes and correct them. If the shaded words are correct, write *C*.

C

I'm a teenager and I know this: ~~the~~ teenagers think a lot about the money. We want money
1.   2.   3.   4

to buy a new jeans or sneakers. Or we want money to go out with our friends. We sometimes
5.

want to go to the restaurant or to a movie. Most of the my friends try to get a job in the
6.   7.   8.

summer to make some money. At the beginning of every summer, my friends always say, "I
9.

need a job. Do you know where I can find it?"
10.   11.

One of my friend found a summer job at Bender's. Bender's is small bookstore. Another
12.   13.   14.

friend found a job at a summer camp. But I have the other way to make money. I prefer to
15.

work in my neighborhood. Most of people in my neighborhood are working or elderly. I ask
16.

my neighbors for work. Some neighbors pay me to take care of the lawn in front of their house.
17.

Another neighbors pay me to clean their garage. In the winter, I shovel a sidewalks in front of
18.   19.

their houses. I like these jobs. I love a music, and I listen to my favorite music while I work.
20.

What do I do with the money I get from my jobs? I buy songs on Internet. I used to buy
21.   22.

CDs, but I only liked a few songs. Some of songs on the CDs were great, but I never listened to
23.

anothers. Now I can download the songs I like and not pay for all the others songs on a CD.
24.   25.   26.

This helps me save money. With the money I save, I can buy the other things I want.
27.

PART 3 Write About It

1. Do you think kids should get an allowance from their parents? How much? Does it depend on the child's age? Should the child have to do chores for the money? Write a few paragraphs explaining your point of view.

2. Write a short essay giving advice to teenagers on how to earn and save money.

PART 4 Edit Your Writing

Reread the Summary of Lesson 14 and the editing advice. Edit your writing from Part 3.

Spelling and Pronunciation of Verbs

Spelling of the -s Form of Verbs

Rule	Base Form	-s Form
Add -s to most verbs to make the -s form.	hope eat	hopes eats
When the base form ends in ss, zz, sh, ch, or x, add -es and pronounce an extra syllable, /əz/ or /ɪz/.	miss buzz wash catch fix	misses buzzes washes catches fixes
When the base form ends in a consonant + y, change the y to i and add -es.	carry worry	carries worries
When the base form ends in a vowel + y, do not change the y.	pay obey	pays obeys
Add -es to go and do.	go do	goes does

Three Pronunciations of the -s Form

Rule		
We pronounce -s as /s/ if the verb ends in these voiceless sounds: /p t k f/.	hope—hopes eat—eats	pick—picks laugh—laughs
We pronounce -s as /z/ if the verb ends in most voiced sounds.	live—lives grab—grabs read—reads	run—runs sing—sings borrow—borrows
When the base form ends in ss, zz, sh, ch, x, se, ge, or ce, we pronounce an extra syllable, /əz/ or /ɪz/.	miss—misses buzz—buzzes wash—washes watch—watches	fix—fixes use—uses change—changes dance—dances
These verbs have a change in the vowel sound.	do/**du**/—does/**dʌz**	say/**seɪ**/—says/**sɛz**/

continued

Spelling of the *-ing* Form of Verbs

Rule	Base Form	*-ing* Form
Add *-ing* to most verbs. **Note:** Do not remove the *y* for the *-ing* form.	eat go study carry	eating going studying carrying
For a one-syllable verb that ends in a consonant + vowel + consonant (CVC), double the final consonant and add *-ing*.	p l a n C V C s t o p C V C s i t C V C g r a b C V C	planning stopping sitting grabbing
Do not double the final *w, x,* or *y*.	show mix stay	showing mixing staying
For a two-syllable word that ends in CVC, double the final consonant only if the last syllable is stressed.	reFER adMIT beGIN reBEL	referring admitting beginning rebelling
When the last syllable of a multi-syllable word is not stressed, do not double the final consonant.	TRAVel Open OFfer LIMit deVElop	traveling opening offering limiting developing
If the word ends in a consonant + *e*, drop the *e* before adding *-ing*.	live take write arrive	living taking writing arriving
If the word ends in *ie*, change the *ie* to *y* and add *-ing*.	die tie	dying tying

Spelling of the Past Tense of Regular Verbs

Rule	Base Form	-ed Form
Add -ed to the base form to make the past tense of most regular verbs.	start kick	started kicked
When the base form ends in e, add -d only.	die live	died lived
When the base form ends in a consonant + y, change the y to i and add -ed.	carry worry	carried worried
When the base form ends in a vowel + y, do not change the y.	destroy stay	destroyed stayed

For a one-syllable verb that ends in a consonant + vowel + consonant (CVC), double the final consonant and add -ed.	s t o p
	   C V C
	p l u g
	   C V C
		stopped
		
		plugged

Do no double the final w or x.	show mix stay	showing mixing staying
For a two-syllable word that ends in CVC, double the final consonant only if the last syllable is stressed.	reFER adMIT beGIN reBEL	referring admitting beginning rebelling
When the last syllable of a multi-syllable word is not stressed, do not double the final consonant.	Open HAPpen deVElop	opened happened developed

Pronunciations of Past Forms that End in -ed

The past tense with -ed has three pronunciations			
We pronounce -ed as /t/ if the base form ends in these voiceless sounds: /p, k, f, sʃ, tʃ/.	jump—jumped cook—cooked	cough—coughed kiss—kissed	wash—washed watch—watched
We pronounce -ed as /d/ if the base form ends in most voiced sounds.	rub—rubbed drag—dragged love—loved bathe—bathed use—used	charge—charged glue—glued massage—massaged name—named learn—learned	bang—banged call—called fear—feared free—freed stay—stayed
We pronounce an extra syllable /əd/ or /ɪd/ if the base form ends in a /t/ or /d/ sound.	wait—waited hate—hated	want—wanted add—added	need—needed decide—decided

Irregular Noun Plurals

Singular	Plural	Explanation
man woman tooth foot goose	men women teeth feet geese	Vowel change (**Note:** The first vowel in *women* is pronounced /ɪ/.)
sheep fish deer	sheep fish deer	No change
child person mouse	children people (OR persons) mice	Different word form
alumnus cactus radius stimulus syllabus	alumni cacti (OR cactuses) radii stimuli syllabi (OR syllabuses)	*us* ⟶ *i*
analysis crisis hypothesis oasis parenthesis thesis	analyses crises hypotheses oases parentheses theses	*is* ⟶ *es*
appendix index	appendices (OR appendixes) indices (OR indexes)	*ix* ⟶ *ices* OR ⟶ *ixes* *ex* ⟶ *ices* OR ⟶ *exes*
bacterium curriculum datum medium memorandum criterion phenomenon	bacteria curricula data media memoranda criteria phenomena	*um* ⟶ *a* *ion* ⟶ *a* *on* ⟶ *a*
alga formula vertebra	algae formulae (OR formulas) vertebrae	*a* ⟶ *ae*

Spelling Rules for Adverbs Ending in -*ly*

Adjective Ending	Examples	Adverb Ending	Adverb
Most endings	careful quiet serious	Add -*ly*.	carefully quietly seriously
y	easy happy lucky	Change *y* to *i* and add -*ly*.	easily happily luckily
e	nice free	Keep the *e* and add -*ly*.*	nicely freely
consonant + *le*	simple comfortable double	Drop the *e* and add -*ly*.	simply comfortably doubly
ic	basic enthusiastic	Add -*ally*.**	basically enthusiastically
ll	full	Add -*y*	fully

Exceptions:

 * true—truly

 ** public—publicly

Metric Conversion Chart

Length

When You Know	Multiply by	To Find
inches (in)	2.54	centimeters (cm)
feet (ft)	30.5	centimeters (cm)
feet (ft)	0.3	meters (m)
miles (mi)	1.6	kilometers (km)
Metric:		
centimeters (cm)	0.39	inches (in)
centimeters (cm)	0.03	feet (ft)
meters (m)	3.28	feet (ft)
kilometers (km)	0.62	miles (mi)
Note: 12 inches = 1 foot 3 feet = 36 inches = 1 yard		

Weight (Mass)

When You Know	Multiply by	To Find
ounces (oz)	28.35	grams (g)
pounds (lb)	0.45	kilograms (kg)
Metric:		
grams (g)	0.04	ounces (oz)
kilograms (kg)	2.2	pounds (lb)
Note: 1 pound = 16 ounces		

Volume

When You Know	Multiply by	To Find
fluid ounces (fl oz)	30.0	milliliters (mL)
pints (pt)	0.47	liters (L)
quarts (qt)	0.95	liters (L)
gallons (gal)	3.8	liters (L)
Metric:		
milliliters (mL)	0.03	fluid ounces (fl oz)
liters (L)	2.11	pints (pt)
liters (L)	1.05	quarts (qt)
liters (L)	0.26	gallons (gal)

Note:
1 pint = 2 cups
1 quart = 2 pints = 4 cups
1 gallon = 4 quarts = 8 pints = 16 cups

Temperature

When You Know	Do this	To Find
degrees Fahrenheit (°F)	Subtract 32, then multiply by $\frac{5}{9}$	degrees Celsius (°C)
Metric:		
degrees Celsius (°C)	Multiply by $\frac{9}{5}$, then add 32	degrees Fahrenheit (°F)

Note:
32°F = 0°C
212°F = 100°C

Make and *Do*

Some expressions use *make*. Others use *do*.

Make	Do
make a date/an appointment	do (the) homework
make a plan	do an exercise
make a decision	do the cleaning, laundry, dishes, washing, etc.
make a telephone call	do the shopping
make a meal (breakfast, lunch, dinner)	do one's best
make a mistake	do a favor
make an effort	do the right/wrong thing
make an improvement	do a job
make a promise	do business
make money	What do you do for a living? (asks about a job)
make noise	How do you do? (said when you meet someone for the first time)
make the bed	

Prepositions of Time

- **in** the morning: He takes a shower *in* the morning.

- **in** the afternoon: He takes a shower *in* the afternoon.

- **in** the evening: He takes a shower *in* the evening.

- **at** night: He takes a shower *at* night.

- **in** the summer, fall, winter, spring: He takes classes *in* the summer.

- **on** that/this day: May 4 is my birthday. I became a citizen *on* that day.

- **on** the weekend: He studies *on* the weekend.

- **on** a specific day: His birthday is *on* March 5.

- **in** a month: His birthday is *in* March.

- **in** a year: He was born *in* 1978.

- **in** a century: People didn't use cars *in* the 19th century.

- **on** a day: I don't have class *on* Monday.

- **at** a specific time: My class begins *at* 12:30.

- **from** a time **to** (OR **till** OR **until**) another time: My class is *from* 12:30 *to* (OR *till* OR *until*) 3:30.

- **in** a number of hours, days, weeks, months, years: She will graduate *in* three weeks. (This means "after" three weeks.)

- **for** a number of hours, days, weeks, months, years: She was in Mexico *for* three weeks. (This means during the period of three weeks.)

- **by** a time: Please finish your test *by* six o'clock. (This means "no later than" six o'clock.)

- **until** a time: I lived with my parents *until* I came to the U.S. (This means "all the time before.")

- **during** the movie, class, meeting: He slept *during* the meeting.

- **about/around** six o'clock: The movie will begin *about* six o'clock. People will arrive *around* 5:45.

- **in** the past/future: *In* the past, she never exercised.

- **at** present: *At* present, the days are getting longer.

- **in** the beginning/end: *In* the beginning, she didn't understand the teacher at all.

- **at** the beginning/end of something: The semester begins *at* the beginning of September. My birthday is *at* the end of June.

- **before/after** a time: You should finish the job *before* Friday. The library will be closed *after* six o'clock.

- **before/after** an action takes place: Turn off the lights *before* you leave. Wash the dishes *after* you finish dinner.

Verbs and Adjectives Followed by a Preposition

Many verbs and adjectives are followed by a preposition.

accuse someone of	(be) familiar with	(be) prepared for/to
(be) accustomed to	(be) famous for	prevent (someone) from
adjust to	(be) fond of	prohibit (someone) from
(be) afraid of	forget about	protect (someone) from
agree with	forgive someone for	(be) proud of
(be) amazed at/by	(be) glad about	recover from
(be) angry about	(be) good at	(be) related to
(be) angry at/with	(be) grateful to someone for	rely on/upon
apologize for	(be) guilty of	(be) responsible for
approve of	(be) happy about	(be) sad about
argue about	hear about	(be) satisfied with
argue with	hear of	(be) scared of
(be) ashamed of	hope for	(be) sick of
(be) aware of	(be) incapable of	(be) sorry about
believe in	insist on/upon	(be) sorry for
blame someone for	(be) interested in	speak about
(be) bored with/by	(be) involved in	speak to/with
(be) capable of	(be) jealous of	succeed in
care about	(be) known for	(be) sure of/about
care for	(be) lazy about	(be) surprised at
compare to/with	listen to	take care of
complain about	look at	talk about
concentrate on	look for	talk to/with
(be) concerned about	look forward to	thank (someone) for
consist of	(be) mad about	(be) thankful (to someone) for
count on	(be) mad at	think about/of
deal with	(be) made from/of	(be) tired of
decide on	(be) married to	(be) upset about
depend on/upon	object to	(be) upset with
(be) different from	(be) opposed to	(be) used to
disapprove of	participate in	wait for
(be) divorced from	plan on	warn (someone) about
dream about/of	pray to	(be) worried about
(be) engaged to	pray for	worry about
(be) excited about		

Direct and Indirect Objects

The order of direct and indirect objects depends on the verb we use. It also can depend on whether we use a noun or a pronoun as the object.

Group 1

Pronouns affect word order. The preposition used is *to*.

Patterns:
He gave a present to his wife. (DO to IO)
He gave his wife a present. (IO/DO)
He gave it to his wife. (DO to IO)
He gave her a present. (IO/DO)
He gave it to her. (DO to IO)

Verbs:

bring	lend	pass	sell	show	teach
give	offer	pay	send	sing	tell
hand	owe	read	serve	take	write

Group 2

Pronouns affect word order. The preposition used is *for*.

Patterns:
He bought a car for his daughter. (DO for IO)
He bought his daughter a car. (IO/DO)
He bought it for his daughter. (DO for IO)
He bought her a car. (IO/DO)
He bought it for her. (DO for IO)

Verbs:

bake	buy	draw	get	make
build	do	find	knit	reserve

Group 3

Pronouns don't affect word order. The preposition used is *to*.

Patterns:
He explained the problem to his friend. (DO to IO)
He explained it to her. (DO to IO)

Verbs:

admit	explain	prove	report	suggest
announce	introduce	recommend	say	
describe	mention	repeat	speak	

Group 4

Pronouns don't affect word order. The preposition used is *for*.

Patterns:
He cashed a check for his friend. (DO for IO)
He cashed it for her. (DO for IO)

Verbs:

answer	change	design	open	prescribe
cash	close	fix	prepare	pronounce

Group 5

Pronouns don't affect word order. No preposition is used.

Patterns:
She asked the teacher a question. (IO/DO)
She asked him a question. (IO/DO)

Verbs:

ask	charge	cost	wish	take (with time)

Capitalization Rules

Rule	Example
The first word in a sentence	**M**y friends are helpful.
The word "I"	My sister and **I** took a trip together.
Names of people	**A**braham **L**incoln; **G**eorge **W**ashington
Titles preceding names of people	**D**octor (**Dr.**) **S**mith; **P**resident **L**incoln; **Q**ueen **E**lizabeth; **M**r. **R**ogers; **M**rs. **C**arter
Geographic names	the **U**nited **S**tates; **L**ake **S**uperior; **C**alifornia; the **R**ocky **M**ountains; the **M**ississippi **R**iver NOTE: The word "the" in a geographic name is not capitalized.
Street names	**P**ennsylvania **A**venue (**Ave.**); **W**all **S**treet (**St.**); **A**bbey **R**oad (**Rd.**)
Names of organizations, companies, colleges, buildings, stores, hotels	the **R**epublican **P**arty; **C**engage **L**earning; **D**artmouth **C**ollege; the **U**niversity of **W**isconsin; the **W**hite **H**ouse; **B**loomingdale's; the **H**ilton **H**otel
Nationalities and ethnic groups	**M**exicans; **C**anadians; **S**paniards; **A**mericans; **J**ews; **K**urds; **I**nuit
Languages	**E**nglish; **S**panish; **P**olish; **V**ietnamese; **R**ussian
Months	**J**anuary; **F**ebruary
Days	**S**unday; **M**onday
Holidays	**I**ndependence **D**ay; **T**hanksgiving
Important words in a title	*Grammar in Context; The Old Man and the Sea; Romeo and Juliet; The Sound of Music* NOTE: Capitalize "the" as the first word of a title.

Uses of Articles

No Article	Article
Personal names: 　　John Kennedy	The whole family: 　　the Kennedys
Title and name: 　　Queen Elizabeth	Title without name: 　　the Queen
Cities, states, countries, continents: 　　Cleveland 　　Ohio 　　Mexico 　　South America	Places that are considered a union: 　　the United States Place names: the _____ of _____ 　　the District of Columbia
Mountains: 　　Mount Everest	Mountain ranges: 　　the Rocky Mountains
Islands: 　　Staten Island	Collectives of islands: 　　the Hawaiian Islands
Lakes: 　　Lake Superior	Collectives of lakes: 　　the Great Lakes
Beaches: 　　Palm Beach 　　Pebble Beach	Rivers, oceans, seas: 　　the Mississippi River 　　the Atlantic Ocean 　　the Dead Sea
Streets and avenues: 　　Madison Avenue 　　Wall Street	Well-known buildings: 　　the Willis Tower 　　the Empire State Building
Parks: 　　Central Park	Zoos: 　　the San Diego Zoo
Seasons: 　　summer　　fall　　spring　　winter 　　Summer is my favorite season. **Note:** After a preposition, *the* may be used. In (the) winter, my car runs badly.	Deserts: 　　the Mojave Desert 　　the Sahara Desert
Directions: 　　north　　south　　east　　west	Sections of a piece of land: 　　the West Side (of New York)

continued

No Article	Article

School subjects:
   history   math
	Unique geographical points:
	   the North Pole the Vatican

Name + *college* or *university*:
   Northwestern University
	The University/College of _____
	   the University of Michigan

Magazines:
   Time   *Sports Illustrated*
	Newspapers:
	   the *Tribune* the *Wall Street Journal*

Months and days:
   September   Monday
	Ships:
	   the *Titanic* the *Queen Elizabeth II*

Holidays and dates:
   Mother's Day
   July 4 (month + day)
	The day of month:
	   the fifth of May
	   the Fourth of July

Diseases:
   cancer   AIDS
   polio   malaria
	Ailments:
	   a cold a toothache
	   a headache the flu

Games and sports:
   poker
   soccer
	Musical instruments, after *play*:
	   the drums the piano
	Note: Sometimes *the* is omitted.
	   She plays (the) drums.

Languages:
   English
	The _____ language:
	   the English language

Last month, year, week, etc. = the one
before this one:
   I forgot to pay my rent last month.
   The teacher gave us a test last week.
	The last month, the last year, the last
	week, etc. = the last in a series:
	   December is the last month of the year.
	   Vacation begins the last week in May.

In office = in an elected position:
   The president is in office for four years.
	In the office = in a specific room:
	   The teacher is in the office.

In back/in front:
   She's in back
   of the car.
	In the back/in the front:
	   He's in the back of the bus.

Irregular Verb Forms

Base Form	Past Form	Past Participle	Base Form	Past Form	Past Participle
be	was/were	been	fight	fought	fought
bear	bore	born/borne	find	found	found
beat	beat	beaten	fit	fit	fit
become	became	become	flee	fled	fled
begin	began	begun	fly	flew	flown
bend	bent	bent	forbid	forbade	forbidden
bet	bet	bet	forget	forgot	forgotten
bid	bid	bid	forgive	forgave	forgiven
bind	bound	bound	freeze	froze	frozen
bite	bit	bitten	get	got	gotten
bleed	bled	bled	give	gave	given
blow	blew	blown	go	went	gone
break	broke	broken	grind	ground	ground
breed	bred	bred	grow	grew	grown
bring	brought	brought	hang	hung	hung
broadcast	broadcast	broadcast	have	had	had
build	built	built	hear	heard	heard
burst	burst	burst	hide	hid	hidden
buy	bought	bought	hit	hit	hit
cast	cast	cast	hold	held	held
catch	caught	caught	hurt	hurt	hurt
choose	chose	chosen	keep	kept	kept
cling	clung	clung	know	knew	known
come	came	come	lay	laid	laid
cost	cost	cost	lead	led	led
creep	crept	crept	leave	left	left
cut	cut	cut	lend	lent	lent
deal	dealt	dealt	let	let	let
dig	dug	dug	lie	lay	lain
dive	dove/dived	dove/dived	light	lit/lighted	lit/lighted
do	did	done	lose	lost	lost
draw	drew	drawn	make	made	made
drink	drank	drunk	mean	meant	meant
drive	drove	driven	meet	met	met
eat	ate	eaten	mistake	mistook	mistaken
fall	fell	fallen	overcome	overcame	overcome
feed	fed	fed	overdo	overdid	overdone
feel	felt	felt	overtake	overtook	overtaken

continued

Base Form	Past Form	Past Participle	Base Form	Past Form	Past Participle
overthrow	overthrew	overthrown	stick	stuck	stuck
pay	paid	paid	sting	stung	stung
plead	pled/pleaded	pled/pleaded	stink	stank	stunk
prove	proved	proven/proved	strike	struck	struck/stricken
put	put	put	strive	strove	striven
quit	quit	quit	swear	swore	sworn
read	read	read	sweep	swept	swept
ride	rode	ridden	swell	swelled	swelled/swollen
ring	rang	rung	swim	swam	swum
rise	rose	risen	swing	swung	swung
run	ran	run	take	took	taken
say	said	said	teach	taught	taught
see	saw	seen	tear	tore	torn
seek	sought	sought	tell	told	told
sell	sold	sold	think	thought	thought
send	sent	sent	throw	threw	thrown
set	set	set	understand	understood	understood
sew	sewed	sewn/sewed	uphold	upheld	upheld
shake	shook	shaken	upset	upset	upset
shed	shed	shed	wake	woke	woken
shine	shone/shined	shone/shined	wear	wore	worn
shoot	shot	shot	weave	wove	woven
show	showed	shown/showed	wed	wedded/wed	wedded/wed
shrink	shrank/shrunk	shrunk/shrunken	weep	wept	wept
shut	shut	shut	win	won	won
sing	sang	sung	wind	wound	wound
sink	sank	sunk	withdraw	withdrew	withdrawn
sit	sat	sat	withhold	withheld	withheld
sleep	slept	slept	withstand	withstood	withstood
slide	slid	slid	wring	wrung	wrung
slit	slit	slit	write	wrote	written
speak	spoke	spoken			
speed	sped	sped			
spend	spent	spent			
spin	spun	spun			
spit	spit/spat	spit/spat			
split	split	split			
spread	spread	spread			
spring	sprang	sprung			
stand	stood	stood			
steal	stole	stolen			

Note:

The past and past participle of some verbs can end in -ed or -t.

burn	burned or burnt
dream	dreamed or dreamt
kneel	kneeled or knelt
learn	learned or learnt
leap	leaped or leapt
spill	spilled or spilt
spoil	spoiled or spoilt

Map of the United States of America

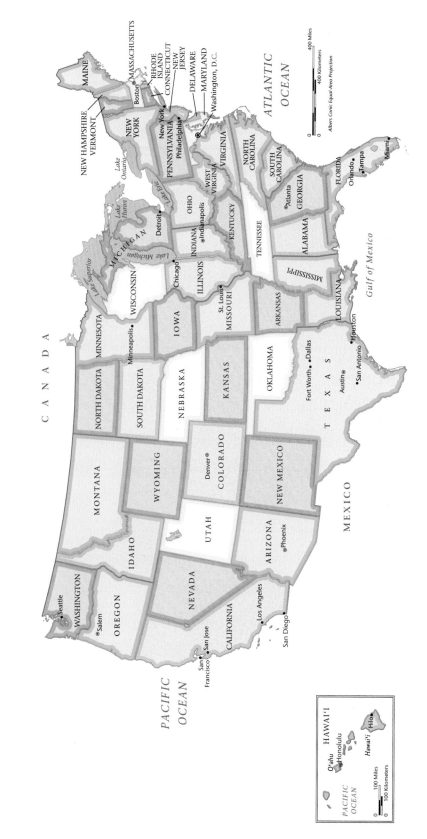

Spelling of Comparative and Superlative Forms

Rule	Simple	Comparative	Superlative
For short adjectives and adverbs, add –er or –est.	tall fast narrow	taller faster narrower	tallest fastest narrowest
For adjectives that end in e, add –r or –st.	nice late simple	nicer later simpler	nicest latest simplest
For two-syllable adjectives that end in y, change the y to an i and add –er or –est.	easy happy early	easier happier earlier	easiest happiest earliest
For one-syllable adjectives that end in consonant-vowel-consonant, double the final consonant and add –er or –est.*	big sad hot	bigger sadder hotter	biggest saddest hottest

Language Note:

* Do not double a final *w*:

      new—newer—newest

Résumé

TINA WHITE

1234 Anderson Avenue

West City, MA 01766

tina.white@e*mail.com

617-123-1234

EXPERIENCE

Acme Computer Services, Inc., Concord, MA

Computer Sales Manager

March 2010—Present

- Managed computer services department, overseeing 20 sales representatives throughout New England.
- Exceeded annual sales goal by 20 percent in 2008.
- Created online customer database, enabling representatives and company to track and retain customers and improve service.
- Developed new training program and materials for all company sales representatives.

West Marketing Services, West City, MA

Office Manager

June 2004—March 2010

- Implemented new system for improving accounting records and reports.
- Managed, trained, and oversaw five customer service representatives.
- Grew sales contracts for support services by 200 percent in first two years.

EDUCATION AND TRAINING

Northeastern Community College, Salem, MA

    Associates Degree Major 2001: Accounting

Institute of Management, Boston, MA

    Certificate of Completion 2004. Course: Sales Management

COMPUTER SKILLS

Proficient in use of MS Windows, PowerPoint, Excel, Access, Outlook, Mac OS X, and several accounting and database systems.

- **Adjective** An adjective gives a description of a noun.

  It's a *tall* tree.　　　　He's an *old* man.　　　　My neighbors are *nice*.

- **Adverb** An adverb describes the action of a sentence or an adjective or another adverb.

  She speaks English *fluently*.　　　　I drive *carefully*.

  She speaks English *extremely* well.　　　　She is *very* intelligent.

- **Adverb of Frequency** An adverb of frequency tells how often an action happens.

  I *never* drink coffee.　　　　They *usually* take the bus.

- **Affirmative** *Affirmative* means "yes."

  They *live* in Miami.

- **Apostrophe** ' We use the apostrophe for possession and contractions.

  My *sister's* friend is beautiful. (possession)

  Today *isn't* Sunday. (contraction)

- **Article** An article comes before a noun. It tells if the noun is definite or indefinite. The definite article is *the*. The indefinite articles are *a* and *an*.

  I have *a* cat.　　　　I ate *an* apple.　　　　*The* teacher came late.

- **Auxiliary Verb** An auxiliary verb is used in forming tense, mood, or aspect of the verb that follows it. Some verbs have two parts: an auxiliary verb and a main verb.

  You *didn't* eat lunch.　　　　He *can't* study.　　　　We *will* return.

- **Base Form** The base form of the verb has no tense. It has no ending (*-s* or *-ed*): *be, go, eat, take, write.*

  I didn't *go*.　　　　We don't *know* you.　　　　He can't *drive*.

- **Capital Letter** A B C D E F G . . .

- **Clause** A clause is a group of words that has a subject and a verb. Some sentences have only one clause.

  She speaks Spanish.

Some sentences have a **main clause** and a **dependent clause**.

MAIN CLAUSE	DEPENDENT CLAUSE (**reason clause**)
She found a good job	because she has computer skills.

MAIN CLAUSE	DEPENDENT CLAUSE (**time clause**)
She'll turn off the light	before she goes to bed.

MAIN CLAUSE	DEPENDENT CLAUSE (***if* clause**)
I'll take you to the doctor	if you don't have your car on Saturday.

- **Colon** :

- **Comma** ,

- **Comparative** The comparative form of an adjective or adverb is used to compare two things.

    My house is *bigger* than your house.

    Her husband drives *faster* than she does.

    My children speak English *more fluently* than I do.

- **Consonant** The following letters are consonants: *b, c, d, f, g, h, j, k, l, m, n, p, q, r, s, t, v, w, x, y, z.*

    NOTE: *Y* is sometimes considered a vowel, as in the world *syllable.*

- **Contraction** A contraction is two words joined with an apostrophe.

    He's my brother.   *You're* late.   They *won't* talk to me.

    (*He's = he is*)   (*You're = you are*)   (*won't = will not*)

- **Count Noun** Count nouns are nouns that we can count. They have a singular and a plural form.

    1 pen–3 pens   1 table–4 tables

- **Dependent Clause** See **Clause**.

- **Direct Object** A direct object is a noun (phrase) or pronoun that receives the action of the verb.

    We saw *the movie.*   You have *a nice car.*   I love *you.*

- **Exclamation Mark** !

- **Frequency Word** Frequency words (*always, usually, generally, often, sometimes, rarely, seldom, hardly ever, never*) tell how often an action happens.

    I *never* drink coffee.   We *always* do our homework.

- **Hyphen** -

- **Imperative** An imperative sentence gives a command or instructions. An imperative sentence omits the subject pronoun *you.*

    Come here.   *Don't be* late.   Please *help* me.

- **Infinitive** An infinitive is *to* + the base form.

    I want *to leave.*   You need *to be* here on time.

- **Linking Verb** A linking verb is a verb that links the subject to the noun, adjective, or adverb after it. Linking verbs include *be, seem, feel, smell, sound, look, appear,* and *taste.*

    She *is* a doctor.   She *looks* tired.   You *are* late.

- **Main Clause** See **Clause**.

- **Modal** The modal verbs are *can, could, shall, should, will, would, may, might,* and *must.*

  They *should* leave.   I *must* go.

- **Negative** *Negative* means "no."

- **Nonaction Verb** A nonaction verb has no action. We do not use a continuous tense (*be* + verb *-ing*) with a nonaction verb. The nonaction verbs are: *believe, cost, care, have, hear, know, like, love, matter, mean, need, own, prefer, remember, see, seem, think, understand, want,* and sense-perception verbs.

  She *has* a laptop.   We *love* our mother.   You *look* great.

- **Noncount Noun** A noncount noun is a noun that we don't count. It has no plural form.

  She drank some *water.*   He prepared some *rice.*

  Do you need any *money*?   We had a lot of *homework.*

- **Noun** A noun is a person, a place, or a thing. Nouns can be either count or noncount.

  My *brother* lives in California.   My *sisters* live in New York.

  I get *advice* from them.   I drink *coffee* every day.

- **Noun Modifier** A noun modifier makes a noun more specific.

  fire department   *Independence* Day   *can* opener

- **Noun Phrase** A noun phrase is a group of words that form the subject or object of the sentence.

  A very nice woman helped me.   I bought *a big box of cereal.*

- **Object** The object of the sentence follows the verb. It receives the action of the verb.

  He bought *a car.*   I saw *a movie.*   I met *your brother.*

- **Object Pronoun** We use object pronouns (*me, you, him, her, it, us, them*) after the verb or preposition.

  He likes *her.*   I saw the movie. Let's talk about *it.*

- **Parentheses** ( )

- **Paragraph** A paragraph is a group of sentences about one topic.

- **Past Participle** The past participle of a verb is the third form of the verb.

  You have *written* a good essay.   I was *told* about the concert.

- **Period** .

- **Phrasal Modal** Phrasal modals, such as *ought to, be able to,* are made up of two or more words.

  You *ought to* study more.   We *have to* take a test.

- **Phrase** A group of words that go together.

  Last month my sister came to visit.   There is a strange car *in front of my house.*

- **Plural** *Plural* means "more than one." A plural noun usually ends with *-s.*

  She has beautiful *eyes.*   My *feet* are big.

- **Possessive Form** Possessive forms show ownership or relationship.

  Mary's coat is in the closet.   *My* brother lives in Miami.

- **Preposition** A preposition is a short connecting word. Some common prepositions include *about, above, across, after, around, as, at, away, back, before, behind, below, by, down, for, from, in, into, like, of, off, on, out, over, to, under, up,* and *with*.

  The book is *on* the table.   She studies *with* her friends.

- **Present Participle** The present participle of a verb is the base form + *-ing*.

  She is *sleeping*.   They were *laughing*.

- **Pronoun** A pronoun takes the place of a noun.

  I have a new car. I bought *it* last week.

  John likes Mary, but *she* doesn't like *him*.

- **Punctuation** The use of specific marks, such as commas and periods, to make ideas within writing clear.

- **Question Mark** ?

- **Quotation Marks** " "

- **Regular Verb** A regular verb forms its past tense with *-ed*.

  He *worked* yesterday.   I *laughed* at the joke.

- **-s Form** A present tense verb that ends in *-s* or *-es*.

  He *lives* in New York.   She *watches* TV a lot.

- **Sense-Perception Verb** A sense-perception verb has no action. It describes a sense. The sense-perception verbs are: *look, feel, taste, sound,* and *smell*.

  She *feels* fine.   The coffee *smells* fresh.   The milk *tastes* sour.

- **Sentence** A sentence is a group of words that contains a subject and a verb and gives a complete thought.

  SENTENCE: She came home.

  NOT A SENTENCE: When she came home

- **Singular** *Singular* means "one."

  She ate a *sandwich*.   I have one *television*.

- **Subject** The subject of the sentence tells who or what the sentence is about.

  My sister got married last April. *The wedding* was beautiful.

- **Subject Pronoun** We use a subject pronoun (*I, you, he, she, it, we, you, they*) before a verb.

  They speak Japanese.   *We* speak Spanish.

- **Superlative** The superlative form of an adjective or adverb shows the number one item in a group of three or more.

  January is the *coldest* month of the year.

  My brother speaks English the *best* in my family.

- **Syllable** A syllable is a part of a word. Each syllable has only one vowel sound. (Some words have only one syllable.)

  change (one syllable)   after (af·ter = two syllables)

  look (one syllable)   responsible (re·spon·si·ble = four syllables)

- **Tag Question** A tag question is a short question at the end of a sentence. It is used in conversation.

  You speak Spanish, *don't you*?   He's not happy, *is he*?

- **Tense** Tense shows when the action of the sentence happened. Verbs have different tenses.

  SIMPLE PRESENT: She usually *works* hard.

  PRESENT CONTINUOUS: She *is working* now.

  SIMPLE PAST: She *worked* yesterday.

  FUTURE: She *will work* tomorrow.

- **Verb** A verb is the action of the sentence.

  He *runs* fast.   I *speak* English.

- **Vowel** The following letters are vowels: *a, e, i, o, u.*

  NOTE: *Y* is sometimes considered a vowel, as in the world *syllable.*

INDEX

Y

PHOTOGRAPHIC CREDITS